W9-APL-214

THE UNTOLD STORY OF
DOUGLAS MacARTHUR

OTHER BOOKS BY FRAZIER HUNT

Blown in By the Draft
The Rising Temper of the East
Sycamore Bend
Custer: The Last of the Cavaliers
Bachelor Prince
This Bewildered World
One American
Little Doc
The Long Trail from Texas
MacArthur and the War Against Japan
Cap Mossman: Last of the Great Cowmen

IN COLLABORATION WITH ROBERT HUNT
I Fought with Custer
Horses and Heroes

THE UNTOLD STORY OF
DOUGLAS MacARTHUR

FRAZIER HUNT

THE DEVIN-ADAIR COMPANY

NEW YORK • 1954

Copyright 1954 by Frazier Hunt. All rights
reserved. No portion of this book may be
reproduced in any form, except by a reviewer
who may quote brief portions in a review,
with written permission of the publisher,
The Devin-Adair Company, 23 East 26th Street,
New York 10, N. Y.
Canadian agents: Thomas Nelson & Sons, Limited, Toronto
Manufactured in the United States of America
by H. Wolff, N. Y.

Library of Congress Catalog Card Number 54–10811

Second Printing

"Great men are like eagles, and build their nests in solitude."

SCHOPENHAUER

*To Arthur MacArthur
a fine young American*

CONTENTS

CONTENTS

PART ONE

The Making
of the Soldier

1880-1930

1

ARMY BRAT

Douglas could never recall any but the vaguest memories of the years at Fort Wingate, the lonely little frontier post in the Territory of New Mexico, close to the Arizona line. He was a babe in arms when in July 1880 the MacArthur family of five made the trek there from the Rio Grande.

It took the train of army wagons eight pitilessly hot days and eight miserably cold nights to cross the high desert plateau. It was Indian country; to the north of the post stretched the vast Navajo reservation, and on west from the Arizona Territory border lay the wild mountainous area of Apache Land.

The Captain's wife and the three little boys took it all in true frontier style. There was no coddling of army wives and army brats in those hard-bitten days. They all shared the hardships, the lonely years and eternal fears with the men in their dusty blue uniforms.

Toward evening the little world about the lonely post of Fort Wingate became afire with color. The boom of the sunset gun rolled across the parade ground after the clear notes of the bugle sounding retreat. Often in later life Douglas MacArthur said that his first conscious memory was the sound of the bugles.

In the Spartan life of the old army the growing child was conditioned by influences and experiences that were tamped down into his subconscious being. And inextricably interwoven with these, his own early memories, were the memories of vivid stories told to him by his father; tales of the Civil War and of the long and colorful years when he served on the Indian frontiers of the Wyoming and Nebraska country.

So it was that the events of his father's early army life became as real to the young boy as his own daily experiences. It was almost as if he could remember far back beyond even his birth: remember Abraham Lincoln, the charge up Mission Ridge, the high mountains of the North West, the mule trains and dusty troopers, marching infantrymen and bearded scouts and the pungent smell of sweaty cavalry horses, the echoes of sunset guns and bugles sounding all the day through from reveille to taps.

On a May day in 1862, when Douglas' father, Arthur MacArthur, was about to turn 17, he had journeyed the long way from Milwaukee to Washington, with a letter of introduction from the Wisconsin governor to Abraham Lincoln. The slender boy was taken to the President by Senator Doolittle, and the tall, gaunt Lincoln had put his arm around the boy's shoulders and explained sympathetically there were no more Presidential appointments to West Point for this June, but that the next year he could have one. And the President added that he had a boy of his own who wanted to go to war.

But the war drums had been beating a full year and young Arthur could wait no longer. His father, Judge Arthur MacArthur, at one time lieutenant governor of Wisconsin, called on his friends in Milwaukee, and the boy was made a first lieutenant and adjutant in the newly organized 24th Wisconsin Infantry. At his first parade formation the young officer's high-pitched voice broke, and he took a good-natured ribbing from his comrades. But a few weeks later when the outfit saw its first service at the brisk little skirmish at Perrysville, Ky.,

4

and then shortly at Stone River, near Murfreesboro, Tenn., the boy adjutant with the high-pitched voice proved his bravery and leadership. He rallied the broken companies and was constantly in the center of the hardest fighting. Fear was not in him. For the next year and more the regiment was to serve in Phil Sheridan's Third Division, and on its battle streamers were such names as Chickamauga, Mission Ridge and Lookout Mountain.

At Mission Ridge the 24th Wisconsin with other regiments of the 3rd Division was standing in ranks at the foot of the steep and dangerous slope that rose in front of them, its wooded face cut by enemy rifle pits and gun emplacements. Generals Grant, Thomas and Sheridan sat their horses to the rear. Suddenly Sheridan was seen to lift his hat, and Captain Parsons, temporarily in command of the Wisconsin outfit, taking the gesture as a command to advance, ordered his regiment forward. As Captain Parsons, the sergeant with the colors and Adjutant MacArthur moved ahead with their own cheering troops close behind, the regiments on their left and right advanced, and shortly thousands of men were sweeping up the ridge, regardless of the murderous fire that poured down on them.

Far up the desperate slope the regimental color bearer of the 24th, still in the van of the advancing line, suddenly collapsed and the flag went down. The 18-year-old MacArthur ran ahead, picked up the flag and shouted for the men to follow him. In a matter of minutes the boy had planted the banner on the crest of the ridge that had shortly before seemed almost invincible.

One or two of the mounted officers at the foot of the long slope, watching the wavering line through their field glasses, saw the gallant incident. A recommendation for a Medal of Honor was made, but somehow it was lost in the whirl of events: it was almost 30 years later in a review of Civil War medals that the oversight was corrected and the then Major Arthur MacArthur of the Regular Army was granted the simple bronze decoration that has no peer in the world.

Shortly after the incident on Mission Ridge, when the greatly depleted regiment found all its field officers either killed or discharged from service on account of wounds, an election was held for a major who would be commanding officer. Without a single protest from any of the older captains, Lieutenant Mac-Arthur was advanced over their heads and chosen major and regimental commander. He was 18½ years old.

By the early spring of '65 the determined Confederate troops found themselves trapped and beaten everywhere by overwhelming power, and young MacArthur knew that the war would soon be over. He wanted a commission in the Regular Army to make soldiering his life's profession. He had not yet turned 20, but he wore the silver leaves of a lieutenant colonel on his shoulders, and he would soon be breveted a colonel of volunteers.

The war had been over only a few weeks when young Mac-Arthur led the proud remnants of his regiment in its homecoming parade down Milwaukee streets. Of the 75 officers who had entrained that rainy afternoon of November 5, 1862, all but 25 had been killed or wounded or taken prisoner. Of the 1,050 men, exactly 334 were still in line.

It was the stories of such deeds and glories that filled the imagination and the memory of the boy Douglas.

2

While he waited in Milwaukee and hoped for an appointment in the newly re-organized Army of the United States, young Colonel Arthur MacArthur read law. The studious habits he acquired never left him. Some ceaseless lash of ambition drove him to use his spare hours in study and in quiet preparation for whatever life might hold for him.

On June 25, 1866, slightly over a year after he had been mustered out of service, he received his commission as a first lieutenant in the re-organized Regular Army. Within three months he was commissioned a captain in the 36th Infantry, then on the Indian Frontier under the command of the grizzled old fighter, Brevet Major General John Gibbon, one-time commander of Wisconsin's famous Iron Brigade. Three years later the 36th was consolidated with the 7th Infantry and shortly afterwards Captain MacArthur was assigned to K

6

Company, 13th Infantry, then at Fort Rawlins, Wyoming Territory.

Once again the young soldier was in Indian country—the beautiful, high country, with its constant excitement and the eternal hope of action that somehow never quite came off. In lonely evenings years later the captain used to tell his sons about these days when he had helped guard the vanishing frontier. Douglas and his brother never tired of hearing the tales of Custer and Wesley Merritt and the incomparable Ranald Mac-Kenzie. The three had been West Pointers of the classes of '61 and '62, and like the young boy colonel from Wisconsin, they had won fame in their youth.

Ordinarily Captain Arthur MacArthur was a reserved man, but in the eyes of his little boys he was the most romantic figure that ever lived. They would never lose the love of country and flag and honor that he implanted in them. And there was another word—duty—that he constantly used.

In October of 1874 Captain Arthur MacArthur and his company were ordered to Jackson Post near New Orleans. In seven years of soldiering in the high Indian country, Arthur MacArthur had discovered that there was much justice on the Indian side. Many years later when stars were on his shoulders instead of captain's bars, the harsh truths that he had learned in the long fruitless campaigns and endless duties on the Indian frontiers were to be of great value in solving the problem of handling the Filipinos and their demands for independence. He passed these lessons down to his sons Douglas and Arthur.

Yankee soldiers were far from popular in the New Orleans country a decade after the war ended. Nevertheless there were many marriages between southern girls and northern men in uniform. During the Mardi Gras festival in 1875 Captain Mac-Arthur met Mary Pinkney Hardy, a lovely young lady from Norfolk who had come down to spend the gay season with friends.

When she returned to the large family home at Riveredge, at the foot of the bridge across the river at Norfolk, in what later was called Berkley, it was not long before the Yankee soldier reported there.

It became a legend that at the wedding, May 19, 1875, two

of the bride's brothers who had attended the Virginia Military Institute and fought for the Confederacy were conspicuous by their absence; it seemed quite sufficient to them that three of the older sisters had already married northerners whom they had met at the family summer home in Massachusetts. Time however was to dull the tiny feud. In the late fall of 1951, when General of the Army Douglas MacArthur paid his first visit to Norfolk since boyhood, he spoke at the dedication of a memorial erected by popular subscription on the site of the old Colonial house where his mother was born. He made proud reference to his mother's brothers who had fought for the Stars and Bars: "From this spot Hardys followed 'Marse Robert's' flag on Virginia's bloody fields—and a Hardy was at 'Old Jack's' elbow that dark night when he fell on the sodden Plank Road near Chancellorsville."

Mary Pinkney Hardy, known in the family as Pinky, on both ancestral sides was from early American stock that had settled in Virginia and North Carolina before the turning of the 18th century. She was born on May 22, 1852, the eleventh of fourteen children, ten of whom grew to maturity.

For many years her father, Thomas Asbury Hardy, was a successful cotton broker in Norfolk, and in 1858 he purchased a vast plantation called Burnside, five miles from Henderson, North Carolina. It may have been that some ray of intuition led the father to anticipate the outbreak of the great civil conflict, and thus provide a refuge for his family when actual war broke.

After the war the family moved temporarily to Baltimore, where Mary and three of her sisters for a time attended the Convent of the Visitation Order in Catonsville, Maryland, although her parents were not Catholics. The rest of her education came from private tutors. Shortly the family returned to the great house on the outskirts of Norfolk. Here the 30-year-old Yankee captain and the lovely 22-year-old southern aristocrat were married by Rev. Father Matthew O'Keefe, the rector of St. Mary's Church—her personal choice at the time. Later the bride was to become permanently associated with the Episcopal Church.

The first son, Arthur, Jr., was born August 1, 1876, while the captain was on detached duty in Washington. Four months later he and his family reported back to his K Company, 13th Infantry, at New Orleans. A second son, named Malcolm, was born in October of '78.

K was moved to the government arsenal at Little Rock the following year, and it was in a pleasant two-family dwelling in Officers Row that Douglas came into the world on January 26, 1880. Five months later K Company joined the rest of the 13th Regiment at Fort Leavenworth, Kansas, but almost immediately K, with four other companies and the regimental band, was ordered to Las Lumas on the Rio Grande in New Mexico, to embark on the eight-day wagon-train journey to distant Fort Wingate.

Two years later the captain was granted the first long leave in his 17 years of regular service, and the family spent six months at the great house in Norfolk. Toward the end of the holiday death struck blindly at the little family. Two faded yellow telegrams that are still preserved tell the story.

BANKERS AND MERCHANTS TELEGRAPH CO.

NORFOLK, VA.

APRIL 9, 1883

TO ADJUTANT GENERAL,

U. S. ARMY

WASHINGTON, D. C.

TWO OF MY CHILDREN ARE ILL ONE DANGEROUSLY AND PERHAPS FATALLY SO I WOULD LIKE TO REMAIN DURING CRITICAL PERIOD AND THEREFORE ASK ONE WEEKS EXTENSION OF MY LEAVE DIRECTLY FROM THE DEPARTMENT

ARTHUR MACARTHUR JR.

CAPT. 13TH INF.

A wire came back granting the request. A second wire was dispatched almost immediately to the Adjutant General:

ONE OF MY CHILDREN DIED LAST NIGHT ANOTHER NOT MENTIONED IN PREVIOUS DISPATCH NOW ILL UNDER THESE CIRCUMSTANCES I ASK TEN DAYS FURLOUGH EXTENSION OF MY LEAVE IF CONSISTENT WITH INTERESTS OF SERVICE

It was the middle son named Malcolm who had succumbed to the virulent outbreak of measles. His death proved a terrible

9

blow to the mother. But gradually the sorrow was forgotten in her growing devotion to her son Douglas. It never failed in it completeness to the day when she died 52 years later.

This devotion between him and his mother was one of the dominant factors of his life. When he was 71 and returned from Korea, exalted by the nation's reaction to his recall, he stood on the spot where the Hardys had lived so long and referred to her as "my sainted mother."

3

The MacArthur family numbered only four when orders came for K Company to march overland from Fort Wingate the 300 miles to tiny Fort Selden, roughly 60 miles above El Paso and the nearby Fort Bliss. It was a matter of accepted army routine that this austere assignment had come to Captain MacArthur.

The single-story, flat-roofed adobe buildings of the little post lay in a windswept bend of the river, on the east bank of the Rio Grande. To the north was the forbidding and waterless desert that for more than 200 years the Spanish had called *El Jornado del Muerto,* the Journey of Death. The Mascalero Apache Indian reservation was a bare hundred miles to the east, across the San Andres Range and the deadly white sands. Beyond the Sacramento Mountains stretched the broad Pecos Valley.

Company K with its two or three officers, its assistant surgeon and 46 enlisted men comprised the lonely garrison. Most of the time Mrs. MacArthur was the only officer's wife at the post, and there were not even the colorful guard mounts and parades to break the deadly monotony. Instead, there was always real danger of marauding Apaches who now and again swept across the bleak mountains and deserts.

For two and a half years the captain and his wife met the endless and weary routine of this tiny isolated post without complaint or slackness of duty. It was unquestionably hard on the health and patience of the Virginia aristocrat who served with him, but she, too, was of the gallant breed of the old army.

10

Douglas grew more and more to resemble her in looks and temperament. Even before the family left Fort Selden, she had begun to implant in his eager mind the idea that he would grow up to be a great man. Some day he must be a general as distinguished as Robert E. Lee.

At the same time his father, poring over his books of evenings, quietly began the education of his boys. Along with the 3 Rs, he instilled in them a stern sense of obligation. They were always to do what was right and just, and forever their country was to come first in their hearts.

Life was far from dull for the two brothers. They had their own little spotted Navajo ponies to ride, and there were hitch-hikes on the mule-drawn water wagon that made its regular trip to the Rio Grande, a mile and a half from the post. And there were visiting officers and mounted details from the cavalry post at Fort Stanton on to the east that guarded the nearby Mescalero Apache reservation. Toward twilight each evening the company would go through the ceremony of retreat and the lowering of the flag, and while the bugle sounded the two little boys would stand at stiff attention.

And there was the time when the few mules and horses of the post, lazily loose-herded by a sleepy sentinel, suddenly were sent into a panic by an object as unaccountable as a gray ghost, or a mirage moving down from the sandy wastes of the *Jornado del Muerto*. By chance the boys were sitting nearby on their pintos, and they were as flabbergasted as the soldier, rubbing his eyes and swearing by the Virgin he had had nothing to drink since last pay day. For there in stately loneliness stood a shaggy camel. Nine-year-old Arthur recognized it by its ungainly shape, and the pair galloped to their father's office to tell him of the visitor.

The captain, knowing his military history, at once recognized the desert phenomenon as a survivor of the herd of camels that Jefferson Davis, when Secretary of War, had brought from Egypt by chartered ship in 1855. They were to serve as pack animals to supply the chain of isolated forts in this vast desert Indian country, but gradually they strayed away from army service.

Late in 1886 the welcome orders came to Captain MacAr-

11

thur that he was to take his K Company to Fort Leavenworth, the great post on the west bank of the Missouri, 20 miles or so north of busy, growing Kansas City.

It was a new and thrilling world the 6½-year-old Douglas now entered. Here was a regular school in which he was registered as a second-grade pupil. So conscientious had been the home tutoring by his father that the older brother Arthur, just turned 10, had no trouble enrolling in the sixth grade.

It was wonderful for the boys to have playmates their own age and to learn games and make friends. And there was an endless flow of excitement in the sprawling post itself. Douglas never tired of watching the mounted troops drill and the artillery battery fire its practice rounds. Then there were the formal afternoon parades when the colonel and his staff sat their fine horses and saluted as the mounted men and the long-barrelled guns and caissons rolled by, and the foot companies wheeled into company front.

The father's once bright hopes for high rank were slowly turning into grave doubts. He was definitely and irreparably behind the Civil War promotion hump. Yet despite these years of discouragement and partial frustration, he never ceased his study and quiet preparation.

When he found out that there was to be a vacant majority in the Adjutant General's department, he asked several of his old army friends for letters of recommendation. A typical reply was the one written to the Adjutant General by Brevet Major General Alexander McDowell McCook, head of the Cavalry and Infantry school and post commander at Leavenworth:

> He is beyond question the most distinguished Captain in the army of the U. S. for gallantry and good conduct in war. He is a student, a master of his profession, has legal ability, which fits him for the position he seeks, is exceptional in habit, temperate at all times, yet modest withal.

That summer of 1889 his appointment as a major arrived, and he was ordered to report for duty in the Adjutant General's office in Washington. He had by now been a captain almost 23 years.

In Washington the newly promoted major missed the busy

routine of a company command, and Douglas and his older brother found no substitute for the color and excitement of Fort Leavenworth or even for the tiny post on the far-away Rio Grande. But there was the exciting competition of school, and much talk soon began of young Arthur's hope to get an appointment to West Point. The father pulled every string he knew, but in the end he had to compromise on an appointment to Annapolis for his elder son.

Douglas now spent many happy hours with his grandfather, the retired judge, Arthur MacArthur, Sr., a gentle old man with wise, kindly eyes. He had first seen the light of day in Glasgow on the 26th of January, 1815, 65 years to the day before the birthday of his grandson, Douglas. The Scots boy with his sturdy, widowed mother had voyaged to Boston on one of the first steam packets. He was graduated in law by the time he was 25, and he hung out his shingle in Springfield, Massachusetts.

Shortly afterward he was made judge advocate of the Western Military District of Massachusetts, and married Aurelia Belcher. A son named Arthur, Jr., born on June 2, 1845, was four years old when the family left for the booming western city of Milwaukee.

Four years later the energetic young lawyer was elected lieutenant governor of Wisconsin and almost immediately found himself in a dangerous and complicated political fight. In order to avert bloodshed he retired as acting governor after the State Supreme Court had debarred the incumbent. As a result of his cool-headed action in stepping aside and protecting the good name of Wisconsin, he gained many admirers. When his term as lieutenant governor ended, he was made judge of the Second Judicial Circuit. In 1870 President Grant appointed him a justice of the United States Court of the District of Columbia, and he served on the high bench for 18 years. He had only recently retired from the federal bench in 1889 when his army officer son, Arthur, Jr., and his family settled down in the capital for a tour of duty. In September 1893, about the time his eldest soldier-son and namesake was assigned as assistant adjutant general to the Department of Texas at Fort Sam Houston in San Antonio, the Judge journeyed to Atlantic

13

City for a few days by the sea. He died there in the midst of his little holiday.

4

Douglas was lacking three months of 14 when the three Mac-Arthurs detrained at San Antonio. The new West Texas Military Academy had just commenced its first year, and he was immediately enrolled there. It meant much to the boy to be back again where there were troops and the colorful trappings of army life. Fort Sam was one of the most important posts of the entire Army at this time, and by a big margin it had the largest garrison of any military reservation the boy had known.

There were pleasant quarters for the major and a maid for his wife, and life was good. Yet somehow the MacArthurs seemed to live a quieter life than most of the other officer families. With them there was no constant exchange of calls and teas and dinner parties. Of evenings the major, now approaching his 50s, continued his endless studies.

An interesting sidelight on this extraordinary man is found in his efficiency report dated "Adjutant General's Office, Washington, May 1, 1890." In the section under the heading *Remarks* is a report of his personal qualifications written out by Major MacArthur himself, in answer to a request by the Department. It read:

> Investigations in Political Economy pursued for many years, through writings of modern economists including Adam Smith, Thomas Robert Malthus, David Ricardo, John Stuart Mill, Carey, Bagehot, Leslie, Jevons and many other standard writers.
>
> Special inquiry made into the colonial and revolutionary period of American history, the formation and adoption of the present Constitution, and the subsequent Constitutional development of the Republic; together with a comparison of the American and English constitutions.
>
> Also quite an extensive examination into the civilization and institutions of China.

From his first year at the little military school, young Douglas, too, proved his flair for scholarship and for general intellectual attainment. When he graduated in 1897 as valedictorian, his 4-year average was 97.33. He had already learned the art of concentration, and it was clear that he had an unusually fine mind.

He was not a rugged, closely knit youth, but in his slender body was the spirit that his father had possessed at this age on his first battlefield. Fifty-five years after Douglas graduated, a classmate, Garahl Walker, wrote out these few words of reminiscence:

I thought he was too light for the football team; however, they took him and made him quarterback which did not require so much weight but brains and nerve. He held the job down. The scrimmages were hard on him. You could see his lips turn blue but he would get up and fight it again. I know all the boys believed in him and I wish they were living to see the fight he is making now.

Certainly he had perfect physical coordination and always a determined will to win. He played shortstop on the baseball team and developed into a star.

During his four years at the Academy Douglas was a day student. A school rule restricted the appointment of the various cadet officers to boys who were regular boarders, and he had to be satisfied with the rank of first sergeant of A Company, but this did not keep him from organizing and training the prize-winning drill squad.

As far back as he could remember, his father had expounded to him the glories of West Point and had gone about the task of lining up an appointment. Time and again the major brought to his home some recently graduated young shavetail to tell his son of the customs and regulations of the Academy, the type of entrance examinations and the courses of study. Major MacArthur still looked to his home town of Milwaukee and the Congressman there to give his son the golden chance at an appointment.

Douglas was ready now for the great test. He was 17½ and physically developed and mentally mature. His character was set. He was reserved and studious. He had learned to keep his eye on the ball. He knew exactly what he wanted to do and where he wanted to go. West Point was the immediate goal.

First of all he must get an appointment, but there seemed to be no opening in sight. Finally a note came from Congressman Theobald Otjen, of Milwaukee, explaining that he would hold a competitive examination for a West Point candidate and alternate in the late spring of 1898. He would be glad to have the son of his old friend enter the competition.

In January 1897 Major MacArthur had been advanced from assistant adjutant general to adjutant general of the Department of Texas. In September he was promoted to lieutenant colonel, and the following month he was assigned to the Department of the Dakotas at St. Paul.

In order to forestall any question about the correctness of Douglas entering the competitive examination for the West Point appointment, it was decided that he and his mother would establish their residence in Milwaukee while the father proceeded alone to his new post in St. Paul. So for more than a year Mrs. MacArthur and Douglas occupied comfortable quarters in the old Plankington House, and he studied intensively for the tests.

On a February day in 1898 the country was shaken with the report of the blowing up of the battleship *Maine* in Havana harbor, and on April 7 war was declared.

Lt. Colonel Arthur MacArthur lost no time in getting in touch with his friend Major General Henry Clark Corbin, Adjutant General of the U. S. Army. He was first assigned to Tampa and then to Chickamauga Park as adjutant general of the 3rd Army Corps. On June 1, 1898, the day before he was 53, the hoped-for telegram arrived that announced his appointment as brigadier general of volunteers:

YOU HAVE BEEN CONFIRMED AND COMMISSION SIGNED BY PRESIDENT SECRETARY WAR DIRECTS YOU REPORT GENERAL MERRITT SAN FRANCISCO FOR DUTY WITH EXPEDITION FOR PHILIPPINES.

H. C. CORBIN,
ADJUTANT GENERAL

The new brigadier general immediately wired the news to his wife in Milwaukee, but her pride and happiness over his star was dimmed by her fears that he might not be able to withstand the rigors of a tropical campaign.

16

Four days after the telegram arrived, Douglas, now 18, began to take the competitive examination for the appointment to West Point. When the marks were announced he led off with an average of 93.3%, and his nearest competitor rated 77.9.

But despite the unusually high scholastic marks he made in the competitive examination, his actual entrance into the Military Academy was postponed until June 1899, when his predecessor graduated. He decided to take special instruction under a Professor McLenagan, principal of the West End High School. For some months he took courses in chemistry, physics and other studies that required laboratory equipment. Outside the school rooms he continued to study advanced algebra, English and history.

On July 31, 1898, his father arrived in the Philippines with 4,700 men of the Third Expedition. In August General Merritt ordered the city surrounded and the Spanish garrison attacked. The underfed, underpaid and neglected Spanish troops put up only a token defense, and with a small loss of life the Americans took over Manila. To the new brigadier general the victory brought the rank of major general of volunteers.

Now came reports that trouble was brewing between the Americans and General Emilio Aguinaldo's native troops, who claimed that they had won their national independence, and that the new white conquerors should turn over to them their Pearl of the Orient.

On the morning of February 5, 1899, cable dispatches reported that fighting had broken out on the northern edge of Manila, and MacArthur's army division was advancing to the northward. His six volunteer regiments drawn from the farms and ranches and small towns west of the Mississippi responded gallantly to his spirited leadership.

Among the officers in his division there were three who especially won his friendship and admiration. Of these, two were from the Regular Army: Captain J. Franklin Bell, his roving scout, and Captain Peyton C. March, his own senior aide. The third officer was a stubby, picturesque fighting man, Frederick Funston, colonel of the 21st Kansas Volunteers. All three were to profit by their services under the generous MacArthur. Within the year Bell would rise from a captain in the regulars to a brigadier general of volunteers; March from a captain to a full colonel of volunteers; and Funston, trained in the hard school of the Cuban insurrection, from the colonel of the 20th Kansas to a brigadier general of volunteers. There was another young officer who had caught MacArthur's eye—a dashing lieutenant of the Signal Corps, a Milwaukee lad named Billy Mitchell, son of the Wisconsin Senator who had served beside Arthur MacArthur in the 24th Wisconsin.

The hard-fighting soldier was overjoyed at the prospect of his youngest son entering West Point in June 1899. "He told me that he started Douglas towards West Point the day he was born," General Peyton C. March, Chief of Staff during World War I, recalled five decades after Douglas entered the Academy.

Late in May 1899, as Douglas and his mother journeyed eastward to West Point, they read newspaper dispatches of the severe fighting going on at that moment north of Manila. General MacArthur had suddenly emerged as one of the heroes of this war.

Strange and unaccountable consequences, however, were to come from this well-deserved publicity.

2

THE LONG GRAY LINE

Douglas had no trouble passing the West Point entrance examinations. On his physical report was written *Normal*.

His height was marked down as 5 ft., 10$\frac{1}{10}$ in. He weighed 133 pounds, and he was 19 years and 4 months old. The report bore the date of June 3, 1899.

Soon after his entrance his mother embarked on the somewhat unusual procedure of settling at the old West Point Hotel toward the north end of the Military Reservation and off limits to the cadets. Until two years later, when her husband returned from his three-year tour in the Philippines, she spent much of her time there.

At this particular period physical hazing, "exercising," as it was called in the cadet vernacular, was probably about as severe as ever in the long history of the Academy. On July 1, 1899, the members of MacArthur's plebe class finished with "beast" barracks and their initial breaking-in by the lordly first classmen or seniors. They were in summer camp under the mercies of the yearlings or sophomores, who had recently completed their own plebe year and been "recognized." Only the members of the yearling class were permitted by custom to indulge themselves in exercising the new cadets.

At the time, the newspapers were filled with cables regarding the Luzon fighting and the fine part General MacArthur was playing in the campaign. To certain of the more perverse yearlings this was excuse enough to turn on his tall, serious son, who, like all good plebes, was doing his level best to mind his own business.

His tentmate was Frederick H. Cunningham from Utica, who had graduated that June from Hamilton College. After Cunningham had been in camp for six weeks he resigned—largely in disgust over the hazing he had witnessed—and on August 20 of this year of 1899 there appeared in the then powerful *New York Sun* an unsigned letter to the editor. It described the various forms of West Point hazing, including the practice of calling out a plebe and forcing him to fight with bare fists the best boxer of his weight and height in the yearling class. The unfair part of the custom was that if the plebe happened to win, he would have to fight another third classman, and on and on until he finally was whipped.

Shortly before Cadet Cunningham had resigned, there occurred one of a number of futile Academy investigations into this problem of physical hazing. The superintendent and the commandant had on a Sunday called the plebe class to a room in the Academic Building and taken aside and interrogated several of the cadets who were under suspicion of having been badly hazed. MacArthur was one of those who were questioned. He refused to divulge the names of any of the yearlings who had exercised him.

With the cadets back in barracks in the fall and the academic year begun, the serious exercising was ended, and the Academy resumed the even tenor of its isolated ways. Apparently the hazing episodes of this particular summer of 1899 had been forgotten. It was not until a year later that a storm of violent public protest and censure hit West Point, mostly centering on indignities practiced on certain members of the class preceding MacArthur's.

In this plebe class of 1898 was an unfortunate boy, Oscar Lyle Booz from Bristol, Pa. Young Booz apparently was generally disliked by the upperclassmen, and life was made unpleasant for him. It was probably true that the persistent hazing he received and the calling-out fights he experienced were reflected in his poor scholarship and his being dismissed in the first-term examinations.

Almost two years later the young man died of tuberculosis at his home in eastern Pennsylvania. The Congressman from his district rose in the Lower House and bitterly charged that West Point hazing was the cause of his death.

Douglas was a third classman, or yearling, that fall of 1900, when this scandal which had occurred two years previously was played up in the metropolitian papers. Already Douglas had made his mark at the Point, standing No. 1 in his class and showing the superiority and leadership that was to mark his half century of soldiering.

On December 11, 1900, President McKinley ordered a special court of inquiry to convene at once at West Point, "to investigate the alleged treatment of former Cadet Oscar L. Booz" and "the extent to which new cadets are now subject to such treatment."

The preliminary days of the hearing were almost exclusively concerned with the Booz matter that had occurred in the summer of 1898, the year before MacArthur's class entered. But before long the testimony switched to more recent episodes, and soon the hazing of young MacArthur became one of the principal matters of investigation.

On January 18 his case was taken up in great detail. His

20

answers to the questions were shrewd and carefully worded. It was evident from the start that he was determined not to involve any upperclassman still in the Academy, and to minimize the incident in every way possible, thus protecting the good name of West Point at any cost save that of giving false testimony. After he was sworn by the Chairman of the Congressional Committee, the questions and answers began:

Q Mr. MacArthur, we have received a great deal of evidence that you were severely hazed. The committee is desirous of having you tell your own story in your own way, giving to us the names of the cadets by whom you were hazed, the date, as near as you can, the time, the place, and the physical effect on you personally of the hazing at that time.

A I cannot tell exactly the time; it was after I had been a plebe about a month, I should say.

Q And the year, please?

A 1899. The hazing I underwent I have seen something about; I have heard accounts of it in the newspapers, and elsewhere, and, like all such matters that start out as a comparatively small thing, it has grown to very large proportions. The hazing that I underwent was in no way more severe or more calculated to place me in a serious physical condition than has ordinarily taken place. I was not in any physical condition that would tend to injure me at all. I have heard it stated, in fact I have seen it in the newspapers, that I was at one time hazed until I suffered severe convulsions. No such affair took place. I was hazed at the time in question until I was quite tired; I might say more than that. As far as my physical muscles were concerned I did not have complete control of them, but as far as being in convulsions, or in any way delirious, or anything of that kind, or out of my head, I most emphatically deny it. . . . I was not obliged to attend hospital for any cause during plebe camp. On the night in question I think I was suffering with a case of exaggerated cramps. That is the only thing I could call it. The place of exercising was over in camp, in one of the "A" company tents. I did not exercise, I do not think, longer than men frequently have and suffer no consequences at all. I was not in a condition of nausea that would cause any bad effects. . . .

Q What did your exercising consist of?

A It consisted of eagling. (Continued squatting to the heels, and then rising, with the arms fully outstretched.)

21

Q How many, please?

A I don't know; I would say, at a rough estimate—well, I could not even make a rough estimate. I did not keep track.

Q Have you any recollection?

A Eagling was interspersed with other exercising; I would do one and then the other.

Q How many, should you say, in all?

A I should say, perhaps, 250 would be a good estimate.

Q And what else, please?

A Hanging from a stretcher. (Hanging by the hands from a tent pole.)

Q How long did you have to hang from a stretcher?

A I should say two minutes at a time.

Q In all, how many minutes?

A I don't know. The whole performance, I should say, took an hour, and was about equally divided between the different exercises.

Q What were the others?

A Eagling, hanging from stretcher, what is known as dipping, and I think that was all. . . . (Dipping consisted in lying face down on the floor, and then pumping up and down with the arms.)

Q You say you were suffering from cramps at the time you exercised?

A Afterwards.

Interminably the questioning went on. The 20-year-old boy was pitted against distinguished and experienced probers, but he continued to shield the cadets still in school who might have taken part in his hazing. Nor would he admit until driven to a corner that he suffered from anything more than cramps, and that the word "convulsions" was the proper one to describe his own condition when he finally returned to his tent. But he could not dodge some of the expertly framed questions.

Q Did you consider it cruel at that time?

A I would like to have you define cruel?

Q All right, sir. Disposed to inflict suffering; indifference in the presence of suffering; hard-hearted; inflicting pain mentally or physically; causing suffering.

A I should say perhaps it was cruel, then.

Q You have qualified your answer. Was it or was it not cruel?

A Yes, sir.

Q And you did not expect it was part of the essential education of an officer to be subjected to such cruelty?

A I do not think it is essential; no, sir. . . .

Q And you believe that an Army officer, or a man who may become an officer of the United States Army should not treat one of his fellow-officers, or some one who is going to be a fellow-officer, in that cruel manner?

A I should say not; no, sir.

A week later in the final testimony taken by the court of inquiry in Chicago, the lid was blown off the entire MacArthur episode by his former tentmate, Cunningham, the plebe who had resigned from the Academy after being there less than two months, although he had never once been exercised. His testimony was from the beginning pointed toward the Mac-Arthur hazing.

Q Do you remember an occasion when MacArthur had been in a tent being exercised and on returning to your tent was overcome?

A I do.

Q What time in the evening was it?

A We returned from mess and I went to the sink; I knew that he had been summoned to report to some tent on the company street —Company A. When I returned from the sink he was gone; it was probably about half past 7 or 8 o'clock.

Q And when did you see him?

A I saw him reel into the tent about an hour later.

Q Then what took place?

A I got up and caught him as he fell.

Q And what did you do to him?

A I laid him gently on the floor of the tent.

Q In what condition was he then?

A He was lucid.

Q Was he in violent convulsions?

A He classified them as cramps.

Q I am asking you to tell what you thought.

A I think if you saw him in the same condition on the street you would call them convulsions.

Q Was his body writhing?

A Yes, sir; he showed the most activity, however, in his limbs.

Q To what extent were his limbs in motion?

A To such an extent I had to hold them to keep them still, and finally he asked me to throw a blanket under them in order that the company officers could not hear his feet striking the floor. He had no control over them.

Q Did you put a blanket under them?

A I did.

Q Was there anything put in his mouth?

A There was nothing.

Q Did he ask for anything to put in his mouth?

A He suggested that if he cried out, to prevent his cries being heard, that we put a blanket in his mouth. There was no suggestion of cotton at all.

Q Was there anybody else in the tent besides yourself and MacArthur?

A I cannot distinctly remember now; I am not sure; but I think Smith, M., was on guard that night; I am not sure, but I know as soon as MacArthur returned his inquisitors came around back of the tent and were much concerned over what they had done.

Q What did they do?

A As near as I can remember they did almost everything in the exercising line.

Q I mean, what did they do back of the tent?

A I believe Barry (who was the yearling who had done most of the hazing and was later sent home) ordered someone—a fourth-class man—

Q Do you mean Barry?

A Yes, sir, Barry. He ordered someone to go to the tank and get water for him, and when it was brought he used it so far as he could bathing his head.

Q Do you remember his condition in the morning?

A He got up feeling very—well, he felt, to use a slang expression, very "all in."

Q What is the meaning of that?

A He did not feel like doing anything. He was urged by some— I do not know the names of them—to go on sick report, but he would not do it.

Q He turned out for drill and other duties as if nothing had happened, did he not?

A Yes, sir. . . .

Q You think that MacArthur was let alone after that?

A Yes; I know he was, because I heard—I do not know who it was told me, but I heard it—the next morning that by his plucky

24

work the night before in the soiree that he had got a bootlick on the whole corps.

Q Do you know who it was?

A I am under the impression it was Barry.

Q The exerciser?

A Yes; he came around with the statement that he was making no apologies or did not apologize for things of that sort, and then he followed it with that remark.

Q Is it fair to say that they indicated a deep concern over the severe hazing that MacArthur had had the night before?

A It would indicate a slight worry on the part of those who had indulged in it.

Q What was meant by bootlick; you said that Barry had told MacArthur that he had received a bootlick from the whole corps?

A That he had got a bootlick on the whole corps.

Q What did that mean?

A It means admiration for his plucky resistance of the night before and that they were proud of him, and they would practically give him the glad hand after that, and I believe that the effect of it after that was that he was not hazed.

Q You said physically MacArthur was a pretty good man?

A Yes, sir.

Q He is not what you would term an athletic man, physically, is he?

A He is tall; his muscles are long, not bunchy; he would make a good baseball player, and he is a good boxer.

Q If he was a good boxer and athlete why didn't he resist this brutal hazing, and fight? He understood, did he not, that this was his alternative? Can you imagine why?

A No; save that he did not want to; and then, too, I believe the fact that his mother was at the post led him to put up with more than he otherwise would have done.

Q Now what offense against the upper class code had MacArthur committed the first time that you say he was hazed?

A MacArthur's real offense was that he was the son of General MacArthur.

Q That was a continuous offense, then?

A Yes; he didn't get over that.

Q Do you know of any charge they made against him?

A Yes, they said he did not brace. MacArthur always walked erect and was not slouchy—he could not walk slouchy if he tried.

Q Was MacArthur the sort of man who was vain of his ancestry?

A No, sir; there was not a finer fellow in the class.

25

It was clear that MacArthur had taken the worst they could give him, including the terrible sweat bath; that he never gave up or tried to dead beat; that he had protected the upperclassmen still in the Academy who might have been involved, and used only the names of three yearling cadets who had been discharged.

Out of it all was to come a calm resolve on his part that he would never haze a fellow cadet, and that if the chance ever came he would do everything he could to abolish the evil and stupid custom.

2

Early in September of his plebe year when the academic year began and the classes returned from the tent camp to barracks, MacArthur was approached by a first classman named Hyde and asked if he would room with him.

It was a most unusual proposition, and Douglas must have been a little flattered by the invitation from an ordinarily inaccessible first classman, whom he was not supposed even to address. Living West Pointers of the time can remember no similar case. It was to work out all to the good for the plebe. Regulations permitted a first classman's lights to be on until 11 o'clock, instead of the usual "Lights Out" one hour earlier. This extra study period was well used by Douglas.

Each evening after supper, weather permitting, Douglas invariably walked for a half-hour with his mother. That she spent most of her time during this two-year period at the old Carney Hotel on the post caused no particular comment. Later the Corps would chuckle over the assumed (but highly exaggerated) rivalry that supposedly existed between Mrs. Arthur MacArthur and Mrs. Frederick Dent Grant, daughter-in-law of General U. S. Grant, over the scholastic and military competition of their sons.

After the graduation parade in June 1900, the remaining three classes gathered to hear the reading of the names of the cadet officers and non-coms appointed for the summer camp. Of the new yearling class Grant's name was read first in the list of temporary corporals with MacArthur's name second; later, at the end of the summer camp when the permanent appointments were made for the scholastic year, the order was reversed, and Douglas became senior corporal. It was the highest cadet rank he could attain as a third classman.

When the scholastic standings for the first year were posted young MacArthur stood No. 1 in the order of merit for his class. Grant was second. He had beaten MacArthur only in French.

Early in the summer camp the yearling corporal caught the eye of the tactical officer of A Company, Captain Edmund M. Blake, Field Artillery, who was standing with Cadet Captain Charles Burnett, of A, watching Corporal MacArthur drill a squad of awkward plebes. Finally Blake turned to the cadet captain and said, "There's the finest drill master I have ever seen."

West Point at this time was a completely isolated and self-contained institution. Cadets were absorbed with their own problems and activities. But it was a little different with MacArthur. The presence of his mother during his first two years there not only furnished him with a terrific stimulant and driving power but kept him in touch with the outside world.

In the summer of 1900 he and his mother were thrilled over the announcement that the General had been appointed the first military governor of the Philippines. Heavy criticism had been brewing throughout the United States over the failure to end the bitter Philippine struggle for independence, and the McKinley administration in Washington was deeply worried. It was thought that the appointment of the popular general would go far to quiet suspicion at home.

A few months after the MacArthur appointment the Second Philippine Commission under the chairmanship of Judge William Howard Taft arrived in Manila. Obviously Taft had been sent out by the McKinley Republican administration to push rapidly toward civil government and conciliation at any cost; General MacArthur, however, believed that with the revolt still active and dangerous the time was not ripe for any sentimental experiments in self-rule, no matter how much the Administration back home wanted the fighting to stop.

He had already taken a number of broad and liberal steps

27

toward the advancement of the Filipinos to ultimate citizenship and self-government. He had instituted the fundamental right of *habeas corpus*. He had assigned army officers to build roads, hospitals and schools, and some of his people were acting as school teachers. He was a just and humane man. But his belief that more time was needed before the power of the governing military should be reduced was in direct opposition to the theories and political necessities of Judge Taft.

Shortly after the Treaty of Paris had legally transferred the Philippines to the United States, President McKinley found to his surprise that a first-class rebellion was included in the purchase price of $15,000,000. When the subsequent violent outbreak came, the President and his advisors figured that it could be put down in six months with 30,000 men. But this became a year and 65,000 men, and the guerilla fighting was harsh and continued. And now into the alarming situation was injected the genial Taft, with orders from Washington that for political reasons he must get the little war off the front pages at the earliest possible moment.

It was decided that on July 4, 1901, General MacArthur would turn over complete authority to the new civil government, to be headed by Judge Taft. Shortly before this date an incident occurred which played directly into Taft's hands and fortunately helped to end the bitter, costly struggle. It still constitutes one of the most fabulous chapters in the whole history of the United States Army—the capture of the insurgent leader, General Aguinaldo, by Brigadier General Funston, U. S. Volunteers, and a group of four U. S. Army officers, with a company of loyal Macabebe Scouts. The Scouts were posing as *insurrectos* bringing the captured American officers to Aguinaldo's headquarters, deep in the inaccessible mountains of Isabela Province. At the moment that the Macabebes were being received they overpowered the little Filipino garrison guarding Aguinaldo. MacArthur had had an active part in planning and authorizing the bold enterprise, and when it had been successfully concluded by seizing the Filipino leader, he saw to it that the volunteer officer, Fred Funston, was promoted to be a brigadier general in the Regular Army.

Later Funston was to name his only son after his benefactor.

Eventually he was to incorporate his experiences in both the Cuban and Philippine insurrections into a fascinating book, *Memories of Two Wars*. Its dedication bore the words:

> To the Memory of
> ARTHUR MACARTHUR FUNSTON
> the little boy who in happy days gone by
> often sat on my knees and, open-eyed and
> wondering, listened to the story of the
> cruise of the *Dauntless* and to accounts of
> midnight rides in the Philippines; but who
> now sleeps forever in the national cemetery
> of the Presidio of San Francisco, under the
> shadow of the flag his childish heart so loved.

At dawn one morning the captured Aguinaldo was transferred from the little American gunboat *Vicksburg* to a launch and taken to General MacArthur's quarters at Malacañan Palace on the Pasig river in Manila. He was received with extreme kindness and generosity. So touched was the Filipino leader that he soon voluntarily issued a proclamation advising the Filipinos to give up their struggle and accept the sovereignty of the United States. The U. S. General's handling of the entire delicate situation was to give to the name MacArthur a special place in the hearts of millions of Filipinos.

One incident shortly after Aguinaldo's proclamation advising his followers to lay down their arms was to have an odd bearing on affairs that occurred many years later. Hiding in the hills of Bataan, along with a few hundred ragged, sick and hungry *insurrectos* under General Mascardo, was a 19-year-old major of the Philippine Army named Manuel Quezón. Racked by fever and almost totally incapacitated, he gave himself up to an American lieutenant stationed in the little port of Mariveles on Bataan, who arranged for him to cross the Bay to Manila.

Soon he was shown into the office of the military governor and through the interpreter, Fred Fisher, he explained to General MacArthur that he had been ordered to find out if Aguinaldo had really surrendered. General MacArthur quietly waved him to a room across the hall, and Quezón entered to find himself alone with his hero, General Aguinaldo.

The meeting not only with his beloved chieftain but with

29

the kindly General MacArthur had a profound effect on young Major Quezón. Many years later it was to reflect directly on his relation with General Douglas MacArthur and in his intense and unswerving loyalty to the United States government.

3

During that summer of 1901 Douglas spent his first and only West Point furlough with his mother in Milwaukee. There his father hurriedly joined them after his arrival in San Francisco. Three years had passed since the family had been together.

Douglas stood No. 1 in scholarship at the end of his yearling year and again was appointed the ranking cadet of his class—senior first sergeant of A Company.

As a proud junior or second classman, he could also wear the big A that he had won in baseball. The class of 1901 had graduated in February, and Stephen Abbot, of the class of 1902, was chosen captain of the ball team. Abbot was re-elected captain the following year, and Douglas played on both his teams.

"He was a heady ballplayer, and we used him as a fielder," Abbot declared a half century later. "He was far from brilliant, but somehow he could manage to get on first. He'd outfox the pitcher, draw a base on balls or get a single or outrun a bunt—and there he'd be on first."

In 1902 Douglas was granted a special leave, and in his full-dress uniform with his shining gold chevrons of first captain, he stood as best man for his older brother, Arthur, Jr. The wedding took place at Newport News, Virginia, and it was the first time in several years that the four MacArthurs had been together. The bride of the young naval officer was Mary McCulla, daughter of a famous admiral who had served in Philippine waters the time General Arthur MacArthur had been there. She was to prove a valiant and devoted champion of the army family, and she and Douglas were to survive them all. During periods totalling ten years, Mrs. MacArthur lived with her, and no daughter could have been kindlier or more loyal than this gentle navy girl.

Even in this period, while Douglas was still in West Point, it was evident that he greatly resembled his mother not only in looks but in temperament. He shared with her a rare quality that can only be described as intuition. Arthur, Jr., on the other hand, was far more like his father. He had his father's careful and methodical mind, and he reached his conclusions by cautious analysis and study.

Douglas, however, seemed to have so trained and organized his mental processes that in approaching a problem he could leap across space and arrive at a conclusion that was often uncanny in its accuracy. He could then leisurely marshal his facts and justify his conclusion in reverse. His swift and flashing decisions were apparently the composite result of a logical mind, an uncanny sense of psychological awareness and an equally important code of moral values. These qualities were his in part from a fine inheritance of body and mind and from his long training by his parents in correct values of moral integrity. To these he added the practice of rigid self-discipline.

Many years later a senior officer, Lt. General Robert C. Richardson, who had served three years with him as a fellow cadet, described in a few words the MacArthur of West Point days: "He had style. There was never another cadet quite like him."

A half-century after their graduation, MacArthur's yearling roommate, Colonel George Cocheu, was asked what sort of a person Douglas was as a cadet. "Think of the sort of man he is today," he replied, "and you have exactly the picture of what he was when he graduated in 1903."

During a part of his last year his eyes bothered him, and while he was in the hospital his name was included in a list of "goats" who must take a special examination in mathematics. Indignantly he put on his dress uniform and announced to his roommate that unless his name was removed from the obnoxious list he would immediately resign. He would go directly to the home of the professor who was head of the department, even though his house was out of bounds for cadets and the act might lose him his chevrons as senior captain.

"Think what your father would say if you resigned so soon before graduation," his roommate argued.

"My father will agree that I did the right thing," Douglas insisted.

31

The professor personally admitted him. Douglas saluted and then briefly said that his instructor had no right to put his name on the "goat" list, and that if it were not withdrawn before classes opened the next morning, he would submit his resignation from West Point. He pointed out that his standing was so high that he could be marked as failing completely in the weekly test without his rating for the year being affected. The professor answered that he was not acquainted with the case, but he would look into it.

Before classes were called that next morning, a messenger came with the report that MacArthur's name had been removed from the "goat" sheet. It might seem a trifling matter, but to young MacArthur it was of the essence of personal honor. He had worked hard for almost four years to keep his superior scholastic record absolutely clean, and rather than have it unjustly marred by a mark of failure at the end, he was prepared to resign.

The previous June, when the graduation exercises of the class of 1902 were over, the list of new cadet appointments was read off. There was not the slightest surprise when Douglas MacArthur's name was called out as first captain. It was the supreme military honor that West Point could give him.

It had come to Robert E. Lee, far back in 1828: he stood second in scholarship in the little class of 36 that graduated in 1829. Fifty-six years later a tall, square-shouldered cadet from Missouri named John J. Pershing heard his name called out as first captain for the coming year of 1885: his scholarship standing was 29 in a class of 76. Three years after the high honor touched Douglas MacArthur, a slender cadet named Jonathan Wainwright was singled out to lead the Corps: he stood 24 in a class of 77. Both Pershing and Wainwright were to play important parts in MacArthur's future.

He had had no serious competitor in the military side, but in the final scholastic listing for his third year he lost his lead to Cadets Fiske and Leeds; he stood third, with his rival U. S. Grant III two slots below. That fall, as a first classman, he took time out to manage the football team, but when spring came he did not go out for baseball. He had satisfied his need to

32

win his A, and the fight to recapture first place in scholarship called for his best efforts.

He had never been the slightest degree interested in being rated the most popular cadet, but he was easily the outstanding one. Only a few times in its more than 150 years of history, has the first captain stood No. 1 in scholarship. Douglas was to have this honor and the additional one of having made the highest marks registered in a quarter-century. At times this period of reckoning has been stretched by MacArthur enthusiasts to cover a century, but the Academy's curriculum has several times been changed so that accurate comparisons in grades and standing are impossible.

At the graduation exercises his father and mother were asked to sit on the platform with other notables, but they chose to sit to the rear of the graduating class among other parents and relatives.

When the address was ended, First Captain MacArthur led the line of 93 graduates from their seats in the front rows. After he saluted and accepted his diploma, there was an outburst of applause. He turned quickly from the rostrum and instead of returning to his seat he walked straight on to the rear. He handed the diploma to his father and smiled down at his mother.

A life-time later he was to put into words what West Point meant to him:

Tokyo
15 March 1947

Nearly 48 years have gone since I joined the long grey line. As an Army "brat" it was the fulfillment of all my boyish dreams. The world has turned over many times since that day and the dreams have long vanished with the passing years, but through the grim murk of it all, the pride and thrill of being a West Pointer has never dimmed. And as I near the end of the road what I felt when I was sworn in on The Plain so long ago I can still say—"that is my greatest honor."

MacArthur

"THE POWER
THAT RULES THE PACIFIC . . ."

There was never the slightest doubt in Douglas' mind but that he would choose the Engineers.

In those days the ten top-ranking Academy graduates had the privilege of picking the branch of the service they desired to enter, and almost automatically they chose the Corps of Engineers, where promotion was swifter and where there were many special considerations. The corps elite at this time consisted of 153 officers, with a brigadier general in command and six full colonels occupying the senior posts.

Besides choosing the Engineers it was almost inevitable that Douglas asked for assignment in the Philippines. Here his father had won his great fame, and it was the only spot where there was a chance of taking part in active fighting. There was bitter guerilla warfare in many parts of the Islands, and in Mindanao and Jolo the Moros were stubbornly contesting the American occupation. If a young officer was lucky, he might still see some real action.

On September 21, 1903, Douglas joined the 3rd Battalion of Engineers at San Francisco. Ten days later he sailed on the transport *Sherman* for Manila. With him were several of his classmates, including Second Lieutenant U. S. Grant III and a detachment of engineer troops. His first detail was with Company M of that outfit, quartered in the Luneta barracks in Manila.

During the year he spent in the Islands he saw engineer duty on Leyte, Samar, Panay and Cebu and headed a surveying crew that ran its traverses in the steaming wooded hills around the port of Mariveles on Bataan peninsula in Luzon. In May 1904 he was ordered before a promotion board in Manila. His general average of 88.1 more than qualified him, and he was promoted to first lieutenant. Five months later he boarded the transport *Thomas* for San Francisco.

It had been a busy and profitable year for him. The lure of the Islands had entered his blood, and he had caught the vision of his father and the little group of able and far-sighted men both in the army and in the new civil government who had determined to build here in the Western Pacific a sturdy outpost of American influence. It would be a living example of how a rich country of good will could help turn a backward and impoverished land into a fine and progressive nation that some day might attain complete independence.

Since Douglas was a boy of 14 in San Antonio his father had been making clear to him the vast, unfolding picture of the changing East. He had watched Japan in 1894 start her first war against decadent China and win (1895) the strategic island of Formosa. As a cadet at West Point he pondered the significance of Secretary of State John Hay's Open Door policy of September 6, 1899, and his subsequent prediction, "As goes China, so goes the world." And he had read and digested the speech of Senator Albert J. Beveridge on January 9, 1900, that had enunciated the principle, "The power that rules the Pacific . . . is the power that rules the world."

In February 1904 when Admiral Togo surprised the Russian fleet outside the harbor of Port Arthur, MacArthur had tried without success to wangle his way to the fighting along the Yalu river that eventually developed into the great siege of Port Arthur.

Within three months after he had arrived in San Francisco and was assigned to the Golden Gate harbor defenses, his father was ordered to Tokyo as military attaché to the American Legation, and chief military observer with the Japanese Army in Manchuria. Douglas would have given an arm to go along.

Actually his father missed all but the shouting, for the Japanese entered Mukden on March 10. But he made the most of his opportunity to correlate the work of the several American

35

observers present. One of them was a rugged 42-year-old captain of cavalry, John J. Pershing; and another officer was a wiry, slender field artilleryman, Captain Peyton C. March, who had been MacArthur's aide in Luzon in the summer of 1899.

General MacArthur's reports were not limited to the narrow scope of battle tactics or even strategy. He saw the vast changes that were taking place in the Far East, with Manchuria and Korea as the immediate prizes and all China and the Western Pacific as the ultimate goals of Japanese conquest. He was fully aware that the victory of Japan did not mean the final elimination of Russia in the contest for the mastery of China.

His reports were read and pondered in various offices in Washington, and President Theodore Roosevelt wanted more and more of such penetrating analyses. So it was that the elder MacArthur received a unique assignment: to make a complete study of all the colonial lands of the Far East. His reply to the singular orders was as follows (the "Second Division" in later years became G-2—Intelligence Section):

Yokohama, Japan
October 27, 1905

Chief Second Division,
War Department.

Sir: — In executing the order of the War Department, in respect to certain instructional journeys to Asia, my present purpose is to leave Yokohama about October 30, directly for India, stopping briefly at Hong Kong, Singapore, Rangoon, and reaching Calcutta early in December.

In India my itinerary will be North West Frontier at Peshawar and Quetta, and thence, via Bombay, Hyderabad, Bangalore and Madras to Colombo—thence returning north by way of Java, Siam and Indo China. I hope to be in Shanghai about April 1, and thereafter remain in China six weeks or two months . . .

Before writing this letter, a personal appeal from the General to an old War Department friend in Washington had worked the magic trick, and the 25-year-old Douglas, then serving in San Francisco, was lifted high into the blue by a telegram that read:

36

SPECIAL ORDER   WAR DEPARTMENT,

NO. 222   WASHINGTON, D. C.

OCT. 3, 1905

FIRST LIEUTENANT DOUGLAS MACARTHUR, CORPS OF ENGINEERS, IS RELIEVED FROM PRESENT DUTIES, AND WILL PROCEED TO TOKYO, JAPAN, AND REPORT IN PERSON TO MAJOR GENERAL ARTHUR MACARTHUR, U.S.A., FOR APPOINTMENT AS AIDE-DE-CAMP ON HIS STAFF.

BY ORDER SECRETARY OF WAR.

J. C. BATES,

MAJOR GENERAL,

ACTING CHIEF OF STAFF

Douglas sailed on October 10, exactly two days before the formal signing of the Treaty of Portsmouth, which President Theodore Roosevelt had induced the Russian delegates to accept. To the President and his advisors the Island Kingdom apparently offered less immediate menace than the awakening Empire of Russia.

Some dream of ultimate Russian expansion and conquest had long aroused the concern of British statesmen and pointed them toward a pro-Japanese policy that in turn was *sold* to Washington. There was no underestimating the possible menace of Russia in the inner circle of imaginative men around Theodore Roosevelt. If Russia's march into the heart and fringes of the Asiatic continent could be stopped by Japan in Manchuria, then it would be well worth the shady trick of turning Korea over to Japan as her pay. Japan could block Russia, but it hardly seemed plausible in 1905 that Japan would ever stand squarely against the growing power of America.

Major General Arthur MacArthur was one of the few army officers with the breadth of background and mind capable of an adequate first-hand survey of the vast and complicated Orient. He possessed the necessary equipment to make a careful report on its billion restless people, already beginning to dream of throwing off the domination of European powers. He had helped the Filipinos take their first faltering steps toward independence. He had been in close contact with the Japanese military leaders, and he had caught the true temper of the

37

underlying struggles for Korea and Manchuria and China. He knew that Russia, so recently driven back across the Amur river into Siberia, would again enter the rich plains of Manchuria, and that in the possibly not-too-distant future the battle for global supremacy might well be fought in this Far Eastern world.

The nine months used in the great tour, which swung from Tokyo to the Khyber Pass in the Himalayas and then back in an arc that touched Java and southeast Asia, was without question the most important single factor of preparation in Douglas MacArthur's entire life. Never was Europe or the Atlantic to hold in his eyes the true historic significance or the sense of destiny that these lands of the Western Pacific and the Indian Ocean now assumed. The things he saw and learned, the deep impressions he gained, were to become a part of him, to color and engage all the days of his life.

Thus at 26 he saw clearly and became thoroughly convinced that the very existence and future of America were irrevocably tied up with Asia and its island outposts.

He was not to return to the Western Pacific for 16 years. But never would he escape from the hold that the world of the Far East had fastened upon him.

2

Back in San Francisco in August 1906, he helped his father with his final reports and then hurried on to Washington and the Engineer School at Fort Belvoir. During that winter season he served as a special White House aide to President Theodore Roosevelt at official functions. But events that were shaping up around his father deeply disturbed him.

Before Arthur MacArthur had returned from the Far East he had been made a lieutenant general—the twelfth in the entire history of the Army—with the provision that the rank was to be abolished with his own retirement. He was well aware that this high honor had been given him in place of the post of Chief of Staff. This coveted promotion had fallen to James Franklin Bell, who was just under 50, and who had been one of MacArthur's finest officers in the Luzon fighting.

At the end of January 1907 a wire from the Adjutant General was sent to the old soldier, again in command at San Francisco, stating that the present large geographic army divisions would soon be abolished, but that if he so desired, he might have the Department of the East, with headquarters on Governor's Island in New York harbor.

The upshot of the matter was a most unusual letter that General MacArthur addressed to Secretary of War William Howard Taft. It read in part:

Dear Mr. Secretary:

I have been painfully conscious for some time that my present assignment is not compatible with the traditions of the Lieutenant Generalcy. The further purpose to abolish Divisions, and thereby reduce me to command of a Department, emphasizes the incongruity. It, therefore, seems to me, the sooner the depressing condition is terminated, the better it will be for all the interests involved. This purpose can be accomplished in two ways, viz:

1. By my retirement from active service.

2. By my assignment to special duty, with station outside Washington, and not at the Headquarters of a geographical command. . . .

I doubt, Mr. Secretary, if you fully realize the professional aspect of the decision which now confronts me. The office of Lieutenant General which I now hold, was originally intended to subserve only the highest purposes of military expediency. In consideration of past achievements and of the possibilities of usefulness in future emergencies, the place has perhaps, at times, been unduly magnified; but, on the other hand, it is now so much depressed that in effect it has become merely a title. By process of current events it has been mediatized, and divested of prestige, dignity and influence.

I am reasonably concerned in respect of the partial restoration of the first two of the foregoing attributes; and as such a result can be accomplished without interfering in any way with the policy of the Department to have the army represented in Washington by a junior officer, I am decidedly of the opinion that such a readjustment of the professional status of the Lieutenant Generalcy would be of material advantage to the service.

I would, therefore, be very much obliged if you will give the matter such consideration as may be possible, and would thereafter advise me of your view in the premises as soon as convenient.

In the meantime I remain,

Very respectfully,
Arthur MacArthur

Mr. Taft replied promptly that he "would be glad to have a statement on the project which you offer to submit as a basis of discussion."

Lt. General MacArthur immediately proposed that he be ordered to Milwaukee, where he would write his final report on his visit to Asia. Shortly afterward the delicate and somewhat humiliating matter was brought to a close by an order from J. Franklin Bell, Chief of Staff, directing his old mentor "to proceed to Milwaukee, Wisc., there to perform such duties as may hereafter be assigned . . . by the War Department." He would officially retire June 2, 1909.

Douglas deeply felt the sense of frustration and futility that he knew was plaguing his father. The only possible contribution he could make was to request assignment to a station close by so that he could be near him. He was successful, and on August 10, 1907, he reported to the Engineering Office at Milwaukee under the command of Major W. V. Judson. He lived with his father and mother in the comfortable old three-story mansion on North Marshall Street that his father had rented when he had first been transferred there.

For some reason, which evidently grew out of a definite grating of personalities, Douglas did not quite hit it off with Major Judson. It was natural for the older officer to be somewhat envious of the younger whose family stood so high in Milwaukee social circles and in the esteem of local citizens. The matter came to a head on an official inspection trip to Manitowoc in northern Wisconsin. When the two men registered at the hotel, the senior officer was assigned a small room, and Douglas was led to the best room in the hotel.

Major Judson was aghast at the hotel clerk's affront to his rank and age. He upbraided Douglas and demanded how such a thing could have happened. The young officer explained that possibly the name MacArthur carried some special weight in this part of the world. There was heat attached to the discussion, and it appears that Douglas made little effort to soothe the ruffled feathers of the major.

The upshot of the episode was that Douglas shortly asked to be relieved, and he subsequently was sent to duty at Fort Leavenworth. Major Judson is said to have dropped a note containing derogatory remarks about MacArthur to the officer commanding the 3rd Battalion of Engineers there, with the result that Lieutenant MacArthur was assigned to the worst company in the battalion. But within three months he had whipped the company into an outstanding outfit, and had won the confidence of the commanding officer of the battalion.

In Major Judson's efficiency report, put in after MacArthur had left Milwaukee, he sharply criticized him for "lacking in zeal to learn." When this was brought to MacArthur's attention, he promptly protested and demanded of the commanding general of the Corps of Engineers a complete appraisal of the case, and that a report on his zeal and devotion to duty be made by each of the half-dozen officers under whom he had served. Most favorable reports quickly followed, and Major Judson's criticism was soon forgotten.

This was the first time that Douglas MacArthur experienced the envy and jealousy of older men, but it was to be far from the last.

3

In many ways the assignment to Leavenworth was choice. An ambitious young officer, even if he did not actually attend the classes, was in an atmosphere of serious military study. If he chose, he could largely follow the regular courses and lectures both in the Infantry and Cavalry schools and in the Staff College.

First Lieutenant George C. Marshall had become an honor graduate of the School of the Line in June 1907, and the following year he had been one of the top graduates of the Staff College there. He had been retained as an instructor in the junior school and had been assigned to teach a special course in the Department of Engineering. Marshall, almost a year younger than MacArthur, had been sent to the Islands as his first duty after he graduated from the Virginia Military Institute in 1902, and there he had immediately caught the eye of Major General J. Franklin Bell, at the time commanding general of the Department of the Philippines. Bell had maneuvered the unusual appointment of Marshall to the Infantry and Cavalry schools, where, although he was by far the junior member of the class of 1907, he finished as an honor graduate.

Marshall was ambitious, quick-witted and self-assertive, and he definitely believed in his own future. He had no particular gift for friendship, and his relation with Douglas MacArthur during the two years they served together in Fort Leavenworth was formal and without warmth.

Several unattached young officers of the Corps of Engineers at Leavenworth at this time secured an apartment in one of the houses that had been built as double quarters and set up an engineer mess that was called The Rookery. Douglas lived in a small two-room suite on the second floor, and saw to it that the youngest lieutenant present served as mess officer. Altogether it was a pleasant and gay little club, with always a young bachelor or two from either the cavalry or infantry invited in as a member.

During the years Douglas spent at Leavenworth, dating from the time he was 28 until he was 32, he appeared as the *beau idéal* of a young soldier thirsting for action. Most of his evenings were spent in quiet study, but on week ends there were parties on the post, in the city of Leavenworth and in nearby Kansas City. He drank very little, but now and again he sat in at a poker game that was fitted for the pocketbooks of young lieutenants. More than 40 years later officers would remember him at the end of a pleasant stag dinner singing his favorite song, "Old soldiers never die—they just fade away."

During the last two years of his tour of duty an outstanding young engineer officer, John C. H. Lee, occupied the room adjoining MacArthur's quarters, and his intimate association with Douglas left many indelible impressions on the younger man. Years later when he had won great honor as head of Services of Supply in the European theatre during World War II and had three stars on his shoulders, General Lee would spin yarns of the pranks of old Leavenworth days.

One had to do with the officers' ball team on which Douglas played and which he helped manage, and with the annual visit of the ball club of the Kansas City Country Club. At the first of the series of games on the post, the Leavenworth strategy was to entertain the visitors so lavishly with food and drink at the luncheon before the game that they were easily outplayed and roundly beaten.

The following year the Kansas City contingent ate and drank heartily, but secretly held back from the feast some of their best players. This time they overwhelmed the Army team. The score in the series was now 1 and 1.

At the luncheon preceding the third annual game, MacArthur humorously introduced two presentable young men as recent graduates who had been stars on the West Point team. It was observed that the pair of young officers had little to say, and the game had become a whopping victory for the Army before it was discovered that the alleged young West Pointers were a pair of Texas bush ringers imported at the cost of a $20 bill—when $20 was considerable money.

Douglas kept a riding horse and tried his hand on the Engineers' polo team, which could hardly compete with the ardent cavalry players. He was particularly competent in his lectures delivered in the latter part of his tour of duty. His real interest inevitably lay within his own profession.

At dinner one evening in the Rookery mess one of the new instructors was bewailing the custom of the question-and-answer period that followed each school lecture.

"I'll tell you how I handle it," Douglas piped up. "At the end of my first lecture in a new course I announce that now is the time for the question period. Then I explain that my soldier father used to say that when he was at Leavenworth there were three kinds of students who ask questions. The first group comprise the lazy students who want the instructor to do their work for them. The second group consist of the fawning students who seek to gain the instructor's favor by flattering him. The third group are the so-and-sos who wished to embarrass the instructor. Then I add quickly, 'Are there any questions?'"

Douglas had been at Leavenworth two years when he reported to a promotion board at the Army Building in New York and on February 27, 1911, was made captain of engineers. He was now adjutant of the 3rd Battalion, and in addition he served as quartermaster and commissary officer, engineer officer, and disbursing officer and was in charge of the engineer depot at Leavenworth. As a sort of extra duty in November 1910 he had been assigned as "member of a Board of Officers to report on certain changes in the pontoon equipage."

The last two years of his service at Leavenworth were filled with odd details that added up to his education as a thoroughly competent combat engineer officer. For one thing, he spent several weeks on an official visit to the Panama Canal Zone, busying himself in the study of that vast engineering project.

There was much social activity around the Panamanian capital city, and a legend persists that he left the heart of at least one of the young ladies he had been squiring in a very shattered condition. He was to remember in particular many evenings he spent at the home of Captain Robert E. Wood of the West Point class of 1900, later head of Sears, Roebuck & Co. They had known each other at West Point and were to be firm friends for the rest of their lives.

From March 7 to July 15, 1911, Captain MacArthur served with the Manoeuvre Division that had been activated in San Antonio as a result of tense Mexican-American relations along the border. The next year he was made a regular instructor in the Department of Engineering at the Fort Leavenworth Service Schools. It was a step up, but he had had more than enough of the wind-swept plains of the Kansas post. He had tried shortly after his arrival for an assignment as an instructor in the Engineering Department at West Point, but for some reason he had been blocked by the superintendent, Colonel Hugh Lenox Scott. To add now to his general discontent, he was deeply concerned over the declining health of both his father and mother.

Early in the morning of September 6, 1912, an orderly from the Officer of the Day's office knocked at the door of his quarters. The telegram the messenger handed him was brief: his father had died suddenly while addressing the comrades of his old Civil War regiment.

As Douglas made his hurried preparations to join his mother in Milwaukee, he recalled a remark his father had made: "I have received every honor my country could give me, save that of dying at the head of her troops."

5

He was met at the depot in Milwaukee by Brigadier General Charles King, a devoted family friend and old comrade-in-arms of General Arthur MacArthur and a military historian and novelist. That same morning King had written out an official report of the General's death and dispatched it to the Adjutant General in Washington. It read in part:

> At ten o'clock on the evening of Thursday, Sept. 5, while addressing at a banquet the survivors of the 24th Wisconsin, his old regiment from '62 to '65, Lieut. General MacArthur suddenly expired.
>
> For over a year the General had suffered from hyper-acidity of the stomach. Of late his condition had aroused the anxiety of Mrs. MacArthur and of their neighbor, myself. The day had been the hottest of the season; the General had taken little nourishment for three days previously, and, fearing the result, Mrs. MacArthur begged him not to go, but aided him to dress when she found he could not be dissuaded. She was, therefore, measurably prepared for the announcement over the telephone that the General had been taken seriously ill, and came bravely forward to meet me when a few minutes later it became my duty to break the news. She herself asked at once, "Is he dead?" and was answered simply in the affirmative. For an instant she bowed her head; then quietly walked to her room with the family physician; was presently joined there by my wife, and the pastor of the Emmanuel Church. With her own hand she wrote the dispatches to her sons, and the newspaper story of her screaming and swooning is absolutely untrue.
>
> On my return from the telegraph office I received a message from Mrs. MacArthur asking me to take charge of preparation for the funeral and asking me to call at ten in the morning.

It was then that Mrs. MacArthur told me, as I already had heard from her own lips, that the General desired not to be buried in his uniform, and added that he had explicitly told her he wished his funeral to be as simple as it could be made and utterly devoid of military display. . . .

Only two additional items needed to be added, and they were included in the subsequent report by General King: apoplexy was assigned as the official cause of his death; and the flag of his country was placed upon his casket and buried with him.

Forty years later a lone figure still lived in Milwaukee who had witnessed the dramatic scene of the General's passing. He was Colonel Horace Martin Seaman, who had been colonel of the 4th Wisconsin Regiment during the Spanish War. On this tragic evening in 1912 he had been invited to sit at the speakers' table as a representative of the Wisconsin National Guard.

Colonel Seaman distinctly recalled how the ninety veterans had sung their campaign songs and greeted their comrades. Finally the dinner was over, the invocation pronounced and the speeches started. Then it came the turn of the old soldier who as a slender youth of 19 had commanded the regiment through its last year and a half of battle.

"Comrades," the General began slowly, "I am here against the advice of my physician, but I could not stay away on this great anniversary of our starting to the war. Little did we think a half century ago that so many of us would be permitted to gather in this way."

He seemed to falter and his face lost its color.

"Comrades," he gasped, "I cannot proceed—I—."

He crumpled up on the table in front of him, and the old men who as youths had followed him up Mission Ridge and into the fire on a dozen battlefields tenderly watched over him.

The regimental surgeon, Dr. William J. Cronyn, who had bound up their wounds in the long ago, hurried forward and examined the General.

"Comrades, the General is dying," he said simply.

Someone in the middle of the room began to repeat the Lord's prayer, and the others followed.

46

Captain Parsons took down the flag that hung behind the speaker's stand and laid it over the body of the General. Then the captain himself faltered and Colonel Seaman held him up. His lips were white and he had difficulty whispering to the younger man: "I—I can't move. I—I've had a stroke."

Two weeks later Captain Parsons, too, was dead.

6

The eldest son, Lt. Commander Arthur MacArthur, had sped to Milwaukee for the funeral and remained with his mother as long as his leave would permit. Before he returned to his navy duty, Douglas assured him that, for the time being at least, he would somehow find a way to be with their mother and to look after her.

But it proved far more easily said than done. He immediately asked for reassignment, but he was blocked by a red-tape rule that an officer of the Engineer Corps attached to an army service school was removed from the jurisdiction of his branch. Any change in station had to originate with the local officer in command. In the end the distraught son took his pride in his hand and wrote straight to the Director of the Army Field Engineering School at Leavenworth.

His letter asking for immediate transfer because of the serious illness of his mother was so compelling that the commanding officer of the school wrote Washington that, while he was loath to lose the services of Captain MacArthur, he would recommend that the request be granted.

Back down the long list of official stations the document gathered its additional endorsements. On November 4 the eighth and final endorsement was signed by the acting chief of engineers, in Washington, D. C. Captain MacArthur was duly relieved from duty at Fort Leavenworth and assigned to Washington.

A few days later he started with his mother on the exhausting train trip to that city. For the moment he was primarily absorbed with the grim task of helping his mother to live.

4

A WILD NIGHT IN VERA CRUZ

Captain MacArthur had been in the capital exactly a month when he was assigned to temporary duty with the General Staff. This top group consisted at this time of 38 officers, 10 of whom were ordinarily on leave or on detached duty. It was the brains of the Army, when it came to planning wars or deciding matters of highest importance. Its exact duties were still a bit nebulous, for the old branches comprising the several services such as Infantry, Cavalry, and Artillery still functioned separately, each branch zealously guarding its own prerogatives.

The 32-year-old MacArthur immediately caught the eye of Major General Leonard Wood, who in 1910 had succeeded J. Franklin Bell as Chief of Staff. MacArthur proved at once that he was alert, of broad military background and knowledge and not afraid to present his own ideas. During his years at Leavenworth he had assiduously followed the various classes in the School of the Line and the Staff College, and he had familiarized himself with the textbooks and studies used in the several courses on tactics, strategy and staff organizations. It was almost as if he had been a continuing student officer at the schools. He had rubbed minds with the keenest of the instructors, and he was now fully prepared for larger duties.

That first winter in Washington he and his mother kept house together in a modest apartment in the Hadleigh at 16th and U. She began slowly to improve and once again to take a keen interest in his advancing career. He spent as much time with her as he could, and save for rare occasions he remained at home evenings sternly working on various general staff problems and studies. There still remained many books in his father's library for him to read.

On May 3, 1913, he was relieved from duty with the General

Staff and assigned to the superintendency of the State, War and Navy Building. This was a sort of routine station in the training of top junior officers in the Corps of Engineers. Four months later he received the unusual distinction of being assigned as a regular member of the General Staff. He was no longer merely on "temporary duty with the General Staff."

General Wood's method of operation was to hand out the various policy problems and subjects under discussion to small sections or to individuals and at subsequent meetings to receive the reports and then ask questions. He discovered that often Captain MacArthur did not agree with the older officers and that he had the courage to present his minority opinion. Soon the Chief of Staff began to go over the heads of the older officers and accept the conclusions of this clear-thinking junior.

The result was inevitable. Before long Douglas found that while he had gained the approval of the exacting Chief of Staff, he had won the quiet envy and dislike of many members of this group of senior officers. He was disturbed, but it was not in his nature to worry about such matters.

By the turn of 1914 the problems involved in the Mexican revolution and particularly in the depredations by both rebel and federal Mexican soldiers had culminated in an insult to the American flag by Mexican officials at Tampico. As a result the port of Vera Cruz was unofficially blockaded by U. S. warships, and the German steamer *Esperanza* was denied the right to land its cargo of war materials destined for the Mexican Army.

Major General Frederick Funston, commanding general of the Department of Texas, was ordered to Galveston to take field command of the elements of a U. S. provisional division concentrated there. On April 21 bluejackets and marines from the U. S. fleet landed in Vera Cruz.

In Washington lights burned all night in the State, War and Navy Building. The Army General Staff sat late, considering the possibility of sending an expeditionary force into Mexico. In such an event Major General Leonard Wood would command the field army. He was ordered to Governor's Island, where he assumed command of the Eastern Department and the duties of bringing up to full strength the 1st U. S. Regular Division.

On April 22, 1914, the day before Wood left Washington, he conferred with Lindley M. Garrison, Secretary of War. It was decided that Captain MacArthur should immediately be sent to Vera Cruz to study the lay of the land and observe and report on all matters that might be useful to General Wood and the War Department. The selection of MacArthur for this assignment caused considerable resentment among the members of the General Staff, who were all senior to him. But Wood knew precisely what he wanted. Arrangements were made for MacArthur's transportation on the battleship *Nebraska,* sailing shortly from New York.

Four days later, four transports loaded with troops under command of Major General Funston dropped anchor in Vera Cruz harbor, and the following morning docked and the troops began disembarking. The city was already in the hands of U. S. marines and bluejackets.

2

The *Nebraska* arrived on May 1 and MacArthur asked permission to go ashore in the first launch. He at once paid his respects to his father's old friend, General Funston, and presented his orders from the Chief of Staff. His official position was a little incongruous. Until definite telegraphic orders arrived later, assigning him as assistant to the engineer officer of the force, he was an unattached and independent agent of the General Staff and the War Department, subject only to the general regulations covering the command.

Funston had only recently received his own confidential orders from the Secretary of War. It included the following:

. . . The Secretary of War further directs that you strictly limit your action in taking over the control of Vera Cruz to the occupation of the city and so much of its environs as you find in the possession of our forces, and that you under no circumstances extend those limits beyond these necessities and that you do not initiate any activities or bring about on your own initiative any situations which might tend to increase the tension of the situation or embarrass your government in its present relation with Mexico, without implicit orders and directives from the Secretary in each case. Even should your judgment indicate that something other than what is now being done should be done you will before acting communicate fully with the Department and await instructions. . . .

The order was written while MacArthur was on the high seas, and he knew nothing about it. Since its content was most confidential, General Funston in his friendly interview made no reference to it.

Shortly after his arrival MacArthur contacted an old friend from Washington days, Captain Constant Cordier, an energetic infantry officer, who shortly put him in touch with a Mexican who had some valuable information for sale. The meeting led to an extraordinary and dangerous mission on the part of Captain MacArthur some four days after his arrival at Vera Cruz. Since he had no official status with the Expedition, he kept the priceless information he had obtained strictly to himself, save for Captain Cordier and one or two close friends. He was still acting as an independent agent of the General Staff and General Wood. Captain Cordier, who had given the original tip, now wrote out on his own authority a long letter to General Wood, still at Governor's Island and busy with the prospect of taking over the Expedition should hostilities open. Cordier's letter was the first mention of the affair, and it recited the main events of the undertaking. Its closing paragraphs read:

I am taking the liberty of sending you this personal letter in order that a daring reconnaissance of Captain Douglas MacArthur, General Staff Corps, may properly be brought to your attention. In my opinion, his splendid and hazardous undertaking calls for the bestowal of a Medal of Honor. . . .

. . . It was a test of supreme courage; and, in my opinion, it stands out boldly as the only distinguished exploit since the landing of our Army on Mexican soil. If any deed of daring merits the Medal of Honor surely MacArthur's audacious undertaking is one.

The passionate nature of Captain Cordier's appeal might have been due partly to his disgust at the bundle of recommendations for the Medal of Honor that were being pre-

51

sented almost haphazardly in behalf of sailors and marines after the limited fighting that took place in Vera Cruz on April 22. A total of 47 navy personnel, including Rear Admiral Frank E. Fletcher, profited in the wholesale distribution of the country's highest award. The Marine Corps had to be satisfied with nine medals, one being given to Major Smedley D. Butler.

Four months later, a full month after his return to Washington, Captain MacArthur was requested by General Wood to write out his own report of the occurrence. It was in the nature of an order and MacArthur somewhat reluctantly did so. His report is quoted in full:

September 30, 1914

From: Capt. Douglas MacArthur, General Staff
To: Major General Leonard Wood
Subject: Detailed report of reconnaissance from
Vera Cruz to Alvarado on the night of May 6, 1914.

1. This report is supplementary to the general one made to you under date of May 9, 1914. It has not been rendered before as I did not realize the matter was under consideration.

2. The general purpose of the reconnaissance was the location of locomotives suitable for road use on the narrow gauge line of the Inter-Oceanic Railroad. Due to the great shortage of animal transportation, the command at Vera Cruz was practically immobile. Freight and passenger cars were in abundance, but no road motive power. Every effort was being made to remedy this state of affairs so that in case of field operations, which appeared imminent, the command would not be tied to Vera Cruz.

3. Through the maudlin talk of a drunken Mexican, I received an inkling that a number of engines were hidden somewhere on the line connecting Vera Cruz and Alvarado. This man was sobered up and found to be a railroad fireman and engineer on the Vera Cruz and Alvarado R. R. He consented after certain financial inducements had been offered, to assist me in accurately locating the engines.

4. At this time I occupied at Vera Cruz a unique and rather difficult status. I had been ordered there before the Fifth Brigade left Galveston as one of the prospective Assistant Chiefs of Staff of the First Field Army. My orders were defined in a letter from the Secretary of War to the Secretary of the Navy under date of April 23, 1914, in the following words:

"I am very desirous of sending down for purposes of observation and reconnaissance a representative of the War Department. This officer is Captain Douglas MacArthur, of the General Staff, who, in case of any aggressive movement by the Army in regard to Mexico, will function as one of the General Staff officers of the Commanding General. In order to facilitate his observations and his passage to Vera Cruz, I would appreciate very much if the Admiral Commanding be requested to extend such privileges to him as may be possible and that the Battleship *Nebraska* which it is expected will touch at New York tomorrow be directed to take him on board as a passenger."

On arrival at Vera Cruz, the headquarters of the Fifth Brigade did not recognize me as an official member of their command, as I had no orders assigning me thereto. They took the attitude that I was an independent staff officer functioning directly under you. I was permitted to exercise my own judgment in regard to fulfilling my general orders and instructions, subject to only such limitations as were prescribed by the Military Governor for all those domiciled in Vera Cruz. In undertaking this reconnaissance, therefore, I was thrown entirely on my own responsibility, as it was not feasible or safe to communicate the question to you for decision. The object of the trip not being aggressive, but merely for the purpose of obtaining information, my general instructions as given above seemed to cover the very contingency, and I accordingly made my plans.

5. The Alvarado Railroad is a narrow gauge road connecting Vera Cruz and Alvarado, distant about 42 miles. The principal towns en route are Tejar, Medallin, Paso del Toro, Laguna, La Piedra, and Salinas. We held the line as far as Tejar, nine miles out. About four miles beyond Tejar, at Paso del Toro, the Alvarado line is crossed by the broad gauge line connecting Vera Cruz and the Isthmus of Tehuantepec. This latter line after leaving Vera Cruz passes through the town of Boca del Rio, where it crosses the Jamapa River, before reaching Paso del Toro. From Vera Cruz to Paso del Toro, therefore, these two railroad lines formed roughly the two halves of an ellipse. We did not hold the Isthmus line beyond the outskirts of Vera Cruz.

6. Mexican troops in force were reported near Tejar and in order to avoid them I determined to proceed along the Isthmus line as far as Paso del Toro and then change to the Alvarado line. My general plan was to leave Vera Cruz alone on foot at dusk and to join my Mexican engineer who was to have a hand-car on the Alvarado line manned by two Mexicans. From there we

were to push along the line until the engines were located and their condition ascertained. All three of the Mexicans were railroad men and their affiliations and experience enabled them to obtain the hand-cars and have them at their appointed places. For their services I agreed to give them $150.00 gold, payable only after my safe return to Vera Cruz. Captain Cordier of the 4th Infantry was the only person outside of these men who knew of the plan.

7. The night was squally and overcast. At dusk I crossed our line unseen near the wireless stations, where a detachment of the 7th Infantry was encamped. I was in military uniform with no attempt to disguise and with absolutely nothing on me in addition to my clothes except my identification tag and my automatic revolver with ammunition. I found my engineer with a broad gauge hand-car in the appointed place. I carefully searched him and after some demur on his part removed his weapons, a .38-caliber revolver and a small dirk knife. As a further precaution against his possible treachery I had him search me so that he might better realize that there being nothing of value on me my death would afford him no monetary return. The essence of the transaction for him, therefore, became my safe return to Vera Cruz when he would receive his pay.

8. We proceeded as far as Boca del Rio without incident, but at the Jamapa River found the railroad bridge down. I decided to leave the hand-car, concealing it as well as possible. After searching the bank of the river for a short distance, we discovered a small native boat by means of which we paddled across, landing well above the town so as to escape observation. On landing we located, after some search, two ponies near a small shack and mounted on them we followed the trail along the railway until near Paso del Toro. We then made a detour and hit the Alvarado line below the town. The two Mexican firemen were awaiting us with the hand-car. We secreted our ponies and after I had searched the two newcomers and found them unarmed we pushed on. Mile after mile was covered with no sign of the engines. The line is studded with bridges and culverts and my crew protested violently at crossing them without investigating their condition. Time was so short, however, that I dared not stop for such steps, and had to take them in our stride. I was obliged to threaten my men to the point of covering them with a revolver at the first bridge, but after that I had no further trouble with them. In fact, after getting into the spirit of the thing their con-

duct was most admirable. At every town we reached I took one man and left the car which was run through to the far side by the other two. I fastened myself by a lashing to the man acting as my guide so as to insure us against separation and together we made a circuit of the town, joining the car on the far side. This took time, but was the only way I could avoid detection.

9. We reached Alvarado shortly after one o'clock and there found five engines. Two of these were switch engines and worthless for our purpose. The other three were just what we needed —fine big road pullers in excellent condition except for a few minor parts which were missing. I made a careful inspection of them and then started back.

10. At Salinas, while moving around the town with one of my men as described above, we were halted by five armed men. They were on foot and wore no uniforms. They were not soldiers and were evidently one of the marauding bands that infest the country with brigandage as a trade. We started to run for it and they opened fire and followed us. We outdistanced all but two and in order to preserve our own lives I was obliged to fire upon them. Both went down. I was fearful lest the firing might have frightened away my hand-car men, but after some search we found them awaiting us about a mile beyond the town.

11. At Piedra, under somewhat similar circumstances and in a driving mist, we ran flush into about fifteen mounted men of the same general type. We were among them before I realized it and were immediately the center of a melee. I was knocked down by the rush of horsemen and had three bullet holes through my clothes, but escaped unscathed. My man was shot in the shoulder, but not seriously injured. At least four of the enemy were brought down and the rest fled. After bandaging up my wounded man we proceeded north with all speed possible.

12. Near Laguna we were again encountered and fired upon by three mounted men who kept up a running fight with the hand-car. I did not return this fire. All but one of these men were distanced, but this one man, unusually well mounted, overhauled and passed the car. He sent one bullet through my shirt and two others that hit the car within six inches of me, and I then felt obliged to bring him down. His horse fell across the front of the car and on the track and we were obliged to remove the carcass before proceeding.

13. At Paso del Toro we abandoned the hand-car, found the two ponies where we had left them and made the best of our way

back to Boca del Rio where we returned the animals from whence we had procured them.

14. We found the boat where we had left it and started to cross the Jamapa River, but when near the shore the boat struck a snag in the darkness and sank. Fortunately the water at this point was something less than five feet deep, for in our exhausted physical condition I do not believe we would have been capable of swimming. As it was I was hard put to it to keep my wounded man's head above water. Day was breaking when we reached the bank, but so wearied were we that we were unable to move on for nearly half an hour. We then located our first hand-car and ran in close to Vera Cruz where we crossed the American lines unobserved.

15. None of the men we encountered were Mexican troops. All were guerillas undoubtedly bent on general mischief. Owing to the darkness I was not recognized as an American soldier and in consequence no alarm was ever felt for the engines. Months later when traffic was partially resumed I saw one of them running to Tejar from Alvarado.

[Signed] *Douglas MacArthur*
Captain, General Staff

3

On December 3 General Wood forwarded his own formal report to the Adjutant General. He carefully explained that Captain MacArthur had been sent to Vera Cruz "with general instructions to obtain, through reconnaissance and other means consistent with the existing situation, all possible information which would be of value in connection with possible operations."

The closing paragraph of General Wood's report was definite and unmistakable:

It will be noted that while Captain MacArthur in making this reconnaissance was carrying out the general instructions which had been given him to obtain all possible information, he voluntarily performed at the risk of his life a most gallant and hazardous act, an act calling for more than could reasonably have been expected in the way of risk of life. This service was performed before he was assigned to duty with the 5th Brigade, and before any official information had been received as to an armistice. In other words, the reconnaissance was made during the period of practical hostilities. Captain MacArthur displayed great gallantry and enterprise, and I believe that the services performed clearly entitles him to a Medal of Honor, and I recommend that one be awarded him.

The first endorsement to the document was an order from the Adjutant General that it be sent to Major General Funston at Galveston, by order of the Secretary of War, "for remarks." The grizzled little fighter, with ill health already beginning to dog his steps, must have been slightly embarrassed to be forced to report on the activities of the son of the man whom he had looked up to as his military mentor. But he was as ruggedly honest as he was brave, and he bluntly stated his case:

1. Until after the return of the expeditionary force from Vera Cruz, and the entire severance of my connection therewith, I had not the slightest information regarding the reconnaissance made by Captain MacArthur, and I have no knowledge except what is to be obtained from these papers.

2. As the reconnaissance was made to the theory that Captain MacArthur was not a member of my command at the time, I am at a loss to know how I can properly make official recommendation on the subject. As a matter of personal opinion I should say that the risks voluntarily taken and the dangers encountered were of a most exceptional nature, and that the awarding of the Medal of Honor would be entirely appropriate and justifiable.

3. I do not consider this the occasion to enter into a discussion of the advisability of this enterprise having been undertaken without the knowledge of the commanding general on the ground, who from the first was acting under definite, confidential instruction from the Secretary of War, and who understood thoroughly that without specific instructions nothing was to be done that might lead to a resumption of hostilities. However, it must be presumed that Captain MacArthur was acting in good faith, and any error of judgment he may have made in undertaking the hazardous expedition should not, in my opinion, cause him to lose the appropriate reward. In the enclosed letter of Captain Cordier to General Wood are several errors of statement as to conditions at Vera Cruz and our activities there, but I do not believe it necessary to go into them, as having no direct bearing on the question under consideration.

The papers and their endorsements were returned to the Chief of Staff, General Hugh L. Scott, who immediately appointed a board of three officers from the War College to report on the award. Four days after these orders had been issued, Captain William G. Ball, aide-de-camp to General Funston, discarded military procedure and wrote a note directly to the Chief of Staff, General Scott. It is important only in that it makes clear that through Ball, as representative of General Funston, Captain MacArthur had kept in touch with the command. And it proved that MacArthur's brother officers of his own rank who were on the scene and understood his exploit not only applauded his deed but were the ones who were demanding that appropriate reward be given him. One part of Ball's letter read:

> I learned of the reconnaissance immediately after its accomplishment, but made no mention of the matter; as it was imperative that the information that had been obtained should be kept as secret as possible. This information became practically the basis of our future plans, and our first aggressive steps would have been to seize the engines that Captain MacArthur located, and thus make it possible to supply the column when it advanced. The practical importance of this information, if we had moved into Mexico, cannot be overestimated. I am thoroughly familiar with all the conditions surrounding the reconnaissance, and unhesitatingly pronounce it one of the most dangerous and difficult feats in army annals. I was impressed then—and I am now—that this officer clearly earned a Medal of Honor, and so expressed myself at the time. I believe that a grave injustice will be done if such action is not taken.

The board met on February 2, 1915, and one week later submitted its findings.

The opinion praised MacArthur's zeal and initiative but questioned the propriety of undertaking the enterprise without the knowledge of the commanding general on the ground. It feared that to bestow a medal in this case might encourage other staff officers to similar indiscretions. Its final paragraph read: "It is recommended that the Medal of Honor be not awarded." Colonel Charles G. Treat of the General Staff, who had been Commandant of Cadets during MacArthur's last two years at the Academy, was senior member of the board. Lt. Colonel William H. Johnston concurred with his findings, but Major P. D. Lochridge, West Point 1887, submitted a minority report against granting the award, on the grounds that there was not sufficient proof and the qualification of "above and beyond the call of duty" was not fulfilled.

Captain MacArthur was incensed. Three days after the board had announced its findings he wrote a straightforward memorandum to the Chief of Staff. It took inner fortitude for him to protest against the findings of his seniors, particularly as he was personally involved in a matter as delicate as a Medal of Honor for himself. But to him this was a moral issue far beyond the matter of a medal or of his own disparagement. He had been a captain for less than four years, yet he dared oppose the highest authority in what he felt involved the honor and justice of the Army. It was the first time he was openly to go against the rigid narrowmindedness and lack of imagination that prevailed in sections of the General Staff and in the high command at that time.

General Scott directed that the Assistant Chief of Staff, Brigadier General Tasker H. Bliss, review the findings and express an opinion on the board's negative decision. On the back of the order disavowing the medal Bliss attached his signature with the single word "Approved." He stood by the board's findings.

Beneath the line and under his signature General Scott wrote "Approval recommended."

A third endorsement graced the page. It was marked "Approved; Henry Breckenridge, Asst. Secretary of War."

The young captain had lost, but he had gone down fighting. To many in the army inner circles his protest seemed rash and impertinent; to others it was courageous and commendable.

There was no question of the propriety of what he did in the mind of the elderly lady who presided over the pleasant apartment they shared together.

He had lost this fight, and he would lose many more that were to come, but he must hold steadfast to his sense of duty, and to the high moral issue of right and wrong.

He must dedicate himself to his country and his career. The two marched together. They were of the same piece, of the same identical pattern.

5

RAINBOW OVER FRANCE

The First World War had been going on for exactly four days when, on August 10, Captain MacArthur was ordered to return on the earliest available transportation from Vera Cruz to his duties in Washington.

Lindley M. Garrison, the harassed Secretary of War, and his 28 General Staff officers on actual duty in the capital had innumerable problems crowding down on them. The Staff consisted of two groups—the War Plans Division and the Mobile Army Division. MacArthur was assigned to the latter, whose function was the broad supervision of the Army in being, the realistic planning for additional forces and the eventual procurement of new equipment and munitions.

In the summer of 1915 General Wood, commanding general of the Eastern seaboard area, pushed through his first Plattsburg Officers' Training Camp, and MacArthur immediately became its champion on the General Staff. In February of 1916, with the national election still nine months off, Secretary of War Garrison and Assistant Secretary Breckenridge resigned as a protest against President Wilson's refusal to adopt a realistic approach to preparedness. Three weeks later the President announced the appointment of Newton D. Baker, former mayor of Cleveland, as the new Secretary. The appointment was in the nature of a political earthquake.

It did not take MacArthur long to penetrate the quiet exterior of this soft-spoken, almost diffident lawyer, who was immediately branded by the anti-administration press as a pacifist tool of President Wilson. The young officer soon realized that here was a clear, brilliant mind, with the fine ability to make instant and positive decisions.

Even the fact that the Pancho Villa raid across the border into Columbus, New Mexico, came when he had been less than 24 hours in office, did not faze the new Secretary of War. He found in Generals Scott and Bliss, the Chief of Staff and the Deputy Chief, the exact type of cool and experienced advisors he could trust. He took their advice about a punitive expedition into Mexico and their choice of Brigadier General John J. Pershing as its commander.

But he needed at his finger-tips some keen, imaginative and highly intelligent younger man who could match his own swift and uninhibited mind and answer the innumerable questions of a purely military nature that were constantly cropping up. He found his man in Douglas MacArthur, now a major.

It took Baker less than a month to grasp the need of preparedness as an over-all national policy, and he quietly went about the difficult business of winning over the President. The next step was to build up a strong public opinion behind the whole idea. On June 30, 1916, he had MacArthur detailed as military aide to the Secretary of War, and placed in charge of the almost non-existent Bureau of Information of the War Department. A week later, with the additional title of press censor attached to his name, MacArthur was made liaison with the newspapermen who regularly covered the War Department.

MacArthur did not make the national policy, but he did explain it to the country. He spent much time with the Secretary of War, and from him Mr. Baker learned many things that had to do with the imponderables of war and army service. He learned to respect and trust MacArthur, and he became a ready convert to the idea that the existing National Guard, with its recent experience on the Mexican border, could be expanded through volunteer enlistment and turned into reliable and effective combat divisions.

MacArthur became at once a sort of unofficial leader of the pro-Guard group. As part of the heritage from his father came a passionate belief in the citizen soldier. The son now felt that if and when war came, Guard divisions should be sent to France simultaneously with the Regular Army outfits. His idea found a ready approval in the Secretary's active mind, and it was passed on to the country through newspaper correspondents and the special writers who found it pleasant and profitable to drop in for a chat with the affable censor. How deeply they appreciated what MacArthur was doing for them was proved by a spontaneous document they sent to Mr. Baker two days before the United States declared war against Germany.

The letter was signed by the 29 men who were among the most distinguished representatives of their profession in Washington. It read:

Washington, D. C., April 4, 1917

The Honorable Newton D. Baker,
Secretary of War
Dear Mr. Secretary:

It seems quite likely that the days of action before us will see many changes in the corps of newspaper correspondents who have been assigned to the War Department for many months past. Some of us will go a-soldiering and others into fields of activity connected with the war. Changes will come, too, in the assignment of army officers whom we have learned to know here in the Department, and before that time comes, we of the Fourth Estate wish to address to you, and through you to Major Douglas MacArthur, our appreciation of the way he has dealt with us for all these months in his trying position of military censor.

We feel no doubt of what the future holds for Major MacArthur. Rank and honors will come to him if merit can bring them to any man; but we wish to say our thanks to him for the unfailing kindness, patience and wise counsel we have received from him in the difficult days that are past.

Our needs have compelled us to tax that patience at all hours of the day and night. We have never failed to receive courteous treatment from him. Although the censorship imposed was but a voluntary obligation upon the press, it has been kept faithfully, and we feel that it has been largely because of the fair, wise and liberal way in which Major MacArthur exercised his functions that this was possible. He has put his own personality into the task.

No man can ever know to what extent the cordial relations the

Major has maintained with the press may have influenced national thought on military matters. It is unquestionable that his hours given to our conferences have never been wasted; they have born fruit in what we in our turn have written and if wise decisions are reached eventually as to the military policy of our country, we cannot but feel that the major has helped, through us, to shape the public mind.

Respectfully,

Edwin M. Hood, A.P.

George N. Gavin, I.N.S.

Carl D. Groat, U.P.

Richard V. Oulahan, N.Y. Times

Lawrence Hills, N.Y. Sun

A. N. Jamieson, Central News

Grafton S. Wilcox, Chicago Tribune

Lewellyn Brown, N.Y. Herald

Frank W. Connor, N.Y. World

Irwin Barbour, N.Y. American

L. W. Moffett, Cleveland Daily Iron Trade

L. Ames Brown, Philadelphia Record

Stephen I. Early, A.P.

Hal H. Smith, N.Y. Times

Albert W. Fox, N.Y. Sun

Matthew F. Tighe, N.Y. American

T. Holman Harvey, U.P.

Arthur Sweetser, A.P.

R. M. Boeckel, I.N.S.

K. L. Simpson, A.P.

J. K. Dougherty, Washington Times

Leroy T. Vernon, Chicago Daily News

W. E. Brigham, Boston Eve'g Transcript

R. A. Zachary, Brooklyn Daily Eagle

Harry B. Hunt, Scripps-McRae Newspapers

Alfred J. Clarke, Washington Star

E. L. Conn, Foreign Affairs News Service

O. McKee, Jr., N.Y. World

Aaron B. Rosenthal, Milwaukee Journal

While it made very pleasant reading for MacArthur, he knew that the letter would arouse more envy among some members of the General Staff who were his senior in years and rank. After all, his concern at the moment was how to shake loose from the General Staff and be assigned to duty with the Line and thus with luck get to France and into action.

He saw Pershing arrive from the Mexican border on May 10, 1917, and two weeks later secretly slip off for France with his small staff. But the young major had little time for wishes or regrets; he had the national draft to promote and sell to the public, and he had his friendly newspapermen waiting for their daily ration of copy and advice.

2

When war broke on April 6, 1917, the two oldest officers on the active list who were attached to the War Department, were Major General Tasker H. Bliss, Chief of Staff, and his West Point classmate of the class of 1875, Brigadier General William A. Mann, chief of the militia division of the General Staff. The Secretary found that General Mann's ideas regarding the citizen soldier and the National Guard were closely in accord with those of Major MacArthur. The two soldiers, one 63 and the other just turning 37, thought that both the Regular Army and the National Guard should be expanded and incorporated into the federal service, along with a drafted National Army that would be swiftly built up.

Baker saw the wisdom of the over-all proposal and gave it his full support. There was heavy pressure from France urging that for morale purposes a Regular Army division should be sent overseas as quickly as possible. So tragic was the condition of national unpreparedness that the 1st Regular Division was the single outfit that approached a fair state of readiness.

When the decision had been reached regarding the 1st Regular Division, the next problem facing the Secretary was which army divisions should immediately follow. Some years later Mr. Baker, in reply to an inquiry by Brigadier General Henry J. Reilly, the official historian of the 42nd Division, wrote the following report:

64

Where American troops saw service in France in 1917-1918.

When the problem arose as to which National Guard division should be sent to France first, we faced the situation that New York and Pennsylvania were the only states that had complete National Guard divisions and were, therefore, in the most advanced stage of preparation for overseas service. We had not gone very far in the war, and public psychology was still an uncertain and mystifying factor. If we sent the New York National Guard first, we might have encountered two kinds of comment; first, from the people of New York who might have said why send our boys first; or, we might have had comment from other states charging that we were preferring New York and giving it first chance. I disclosed my puzzle to Major MacArthur, who was attached to my office at the time. He suggested the possibility of our being able to form a division out of the surplus units from many states, the major part of whose National Guard organizations were in multi-state divisions.

I sent for General Mann, who was Chief of the Militia Division, and asked him whether there were enough surplus units to organize such a division and told him why I wanted to have a division which would represent as many states as possible. General Mann responded that it would be very easy to form such a Division and pointed out some of the states from which elements could be drawn. Major MacArthur who was standing alongside said, 'Fine, that will stretch over the whole country like a rainbow.' The Division thus got its name.

When General Mann returned to my office a little later with the details of his plan for the Division, I said to him that I wanted him to prepare the plans, organize the Division, and take it overseas as its commanding general on one condition, which was that he should take Major MacArthur as his chief of staff. I have rarely seen anybody filled with greater enthusiasm than he was for both these suggestions.

3

It was great news that Douglas MacArthur carried home that night to his mother. He knew that while General Mann would for a time have the rank and honor of being the commanding general of the unique division, it actually was and would continue to be his own outfit. He would now hold the rank of full colonel in the National Army.

Second only to the 1st Division, the Rainbow sponsors had the initial good fortune to pick and choose their senior officers from the flower of the Regular Army. For their two infantry brigade commanders the Mann-MacArthur team chose Colonel Robert A. Brown, West Point 1885, and Colonel Michael J. Lenihan, class of 1887. The fact that Colonel Brown had served as aide-de-camp to Douglas MacArthur's father in the Philippines in 1901-02 possibly had something to do with his appointment.

For the artillery brigade commander they picked Major Charles P. Summerall, class of 1892, who also had served under Major General Arthur MacArthur in the Philippines and as a first lieutenant in the famous Reilly's Battery of the 5th Field Artillery during the Boxer uprising in Peking in 1900. Major Summerall was at the moment in charge of field artillery affairs in the Militia Bureau of the War Department.

These three brigade commanders were all made brigadier generals in the National Army on August 5, 1917. On that same date Major Douglas MacArthur of the Corps of Engineers became a colonel of infantry in the National Army. At last he was in the Line.

The majority of the senior officers of the divisional staff were from the Regular Army, and a number of unit commanders also had been in the regular service. Among these was Major Robert E. Wood, West Point 1900, who had retired in 1915 after serving ten years with distinction on the Panama Canal Commission. Wood was made a colonel and was designated as commanding officer of the 117th Train Headquarters and the military police. Shortly after arriving in France he and several other crack officers were looted from the Rainbow and attached to Pershing's G.H.Q.

In a rather special way the Rainbow Division was a tight and proud outfit. Henry J. Reilly, the unusually able colonel of the 149th Field Artillery regiment from Illinois, had been three years with MacArthur at West Point, graduating in 1904; after ten years of active service as a cavalryman, he resigned to become a war correspondent for the Chicago *Tribune* and a pleader for preparedness. And there was Grayson M. P. Murphy, who had been a West Point classmate of MacArthur's, eventually resigning from the Army to enter Wall Street. With the coming of the war he went to Europe as an American Red Cross Commissioner, but when the Rainbow arrived in France, he insisted on retiring from his high post and joining the division and was assigned Assistant G-3 of the staff.

One of the battalion commanders of the old New York 69th Infantry—now designated as the 165th—was a brilliant young lawyer, William J. Donovan, soon to be dubbed "Wild Bill." At the end of the war he was called "the bravest of the brave" by Father Duffy, famous chaplain of the regiment. Donovan was the only soldier in the A.E.F. to win every United States decoration, including the Medal of Honor, the Distinguished Service Cross, the Distinguished Service Medal and two Purple Hearts.

The list of superior men in the division was almost endless; Colonel Ben Hough of the 166th Ohio and Colonel Bill Screws of the 167th Alabama. (How these proud bucks enjoyed answering the inevitable question, "Where you from, Buddy?" with their standard reply, "We're from Alagoddambam.") Then there was Colonel Robert H. Tyndall of the 150th Indiana Field Artillery; and Colonel George E. Leach of the 151st Minnesota Field Artillery; Colonel William Kelly, of the 117th Engineers, a West Pointer and a regular major of the Corps of Engineers, who had graduated No. 2 at the Academy the year MacArthur entered; and Colonel E. R. Bennett, of the 168th Iowa, who wore himself out in the fighting and handed over his splendid regiment to Lt. Colonel Matthew A. Tinley. Both Bennett and Tinley, as well as all three of the battalion majors, had served in the old 52nd Iowa Volunteers under General Arthur MacArthur in his famous 8th Division during the Philippine Insurrection. There were other superb officers who helped the Rainbow to win fame and immortality.

At Camp Mills on Long Island Colonel MacArthur worked day and night in a wooden shack that housed the division staff during August and September 1917 to whip the 27,000 men into shape. His goal was not only for the Rainbow to be the second complete division to arrive in France, but to take with it sufficient extra clothing and equipment to last six months.

But New England's 26th Division, raised from Guard units

of the several states in that part of the country, beat the Rainbow to France by several weeks. More than half the 2nd Regular Division also preceded the Rainbow overseas. Hard luck seemed to dog the 42nd, for a large part of the supplies it had so carefully garnered and carried along—including 50,000 pairs of heavy shoes—were confiscated by other outfits or lost in the great war shuffle in France. And when the drivers and mule skinners from the division wagon trains and the artillery batteries went to the port of St. Nazaire to pick up their carefully selected American horses and mules, they got only bony, third-rate left-overs raked in from the tiny farms of France and Spain. But by this time they had learned to swear and repeat the endless refrain *C'est la guerre.* For nothing really mattered much as long as the division shared the honor of being one of the first four outfits to get to France.

MacArthur sailed on the *Covington,* the former *Kaiser Wilhelm der Grosse,* leaving Hoboken October 18, 1917. He had had no single day of leave, not even a Sunday off, since that morning in early July when he first spoke the magic word "Rainbow."

The outfit with the beautiful name soon took on much of the color, dash and unique flavor of its chief of staff and founder. All his life the division was to occupy a peculiar place in MacArthur's heart. In the years to come he was never too busy to open his door to any man who had worn the Rainbow's colorful patch on his sleeve.

His father had felt the same way about the men who had served with him in the 24th Wisconsin in the Civil War, and about the soldiers of the six Western regiments that had comprised his famous 8th Division in the Philippines.

From his father he had inherited, along with this pride of outfit, a sense of leadership that was of the essence of the elusive and deathless thing called soldiering.

4

The orders that were handed Colonel MacArthur when the *Covington* tied up to the dock at St. Nazaire on December 1 were extremely disconcerting.

The infantry regiments aboard the ships in this initial convoy were to be unloaded immediately and shipped in the miserable little "40-and-8" French boxcars to training areas south of Toul, in eastern France. But the artillery brigade aboard the *President Lincoln* was not to be disembarked.

The original plan had been for the brigade to move to the artillery training sector at Coëtquidam, in the Breton peninsula, site of the French military school, where it would receive its quota of French 75s for the regiments from Illinois and Minnesota, and the new 155s, or heavies, for the Indiana outfit. But now came the new orders, and Brigadier General Charles P. Summerall and his three regiments could cool their heels aboard ship, while they cursed and wondered.

MacArthur sensed that there was more behind the order than met the eye. He sought immediate clarification from G.H.Q.

Then the blow fell: I Corps, that was being organized in Chaumont, would consist of three divisions, with the fourth division—the 42nd now arriving—to be used as replacements. It foretold the end of the Rainbow for 27,000 proud men.

MacArthur quietly passed on to Brigadier General Summerall the alarming news that the Rainbow was to be a replacement division. MacArthur knew the quality and imagination of the artillery colonels, and he knew how deep was Secretary Baker's personal affection for the division. There was still no censorship in France for private cables to the United States, and overnight dispatches started arriving at the Washington offices of certain highly placed Senators and Representatives. A day or two later important callers began dropping in at the offices of the Secretary of War and the Chief of Staff. This rape of the Rainbow must be called off. The 42nd Division already had helped glue the nation together in its great war effort, and it must not be broken up.

It is uncertain how much Pershing personally resented the obvious pressure that had been brought on the War Department to cancel his orders that the 42nd be turned into replacements: but there were unquestionably certain members of his G.H.Q. who blamed the whole affair on MacArthur and never forgave him for what they considered his interference.

Among these high staff officers that had this feeling were Pershing's G-3, Major General Fox Conner, and Adjutant General "Corky" Davis. Most of this tight group were known as "The Ninety-eighters" from their West Point class. They had been prominent in the Leavenworth schools, and they had long distinguished themselves as staff officers. At the end of the war the little G.H.Q. crowd that had never been quite reconciled toward the brilliant young MacArthur was joined by the then Colonel George C. Marshall.

The infantry regiments of the 42nd had been in training camps a bare ten days when orders came to march overland, as far as 50 kilometers in some cases, over sleety, slippery roads in zero weather. Many of the men were without underwear, and there were others who had no overcoats. Some 400 men of New York's 165th Infantry were left behind because their shoes were too worn to undertake the desperate march.

Herbert Corey, one of the stern and experienced American correspondents in France at that time, listened to MacArthur rail against the intolerable situation. So wrought up was he that he told Corey he might make full use of the information. Corey wrote a bristling, indignant story and submitted it to G.H.Q. censorship. It was promptly turned down. Again Corey submitted it. It was refused. Corey kept at it until the division got adequate clothing.

On December 15 Major General Mann, who had the honor of organizing the division and taking it to France, was relieved by Charles T. Menoher, a regular colonel in the Field Artillery, who had been a classmate of General Pershing. MacArthur soon won the complete confidence of this new commanding officer. Never as long as MacArthur was Chief of Staff did General Menoher interfere with his practical operation of the division.

5

By middle December the Rainbow was settled in scattered villages and farms along the valley of the Meuse river, prepared to accept the prospect of a dreary Christmas. It was the coldest winter that France had had in many years, and the billets, crowded with American troops who were poorly clothed and even short of adequate blankets, were bitterly uncomfortable.

Two days before Christmas General Pershing appeared at the division headquarters for his initial inspection. At Camp Mills MacArthur had lifted an enterprising young second lieutenant, Walter B. Wolf, from Reilly's 149th Field Artillery, and attached him to his staff as a sort of fifth wheel. Wolf, who hailed from Chicago, had been a *cum laude* and crewman at Yale, and his alert and loyal mind fulfilled MacArthur's rather sharp requirements.

On this cold pre-Christmas day in France when Pershing told MacArthur he wanted to drive around the training area, MacArthur chose Lieutenant Wolf to act as a guide and lead off in a motorcycle side-car. Unfortunately Wolf overran a turn, and Pershing's black Rolls Royce had to back-and-fill and maneuver to get turned around and onto the proper road.

Pershing opened the door of his car and berated the unfortunate Wolf for his error. He was a master at this sort of thing, and the rather diffident Wolf was getting nowhere in his attempt at explanation and apology.

"I think I must share at least half the blame, sir," MacArthur broke in. "Lieutenant Wolf has been on almost constant duty at headquarters and he has had little opportunity to learn every detail of these roads. I am the one really responsible."

General Pershing grunted his acceptance, and in Wolf, MacArthur won a devoted friend for life.

Constantly MacArthur fought to keep the division together. Brigadier General Summerall shortly was ordered to command the artillery brigade of the 1st Division, and a little later Colonel Robert E. Wood and other valuable officers fell to the long arm of G.H.Q. Back in Long Island the Chief of Staff had singled out the highly intelligent and tireless Major William J. Donovan of the 1st Battalion of the 165th New York as a fighting man after his own heart. Donovan had been sent to a French school of the line soon after they reached France, and the commander of the school tapped the brilliant Rainbow officer to remain on as an instructor. "Wild Bill" hurried to MacArthur's Headquarters with his story. He did not want to be an instructor or in fact anything but the best battalion commander in the Rainbow Division.

"Let's go, Bill," MacArthur said to him. "Don't ever let them get you away from the Line. Fighting men are the real soldiers."

MacArthur drove Donovan 40-odd miles to G.H.Q. at Chaumont. He talked his way quickly into the office of the commander-in-chief and presented the case of a fighting Irishman who wanted to continue to be just that. Pershing nodded his approval. He, too, liked fighting men.

On February 14, 1918, orders came for the 42nd to move into a fairly quiet combat sector in the Lunéville and Baccarat areas. The division's four infantry regiments were to battle-train with four French divisions, and all would be under the command of General DeBazelaire of the French 7th Army Corps.

A number of times American units, preparing for night raids or undergoing heavy shelling, suddenly found MacArthur in their midst, a tall, serious figure in a barracks cap, with a riding crop under his left arm and a quiet word of approval on his lips. As a result of his personal leadership in one of these raids General DeBazelaire on February 26 recommended MacArthur for a Croix de Guerre. It was his first combat medal. The second came March 9 when he accompanied a heavy daylight raid by French units and two companies of the 168th Iowa, which 18 years before had served under his father in the Philippines as the 51st Iowa Volunteers. The desperate little affair brought Colonel MacArthur his first Distinguished Service Cross, the second-highest battle decoration his nation could give.

The misty, half-rainy March days were ideal for the Germans to lay down their poison gas barrages. There were no frightening explosions as was the case with ordinary artillery shells, but only a subdued warning whistle and then a queer dull thud as the thin outside casings broke apart and the deadly gas escaped. MacArthur, roaming the damp and dangerous front areas, stepped squarely into a saturated spot. Wolf, now a captain and acting adjutant, managed to get him back to his own quarters. He wanted to take him to the hospital, but MacArthur refused and would not even let him send for the surgeon. It might mean that he would be separated from his command, and he believed that an officer's place was with his troops. Save for passing through the outskirts of Paris on a troop train, he never so much as entered that city, nor did he indulge himself in a single day's leave during the full year and a half he was in France.

On March 21, 1918, the Germans unloosed their great attack in the North against the British Fifth Army, in a desperate gamble to end the war before the American Army was fully ready. The four French divisions with which the 42nd had been in training were withdrawn, and for 82 straight days the Rainbow alone remained in more or less active front-line combat, with battle casualties totaling 2,014 killed and wounded. On June 16 the order arrived for its relief.

The units began at once the march to the loading quays at Charmes and other railheads, some of the outfits trudging 40 miles or more. There was no time for "spit and polish." No new clothing had been issued for months, the transport and equipment were shabby, and the horses were gaunt and miserable.

Since dawn on the day of June 21, Colonel MacArthur and Captain Wolf had been on the loading ramps that led to the open doors of the tiny horse-and-soldier cars strung out in the railroad yards at Charmes. Around 2 in the afternoon General Pershing and some of his staff strode up the ramp. Apparently they had been inspecting the arriving columns, with their battle-scarred wagons and artillery trains moving toward the several loading points.

Pershing was a dozen feet away when he turned loose his crisp, hard voice on MacArthur. Soldiers and junior officers busy on the ramp were close at hand, but there was no effort by the Commanding General of the A.E.F. to keep his words from their ears or to soften the blow he was delivering.

"This division is a disgrace," he barked out. "The men are poorly disciplined and they are not properly trained. The whole outfit is just about the worst I have seen."

MacArthur was aghast. It was rough enough to come under

74

the direct ire of the Commanding General in private, but there were others here to listen to every word spoken and see every gesture made.

"MacArthur," General Pershing continued, "I'm going to hold you personally responsible for getting discipline and order into this division. I'm going to hold you personally responsible for correcting measures with the officers at fault. I won't stand for this. It's a disgrace."

"Yes, sir!" MacArthur answered, as he saluted.

Pershing gave him no chance to explain. The division had been in the muck and misery of the line for almost three months. It had just marched 60 kilometers through mud. But Pershing wanted no explanations.

He turned on his heel and stamped off down the ramp. MacArthur's face flushed and then drained of blood until it was ashen gray. He could not believe what he had heard and seen.

Without a word he walked toward the little town, its narrow streets crowded with men and transport of his division—his disgraced division.

Wolf walked by his side. MacArthur spoke no word. Automatically he returned salutes, but he was as one beside himself. Finally, half exhausted, he took a seat on a bench in the tiny green square. Twilight was descending, and from the rear came the shouts of men loading animals and guns and caissons. Then he began to talk. The division would suffer now. It would be discriminated against. It was utterly unfair.

Wolf tried to make clear that this was Pershing's way, the technique of his rugged discipline. Then why, MacArthur demanded, had he not done it quietly and waited for an explanation? What could Pershing have against him? Could it be some ancient grudge he might have held against his father?

Never did MacArthur find the answer. Time and again Pershing or his people back in G.H.Q. would send inspectors to comb through the division for such little faults as they might discover and report. Finally came the last straw. Late one afternoon a booted and spurred colonel, fresh and immaculate from the Inspector General's office at Chaumont, appeared at division headquarters with minor complaints. MacArthur blazed out at the elegant gentleman, ordering him to get out of the division area under threat that he would personally shoot the trouble-maker if he found him there again!

Apparently MacArthur overwhelmed him by the very fury of his anger. Strange things happen in war.

6

The division was headed now for the bitter fighting along the Marne. The 2nd Division, with its magnificent brigade of marines, and the 3rd and the 26th Divisions had all done valiant work in checking the Boche drive toward Paris. The Rainbow would now be grouped with the 26th from New England and the 32nd from Michigan and Wisconsin to form a great road-block against the coming German attack.

But at the last minute orders were changed, and the Rainbow was assigned to the brilliant, one-armed General Henri J. E. Gouraud and his famous French Fourth Army. Evidence had come to Foch that the Germans were about to launch an all-out attack in the white chalk cliffs and plains of the Champagne to the south of the Marne in a terrific effort to break through to Paris.

On July 4 the division swung to the right toward its new battle destination. Gouraud, alert to the new type of by-pass offensive that the Germans had worked out in their successful rolling back of the British Fifth Army on March 21, 1918, had evolved a completely new theory of defense. The Boche had swiftly broken through and around the heavily manned British front lines and pushed ahead toward the lightly held rear areas. Here in the Champagne the actual forward lines were now manned by skeleton sacrifice units, waiting to fire their rocket signals when the German barrage lifted and the gray-clad troops began their actual assault.

The intermediary line of defense would be held by wired-in pockets with machine guns and ample fire power. Once the Germans succeeded in breaking up or by-passing this middle line of defense nests, they would then come into contact with the main defenses. It was an entirely new idea of defense-in-depth that promised to become a death-trap to those who broke through the first two lines.

July 14 was Bastille Day, the greatest of all French holidays. Wise old Gouraud figured the Boche might attempt their break-through at dawn, and when the day passed bright and quiet, he staged a little supper in the late afternoon at the fortified Ferme de Suippe, which he used as his battle headquarters. MacArthur with the other colonels and general officers of the Rainbow sat down at the long table, interspersed among the men of Gouraud's staff and high officers of the French troops in the sector.

It was a plain but excellent meal, such as only French army chefs in those war days seemed to know how to create almost out of nothing. And when the meal was over, the great General rose and made a speech so touching and so heart-warming that no one there can ever forget it. Candles flickered along the long, pine table, and tears filled men's eyes.

The meeting broke up while the glow of twilight made it still possible for the various commanders to return to their battle stations before night fell.

Luck was with Gouraud, in large measure because of an incredible act of valor on the part of four French reconnaissance soldiers. Late that evening they penetrated the German front lines and drifting far to the rear located the exact position of the main attack force and captured a Prussian who had the written orders for the coming attack. It was clear that the enemy artillery bombardment was to begin exactly at midnight. Four hours later the infantry would start their assault.

Gouraud moved swiftly. He ordered the Allied guns to open at 11:30 P.M., one half-hour before the Boche guns started firing. Every road, gun nest and concentrating area in the enemy's rear was to be shelled without letup. It was a deadly gamble; if the information was wrong, it would tip off the Germans to the complete awareness of the defenders.

MacArthur, watching the Allied bombardment from the entrance of his dugout a little behind the main line of defense, checked the minutes as they slipped by; 12 midnight—and no answering bombardment; 12:05—and still no move; 12:10—and thousands of enemy guns seemed to rip the sky apart and shoot down the very stars. It was the greatest concentration of artillery the world had known. The boom of the big guns on both sides could be heard that night in Paris, almost 100 miles away. France was again in peril.

At 4:17 in the morning the German bombardment of the front lines lifted, and out of the dawn came the gray-clad Boche. The warning rockets exploded in the red skies, and the isolated lookouts, including Rainbow men, went to their death.

Units of all four of the 42nd Division infantry regiments, in their islands along the intermediate position, worked their guns and held their ground. The Germans flowed around them, only to crash into the main defense line. In a few spots the enemy broke through, but everywhere else he was repulsed and driven back. In due time came the French and American counterattacks, and by afternoon the outcome was clear: the last great attack of the Germans in the war had failed. Paris was saved.

MacArthur would never serve again under the old French hero, but there was no question that each appealed deeply to the other. In General Gouraud the American found his ideal battle commander, and from the older man's wisdom and flaming patriotism he took certain indestructible truths that became a part of his philosophy of life and war.

Years later when he was Army Chief of Staff, MacArthur sent a Christmas cable to the aging Gouraud. It read: "Like wine, time only improves the flavor of a great comradeship."

Long before this date, the crippled little hero had attested to his side of the unique friendship. The particular proof lies in a curious document that bears printing:

AMERICAN EMBASSY,
OFFICE OF THE MILITARY ATTACHÉ,
LONDON

May 15, 1919

From: Lt. Col. S.L.H. Slocum
To: The Adjutant General, Washington
Subject: Brigadier General Douglas MacArthur

1. Recently while visiting the French Front and the Army of Occupation, I met General Gouraud, French Army, at luncheon

in Strasburg. After the luncheon General Gouraud came up to me and asked me if I knew General Douglas MacArthur of the American Army. I stated I did know him. He then remarked: "I consider General MacArthur to be one of the finest and bravest officers I have ever served with."

2. I think this should be put on General MacArthur's personal record.

S.L.H. Slocum,
Lt. Colonel

Somehow in those chalk hills and deadly woods of the Champagne and in the terror of the German attack that failed, MacArthur caught a glimpse of the new technique in offensive tactics that he would mull over for a quarter-century to come. Then, when his own moment arrived, he would lift the lesson in tactics into the realm of strategy—and the great by-pass of the Southwest Pacific would be born.

7

It was time for Generalissimo Foch to strike back. The fifth and last great German attack of the spring and summer of 1918 had failed, and the power of decision was now for the first time in almost four years in the hands of the Allies.

On the west side of the deep Marne bulge near the important railhead of Soissons, the 1st and 2nd American Divisions were hurriedly larded between French outfits, and on July 18 a desperate Allied offensive opened. It was never to cease until the signing of the Armistice on November 11.

Two days after the offensive began, the 42nd was withdrawn from the Champagne defensive front and ordered to the Marne to fight under General Degoutte of the French Sixth Army. In the black, murky night of July 25-26, the infantry regiments of the two brigades began to unload from buses and other carriers with orders to relieve at dawn the units of the exhausted 26th New Englanders. For almost a week the men of the U. S. 26th and the 3rd Divisions with a brigade of the 28th had driven the stubborn enemy from the north bank of the Marne toward the high hills across the tiny Ourcq river. To add to the general confusion and uncertainty, General Menoher,

MacArthur's division commander, now received orders that the Germans, who were now pulling out, must be pursued and kept off-base at all cost. It was a frightening and bewildering front, and part of that first morning's fighting was with the bayonet alone under orders that no shots be fired. But the real surprise was the other way around; Rainbow men going forward through the mists suddenly heard the death song of German bullets from hidden machine guns ahead of them and on both flanks.

MacArthur walked the deadly woods and studied the fields of slaughter. He realized the terrible mistake: the Germans were no longer rapidly retreating with only a small rear guard left to cover their withdrawal. Instead, substantial Boche forces had settled down here on these slopes and in these bits of protecting woods, and behind stout stone walls and farm buildings they had planted their heavy machine guns and mortars in a determined defense. No American advances were possible unless made over cleared fields swept by enemy fire. Yet there were orders from higher up that demanded that they cross the river and take the slopes beyond, regardless of the complete lack of artillery preparation to silence the German positions.

No words can describe the terror and death that lay in wait along these poppy-covered hillsides and in the woods and wall-enclosed farms of the green countryside. Doughboys from New York and Ohio, from Iowa and Alabama and special units from a dozen other states stalked the spitting machine-gun nests, only to be cut to shreds by deadly streams spurted at them from some unsuspected direction.

Finally they learned how to crawl forward in twos and threes, Indian fashion, and when some unconquerable little group had reached a nest of stubborn enemy guns, they would throw their hand grenades and then spring on the enemy. It was not strange that few prisoners were taken.

The succeeding five days and nights were full of anguish for MacArthur. He had nothing to do but follow the orders sent down from Corps and Army. Sergy, Mercy Farm, Nesles, Forêt de Fère, Hill 212—these were names and memories that would forever live in his mind. He vowed that he would never be guilty of ordering a brutal frontal attack without full recon-

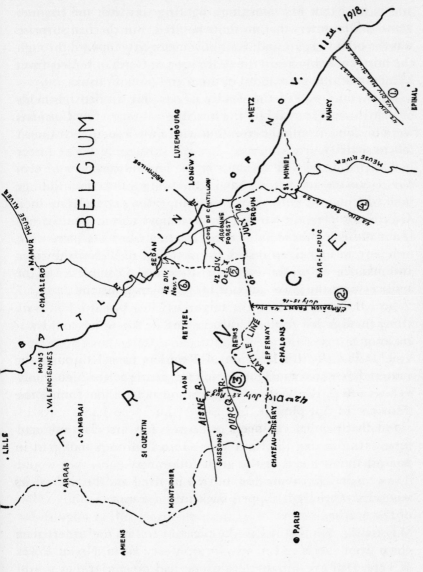

Where the 42nd (Rainbow) Division fought in 1918.

naissance, sure information and adequate bombardment preparation.

It seemed the end would never come. Stubbornly held points would be taken, and then came deadly enemy fire and counterattacks. The same stone farms and bits of woods change hands a half-dozen times. There was neither rest nor hope.

Shortly after midnight on August 1 Captain Wolf, inspecting the battalion and company posts of command, noted unusual activity out front in the German lines. He reported back to MacArthur's command post. Then runners whom Wolf had left behind came in with the word that there was a sudden end to all Boche activity.

MacArthur needed no more proof. He was certain now that the Germans were withdrawing. At 3:30 that morning he walked along the entire division front, calling at each battalion C.P. He ordered the various units to move ahead immediately. They must dog the steps of the retreating Germans.

There was no time to seek the approval of his own division commander or of the corps headquarters. MacArthur alone must assume the grave responsibility for ordering the dawn advance. If he was wrong, he might have to pay for his brash courage with his military career. But he knew he could not be wrong.

That day the 4th Division of Regulars passed through the battered 42nd to harass the enemy retreating to the high southern slopes of the Vesle. The Rainbow was to be denied the privilege of hot pursuit, but MacArthur, who had always insisted that combat engineers could serve as first-class infantrymen, saw to it that the Rainbow's 117th Engineers took part in at least the first half of the great follow-up.

The weary Rainbow now buried its dead and carried off its wounded. Quietly it slipped back into the warm, sunny valley of the Marne.

Here the men bathed in the pleasant stream and revelled in clean, fresh clothing and new equipment and in a great influx of replacements. For the Rainbow had paid a frightful cost for the few kilometers it had gained on the Ourcq and for the glory it had won. In the five days it had suffered casualties in killed and wounded of 5,529, mostly in its four regiments of infantry.

MacArthur, lonely in his heartache and distressed by the mistake that had been made by the high command, now wore a single star on each shoulder. Shortly after the division had left the Lorraine front, word had come to him that he had been nominated as a brigadier general. Later came the devastating news that he was to be sent home to command and train a brigade of the newly organized 11th Regular Division to be formed at Camp Meade, Maryland.

The Rainbow's commander, Major General Menoher, registered his violent protest. Captain Wolf hurried to Chaumont with the plea that MacArthur could not be spared at the very moment when the division was about to bear a goodly part in the coming Champagne offensive. Nevertheless, there were repeated orders for him to leave his beloved outfit. Finally, however, he was permitted to stay on.

The killing and the sleepless rigor of hard battle on the Ourcq had been a little too much for the fatherly Brigadier General Brown of the 84th Infantry Brigade. It called for the stamina and endurance of a younger man. MacArthur would now take over the two regiments of the 84th Brigade, the stout men from Alabama and Iowa. Rebel and Yank, they fought joyously among themselves, but when they faced the enemy, they battled side by side almost as a single unit.

No longer would MacArthur have to worry over the countless details of supply, equipment, transport, training and battle plans for a great square division. He would now have for his own two magnificent regiments with their supporting troops and machine-gun battalions—and always he would insist on a full brigade of artillery to support his attacks.

He could now break with his telephone and his division headquarters. He could fight his brigade on his own feet, try out his own theories of command and leadership. He was 38 and ready for the test.

THE END OF THE RAINBOW

It was an experienced and far wiser division that jumped off on the St. Mihiel front two weeks after the end of the bloody Ourcq fighting.

The clearing out of this strong St. Mihiel salient, which the Germans had held for four years, was a purely professional job for the toughened Rainbow and its comrades in the 1st and 89th Divisions, with the 3rd Division—the famous "Rock of the Marne"—in reserve. By noon of that first murky day the Rainbow men reached the objective set for their initial drive. A thousand prisoners snailed back to the prepared pens in the rear. MacArthur's 84th Brigade had enveloped the stubborn Bois de la Sonnard and then driven straight through it.

By the following noon the division had almost reached its final objectives, and its casualties had remained light. MacArthur, remembering the deadly confusion and mistakes of the Ourcq battle, had vowed that he would have no part in needless slaughter. Never again would a soldier of his be sacrificed unless it was absolutely necessary. He would obey orders, but he would never hesitate to appeal with all his power against instructions he knew were wrong and costly. The commander on the spot must have flexibility and a certain power of decision. He never forgot the terrible lesson he had learned on the Ourcq.

The afternoon of the second day at St. Mihiel a group of high officers, gathered on the top of a small knoll, witnessed one of those rare moments that now and again light up battlefields with a strange glory. There ahead, on down the broad Wouvre plain and scarcely more than a dozen miles away, lay the hazy outlines of the prize city of Metz. It was like a faint mirage floating low on the distant horizon, daring men to seek it out. An army corps brazen enough and of sufficiently desperate courage might drive straight to it, cut the great lines of communication behind the German front and possibly bring the war to a dramatic close. These American officers were quite willing to make a try.

But instead, MacArthur and his brigade were ordered to take over the division's front and organize quickly a sturdy line of defense. Two weeks later the 84th was relieved by its sister brigade, and MacArthur and his Iowa and Alabama boys along with the other units attached to his outfit settled down in the rear areas to rest and recoup.

It was October 1 when the Rainbow moved out toward the vast, shifting battlefield along the 40-mile American front of the Meuse-Argonne. Since September 25 the greatest offensive battle that American troops had ever fought was thundering and roaring ahead. At the start 7 full American divisions were in the front line, and before the battle was over a total of 27 U. S. divisions were engaged. No less than a million Americans would win the right to wear the battle star of this final Meuse-Argonne offensive. A successful break-through to Sedan on the Meuse meant the penetration of the great Hindenburg Line and the probable defeat of the Boche.

Five days after the rested Rainbow began its march forward its units crossed into the battle area, slithering and slipping over the greasy roads and trails, through dripping patches of forests and battered little towns toward the fighting. For nearly a week its men lay soaked and half-frozen in the crowded, muddy woods of Montfaucon, well within the captured territory.

Then on the late afternoon of October 11, they slowly trudged northward over the blasted roads under intermittent shelling, and on midnight of the following day they relieved the completely exhausted 1st Division.

These fortified hills and dangerous woods formed the last of the mighty German defenses in the Argonne. Here was a key part of the final Hindenburg Line, locally known as the Kriemhilde Stellung. It had defied and broken the back of the magnificent 1st Division. Major General Charles P. Summerall had fought his splendid outfit with courage and determination, but

85

deep trenches and endless wire and uncountable enemy cannon and hidden machine guns that spurted streams of hot steel from nowhere were too much for the stoutest of hearts and the bravest of souls.

For his superb leadership Summerall had been rewarded with the V Corps, but the 1st Division had battered itself half to death, and now the Rainbow must take up where it had left off.

MacArthur, often alone, carefully surveyed the desolate and forbidding country that his brigade must fight over. There were rolling hills, partly wooded, with valleys of death between the endless folds of the ridges, and mist and cold and danger were everywhere. He seemed to have a sixth sense when shell fire would lift for a short period and he could hurry on foot across some open bit of country or down some dangerous slope. Squalls of gas and shellfire broke like puffs of wind off shore.

Toward the end of his first day of reconnaissance he was caught squarely in a poison gas attack and made his way back to his C.P. with difficulty. He would carry no gas mask and wear no steel helmet. It was sheer recklessness but it was also a gesture of defiance to the enemy that helped build morale in his own troops, even though it was against definite orders.

This time his gas wound was far worse than the one on the Lorraine front. Major Wolf, his adjutant, feared that the war was over for him. But MacArthur stubbornly refused to be hospitalized.

With uncanny intuition he saw that the position on the right of his brigade line, which Iowa's 168th Infantry must occupy this night for its jump-off at dawn, was actually a kilometer and a half within Boche-held country. This would put it squarely on the line where the supporting American artillery would lay down its preliminary barrage.

MacArthur was violently ill, but there was no moment to lose if the mistake was to be corrected in time. He ordered Wolf to contact corps headquarters immediately and report the ghastly error. At dawn MacArthur left his C.P. and on foot visited the commanders of the advance battalions of his two regiments and checked on the new dispositions he had ordered.

On his right were the splendid fighters of the 32nd Division from Wisconsin and Michigan, who had batttled alongside the Rainbowers on the slopes of the Ourcq. On his left were the stalwarts of the New York and Ohio regiments of the Rainbow. It was a magnificent team.

For the next two days, October 14 and 15, little units of American soldiers, well-spaced and thoroughly experienced, crawled and sneaked and side-slipped from one bit of cover to another. Suddenly they would close in to form squads and platoons for a swift envelopment that would gain them a toe-hold on some slope or deadly hill notched with machine-gun implacements.

By nightfall of the first day Hill 288 was in the hands of the Iowa men. The following day Hill 242 fell, and then the fortified Tuilerie Farm. Every foot of the front areas was dangerous and uncertain. A burst of machine-gun fire would suddenly break the silence, and now and again a battery of enemy 77s would open up on some valley road, or hidden mortars would shell a wooded slope that was sheltering for the moment an advancing platoon. Death, blind and remorseless, whistled and sang its way through the cold mists.

Early one morning Lincoln Eyre, the tall, distinguished correspondent of the New York *World,* with a war reporter of the Chicago *Tribune* [the author] arrived at MacArthur's headquarters. At that very moment the General and Wolf with a soldier or two were approaching the battered old farmhouse from the direction of the front. The General wore a barracks cap and black West Point sweater, and his shoes and puttees were muddy and wet. It was obvious that he was returning from a private reconnaissance of his own.

With the greetings over the little party moved toward the stone building. Someone whispered that MacArthur had had a close call. He had run into one of his own platoons stalking a hidden machine-gun nest off to the left. He was giving the men his benediction when an enemy bullet clipped the left sleeve of his sweater. The *Tribune* correspondent now hurried alongside the General and pointed toward the ravelled sleeve.

"When did brigadier generals get to be expendable?" he questioned.

MacArthur grinned a little sheepishly. Finally he answered.

"Well, there are times when even general officers have to be expendable. Come on inside and we'll rustle some coffee."

His people were making progress but there still remained the deadliest task of all—the Côte de Chatillon. Dominating the whole scene lay this key obstacle, the entrenched Hill of Chatillon, heavily wired, its machine guns enfilading the slopes and valleys surrounding it.

Early the night before, runners from captured Hill 242 had brought word to MacArthur that a patrol had discovered that the deep belt of wire entanglements around the lower slopes of the Côte de Chatillon dribbled out half-way around its northwestern base. With men from Alabama and Iowa planted on its flanks, MacArthur now saw his chance. He directed that during the night all the heavy machine guns in his brigade be concentrated for a long barrage, while artillery battalions would open with their heaviest possible fire. He knew, however, that observation would be most difficult in the hazy mist of the morning.

It was midnight and raining when MacArthur finished drawing up his plans for the attack. Suddenly the door of his advanced C.P. opened and General Summerall, V Corps commander, entered the candle-lit room. He was haggard and muddy and tired. A plate of cold food and a mess cup of steaming black coffee was set out for him. Finished, he pushed back from the rough table.

His voice was low as he spoke directly to the brigade commander. "You will give me Côte de Chatillon tomorrow or turn in a report of 5,000 casualties."

MacArthur brought his heels together. "This brigade will capture Côte de Chatillon tomorrow, sir, or you can report every man in it as a casualty. And at the top of the list will be the name of the brigade commander."

Tears came to the eyes of the grizzled old soldier. He seemed stunned and uttered no word. He had served under Douglas MacArthur's warrior father. It had taken an iron will on his part to order the attack that might bring death to hundreds and even to the son of his dear friend Arthur MacArthur. War was a grim and ugly business.

As silently as he entered, he opened the door and stepped out into the black night.

2

At dawn MacArthur, still ill and shaken from his gas wound, moved out for the final word with his battalion commanders. At 5:30 he watched the First Battalion of the 168th Iowa move out from the Tuilerie Farm. Some time later a provisional battalion of the 167th Alabama stalked stealthily to the right toward the opening in the wire.

And now the two battalions moved cautiously forward through the mist, while a curtain of fire was set down ahead of them. Like the arms of a great pincer the attackers closed in on both sides of the fortified hill that for days had defied the best that the Americans had to throw against it.

Suddenly German defenders in their trenches and nests found men in khaki among them—hard, pinched-cheeked, dirty men, with bloodshot eyes and cold steel in their hearts. And death came swiftly to these Boches, and the key to victory belonged to the soldiers from a far-away land.

Thus fell the Côte de Chatillon. MacArthur in later years could never even mention the name without visible emotion.

3

That night the least chewed-up battalions of the 84th Brigade took over the front line positions that they had won at such cost. For MacArthur's men had been forced to pay a heavy price for the victory. B and C Companies of the Iowa regiment welded together and commanded by a lieutenant could muster only 70 men out of their original 500. The entire 1st Battalion had only 300 men and 6 officers remaining. In three days the 168th Iowa Regiment alone had lost 1,150 men and 25 officers.

The toughest nut of the Kriemhilde Stellung was cracked, but the Rainbow must now step aside and watch the 2nd Division with its deathless Marine Brigade step in and take up the pursuit. There was fighting enough and honor enough for all.

Ten days after the Côte de Chatillon fell, and while the division replaced its terrible losses, it was transferred from Summerall's V Corps. That same cold, muggy day Summerall, the splendid old soldier, who was universally recognized as one of the finest battle commanders in France, wrote a formal letter to the commander of the 42nd Division. It had to do principally with the exploits of the 84th Brigade, and copies eventually would go forward to the great G.H.Q. of the American Expeditionary Force. He wrote:

> This Brigade [the 84th], under the command of Brigadier General Douglas MacArthur, has manifested the highest soldierly qualities and has rendered service of the greatest value during the present operations. With a dash, courage and a fighting spirit worthy of the best traditions of the American Army, this Brigade carried by assault the strongly fortified Hill 228 on the Kriemhilde Stellung and unceasingly pressed its advance until it captured the Tuilerie Ferme and the Bois de Chatillon, thus placing itself at least a kilometer beyond the enemy's strong line of resistance. During this advance the enemy fought with unusual determination with a first class division and in many instances resorted to hand to hand fighting when our troops approached his rear.—The conduct of this brigade has reflected honor upon the Division, the Army and the States from which the Regiments came.

4

The final ten days before the Armistice of November 11 were in the nature of a weird and almost unearthly anti-climax.

After the brief but utterly exhausting period spent in breaking through the last Hindenburg Line, the 42nd Division was permitted to recoup itself. It was now attached to I Corps and ordered to drive with little short of abandon toward the great German rail center of Sedan—where 48 years before the French armies of Napoleon III had suffered complete defeat.

So it was that across the cold and miserable country, still

held by stubborn pockets of German resistance, the two infantry brigades, covered by their artillery trailing close behind, slogged and fought their way toward Sedan and the Meuse river. There was much sickness and exhaustion, and the battle casualties continued to mount.

Almost as deadly to morale as the hidden enemy fire were the latrine rumors of an early peace. Added to freezing nights in the open and the pinched rations, was the factor of general confusion and uncertainty. At times the fighting seemed to be almost automatic.

Across the wide front and straddling both sides of the Meuse river, the American divisions, now more or less on their own, lunged ahead against a still obstinate enemy. On the afternoon of November 5 General Fox Conner, G-3 of Pershing's G.H.Q., drove to Lt. General Hunter Liggett's First Army Headquarters with the information that he had just received a telephone call from General Pershing indicating that he wanted the First Army, with its I and V Corps, to capture Sedan.

Here, at the First Army, miles to the rear of even the two corps headquarters, Colonel George C. Marshall, now assistant chief of staff and G-3—chief of the operations section—of the First Army, wrote out the strange order, under the prompting of General Fox Conner. But the junior officer, Marshall, was in no way to be held responsible for the subsequent happenings. Since Lt. General Liggett was absent, the order was held up until the arrival of Brigadier General Hugh A. Drum, the chief of staff of the First Army. It was dispatched sometime that evening, but there was bitter night patrol fighting on out ahead, and nothing was done at the two corps headquarters until the following day. The order read:

Memorandum for Commanding Generals, I Corps
V Corps

Subject: Message from the Commander-in-Chief

1. General Pershing desires that the honor of entering Sedan should fall to the First American Army. He has every confidence that the troops of the 1st Corps, assisted by the 5th Corps, will enable him to realize this desire.

2. In transmitting the foregoing message, your attention is in-

vited to the favorable opportunity now existing, for pressing our advantage throughout the night. Boundaries will not be considered binding.

By command of Lieutenant General Liggett

Official:
G. C. Marshall,
A. C. of S., G-3

Largely as a result of the intemperate final sentence in the order—"Boundaries will not be considered binding"—there now occurred one of those unforeseen and bitter incidents that sometimes happen. In these rare instances officers and men, exhausted, confused and yet inspired by the pride and courage of their individual outfit, are somehow able to call on unknown reserves of endurance to drive them on to ends so ambitious that they border on folly.

Briefly, the position on the morning of November 6 was about as follows: The French 40th Division held the left of an advancing American line that, reading from left to the right, comprised the 42nd and 77th U. S. Divisions of the I Corps, commanded by General Joseph T. Dickman; then on the right the 1st, 2nd, and 89th Divisions of the V Corps under General Summerall. The 42nd Division at this moment possibly faced the toughest enemy resistance on its front of any of the several divisions in this area. It was nearest to Sedan.

At midday of November 6 General Summerall, V Corps commander, strode into the 1st Division's C.P., bringing with him the request made by Pershing. General Frank Parker, the able and driving commander of the 1st Division, immediately set his tired but game regiments into motion. As well as anyone in the whole A.E.F. he knew Pershing's great pride in the 1st. The concluding sentence in the order, *Boundaries will not be considered binding,* gave the division commander all the latitude anyone could ask.

Immediately General Parker ordered his division to drive in five columns toward the prize city. Luckily the 77th escaped most of the galling humiliation of having the columns of another division, without definite authority, march straight through its own area. To the Rainbow, however, the sudden intrusion of the 1st Division troops cutting across its positions brought a flaring of temper and pride that narrowly missed having tragic consequences.

By nightfall of this memorable November 6 the Rainbow's 84th Brigade found itself stretched out along high ridges that overlooked the Meuse river, with the city of Sedan only a few miles ahead. Late that afternoon MacArthur had received the order to push the final drive toward the prize, regardless of the night march involved and without consideration for the exhausted condition of his men. He knew there was a strong force of the enemy directly between him and the river, and he would accept no part in the losses that a night advance would cause. He dispatched Major Wolf to the Division C.P., explaining the situation and asking permission not to move until early the following morning. He then lay down in the hope of gaining a little sleep.

Sometime after midnight he was awakened by his adjutant accompanied by a colonel of the staff of the 1st Division, who explained that despite the unknown dangers of the night, the elements of the 1st were now crowding the roads of MacArthur's area, and that as a result of the precipitate drive the advancing 16th and 18th Infantry Regiments of the 1st had overrun their own wagons and supply trucks and were completely out of food.

MacArthur ordered that his own scanty rations be divided with the brother regiments. Then in the cold and hazy uncertainty of the pre-dawn he decided that he must personally warn his own troops of possible collision. He feared that the unorthodox relaxing of division boundaries might lead to bloodshed. In the confusion of battle, Americans might well fire into unidentified American columns which had crossed division lines. He had best do this important job himself, and he started off with Wolf.

Morning was just breaking when the two officers were suddenly surrounded by a strong patrol of American soldiers. A young lieutenant, with his pistol cocked, declared them captives. His suspicions had been aroused by the odd barracks cap MacArthur was wearing and the long woolen muffler wrapped round his neck; the lieutenant and his men had been warned of possible spies wearing American uniforms, and their exhausted nerves inclined to make them trigger-happy.

Quietly the General explained the identity of himself and his adjutant. The young officer answered that he belonged to the 16th Infantry of the 1st Division. He had his orders, and he must take the two officers back to his own battalion commander. At that moment MacArthur saw emerging through the mist and far down the slope a column that almost certainly was made up of his own troops. He suggested his captors take him there, and when they reached the heavy patrol of the 42nd, the lieutenant saluted, apologized a little awkwardly and went his way.

A day later General Liggett, the First Army commander, wisely untangled the dangerous snarl by angrily ordering the 1st Division out of the Rainbow's area. To the French Army rightfully went the honor of recapturing Sedan, and thus at least partially avenging the great military humiliation it had suffered there so many years before.

So in the end MacArthur and his weary men and the rest of the exhausted 42nd Division reversed their direction, began a side-slip to the rear and east and headed for the pontoon bridges that had been flung across the Meuse. It took all of MacArthur's leadership to keep his tired and ragged footsloggers in hand. The fine razor's edge of their discipline and pride had been nicked and dulled by the rumors of peace and the subsequent feeling that they had been cheated of the honor of capturing Sedan.

Around 9 o'clock on the evening of November 10 MacArthur came into his temporary C.P. and heard the news that the formal armistice was set for 11 o'clock the following morning. The division was now close to Buzancy, and not far away from the scene of one of its greatest victories. MacArthur went on foot from one outfit to another carrying the news that apparently the war was over. But the men were so tired that their tide of emotion had long ago spent itself.

That night he found 60 wounded Americans who had been prisoners of the Germans and with some 200 wounded Boche had been housed in a makeshift hospital. They all had been

94

hastily abandoned when the retreating enemy was forced out of the area.

MacArthur and his exhausted troops welcomed the armistice but it seemed to come as an anti-climax. In his own heart there was no exaltation, only compassion. He had not thought it would be this way on the eve of the final victory for which he and his men had fought so valiantly.

5

Major General Menoher had now been rewarded by receiving command of a corps. For the next two weeks, while the division fought through the final days and began its advance into Germany, MacArthur, as the senior officer present, commanded the division. He showed no outward sign of his disappointment that he had not been made a major general. He knew that both his old division commander, General Menoher, and his former corps commander, General Summerall, had made every possible effort to have him promoted.

The marching columns had barely reached Luxembourg when MacArthur received a personal letter that had arrived in the carrier pouch from G.H.Q. at Chaumont. It read:

AMERICAN EXPEDITIONARY FORCE

OFFICE OF THE COMMANDER-IN-CHIEF

(Personal)   *France, Nov. 29, 1918*
My dear General MacArthur:

It gives me great pleasure to inform you that on Oct. 17, I recommended you for promotion to the grade of Major General, basing my recommendation upon the efficiency of your service with the American Expeditionary Force.

The War Department discontinued all promotions of General Officers after the signing of the Armistice, and I regret that you will not therefor receive the deserved recognition of your excellent services.

Sincerely yours,
(Signed) *John J. Pershing*

There were additional evidences of the regard of his superiors for MacArthur. The dead had hardly been buried in front of the Côte de Chatillon, near the end of October, when the

Rainbow's commander, Major General Menoher, dispatched a letter to his West Point classmate, the Commander-in-Chief of the American Armies, on the subject of the "Distinguished Services of Brigadier General MacArthur."

It is a long document, covering more than 2,000 words, and there is a fire and passion about it. It began:

I do not feel that my duty with the 42nd Division has been completed and that I am free to assume another command without recording the services rendered by the former Chief of Staff and one of the present infantry brigade commanders of the Division, General Douglas MacArthur, throughout the period during which I commanded the 42nd Division. These services, rendered constantly, for over a year, and in the large part amidst active operations in the field, have been so soundly, brilliantly and loyally performed that in the recognition of them I see only a fair appraisal of the example of energy, courage and efficiency which General MacArthur has set to the 42nd Division and to our entire Army in France. The contributions made to our military establishment by this general officer while under my command have already had far-reaching effects. He has stood for the actual physical command of large bodies of troops in battle, not of a day but of days' duration, and I believe has actually commanded larger bodies of troops on the battle line than any other officer in our Army, with, in each instance, conspicuous success. He has developed, combined and applied the use of the infantry and correlated arms with an effect upon the enemy, a husbandry of his own forces and means and a resourcefulness which no other commander in the field has. . . .

For his field leadership, generalcy and determination during three days of constant combat (in front of the Côte de Chatillon), I was happy to recommend to you for a second time that he be made a Major General, which recommendation the Corps Commander, General Summerall, entirely concurred in and approved. For his gallantry and determination in the field, though again suffering from gas poisoning, I recommended General MacArthur for a palm of the Distinguished Service Cross, which action General Summerall also endorsed with his approval. . . .

This record represents the unremitting endeavor of a very brilliant and gifted officer who has, after more than a year's full service in France without a day apart from his division or his command, and although twice wounded in action, filled each day with a loyal and intelligent application to duty such as is, among officers in the field and in actual contact with battle, without parallel in our Army. . . ."

General Menoher's extraordinary letter of commendation bore the date of October 30. The war ended twelve days later. Five days after the signing of the Armistice an officer reported at the Rainbow's headquarters with personal orders to supervise a special board to consider recommendations for the Medal of Honor within the division.

There was little time to do anything about the matter until the division was settled in its pleasant billets along the Rhine. Shortly the board of awards was selected by the division headquarters, and Major Walter Wolf was made recorder.

Among a number of the younger officers there was a determined feeling that their former chief of staff and present commander of the 84th Brigade must not be overlooked. On December 17 the special board sent in its recommendation of nine names for the Medal of Honor. No. 1 on the list was Brigadier General Douglas MacArthur.

It was a month later when the final report from Army Headquarters reached the Rainbow. It read:

1. Recommendations for the award of the Medal of Honor to the following member of your Command are disapproved.
Brigadier General Douglas MacArthur
[2 additional names]
2. The acts recited in these cases are judged not to meet the standard set for the award of the Medal of Honor.

> By command of General Pershing,
> J. A. Ulio
> Adjutant General

The members of the special board of awards for the division were shocked and embittered. Most of them had heard rumors of the enmity against General MacArthur that was said to have existed on the part of certain senior members of Pershing's G.H.Q. staff. To cross out the No. 1 name on its carefully selected list, when each member of the division's board of awards personally knew of numerous incidents of his leadership "above and beyond the call of duty," seemed to reflect such a feeling of personal hostility that the board presented a written protest. But it was of no avail.

It was the second time that Douglas MacArthur had seemingly won and yet been denied his country's highest award for valor.

April 11, 1919, saw the first shipload of men of the famed 42nd pulling out from Brest. The last units left France on the 18th—eighteen months to a day from the date of the departure of the first convoy of the division from Hoboken.

It was the end of the Rainbow.

7

BACK TO WEST POINT

MacArthur was back in Washington but a few days when General Peyton C. March, Chief of Staff, sent for him.

March, abrupt, incisive and highly intelligent, had, it will be remembered, served in the Philippines in 1899 as a sort of super-aide to General Arthur MacArthur. At a farewell dinner to his staff and his senior officers in Malacañan Palace in June 1901, General MacArthur, then military governor of the Islands, singled out March and J. Franklin Bell as the two officers most likely to reach the top of their profession. In 1906 Bell became Chief of Staff of the newly reorganized U. S. Army; and in 1918 Secretary of War Baker brought March back from France, where he had been Pershing's chief of artillery, and made him Army Chief of Staff.

On this May day in 1919 when MacArthur, a temporary brigadier general, reported to the Chief of Staff's office, General March told him that he would make him superintendent of West Point on condition that MacArthur approved of certain ideas that March wished to be carried out. When March at

20 had entered West Point in 1883, he was already a graduate of Lafayette College, so that much of the military academy's scholastic work had not been difficult for him.

"West Point is 40 years behind the times," he bluntly told MacArthur.

Then he went on to explain that because the war's demand for officers had reduced the 4-year course to a single year, much of the spirit of the fine, old Academy had been lost. A complete job of rehabilitation was necessary. The present outlook was that Congress would authorize a 3-year course, and plans would have to be made with that goal in view. Among other changes March demanded that all physical hazing be stopped.

MacArthur promptly answered that he would be very happy to take on the difficult assignment. March suggested that he consider Lt. Colonel Robert M. Danford, Field Artillery, for his commandant. Colonel Danford, who came from the tiny river town of New Boston, Illinois, on the Mississippi, had literally left the plow to enter West Point and an army career. He had graduated in 1904, and MacArthur remembered him well and favorably from the three years they had been fellow cadets.

A talk with Danford proved to MacArthur that they saw eye to eye regarding the need of modernizing the Academy from top to bottom, including the abolishment of hazing. To reorganize the scholastic side alone would be a long and hard fight that would bring out the opposition of certain high-ranking members of the permanent academic staff, as well as that of many older officers and certain elements in Congress.

On June 12 MacArthur settled his mother in the comfortable quarters at West Point that had been built almost a hundred years before for Superintendent Thayer. During the war period Mrs. MacArthur had been living with her older son's family at the naval base in San Diego, and it would be pleasant for her to be mistress of this distinctive home.

MacArthur's third annual report as superintendent contains an accurate description of the problems he faced:

When I assumed command on June 12, 1919, I found there two classes in the Academy, each of them under instruction less

99

than a year. It is no exaggeration to describe conditions with respect to the course of training at that moment as chaotic.

Orders had been issued to prepare the first of the two Fourth Classes for graduation in 1920, and the second in 1921. These orders were modified in May, 1919, by changing the curriculum to a three-year basis for graduation.

But the Act making appropriations for the fiscal year ending July 30, 1921, was passed, carrying the provision that the course of instruction should be four years. Thus within a single year, preparation had to be made for three different courses of training preparatory for graduation at different periods.

This uncertainty with respect to the curriculum was not the only reason for the chaotic conditions. The morale of the cadet body was low. Following the armistice, 24 cadets resigned from the Fourth Class A (entered in June, 1918)—and 85 from the Fourth Class B (entered in November). The education qualifications for admission had been largely discarded in the case of cadets who entered in November, 1918, and 73 failed in the spring tests.

The traditional disciplinary system, so largely built around the prestige and influence of the upperclassmen, was impossible in a situation where there were no upperclassmen. Cadet officers had never known the example of cadet officers before them, and the body of the Corps had a most imperfect idea of the standards of bearing and conduct which have been characteristic of the cadet for over a century. The old West Point could not have been recognized in the institution as it appeared in June 1919. It had gone; it had to be replaced.

We had the buildings and equipment for a great military institution; we had the traditions of the old West Point implanted in the character of its graduates; we had the experience of the World War to point the way; we had the assurance of loyal and devoted service from the fine corps of officers on duty here; and we had a point of departure in the legal establishment of a four-year course of study and training. Our problem was upon these foundations and with these guides and aids to build a new West Point which should continue the fine tradition of the old and should give the most thorough preparation of officer personnel for the next possible future war.

All that first summer of 1919 the new superintendent sat with the Academic Board and thrashed out the scores of problems that had to do with a complete redrafting and modernizing of the various courses. General March had not exaggerated when he had called West Point 40 years behind the times. At once MacArthur met considerable opposition from several older men on the faculty who looked upon him as only a brilliant upstart and outsider. For some weeks MacArthur quietly endured their constant opposition. One of the senior academic colonels especially irritated him by his sniping tactics of continued obstruction. At the opening of one particular session MacArthur had barely finished outlining a certain new idea when the obstreperous colonel jumped to his feet and began his objections. It was a little more than MacArthur could stand.

"Sit down, sir!" he roared, "I'm talking!" And then he gave his offending subordinate a dressing-down the like of which the Academic Board conference room had never before witnessed.

A number of years later when MacArthur was Military Advisor to the President of the Philippine Commonwealth, he outlined some of his original ideas in answer to a letter from a young captain who had just been appointed assistant professor in the English Department at West Point. Time apparently had little changed the fundamental conception he had initiated some years before.

You were good enough to ask my opinion with reference to the objectives of the English Course at West Point. It is unquestionably to so train the cadet that he can clearly and lucidly present his basic thoughts and ideas. It is not the mission of the English Course to create or control those ideas, but it is its clear function to provide him with the medium through which he can present his views in an intelligent and even forcible manner. No man can hope to rise to distinction who cannot do this and no man, however humble his position, should fail to be able to do so. It is the very medium in which modern civilization lives. It is almost like the air you breathe. Without it a man may have the finest judgment in the world, he may be even wise as Solomon, and yet his influence will be practically negligible.

The accomplishment of such a purpose is not confined to proper grammatical, rhetorical or phonetical grouping of words into sentences and paragraphs. There must be the logical connection between the thought in a man's brain and the ability to present it in clear language. How to accomplish this is the detailed duty of your new department.

When I was Superintendent I outlined at much greater length than this letter what I expected to accomplish from the English Department and left the ways and means to that department. The success attained did not even approximate to what I had in mind and I have always felt that there was great room for ingenuity and constructive effort along those lines at West Point. In many ways I regard it as the most important department there and certainly if it could fulfill the objective I have named above, it would be beyond doubt the most useful. The pen is still mightier than the sword.

The human side was only one factor in the many problems that MacArthur faced. He was determined to end the Academy's antiquated attitude toward the cadets and particularly the upperclassman. As swiftly as he could he laid down the rule that the cadets of the three top classes must be treated as responsible young men. He allowed them to smoke pipes and cigars in their rooms. If their scholastic grades were good, he permitted them week-end leaves, and permitted each cadet $5 a week from his pay and allowances.

The chaplain at West Point at the time was a tall, slender, tolerant divine who had been a three-letter man at the University of the South, at Sewanee, Tenn., where he had gained the nickname of Buck; his family name was Wheat. He was chaplain, athlete and warm human being.

The new superintendent found Buck Wheat and his high enthusiasm for various sports to his exact liking. When it came time for spring baseball practice and the chaplain showed what a superb first baseman he was, the General wanted to make him baseball coach. Wheat begged off in favor of an old-time professional, but he was on hand every afternoon for practice.

For a hundred years the Academy had followed a strict custom for Sunday observance. After compulsory chapel and noon dinner, cadets might gather quietly in one another's rooms or take walks, but they must play no games or in any possible way desecrate the Sabbath. Chaplain Wheat watched the boys wistfully looking out of their barracks windows or listlessly strolling about the post, and finally he went to the new super-intendent and laid out his proposal:

Why not permit the cadets to practice ball or tennis or golf on Sunday afternoon, even using the Plain for their quiet exercise? As chaplain he would gladly play with them, and thus soften any personal criticism of the cadets by religious fundamentalists.

MacArthur pushed back his chair and started walking up and down his office. It was a grand idea, he insisted. Get the cadets out of their rooms and into the air and under the blue sky. The better the day the better the deed. He approved 100%. Go to it!

Sure enough, letters of disapproval appeared in the New York papers and a number of complaints went to the War Department, but neither the superintendent nor the chaplain wavered.

MacArthur never lost his affection for Buck Wheat, who, after serving eight years as chaplain at West Point, became head of the English Department there and retired in the early 40s as a full colonel in the Regular Army. For many years one of MacArthur's favorite stories had to do with the chaplain's prowess in various fields of sport. At the Academy there were several Officer Clubs that revolved around such diverse fields as tennis, golf and skeet shooting. At the close of the special season of each sport an informal gathering of the club members took place and the superintendent was asked in to award the silver cups.

Toward the end of MacArthur's tour he was invited to attend the last meeting of the Skeet Club, at which the championship shoot was to be held. In the final elimination only two officers and Chaplain Wheat were still in the running for the cup. Major Simon Bolivar Buckner, Jr., class of 1908, and Captain Omar Bradley, class of 1915, each broke 24 out of a possible 25. Wheat tied the score, so that a shoot-off was necessary.

Again Buckner and Bradley each broke 24 clay pigeons. Wheat, using an old double-barrel hammer gun that was practically a family heirloom, made a perfect score. It was a magnificent display of nerve and perfect coordination.

After the proper toasts were made General MacArthur stepped up to present the silver cup. His sly sense of humor and his magnetic personality were at their best.

"Chaplain Wheat," he began slowly, "sometime this fall I presented you with a cup as the champion golfer in the Officer Corps here at the Point. A little later I had the honor of handing you the championship cup as the best tennis player among the officers at the Academy. We were all proud of you and your records.

"And today I am presenting you this silver cup for being the finest skeet shooter at West Point. But in all sincerity and as your true friend, I must warn you that you have now gone just a little too far. My brother officers here do not particularly mind your winning the championship cups in tennis and golf, but when you presume to win against the Army in a matter of shooting, which is its peculiar field, then, sir, I must tell you with complete frankness that you have gone just a little too far."

The chaplain's only concern regarding the superintendent was that he never attended chapel, despite the fact that it was evident that MacArthur possessed a deep pool of religious mysticism. Toward the end of his three-year tour, the superintendent, however, was now and again prevailed upon to attend the beautiful chapel services, there to listen to the unforgettable organ music of Fritz Mayer and an inspiring talk by Chaplain Wheat.

One of the many MacArthur innovations was intramural athletics, which required every cadet to take part in some interclass sport. With this went a whole new conception of the need for more physical training. Another important change followed the order that most of the summer training of the upper classes should be done at Camp Dix or other camps where there were regular units of the Army. Quietly MacArthur put in requisitions for every new type of army gun, weapon and transport, until he had at West Point the equipment for a full army brigade.

Colonel Danford, the commandant, handled personally all of the direct contact with the cadets, but he and the superintendent always worked in harmony. They both were determined to wipe out the last vestiges of the old custom of exercising or physical hazing. As a cadet Colonel Danford had not been severely hazed, but MacArthur had not forgotten the unreasonable cruelty of his own experience. Neither officer had associated himself with the hazing of plebes during his upperclass years, and they were equally determined now to tear out root and branch the unwarranted and sometimes brutal cadet tradition.

Early in the academic term that began in September 1920, the Class of 1922 became involved in a rather weird chain of incidents. A certain obnoxious and unpopular cadet had been "braced" (made to stand at rigid attention) and harmlessly "crawled" by a third classman. He had immediately fled to the commandant's office with a sorry tale, in which he claimed that he had been so unnerved by hazing that he was failing in his academic courses.

The upperclassman who had crawled him but not actually hazed him physically was given a heavy slug of punishment, and the squealing plebe was not dismissed for his scholastic failure. The Corps was bitter against the plebe for breaking the cadet code, and against the superintendent for permitting the plebe to remain at the Academy, despite the fact that his low grades called for his dismissal.

The unfortunate cadet continued his refusal to conform and openly opposed the Corps. Finally in the summer of 1921, when two of the four classes were transported to Fort Dix, the resentment reached the boiling point.

The first captain at the time was a superior cadet named George Olmsted, who stood No. 2 in scholastic rating in his class. Special care was taken by his classmates to see that Olmsted personally should have no part in or knowledge of the subsequent events.

Late one night the First Class gathered in an unused company barracks at Camp Dix. There in complete darkness it was decided that a small and secret group chosen by the Corps Honor Committee should handle the case of the offending cadet. No names were spoken, so that if anyone present was called up on the carpet he could answer that he could not positively identify any cadet who had a part in the proceedings. Likewise, great care was taken that First Captain Olmsted was not involved in any way.

A purse of money was raised, and in the middle of the night the cadet to be railroaded was quietly taken from his barracks, hustled off to the nearest railroad station, given the money for expenses and a civilian suit and warned never again to show his face around the Corps.

Shortly before this the commandant had left Fort Dix for West Point, so that he was at the Academy when MacArthur heard the news of the affair. The superintendent immediately called in Colonel Danford.

"Get back to Dix as soon as you can and bust Olmsted," MacArthur ordered.

Danford returned at once to the army camp outside Trenton and at mess call had the cadet adjutant read out the orders reducing Olmsted to the ranks and appointing Cadet Charles J. Barrett as first captain.

On giving the seemingly harsh order MacArthur had been guided by the memories of his own sense of duty and responsibility when he had been first captain. If some such unfortunate incident as this railroading had occurred during his time as first captain, he would have personally accepted the full responsibility for any action the Corps might have taken, even though he had had no knowledge or part in it. He saw no reason why First Captain Olmsted should not do likewise.

Late that following spring, shortly before the Class was due to graduate, MacArthur, touched by the manly and dignified way that Olmsted had accepted the unhappy situation, made him a cadet captain. The idea had first been suggested to the commandant by Olmsted's company tactical officer, and Colonel Danford had passed it on to the superintendent.

It was a gesture that the Corps fully appreciated.

2

MacArthur's career was in friendly and generous hands in the War Department as long as Newton D. Baker was Secretary of War and General Peyton C. March was Chief of Staff. On January 20, 1920, he was made a permanent brigadier general, the youngest in the Regular Army. Scores of older officers who had enjoyed temporary high rank during the war and were now reduced to their permanent grades were openly indignant. And many officers of his own generation found the former temporary stars on their shoulder straps replaced by the gold or silver leaves of a major or lieutenant colonel. Only Hugh A. Drum, of the many who were near MacArthur's age, was given the permanent rank of a general officer. One of the officers who had gained considerable reputation in the war and was now reduced to a major on Pershing's staff was George C. Marshall.

When President Harding entered the White House on March 4, 1921, the atmosphere surrounding the War Department at once changed notably as far as MacArthur was concerned. John W. Weeks replaced Newton D. Baker as Secretary of War, and John J. Pershing succeeded March as Chief of Staff. March was not even permitted to finish out his customary four-year tour of duty.

The old Chaumont crowd from France now held down many of the key desks in the War Department and General Staff. Some of them brought to their new jobs their old resentment against MacArthur, now aggravated by the fact that a number of them had lost their war grades and that MacArthur now ranked them. They had been G.H.Q. men in the war and were still Pershing men, and they were envious of the single star that MacArthur wore.

But he had plenty to worry about in the great shift of West Point from a hide-bound military school disrupted by the war to a modern college. His own life continued to be as austere and restricted as it had been. Most of his evenings were spent alone in his study in the superintendent's rambling old house. He had started pretty much as a lone wolf, and as a lone wolf he would continue.

In an outburst of confidence he once said to Colonel Danford, "When a man gets to be a general officer, he has no friends."

MacArthur's routine at West Point was unique. He arrived at his office around 10:30 each morning. After clearing his desk of mail and such items as presented themselves, he took care of the appointments that were scheduled. Around 12:00 he went to his quarters, ate lunch and usually took a siesta. Then he returned to his office, finished off any work or appointments that were left over, and if it was the football or baseball season, he would hustle over to the athletic field and watch the practice.

While football captured his most intense interest, the fact that he had played on the West Point baseball team gave him a peculiar and abiding affection for that game. During the years immediately after the armistice the Academy suffered from a succession of poor baseball teams. For three years straight the Cadets had lost to the Midshipmen and when May 21, 1921, rolled around and the Army won 8 to 7 over the Navy, every West Pointer from the superintendent to the lowliest plebe felt a hilarious joy.

That night during supper word quietly passed through the Corps that there would be a midnight shirt-tail parade despite the most stringent regulations against such action. Promptly at midnight the Corps gathered on the Plain, snake-danced past the superintendent's and commandant's quarters and on to the site of old Fort Clinton. Here guards were placed and while a great bonfire blazed, musical instruments miraculously appeared, and a celebration exploded that could be heard for miles up and down the river.

Major Charles Bonesteel was officer in charge that night, and when he discovered the cadet sentinels, he assured them that he was not making a report but simply wanted to join in the fun. So it was that instead of ordering the cadets to their barracks and reporting the ringleaders, he took part in the celebration and along with the captain of the ball team made a rip-roaring victory speech. When the steam had blown off and dawn began to show, the cadets quietly returned to their rooms.

Later that morning when the commandant dropped in at the

superintendent's office for his regular morning conference, Mac-Arthur greeted him with a broad grin.

"Had quite a party last night, didn't you, John?" MacArthur said, addressing the commandant by his cadet nickname.

"Yes, sir," Danford answered, not quite certain how things would turn out.

"How many did you 'skin,' John?"

"Not a damn one, General."

MacArthur hit the desk with the heels of both hands. "Good!" he pronounced. "You know, John, I could hardly keep from going out there myself."

Now and again his driver would motor him to New York for some special dinner or theatre party. As he returned late one night from an evening in the city, and his car was slowly making its way along the narrow, winding roads on the west bank of the Hudson, a man stepped out from a clump of woods and with a flashlight waved the automobile to a stop. Suddenly he drew a pistol and covered the driver and the General.

"Hand over your money!" he ordered, his flash half-blinding the two men in the car.

"Hold up, huh?" MacArthur questioned.

He was told to dig up his purse and get busy about it. Mac-Arthur was deliberate in his answer.

"You don't get it as easy as that," he said calmly. "I've got around $40 in my purse, but you'll have to whip me to get it. I'm coming out of this car, and I'll fight you for it."

The stick-up man waved his pistol and threatened to shoot. MacArthur shook his head.

"Sure you can shoot me," he went on. "But if you do they'll run you down and you'll fry in the Big House down below. Put up that gun, and I'll come out and fight you fair and square for my purse."

Almost as an afterthought he added: "My name is MacArthur, and I live—"

The man let down the hammer of his gun. "My God! why didn't you tell me that in the first place! . . . Why, I was in the Rainbow. I was a sergeant in Wild Bill Donovan's outfit. Why, General, I'm sorry. I apologize."

MacArthur ordered his chauffeur to drive on. When he arrived at West Point he made no effort to notify the State Police.

4

Within General Pershing's office there were certain critical comments regarding MacArthur's tour at the Academy. In June 1922 he would have finished three years of duty. Ordinarily the assignment was considered a four-year detail, but there was nothing hard or fast about its tenure. It was discovered that MacArthur stood No. 1 on the list of general officers who were due for foreign service. It was as good an excuse as any to relieve him and send him to Manila. In mid-January 1922 the War Department made that official announcement.

It kicked up more fuss than had been expected. There were Letters to the Editor in the New York papers, but the War Department settled all questions by its press release of January 30.

> Brigadier General Fred W. Sladen, commanding Fort Sheridan, Ill., was today appointed Superintendent of West Point to relieve Brigadier General MacArthur on June 30. General MacArthur is assigned to the Philippines.

But a new element now entered. January 14 *The New York Times* printed a dispatch from its Washington office announcing the engagement of Mrs. Louise Brooks and Brigadier General Douglas MacArthur. Mrs. Brooks was described as "the only daughter of Mrs. Edward Stotesbury by her first husband, the late Oliver Cromwell, of New York. She was formerly the wife of Walter D. Brooks, Jr., of Baltimore and Green Spring Valley, Maryland, and had been divorced in France in 1919."

It had been a fast and exciting courtship. The two met at Tuxedo, the society resort west of the Point. Later at a dinner party at the superintendent's home the General's mother, too, was completely charmed by Mrs. Brooks.

Louise Cromwell Brooks was then in her middle 30s, and MacArthur was 6 or 7 years her senior. She had social background, a splendid zest for living, a son and daughter and a stepfather who was one of the richest men in America. And General MacArthur was certainly one of the prize bachelors of the time.

Mrs. Brooks had lived in Paris much of the post-war years, and among all the young women of the American colony she had been one of the gayest and most sought after by the officers of the army set. Her name had been often linked with that of General Pershing, although actually it was the attractive Major John G. Quakemeyer, a bachelor officer on Pershing's staff, who was her most ardent suitor.

And now in the furor caused by the announcement of the Brooks-MacArthur engagement and the order relieving MacArthur of command at West Point, Pershing found that gossip was involving his name in the twin affair. Shortly after a critical Letter to the Editor, regarding MacArthur's relief as superintendent, was published in *The New York Times*, there appeared on page 3 of that newspaper a long story from its Washington office, under the head, *Pershing Denies 'Exile' Order Rumor*. It read:

> "It's all damn poppycock, without the slightest foundation and based on the idlest gossip."
>
> John J. Pershing, General of the Armies and Chief of the War Department General Staff, used these words tonight in characterizing published rumors that he, as an unsuccessful suitor for the hand of Mrs. Cromwell Brooks, had "exiled" General MacArthur to the Philippines.
>
> "There is no ground for that story. It is all damn poppycock. . . . If I were married to all the ladies to whom gossip have engaged me I would be a regular Brigham Young. General MacArthur is being ordered to the Philippines because he stands at the top of the list of officers due for foreign service. He has been due for such service, as a matter of fact, for over a year.
>
> "I do not know whether General MacArthur has any intention of resigning from the army. I haven't had the slightest intimation to that effect from him. But I can say that I do not believe that General MacArthur would resign from the army merely because he was about to be ordered to a foreign post. I know General MacArthur well. He is one of the most splendid types of soldiers I have ever met. All this stuff is idle nonsense."

The wedding was performed February 14, 1922, at El Mirasol, the Spanish villa of Mr. and Mrs. Stotesbury on Ocean Boulevard in Palm Beach. It was a fashionable affair and was duly reported in the society columns of all the leading journals of the country.

The bridegroom was accompanied to Palm Beach by Chaplain Wheat, who was the only representative of the MacArthur family mentioned among the 200 who attended the wedding and the subsequent reception. The absence of the General's mother was a matter of some comment.

8

RETURN TO THE PHILIPPINES

Life as a married man with two attractive step-children was possibly a bit more complicated for MacArthur than he had imagined it would be. His bride was witty, amusing and talented, but her background and her ambitions were quite different from her husband's. And no matter how much personal devotion there was between them, a clash of these two strong personalities was inevitable.

Besides this, the importance of money assumed a dominance it had never before held in the mind of the stern soldier, who had been brought up in a certain gracious austerity. Much of his boyhood had been spent in army posts, where the MacArthurs necessarily lived with care and frugality on the small army pay of the period. Eventually his mother inherited $40,-000 from her father's estate, and this had been cautiously husbanded. His father had little more than his regular pay and as a retired officer during the last three years of his life, his three-quarters base pay.

It was early in October 1922 when their ship docked at Manila. Eighteen years had passed since he had last seen the Pearl of the Orient in the fall of 1904. It was good to be back.

But the intervening years had brought changes. The Filipinos had made great advances in home government, and the independence movement under the tireless and almost inspired leadership of Manuel Quezón was growing stronger.

Along with the growing desire of the Filipinos for complete political freedom and equal social status, a counter movement among the foreign business sections and in much of the American Army and Navy set was driving a dangerous wedge between the two racial groups. It was a conflict over the already outmoded British colonial idea of class and race superiority.

Douglas MacArthur immediately felt the serious impact of what was happening. He knew what it had meant to the Islands when his father had taken into his home the captured General Aguinaldo, head of the Insurrecto movement, and treated him as a brother officer and an equal. And now, 21 years later, the son realized that a full awakening of pride and dignity of race must be part and parcel of the Philippine preparation for ultimate independence.

Time and again he went out of his way to show publicly his friendship and sense of complete social equality with Manuel Quezón and other Philippine officials. The Quezóns were guests of honor at dinner parties at the MacArthur home, and every effort was made to bridge the widening chasm.

MacArthur was shocked to see the increasing acceptance by his American compatriots of a colonial theory that he knew was outmoded throughout the whole Far East. He was a complete realist in his study of the problem. Facts were facts: the age of exploitation and the old ideas of superiority of races were definitely coming to an end.

From the moment of his arrival in Manila he had few illusions about how he would be accepted by certain of the older army colonels and general officers, all his elders. He well understood the undercurrents of army envy and critical appraisal, and they no longer bothered him. He knew, too, that he had

113

loyal friends—at least in the two top American officials in the Islands; Major General Leonard Wood, the governor general, and Major General George W. Read, commanding general of the Department of the Philippines.

When the news of MacArthur's relief from West Point and his assignment to the Philippine Department reached Manila, there was some concern at headquarters about what should be done with him. Major Robert C. Richardson, G-1 on the staff, who handled personnel, and who had been three years with MacArthur at West Point, conceived the idea of having him assigned to the command of a somewhat superimposed and nebulous area to be designated the Military District of Manila.

Richardson also arranged with the help of Manuel Quezón, leader of the Independence movement and speaker of the House of Representatives, for the Philippine Constabulary to turn over to MacArthur its old headquarters building at Calle 1 Victoria for his residence. It was a beautiful 200-year-old structure with lovely gardens and vistas that sat atop the high stone wall surrounding the ancient inner city of Manila. The MacArthurs, at their own expense, renovated the charming and exotic place and moved in. It was called The House on the Wall.

Within the year the War Department in Washington found out about MacArthur's special assignment to the rather fanciful District of Manila, ordered it dissolved and sent him to command the brigade at Fort McKinley. MacArthur fortunately was permitted to remain in his unique home and commute by motor car to Fort McKinley.

In the middle of February 1923, a cable arrived from the General's sister-in-law, Mary McCulla MacArthur, that Mother MacArthur was desperately ill and that the physicians thought she had not long to live. Immediately plans were made to leave on the first ship. It sailed from Manila on February 11, and the whole family, Louise and her young son and daughter accompanied MacArthur on the 10,000-mile journey home.

For a number of years Mrs. Arthur MacArthur had been in more or less precarious health. The long and trying tours in

114

the isolated frontier posts had left their mark on her. Early in the days when her son was superintendent at West Point, she had suffered from an attack of vertigo and had been confined for some time in the post hospital. One morning the post surgeon called at MacArthur's office and solemnly told him he thought his mother could not live more than a few days or weeks at the most. Her heart might play out at any moment.

MacArthur thanked him, and that noon before lunch he walked over to the hospital. He was upset, but he believed that the surgeon's diagnosis was wrong. He felt that he knew his mother and the strength of her courageous spirit far better than the army doctor.

Only once or twice in his life did he ever tell the story: "When I came into her room, I patted her on the back and appeared highly elated. I told her that I had the finest news in the world for her; the doctor had just told me that she had a strong heart, and that she could leave the hospital anytime she wanted to. In less than a week I had her home with me, despite the doctor's dire prophecies. Fifteen years later I was by her bedside when she died."

But on the long trip back to San Francisco and across the continent to Washington, he had no assurance that he would get there in time. He made it, and the sight and touch of her son proved to be exactly what the mother needed. He was grateful all his life for the wonderful care his sister-in-law Mary poured out on his mother throughout the years when he could not be with her. And he was deeply appreciative, too, of the ceaseless interest of Dr. Howard J. Hutter, of the Army Medical Corps, who helped her professionally over the years from 1922 until her death.

Within a few weeks the General's mother was so improved that he and his family were able to start back to Manila. It was not long after his arrival when a cable announced the sudden death from appendicitis of his only brother, Arthur. From now on the devoted Mary would alone have to face the problem of caring for her family and of helping to look after Mother MacArthur as well. No one in the Navy had had a brighter future or was any more beloved by his men than Captain Arthur MacArthur. He had been an extraordinarily brilliant officer.

2

About this time the General's West Point yearling roommate, Major George Cocheu, dropped in at his office at Fort McKinley and found him looking grimly at a sheet of paper on his desk. He tossed it over to Cocheu. It was an order for MacArthur to undertake a complete survey and study of Bataan and draw up a plan of defense for the mountainous and wooded peninsula that lay a scant three miles across the sea channel from Corregidor at the mouth of Manila Bay.

"Why, that's a job for a young engineer officer and not for a brigadier general," Cocheu indignantly remarked. "What are you going to do about it?"

"Obey it, of course," MacArthur answered. "It's an order. What else can I do?"

For weeks MacArthur and his party of surveyors and map makers covered every foot of the steaming, malaria-infected area. Some of it he remembered vividly from the days when as a second lieutenant in the Corps of Engineers he had tramped over its trails and up and down its steep mountainous slopes and through its bamboo thickets.

In September he received a cable from the War Department that he was to be made a major general on January 17, 1925. He would be closing his 44th year when he could pin the second star on his shoulders. Rarely had so young a man gained such high honors in days of peace. The single senior peace-time rank that lay still ahead was that of Chief of Staff of the Army, which carried the four stars of a temporary full general. He still had 20 years of active service before his compulsory retirement at 64. It seemed plenty of time in which to reach the final goal.

In due time he assumed command of the 3rd Corps Area in Baltimore and he and his family settled down in his wife's country estate at Rainbow Hill, Eccleston, Maryland, within easy motoring distance of his office. Washington with its great dinners and social functions was less than two hours distant.

This era was the fabulous period of the stock market boom. For the first time in his life MacArthur found himself knee-deep in a social and financial whirl that was most difficult to resist.

MacArthur was caught in the vortex. But he could not silence the still small voice that pleaded for the austere and sacrificing life of a soldier, dedicated to his country.

3

He had been in command at Baltimore and living in his country home only a few weeks when he was appointed to serve as a member of the military court-martial of the brilliant young air officer, Brigadier General William (Billy) Mitchell. There were 12 members of the court at the start, all major generals, and Colonel Blanton Winship was assigned to act as law member of the court. The case opened on October 28, 1925, in an old brick building at the foot of Capitol Hill in Washington.

His assignment as a member of this particular court was possibly the most distasteful order he had ever received. Billy Mitchell's grandfather had been a close friend of his own grandfather in Milwaukee. Mitchell's father had served as a brother officer with Douglas's father in the 24th Wisconsin Volunteer Infantry during the Civil War until Lieutenant Mitchell had been forced to resign because of eye trouble. The two sons, Billy and Douglas, had become close friends in Milwaukee while Douglas awaited his entrance into West Point and Mitchell was standing by for his orders to Manila. Later each gained fame in the war in France. And now MacArthur must sit in judgment on his own companion in arms and old family friend.

At the opening session three of the members, including Major General Charles P. Summerall, president of the court, were challenged by the defense and excused. The trial opened on Wednesday, and on the following Monday the prosecution rested its case on the assumption that it had proved that General Mitchell had made certain public statements that violated definite orders that he must cease his violent attacks on the lack of air preparedness and against certain army superiors.

117

For four full weeks the defense now presented a string of witnesses who cleverly shifted the hearings completely away from the original case of Mitchell's insubordination. Instead, the War Department and the nation itself seemed to be on trial, with the army fliers as prosecutors. [MacArthur followed much the same course a quarter-century later in the Senate Hearings that were concerned with his own relief from command in Korea: he and his friends brought the real issue to the front so that the ensuing testimony was broadened to include the entire Far Eastern strategy and policy. As in Mitchell's case the effect on national thinking was a vital result.]

As a matter of fact, this long Mitchell trial in 1927 proved a lesson for MacArthur on future air warfare. For a solid month he listened to brilliant and imaginative young airmen in both the Army and Navy state their case for the new weapon of the three-dimensional wars of the future. Over and over again these men of the skies pounded in Mitchell's thesis: "Neither armies nor navies can exist unless the air is controlled over them."

Day after day as the trial dragged along Mrs. Billy Mitchell appeared in the courtroom arm in arm with Mrs. Douglas MacArthur. It was known that the families were devoted friends, and since he was a member of the court, this obvious intimacy of the two wives undoubtedly caused him some embarrassment.

Only a two-thirds vote was needed for a verdict at the end, and after a short recess the court found Mitchell guilty of the charges and sentenced him "to be suspended from rank, command and duty, with forfeiture of all pay and allowances, for five years." This severe sentence was later modified when the Secretary of War granted Mitchell half-pay and allowances.

When the verdict was announced it was assumed by many that MacArthur had voted for conviction. Over the years that followed, certain of his more violent critics assailed him for his part in the persecution of Mitchell.

Since members of any court-martial are sworn to secrecy, there was no proof how MacArthur or anyone else did vote. Certainly he was greatly in sympathy with the new concept of the important part the airplane must have in future wars, and of how strategy and tactics on the land and sea must develop in accordance with the new striking weapon. And so strongly was MacArthur opposed to gag rule of any kind that many intimate friends in later years were convinced that he could only have voted for Mitchell's acquittal.

It was a part of his military philosophy then and later that an officer should not be gagged or silenced for being at variance with his superiors and with the accepted doctrines. In years to come this philosophy of an officer's freedom was to become extremely important in his own life.

4

Despite the social demands on his time, he managed to keep up a fair amount of his reading and study. He was keenly aware of the growing pressure of foreign ideologies that had begun to spread over the country in the guise of liberal ideas. His concern at the moment was the expanding pacifist movement that was very definitely threatening a return of national unpreparedness.

He saw clearly that America was again on the easy road that led to danger and uncertainty, just as she had always been after each war in her history. He had known almost first-hand how deplorable was the lack of national defense following the Civil War, and on down through the miserable little war with Spain. He recalled as vividly as if he had been a part in it, how raw courage had valiantly tried to offset the inexcusable lack of preparedness in the fighting in Cuba and in the involved and desperate campaign in the Philippines.

He had many long conversations with the new Chief of Staff, General Charles P. Summerall, about what might be done to awaken public interest to the fact that the Army had once again been whittled down and starved until its effectiveness was almost neutralized. Dwight F. Davis, Secretary of War, also was deeply concerned, and it was suggested that MacArthur at a great dinner of the Soldiers and Sailors Club at the Ritz-Carlton in New York should make the principal address pointing to the growing danger. Governor Al Smith was a co-sponsor of this serious attempt to awaken public opinion.

119

MacArthur's gift for emotional oratory was now fully developed and there were few voices in America that could approach his lyric quality. There was a prophetic ring, as well, to the talk he delivered at this much-publicized dinner on April 6, 1927:

> With the Red menace in Russia, Poland in disorder, Roumania threatened with secession, France fighting in Morocco, Nicaragua in revolution, Mexico in confusion, and civil war in China, it does not seem unlikely that our streets will again be filled with marching men and our country again have need of our services.
>
> The provisions of our National Defense Act should be fully carried out. Total disarmament is unthinkable. No one would take seriously the equally illogical plan of disbanding our fire department, or disbanding our police department to stop crime.
>
> Our country insists upon respect for its rights, and gives due recognition to the rights of all others. But as long as humanity is governed by motives not in accord with Christianity, we are in danger of an attack directed by unworthy impulses. We should be prepared against brutal attack. Those who would not protect themselves should, as a matter of common decency, be willing to furnish the reasonable protection required by others.
>
> Our nation has shrunk from enforced military service. But between the two extremes has been evolved the conception of citizen soldiery. Upon the successful solution of this problem—the citizen soldier—will depend the very life of the nation. And when the bloody test comes some American chief on the day of victory is going to thank God for what the nation is now building up in its citizen soldiery. . . .

But the entire nation seemed anesthetized by ignorance and inertia and oblivious to the stealthy infiltration of subversive conspiracy. He expounded his beliefs as often as he could, but there was no chance to turn them into anything bordering on a crusade.

[In due time it became apparent that it was during this period of the late '20s and early '30s that MacArthur won the bitter and enduring enmity of two powerful groups within the United States: the Communists and the Pacifists. The latter included many internationalists and well-wishers who violently opposed his belief that national security depends on adequate preparedness.]

120

Even during the seriousness of these days MacArthur's life was a varied one. He had never lost his keen interest in sports, and now and again he attended championship fights and World Series baseball games. In mid-September 1927, after the sudden death of the president of the American Olympic Committee, he was offered that difficult post and the active directorship of the Olympic team. The Army Chief of Staff agreed to place him on detached service, and the next June in Amsterdam the American team won first place with 131 points, with Finland in second place with 62 points.

The day after the victorious team returned to New York General Summerall addressed a letter to MacArthur:

> I can best voice what is universally recognized that you alone are responsible for cementing the bonds between disorganized and factional organizations, infusing a spirit and resolution and will to win in the contestants, and maintaining before the world the noblest ideals of American citizenship. You have not only maintained the reputation that Americans do not quit, but that Americans know how to win.
> With my own warm and deepest gratitude,
>
> Faithfully your friend,
> *Charles P. Summerall*

"Americans do not quit" in this letter referred to an incident when the first boxing contest was decided against the American contender who seemed to have won over his South African opponent. The manager of the American boxing team had immediately withdrawn his men from further competition. But MacArthur ordered the team back into the contest, saying that Americans never quit.

MacArthur on his return had two weeks to cross the continent and embark at Seattle for Manila. The Chief of Staff had directed that he proceed to the command of the Department of the Philippines. He was now assured of a friend in the office of the Chief of Staff. He had ample time to pack and arrange his personal affairs. His wife and her children did not accompany him this time.

Once again in the bright and lovely city of Manila, now with no family responsibilities, he could return to his old routine of aloofness to social demands and after the day's work turn undisturbed to his books and study. The magnetism of his personality was keen and alive, and the quiet austerity of his life in no way reflected any traits of an introvert. Almost invariably there was a frank and cheery good-feeling about him personally that was infectious and stimulating.

He immediately discovered that he was more in accord with the broad and tolerant attitude toward the Filipinos that guided Henry L. Stimson, then governor general, than he had been on his previous tour with that of Major General Leonard Wood.

His return as commanding general of the Department within three short years after his previous tour of duty caused the usual comments and whisperings among some older and less fortunate officers. It did not in the least bother him.

Soon after he had taken over command the adjutant general of the Department came to him with a thick-bound volume of mimeographed sheets and explained that the staff had gathered a collection of all the precedents that had been established by the various commanding generals so that MacArthur would know what to do no matter what the problem might be. "We thought you might be interested in having this," the officer explained proudly.

General MacArthur lifted the bulky volume. "It's a tremendous job you have done," he said. "How many copies of this are there?"

"Exactly six, sir," the officer answered.

MacArthur looked him straight in the eyes and there was no smile showing when he said: "Well, you get all those six copies together and burn them—every one of them. I'll not be bound by precedents. Any time a problem comes up, I'll make the decision at once—immediately."

Long ago he had learned the art of quick decision. His mind was already so steeped in experience and military background that he had no need to hesitate or postpone his conclusions. He walked alone but with a sure and steady step.

There is no record of MacArthur having met Manuel Quezón when he first came to the Islands in 1903, but during his second tour he had started a firm friendship with this leader of the Independence movement. On this return to Manila in 1928, he and the Quezón family renewed their warm friendship.

MacArthur had no sympathy whatever with the line of racial cleavage that was now being drawn by large elements of the American military colony and the upper crust of foreign civilians. He saw that it had increased to an alarming extent even during the few short years he had been back in the States, and he determined that he would show his opposition.

Not long after he arrived on this tour of duty it came to his attention that on the three-decker boats that shuttled back and forth between Corregidor and Manila the top deck was reserved for American officers and their families, and the lower decks were for American enlisted men and their families, and for enlisted and civilian Filipinos.

The civilian engineer on Corregidor who knew most about the secret installations on the rock citadel was a Spanish soldier who had gone over to the Americans in 1898. This engineer could ride on the top deck himself, but his fine Filipino wife and children were relegated to the lower deck. When a U. S. colonel asked the provost marshal on Corregidor to correct this injustice, the officer told him that the regulations regarding boat decks could not be changed.

When MacArthur heard of this he immediately sent for the coast artillery officer who commanded Corregidor.

"But the regulations are clear," the high-ranking officer argued, when the matter was laid before him.

MacArthur blazed out at him: "You change them at once. Understand, at once!"

Little stories like this, indicating MacArthur's fairness toward the Filipinos, began to be repeated over the Islands.

Quezón had had much to do with picking Henry L. Stimson as governor general in 1927. Besides "racial sensitiveness," as Stimson labelled it, an even more disturbing factor in the

123

Philippine situation was the demand of American cordage, sugar and dairy interests that the duty-free entrance of Philippine sugar and copra should be stopped, and that the Islands should quickly be granted full independence.

With the coming of the Hoover administration on March 4, 1929, Stimson was promoted to the cabinet position of Secretary of State. The decision as to his successor in Manila was temporarily postponed by President Hoover. No position within the appointing power of the President was more sensitive or explosive. Many commercial interests were in direct opposition to American pledges and ideals. And in the Islands themselves Quezón and other Filipino leaders were beginning to think that possibly they had gone a little too far and fast in their demands for immediate and full independence, and that they might better go along under the protecting wing of the United States as a commonwealth with free-trade privileges.

Already Quezón was turning to MacArthur for advice and help. The General's concern was primarily involved in defense and in the growing threat of Japan's expansion. It was not his province to be concerned with the time schedule of independence, but he was firm in his belief in the rightness of ultimate Philippine independence, with a strong and lasting tie-in with the United States. These Islands were his second home. Two generations of MacArthur soldiers had proven how deep was their affection for this lovely land.

6

On June 17, 1929, a friendly reporter from a Manila paper brought MacArthur the yellow flimsy of an A. P. dispatch from Reno, Nevada. It read:

Major General Douglas MacArthur was divorced here today by his wife, Mrs. Henrietta Louise MacArthur, on the grounds of failure to provide.

Although the complaint charged failure to provide, and Mrs. MacArthur's testimony had only to do with the allegation, after she left the court room she said: "General MacArthur and I have divorced because we were wholly incompatible to one another.

I have the greatest respect and admiration for him, and we part as friends."

The Manila reporter said that his editor was perfectly willing to kill the story if it would offend the General.

"Put it on the front page if you care to," he answered, giving no sign of his personal distaste. "It doesn't make the slightest difference to me."

A month after the arrival of this dispatch from Reno, MacArthur was handed a long decoded cable marked "Secret." It was marked "For MacArthur's eyes only":

> The President desires to appoint you as Chief of Engineers. He desires a reorganization of the Engineer Corps administration along broad lines to conform to the magnitude and diversity of its activities, greatly increased by the flood control and inland waterway projects. I have assured the Secretary of War and the President of your unswerving loyalty and cooperation in executing his wishes. He is convinced of your organizing ability and professional qualifications. The President desires to know whether you are willing to accept the appointment. Keep this in strictest confidence. Reply in same code.
>
> *Summerall,*
> *Chief of Staff*

It was very difficult to turn down such a request coming from the President. But MacArthur knew that if he accepted the appointment, he would set a roadblock against his chances of ever being made Chief of Staff. Besides, he had long ago ceased thinking of himself as primarily an army engineer; he was a soldier of the Line. He had tasted field command and war, and they had given him a bitter-sweet memory that had become a part of his life.

Carefully but firmly he begged off from the assignment. The great Mississippi river floods had left the engineer-minded President Hoover deeply shaken, and MacArthur had been recommended to him as general officer most competent to reorganize and enlarge the Corps of Engineers.

As the year 1929 drifted into 1930, the Far Eastern world like the European had dark patches of warning in the skies. Germany was about to rearm, Japan was plotting her further conquest of Manchuria and her intrusion into China proper. And America was wallowing in the slough of despair and insecurity.

MacArthur's tour of duty in Manila would be finished in October 1930. On July 7 he cabled the Adjutant General in Washington asking for assignment to the 2nd Corps Area in New York City, whenever that command became vacant. He wired: "I have never before made special application for station, and I earnestly solicit favorable consideration. The most impelling personal reasons dictate the request."

In the same cable he requested permission to make a final inspection trip of China and Japan, and then return home on a commercial liner from Yokohama, without back-tracking to Manila. The following day a reply came granting him the travel permission and assuring him that his request for assignment to the 2nd Corps Area would receive consideration.

In Washington every conceivable kind of pressure was being brought to bear on President Hoover and Secretary of War Hurley by the political friends of a number of the senior major generals for the appointment to succeed Summerall as Chief of Staff. President Hoover was very clear in his mind on one thing: He held unequivocally that "the choice of Chief of Staff by seniority led only to dead ends." He considered vigorous young blood and an independent mind badly needed in this exacting office. And he was determined that the new Chief of Staff must not be tied in with the old army cliques.

In all this reasoning he was completely supported by his able Secretary of War, Patrick J. Hurley, who had made a fine record in the brilliant 3rd Division in France. Hurley had long been impressed by the record and personality of MacArthur, and his favorable opinion was further strengthened by a cablegram from him that he received on May 22. It read as follows:

I have just read in the local papers your letter to Senator Bingham dealing with the Philippine problem, and I cannot refrain from expressing to you the unbounded admiration it has caused me. It is the most comprehensive and statesmanlike paper that has ever been presented with reference to this complex and perplexing problem. At one stroke it has clarified issues which have perplexed and embarrassed statesmen for the last thirty years. If nothing else had ever been written upon the subject, your treatise would be complete and absolute. It leaves nothing to be said and has brought confidence and hope out of the morass of chaos and confusion which has existed in the minds of millions of people. It is the most statesmanlike utterance that has emanated from the American Government in many decades and renews in the hearts of many of us our confirmed faith in American principles and ideals. You have done a great and courageous piece of work and I am sure that the United States intends even greater things for you in the future. Please accept my heartiest congratulations not only for yourself personally but the great nation to which we both belong.

The Secretary's mind had already been made up as to his own choice of Chief of Staff when the President asked for the personal files of the two youngest major generals on the list of those who still had four years to serve before retirement. MacArthur was the youngest of the major generals who still had four years' service ahead of them, and he was the senior of this particular group. The second youngest major general was Hugh A. Drum. After careful study the President agreed to accept Hurley's recommendation of Douglas MacArthur.

Before any announcement of the decision had been made the Secretary of War was summoned late one afternoon to the White House. When he entered the study he found General of the Armies John J. Pershing, who had just returned from a mission in France, in conference with the President. After the usual greetings the President quietly asked Hurley why he had not consulted Pershing regarding the appointment of a new Chief of Staff. It was evident to Hurley that Hoover wanted to be relieved from the pressure General Pershing was exercising.

Hurley replied that Pershing was abroad at the time the decision was made. Then he promptly added: "But even if he had been here in Washington, I probably would not have consulted him, Mr. President."

In a frank and straightforward manner the Secretary explained that he had learned discipline and the chain of command from Pershing. He had never offered unasked advice

127

to his seniors. He understood fully the responsibilities and the duties of a superior officer. He was now General Pershing's superior, and he probably would not have accepted General Pershing's unsolicited advice. This difficult decision regarding the appointment of a Chief of Staff was the Secretary of War's responsibility—subject only to the final decision by the President, his single superior. If the President now wanted to change the appointment, he would gladly accept his orders.

General Pershing rose to his feet and walking to the Secretary's chair patted his shoulder. "Well, Mr. President," he pronounced with emotion, "he is one of my boys. I have nothing more to say."

Later it became known that Pershing had strongly urged the President to appoint either Fox Conner, his chief of staff in the A.E.F., or Hanson E. Ely, who had served as commanding general of the 5th Division in France.

7

On August 5, 1930, a radiogram from Major General Preston Brown, Acting Chief of Staff, was handed MacArthur in his office in Manila. It read:

> President has just announced your detail as Chief of Staff to succeed General Summerall. My heartiest congratulations.

MacArthur was then a few days over 50½ years. It has been said that he was the youngest general officer ever to be appointed Chief of Staff. But in fact, J. Franklin Bell, who owed so much to Douglas MacArthur's father, had been made Chief of Staff in 1906 several months before he was 50; and Major General Leonard Wood was not 50 when he was chosen in 1910 as Chief of Staff by President Theodore Roosevelt.

Certainly no other soldier, regardless of age, had ever brought to the high office the breadth of mind and background and grasp of world affairs that Douglas MacArthur possessed. For many years he had been deliberately preparing himself for this great task. The appointment was a surprise to him and his friends only because he was chosen at this particular time rather than 4 or even 8 years later.

A tempest in the army teapot boiled up immediately. *The*

New York Times let loose an editorial blast against the President's purported statement that "he is the only one of the Major Generals who has a sufficient period to serve in the army before retirement, to serve the full four-year term as Chief of Staff." The paper duly listed the names of ten other major generals who had at least four years more to serve, and added that there were only nine major generals who would have to go on the retired list before the next four years were ended.

Three days later the War Department cleared up the misunderstanding by explaining that what the President had really said was that MacArthur was "the senior ranking general" among those who could serve the full four-year term as Chief of Staff.

But the storm blew itself out long before it reached the Philippines. Whoever plucked the plum would have to face the envy of many officers and their friends.

MacArthur's orders to inspect army installations west of the Mississippi river and then assume office on November 21, 1930, automatically cancelled his contemplated trip to China, Manchuria, Korea and Japan. But his own Intelligence Section, operating out of the Department headquarters in Manila, had kept him fairly well informed of Asiatic affairs. He was familiar with the stealthy Japanese intrusion into the mainland of China. Japan had been slowly building up her economic empire in Manchuria, and he was certain that in time she would find or create the necessary excuse for military adventure.

He knew of the undercover activities of Colonel Doihara, an ambitious Japanese officer. He thought that the Tanaka Memorial, allegedly mapping Japan's future Asiatic advances, was substantially true, and he was familiar with Japan's Twenty-one Demands of World War I days.

It was clear to him that the great decisions regarding the fate of Asia and the Western Pacific were still to be made. The shadow of an ambitious Red Russia in the vast reaches of Eastern Siberia was slowly growing more ominous. Here in Northeastern Asia was the Triangle-of-Destiny, where the fate of China, Russia and Japan might be decided and the future history of the whole world be written.

Already Communist Russia had made great gains in undermining the inner citadels of its enemies. He was disturbed especially by the secret boring from within by Red termites, already working on the insecure pillars of the restless and awakening colonial lands of East Asia—and even on the foundations of his own America. In the Philippines he had followed closely the workings of Russian and Japanese secret agents. He was aware of the growing threat of the vast revolutionary social and political unrest in these lands and peoples of the Far East.

He understood the manifold problems that lay ahead of him as Chief of Staff. The great depression was still on, and he knew that it would be hard to arouse Congress to the needs of even half-way preparedness. As a start he must first straighten out the definite injustices and inequalities in officer pay and promotion and then take up the long fight to modernize the Army itself.

He welcomed the struggles and conflicts that he faced. He recognized no allegiance to anything or anyone save his country. Thoughts and dicta of his father were constantly in his mind. And he was aware, too, of how much he owed his mother. As an intimate member of the family explained many years later: "Somehow or other he had acquired through her the rare and subconscious gift of being able to tune into the great force that exists in the universe, and to draw from it an inner spirit and a sustaining power."

It warmed his heart to know that he could once again take her under his protecting wing. She was now in her 78th year, and although he appreciated the endless sacrifices his sister-in-law, Mary McCulla MacArthur, had made in giving her a home and in caring for her, he felt that once she was installed with him in the Chief of Staff's quarters at Fort Myer, outside Washington, her health and spirits would show definite improvement.

PART TWO

The Fight for
Preparedness

1930-1941

9

THE FIRST BATTLE

It was to a greatly changed America that MacArthur returned in the late fall of 1930, and he was now operating on a much higher and more exacting level of authority.

All during the previous 27 years of his commissioned service he had been receiving orders and policy decisions made by others. Now he would make the over-all decisions and give the orders.

The great depression had been on for almost a year. Millions were jobless, confidence was shaken, and public morale was at the lowest it had been since the panic of 1892-3.

A little over two weeks before MacArthur was sworn in as Chief of Staff, the Democrats had recaptured the Lower House of Congress and put an end to any chance the Hoover administration might have had to work its way out of the economic debacle. The opposition now set its sights on the presidential election of 1932. Any hope of unity or cooperation between the parties was definitely over.

Under the guise of the pressing need for economy in government, certain leaders of the opposition began a frontal assault on the Army and Navy. Consciously or unconsciously they lent their support to an increasing number of pacifists who preached moral disarmament and America's role in leading the way toward permanent peace by stripping bare her own inadequate defenses. MacArthur sensed the very real danger. Yet to oppose the powerful group was to bring on the charge of being a militarist. He was certain that many of the pacifist leaders were innocent tools in the hands of radical and liberal groups and elements that were in many cases definitely Socialist and pro-Bolshevik.

In the late spring of 1931, after he had been Chief of Staff six months, the problem seemed to reach a minor climax in a questionnaire circulated among some 53,000 Protestant clergymen by S. Parkes Cadman, Harry Emerson Fosdick, Daniel A. Poling and seven others through the auspices of *The World Tomorrow,* a powerful church weekly. One question on the list was: "Do you believe that the Churches of America should now go on record as refusing to sanction or support any future war?"

Of the 19,372 replies received, 12,076 (62%) expressed the opinion that the churches of America should not support any future war.

Another question read: "Are you personally prepared to state that it is your present purpose not to sanction any future war or participate as an armed combatant?" To this 10,427—or 54%—answered that they would not sanction war nor participate in it.

The result of the poll was published in the May 1931 issue of the magazine. The June issue was devoted almost entirely to a series of articles by notable pacifists then in America, including the German refugee Albert Einstein. In a more critical section appeared a long letter from MacArthur.

> My predominant feeling with reference to the majority of replies received by your paper from 19,372 clergymen is that of surprise; surprise at the knowledge that so many of the clergymen of this country have placed themselves on record as repudiating in advance the constitutional obligations that will fall upon them

equally with all other elements of our citizenship in supporting this country in case of need.

To exercise privilege without assuming attending responsibility and obligation is to occupy a position of license, a position apparently sought by men who do not avail themselves of the privileges conferred by our democracy upon its citizens, but who, in effect, proclaim their willingness to see this nation perish rather than participate in its defense.

The question of war and peace is one that rests, under our form of government, in Congress. In exercising this authority, Congress voices the will of the majority, whose right to rule is the cornerstone upon which our governmental edifice is built. Under the Constitution, its pronouncement on such a question is final, and is obligatory upon every citizen of the United States.

That men who wear the cloth of the Church should openly defend repudiation of the laws of the land, with the necessary implications and ramifications arising from such a general attitude toward our statutes, seems almost unbelievable. It will certainly hearten every potential or actual criminal and malefactor who either has or contemplates breaking some other law. . . .

Perhaps the greatest privilege of our country, which indeed was the genius of its foundation, is religious freedom. Religious freedom, however, can exist only as long as government survives. To render our country helpless would invite destruction, not only of our political and economic freedoms, but also of our religious freedom. . . .

Any organization which opposes the defense of the homeland and the principles hallowed by the blood of our ancestors, which sets up internationalism in the place of patriotism, which teaches the passive submission of right to the forces of the predatory strong, cannot prevail against the demonstrated staunchness of our position. . . .

This was the beginning of the moral fight MacArthur waged during the years he remained in Washington. Almost exactly a year after his letter to the religious journal, he addressed the graduating class at the University of Pittsburgh. A small radical group had planned an anti-war demonstration and protest against his appearance, and a number of students were actually engaged in starting a mass protest when police appeared and arrested three students. MacArthur was able to deliver his address uninterrupted. He said in part:

Pacifism and its bedfellow communism are all about us. In the theatre, newspaper and magazines, pulpits and lecture halls, schools and colleges, it hangs like a mist before the face of America, organizing the forces of unrest and undermining the morale of the working man.

Day by day this canker eats deeper into the body politic.

For the sentimentalism and emotionalism which have infested our country, we should substitute hard, common sense. Pacifist habits do not insure peace or immunity . . .

It was June 9, 1932, when he spoke these prophetic words. The Bonus Marchers were already beginning to drift into Washington.

2

A number of important matters occurred during the year between the MacArthur letter to *The World Tomorrow* and his speech at the University of Pittsburgh. One was the demand in certain Democratic circles in Congress that big cuts be made in both army and navy appropriations.

But MacArthur entertained no such defeatist ideas. He proposed to keep the little Army intact and abreast of the best military thought in the world. It had been more than 12 years since he had returned from France and the first World War, and he felt the need to catch up with the latest military developments in Europe. On September 4, 1931, he and his energetic aide-de-camp, Captain T. J. Davis, sailed on the *Leviathan* to attend the annual maneuvers in France as the personal guest of General Maxime Weygand, Chief of Staff of the French Army.

The exercises were in the Aisne Valley, adjoining the battlefield of the Ourcq where MacArthur's Rainbow Division had suffered more than 5,000 casualties.

At the close of the maneuvers a group of ranking officers were gathered in a knoll overlooking the rolling country near Rheims and Dormans. Dramatically the French Minister of War, M. André Maginot, strode out in front of the party. He stood six feet four. In a booming voice he asked General MacArthur to step forward. With a flourish the War Minister made a touching little speech and hung the ribbon and medal of the Grand Cross of the Legion of Honor around General Mac-Arthur's neck.

MacArthur was on his way to Yugoslavia on September 18 when the news arrived that the Japanese Army in Manchuria had engineered the Mukden incident and that a one-sided war was now on in the strategic lands north of the Great Wall of China. What he had so long feared had finally happened. He returned to America as soon as he could do so without arousing too much speculation.

He found that Secretary of State Stimson strongly favored imposing moral sanctions on Japan, but when President Hoover by long-distance telephone sought the approval of France and England and was flatly turned down, the Chief Executive argued that a one-nation boycott was tantamount to a declaration of war.

As early as September 1924 a joint board of the Army and Navy had worked out War Plan Orange, a program for action in case of a war with Japan. In broad terms the Plan called for the Army to secure Manila Bay by holding strategic Corregidor and Bataan for four to six months, during which time it was hoped that the Navy would be able to send its fleet with a great train of transports and supply ships to the relief of the bay. Manila would then become a secure base of operations for the ultimate defeat of Japan.

There was much opposition to the plan, particularly among certain army leaders who thought that the Philippines could not be defended, and that the sooner the United States withdrew all its military forces and abandoned its installations, the better off the nation would be.

In March 1934 Congress passed the Tydings-McDuffie Act, which guaranteed full independence to the Philippines in 1946. General MacArthur's conclusion was that in case of war with Japan America's duty was clear-cut and inescapable; it was simply to carry out the pledges embodied in the Tydings-McDuffie Act, in which the United States accepted full responsibility for the defense of the Islands until they attained complete independence in 1946.

In May 1935, while he was Chief of Staff, the joint Army and Navy board again revised the Orange Plan in order to bring it into line with the new Four-Army Plan and with the Navy's conception that in case of war the Pacific Fleet's westward advance across the Central Pacific would have to be by progressive stages.

Five years later when, as Quezón's Military Advisor, MacArthur was deeply concerned with the actuality of building a Filipino force to oppose Japanese aggression, he answered a letter from a brilliant young regular officer about his pessimistic feeling regarding the Army War College he was then attending. It merits being quoted:

> I note a tone of disappointment—almost of frustration—in your critique of the War College Course. The more you become acquainted with the bureaucracy of our governmental departments the more pessimistic you will become. "Red tape," "Bureaucracy," "Routine," "Laissez faire"—whatever you wish to call it—its deadening effect is felt by everyone who comes within the scope of its influence. The great figures that we produce are those who pay little attention to such matters and retain their own freedom of initiative when emergency arises.
>
> I recall my complete disagreement with the Orange Plan when I became Chief of Staff, but I realized at once that I would be wasting my time in trying to educate others to my own point of view. I, therefore, short-circuited by seeing the President personally and telling him that if mobilization became necessary during my tenure of office my first step would be to send two divisions from the Atlantic coast to reinforce the Philippines; two divisions from the Gulf of Mexico to reinforce Panama, and two divisions from the Pacific coast to reinforce Hawaii, and that I intended to defend every inch of those possessions and defend them successfully. This being the case, the Orange Plan was a completely useless document. The President agreed with me entirely.
>
> I presume that the Orange Plan that you spoke of is still the same old plan that was antiquated even before my own tenure as Chief of Staff. Fortunately, the man who is in command at the time will be the man who will determine the main features of campaign. If he is a big man he will pay no more attention to the stereotyped plans that may be filed in the dusty pigeon holes of the War Department than their merit warrants.

It was the aggressive soldier and the independent thinker who wrote these lines. Long before this he broke with prece-

138

dent and all the debilitating checks that are put on courageous and original thinking. His mind was weighed down with no inhibitions or fears of failure or disapproval.

3

Back at his desk in the War Department late in 1931 Mac-Arthur was struck by the almost complete lack of realism in the public's attitude toward the developing world crisis. The Japanese Army was running wild in Manchuria, and the situation in the Far East was so explosive that the United States might easily be drawn into war.

Yet there was a definite and powerful group in the Democratic-controlled Congress, convening on December 7, 1931, that was openly attacking the Army under the guise of economy.

MacArthur's position was most difficult. At the very moment when American armed forces should be enlarged to meet any sudden emergency, he had his back to the wall fighting to protect the little Army he had. The most he asked for at the start of the new Congressional session, when the purse strings were in the hands of the party opposing the Hoover administration, was a new promotion bill that would correct the worst of the injustices of the war hump. Every detail of his plan was assailed, and a bill was being considered that would reduce the officer corps from 12,000 to 10,000.

In the midst of the argument the frightening news was cabled from Shanghai on January 28, 1932, that Japanese marines in the International Settlement had invaded the bordering Chinese section of Chapei, and that a full scale war between Japan and China had begun. Thousands of Chinese civilians in Shanghai were killed by the naval bombardment and by gunfire from Japanese ground troops.

At conferences of the joint Army and Navy board, plans were drawn up to meet as thoroughly as possible any of the numberless emergencies that might occur. Due to the very nature of its task and composition, the Navy was constantly in a state of readiness. But not the Army: Its 12,255 regular officers and 124,301 enlisted men (including 6,000 native Filipino Scouts in federal service) were scattered in scores of posts in Luzon, Hawaii, Alaska and Panama and across the continental United States.

All the winter and spring of 1932 on the home front MacArthur fought the enemies of preparedness. Despite the perilous situation in Asia, the number of regular troops within the continental United States available for combat duty was only slightly more than three times the number of men on the New York City police force. For the time being Representative Ross Collins of Mississippi and his followers centered their major demands for army economy on the dangerous proposition that 2,000 officers must be cut from the list of 12,255. In quiet desperation MacArthur on May 10, 1932, wrote a letter to Minority Leader Snell that obviously was meant largely for publicity use.

> An army can live on short rations, it can be insufficiently clothed and housed, it can even be poorly armed and equipped, but in action it is doomed to destruction without the trained and adequate leadership of officers.
>
> An efficient and sufficient Corps of Officers means the difference between victory and defeat.

But when the first vote was taken on the War Department Appropriation Bill providing for the reduction of 2,000 officers it was passed in the Lower House by a vote of 201 to 182.

MacArthur fought back for almost two months, and on July 12 a compromise bill to cut only 1,000 from the officer list failed to pass by a vote of 175 to 154. The entire Democratic Tammany delegation of New York City, led by Representative Thomas H. Cullen, voted against the bill. The Army was saved.

In its issue of July 16, 1932, the powerful *Army & Navy Journal* said editorially:

> For seven long, dreary months General MacArthur fought the forces of destruction in the Congress.
>
> For four months prior to that time he struggled to prevent budget recommendations which threatened to hamstring the Service and to discourage the advocates of National Defense. The fight he made was not only for the Army, it was for the Navy

and Marine Corps as well; for the pacifists conceived that the Army was the easiest arm to attack, and on its weakening they anticipated it would establish a precedent for a later assault on the sea Services. . . .

Undoubtedly the Army has a conception of the gruelling labor involved, the tactful consideration displayed, the careful thought necessary to counter the moves made by no mean adversaries. Representative Collins, and his inspirational chiefs, Speaker Garner and Representative Byrnes, Chairman of the Appropriations Committee. But its conception fell far short of the facts. Willing to make concessions on travel, subsistence, comforts, Yes, said General MacArthur, but on man-power, No!

Should the Democrats retain control of the House in the next Congress, Representative Collins doubtless will renew his officer cut demands.

The *Journal's* prophecy proved to be correct on both vital counts.

4

The sore had been festering for more than six weeks. During June and July 1932 a group estimated at about 11,000 unemployed, many of whom were not veterans at all, had gathered in Washington, in the hope of compelling Congress to vote immediately for a cash bonus to World War I veterans.

Actually the movement was far deeper and more dangerous than a mere raid on the almost empty federal treasury; it was a well-conceived plot of the American Communist party, backed and instructed by Moscow, to bring about a bloody riot that would involve the U. S. Army and force it to fire on veterans. The hope then was that this action would lead the way to a revolutionary mood that might spread to other cities and eventually involve the entire country which was still suffering from unemployment and depression. There was the long chance that a real revolution might follow. This was in the nature of a dangerous trial balloon. Many of the innocent leaders had no inkling of the true motives of the Red organizers who shortly took over actual direction in Washington. Newspapers dubbed the affair the "Bonus March," and for days on end the press of the country carried stories of the threatening gangs that President Hoover was patiently trying to handle without resort to violence. He succeeded in obtaining funds to buy tickets home for the legitimate veterans and their families. Some 6,000 left the city, but there still remained a hard core of 5,000 irreconcilables.

Assistant Attorney General Nugent Dodds had recently sent to the White House a report from the F.B.I. stating that fingerprints made of 4,334 Bonus Marchers by the Federal Bureau of Investigation showed that 1,069 of them—nearly 25%—were of men who had criminal records ranging from murder and rape to such minor categories as drunkenness. There is ample evidence that the Communists had gained control before the day of the riot. The Chief of Staff and the Army were completely alerted to the grave dangers that existed.

On the morning of July 28, L. H. Richelderfer, president of the Board of Commissioners of the District of Columbia, informed the President that about 50 of the malcontents were occupying several old buildings on Pennsylvania Avenue, and that their tenure interfered with certain government construction work going on. Treasury representatives asked the intruders to move out, but their answer was to bring in a mob of a thousand from outside camps. In the struggle with Washington police that morning a number of police officers were injured, one marcher was killed and a bystander was wounded. In all, 57 persons were seriously injured.

The Police Commissioner appealed at once to the Board of Commissioners of the District of Columbia to ask the President to call out federal troops. Commissioner Richelderfer immediately addressed a message to the President asserting that it would "be impossible for the police department to maintain law and order except by the free use of firearms. . . . The presence of federal troops in small number will obviate the seriousness of the situation, and it will result in far less violence and bloodshed."

At once the President called in Secretary of War Hurley and directed him to take charge, cautioning him to prevent bloodshed but to restore law and order. At 2:55 that afternoon of July 28, Hurley formulated his orders and at the request of General MacArthur issued them in writing:

To: General Douglas MacArthur,
  Chief of Staff, U. S. Army

The President has just now informed me that the civil government of the District of Columbia has reported to him that it is unable to maintain law and order in the District.

You will have United States troops proceed immediately to the scene of disorder. Cooperate fully with the District of Columbia police force which is now in charge. Surround the affected area and clear it without delay.

Turn over all prisoners to the civil authorities.

In your orders insist that any women or children who may be in the affected area be accorded every consideration and kindness. Use all humanity consistent with the due execution of the order.

Patrick J. Hurley
Secretary of War

Six hundred soldiers from nearby units were standing by and ready for instant service. General MacArthur personally instructed Brigadier General Perry L. Miles, commanding the 16th Brigade, to carry out the orders. General Miles, in turn, passed on the detailed instructions to his unit commanders:

We are acting on the order of the President of the United States. The cavalry will make a demonstration down Pennsylvania Avenue. The infantry will deploy in line of skirmishers in the rear of the cavalry. You will surround the area on Pennsylvania Avenue between Third and Fourth Streets, and evict the men in possession there. Use care and consideration toward all women and children who may be in the area.

At this time Army Regulations prescribed that officers serving in the War Department and on the General Staff should wear civilian clothes save on special occasions. So grave did the situation appear to the Chief of Staff that at the last moment he decided to put on his uniform and take personal charge of the delicate operation. Dwight D. Eisenhower, a major on his personal staff, accompanied him in uniform as a sort of special assistant. Another major, George S. Patton, commanded the squadron of the 3rd Cavalry that had been ordered over from Fort Myer.

It was 4:30 in the afternoon when the Regulars began their march down Pennsylvania Avenue, the cavalry leading, followed by six small tanks, a platoon of machine gunners and then the infantry—a scant 600 all told. The brickbats of the Bonus Marchers were answered by tear gas, MacArthur himself getting a lungful. Several cavalrymen were knocked off their horses by bricks, but there was no lessening of the steady pressure of the soldiers though not one shot was fired by the troops.

By 6:30 the two camps on Pennsylvania Avenue had been cleared, and 45 minutes later the camp of John Pace's radical group was set fire by the men themselves, and it was evacuated shortly before the troops arrived. By 9:20 p.m. the soldiers reached Anacostia Flats and slowly pushed out the rioters, who set fire to a number of their own huts. Not a single Bonus Marcher had been seriously injured. The definite show of force, the discipline of the troops involved and the plentiful use of tear gas had turned the trick that had balked the Police Commissioner and caused the Board of Commissioners to call on the President for help.

Somewhere between 10 and 11 o'clock that night, after a personal report to the President, MacArthur returned to his office. Newspapermen were waiting for him, and the Secretary of War suggested he give out a statement. MacArthur explained that he had confined his operations to clearing the marchers out of government buildings and off government property. He believed that only 1 in 10 of the mob was a war veteran. He regarded the rest as insurrectionists. He continued:

> If President Hoover had not acted when he did he would have been faced with a serious situation. Another week might have meant that the government was in peril. He [Hoover] had reached the end of an extraordinary patience and had gone to the very limit to avoid friction before using force. Had the President not acted when he did he would have been derelict in his duty.

The following day police rounded up 36 of the leaders while they were holding a meeting in an abandoned church. Among the men arrested was James Ford, who was identified as the American Communist Party candidate for vice-president. Another of the prisoners was Emmanuel Levin of New York City, who was one of the recognized leaders of the Communist group in the bonus mobs. The Army quietly offered to fill up the gas tanks of the marchers' cars, and with a hot meal from the army rolling kitchens most of the rioters headed for home.

On the Sunday following the Bloody Thursday *The New York Times* carried on its front page this item regarding the trouble:

> The Communist Party, at its Headquarters here, accepted responsibility yesterday for the demonstration that resulted in the bonus-army riots in Washington.
>
> "We agitated for the bonus and led the demonstrations of the veterans in Washington," a spokesman for the party said at the headquarters at 50 East 13th Street. "We stand ready to go to Washington again and fight for the working men. We started the march from here for Washington and we will lead the way again in December."

Never before had General MacArthur faced such violent attacks. With President Hoover he was called an enemy of the working man and of every unfortunate veteran. Mr. Hoover 20 years later reduced the political consequences of the action to a single paragraph in Vol. III of his memoirs:

> The Democratic leaders did not organize the Bonus March nor conduct the ensuing riots. But the Democratic organization seized upon the incident with great avidity. Many Democratic speakers in the campaign of 1932 implied that I had murdered veterans on the streets of Washington. . . .

Even as late as 1949 Mrs. Eleanor Roosevelt in her autobiography in *McCall's Magazine* rekindled the long-smoldering hate and false accusations that had been heaped upon the men who had handled the dangerous situation. Writing in the July issue she said of the exciting period:

> The first march, which had taken place in Mr. Hoover's administration, was still painfully fresh in everybody's mind. I shall never forget my feeling of horror when I realized that the Army

145

had actually been ordered to fire on the veterans. This one incident shows what fear can make people do. Mr. Hoover was a Quaker; and General MacArthur, his Chief of Staff, must have known how many veterans would resent the order and never forget it. He must have known too the effect it would have on public opinion. Yet they dared do nothing else in the face of a situation which frightened them.

The completely erroneous charge that "the Army had actually been ordered to fire on the veterans" was fully answered in the November 1949 *McCall's* by the former Secretary of War, Patrick J. Hurley. But this reopening of old sores 17 years after the event proved once again the force of the anger and resentment that had been engendered.

MacArthur's name had been constantly associated with that of President Hoover's in the criticisms and reprisals that continued for years. The distortion of MacArthur's part in the singular affair was to become one of the myths that grew up around him. Even the later sworn testimony of certain ex-Communists who had helped lead the demonstrations could never quite overtake the bitterness that had been fastened on the soldier.

In 1948 Benjamin Gitlow, admitted former Communist, told of the Red plot in his book, *The Whole of Their Lives*. He wrote:

> On July 5 Earl Browder declared that the veterans were the shock troops of the unemployed. Said he, "The Bonus revolutionary force in Washington is the most significant beginning of the mass struggle against the deepening consequences of the crisis." . . .
>
> On July 28 the government went into action. General Douglas MacArthur, Chief of Staff of the United States Army, stepped in to prevent serious bloodshed after a fight between communist-led veterans and police resulted in the death of one veteran and the shooting of an innocent bystander. It was just what the Communists wanted. It was what they had conspired to bring about. Now they could brand Hoover as a murderer of hungry unemployed veterans. They could charge that the United States Army was Wall Street's tool with which to crush the unemployed, and that the government and the Congress of the United States were bloody Fascist butchers of unarmed American workers.

A year later John T. Pace, another acknowledged former Communist, told his story before a Congressional committee. It would seem to clear up, once and for all, any doubts as to who were the real conspirators and what was the true nature of their plot. He testified:

> I feel responsible in part for this often-repeated lie about President Hoover and General MacArthur. . . .
> I led the left-wing or Communist section of the bonus march. I was ordered by my Red superiors to provoke riots. I was told to use every trick to bring about bloodshed in the hopes that President Hoover would be forced to call out the Army. The Communists didn't care how many veterans were killed. I was told Moscow had ordered riots and bloodshed in the hopes that this might set off the revolution. My Communist bosses were jumping with joy on July 28 when the Washington police killed one veteran. The Army was called out by President Hoover and didn't fire a shot or kill a man. General MacArthur put down a Moscow-directed revolution without bloodshed, and that's why the Communists hate him even today. . . .

The last sentence deserves careful re-reading. It was the beginning of a definite and ceaseless campaign that set MacArthur apart from all the other high army officers as a man *to get,* no matter how many years the Communists and their friends and admirers had to wait or what methods they might have to use.

5

MacArthur returned from a second survey of European armies less than a month before the national elections of November 1932 which resulted in the utter defeat of the Republican party. MacArthur realized that his immediate problem was to hold together his little Army and then to remodel and modernize it, but he knew that he must face the increasingly bitter opposition of the Ross Collins faction and their Senatorial opposite numbers. He saw that now they would probably have behind them the pressure and power of the new occupant of the White House. MacArthur did not have long to wait for the opening attack.

Early in the year, during the lame duck session of the old

147

Congress, he appeared before the military sub-committee of the Senate Appropriations Committee in opposition to the Convery-Taber amendment to the Economy Act, which proposed to deny army retired pay to officers who were drawing incomes of $10,000 or more from private employers. It was all a part of the drive to cut down officers' pensions, a plea that had been bitterly debated in the Lower House. Ross Collins and his followers there were demanding that no officer's retired pay be in excess of $2,400 a year. At the same time there were attacks on the law that granted General of the Armies John J. Pershing a special pension that totalled around $18,000 a year.

This latest attack was a little too much for MacArthur. He vigorously addressed the members of the Senate Appropriations Committee, reminding them how the British Army rewarded their General Douglas Haig, who occupied a position equivalent to General Pershing's in the American Army. Haig was promoted to field marshal and awarded a bonus of approximately half a million dollars in the form of a trust fund, the income of which was to accrue to his family through a period of three generations. In addition to this annual income of around $30,000, he received during his lifetime an annuity of $8,700 a year.

General Pershing, then 72, was spending the winter in Arizona. When word came to him of the fight that MacArthur was putting up, he wrote him a personal note in his own handwriting:

Tucson, Arizona
Feb. 23, 1933

General Douglas MacArthur,
Washington, D. C.
Dear General:

Please allow me to send to you my warmest congratulations upon the way you have succeeded in overcoming opposition in Congress to the Army. I think you have much to be thankful for, as we all have.

And may I also express my appreciation for the way you have defended the Retired List and especially your reference to me.

Yours cordially,
John J. Pershing

As a matter of fact Pershing was a little previous with his congratulations. Shortly after the inauguration of Franklin D. Roosevelt on March 4, 1933, Lewis Douglas, Director of the Budget, appeared in the role of the Army's chief opponent in money matters. Previously Douglas, as a Congressman from Arizona, had been one of the outstanding friends of the Army, and his sudden about-face was of deep concern to Lt. Colonel Irving J. Phillipson, the Chief of Staff's liaison officer with the Congress and the Budget Office.

President Roosevelt's instructions to the Director of the Budget were to balance the budget. Douglas, being intimately familiar with Army costs, immediately turned to the Department of the Army for most of his initial savings.

During the last year of the Hoover administration a cut was made in the pay of all members of the armed services. The budget for the Army had already been brought down to what seemed an irreducible minimum when the new administration appeared with its drastic demands.

On March 28 the Budget Director announced that the funds for the Regular Army and for service overhead for the fiscal year beginning July 1, 1933, should be cut 51% as compared to a normal annual appropriation; the National Guard expenditures reduced 25%; the Organized Reserves 33%; the Reserve Officers Training Corps 32%; the Citizens Military Training Corps 36%; with a 75% loss to the National Board for the Promotion of Rifle Practice. In addition he demanded of the War Department that the information regarding the reductions should be kept secret.

It was at this moment that Providence seemed to take a hand in the matter. On March 31 Congress authorized the establishment of a Civilian Conservation Corps, with the number of enlisted personnel initially fixed at 250,000 but soon after raised to 300,000. The Army was charged with receiving the applicants and organizing them into units which were to be turned over to the Departments of Interior or Agriculture for reforestation work and camp duty.

Within ten days the President saw that only the Army could properly establish and administer the 1,450 camps that were authorized, and he dumped the job in MacArthur's lap.

In an incredibly short time the Army was enrolling 8,500 CCC recruits daily, and pushing them through a three-week conditioning course in which they received immunizing treatments, clothing and equipment. They were organized into work companies of approximately 200 men each.

Seven weeks after the Army's concentration depots opened, 300,000 recruits had gone through the mill and some 1,315 camps were functioning. Each camp was under the direction of two regular officers, one reserve officer and four enlisted men of one of the regular establishmens. A total of 3,109 officers of the Regular Army, 532 officers of the Regular Navy and Marine Corps, and 1,774 reserve officers were required for this special duty.

But despite the extraordinary accomplishment of the services there was no change in the critical attitude of the Director of the Budget or of the anti-defense members of Congress. At the end of April 1933 MacArthur appeared before the House Military Affairs Committee to oppose a bill that would have placed a large number of regular officers on a forced furlough list and reduced their semi-retired pay by 50%—in addition to the previous 15% cut in the pay of all officers. The Chief of Staff pointed out that a second lieutenant furloughed under the bill would receive exactly $54 a month. It was the same old fight to cut back the Officer Corps, but under a new guise and dress. Patiently MacArthur restated his arguments:

> The foundation of our National Defense system is the Regular Army, and the foundation of the Regular Army is the officer. He is the soul of the system. If you have to cut everything out of the National Defense Act (of 1920) the last element should be the Officer Corps. If you had to discharge every soldier, if you had to do away with everything else, I would still professionally advise you to keep those 12,000 officers. They are the mainspring of the whole mechanism; each one of them would be worth a thousand men at the beginning of a war. They are the only ones who can take this heterogeneous mass and make of it a homogeneous group. . . .

Nevertheless, the anti-army drive in Congress went steadily forward. It was a many-sided struggle. Behind the specious argument that the issue was primarily one of saving money, stood the hidden pressure of radical groups within the country who were determined to make America impotent by cutting away the underpinning of her national defense. Injecting itself into this dangerous project was an organized pacifist movement, with the rank and file largely innocent of any real wrongdoing but, nevertheless, influenced by Communist dupes and sentimental busybodies.

From the political angle, apart from the direct secret Red intrusion, it was evident to MacArthur that behind Congress and its demands for economy stood the Director of the Budget and behind him the President of the United States. To the General it seemed that the one hope now of saving the Army and particularly the Officer Corps and Reserves was a personal appeal to the White House. He immediately asked for an appointment with the President.

Roosevelt received him cordially and congratulated him on the excellent work the Army was doing in establishing the CCC camps. MacArthur explained that without the full Officer Corps it could never have been accomplished. Yet, he went on, there was still a concerted action to cut back the officer list. He reviewed the dangerous situation that was developing in Germany and Italy and the steady march of the Japanese in Manchuria and China. It was unreasonable and might actually be fatal to weaken the national defenses at this particular time.

The President, in turn, emphasized the need for the strictest economy and the necessity of trying to balance the budget. MacArthur agreed with the soundness of both items, but he protested that it was dangerous to force the military services to bear so much of the burden, while at the same time the new social services were being expanded without limit.

But the President was obdurate. His conception of his almost unlimited authority became evident as he argued that his Chief of Staff must accept the decisions he had made. The cuts had been ordered, and they must stand.

MacArthur argued that if they were carried out, the Army would definitely be forced below the level of national safety. The morale of the whole Army would suffer grievously and the actual defense of the nation would be in peril.

151

He insisted that he was in no way usurping civil authority. Congress rightly held the purse strings of all expenditures. But this was a matter of life or death for the armed forces and the country. It was the President's duty to throw his great influence on the side of national security.

Sharp words were exchanged. MacArthur, who had prided himself all his life on his cool detachment in the face of conflict, now felt his self-control begin to weaken. He was conscious of the significance of the fight he was making. He could not retreat in his arguments or in his demands. He felt that his country's safety was at stake, and that if necessary he would sacrifice his own professional career. His sense of duty was clear and undeniable.

The President demanded the right to run national affairs as he saw fit. He could not give in, nor could he brook this personal interference.

The tension shortly reached the breaking point. Both men were emotionally exhausted, yet neither would compromise. Finally MacArthur played his last card.

He rose to his feet, and his voice was cold and deliberate.

"Mr. President," he said in effect, "if you pursue this policy, which will lead inevitably to the destruction of the American army, I have no other choice but to oppose you publicly. I shall ask for my immediate relief as Chief of Staff and for retirement from the Army, and I shall take this fight straight to the people."

It was a violent and unprecedented scene. Roosevelt was beside himself with anger.

MacArthur saluted, turned on his heel and walked out of the room. He was so incensed and wrought up that he was physically ill on the White House lawn.

As he drove back to Number 1 Quarters at Fort Myer, he was not at all sure but that the following day would see the end of his army career. For he meant to do exactly what he had threatened.

10

THE FIRST PENALTY FOR OPPOSITION

President Roosevelt never referred to this bitter personal encounter. Instead, he quietly spread the word to drop the fight for some of the proposed Army cuts; that the need of more than 3,000 regular officers for special duty in the CCC camps made it inadvisable to reduce the Officer Corps at this time.

MacArthur kept his victory strictly to himself. He realized that he still faced strong opposition in Congress and in the Bureau of the Budget, and in the New Deal experimenters who were gathering around the White House.

As a matter of fact, his campaign for rebuilding the Army was only started. Within the year he began to move toward its attainment. Slowly he assumed the offensive, and one by one he presented his long-range plans to Congress.

His first real triumph came when he succeeded in having the sum of $5,000,000 allocated to the maintenance of the National Guard raised to $18,000,000. A second victory was an allotment of $10,000,000 from the Public Works Administration for partial motorization of the Field Artillery of both regular and the national guard regiments and for motorizing the field trains of the regular infantry divisions.

The roadblock set against the Army had now been partially broken. But MacArthur had only a year left of his four-year tour of duty as Chief of Staff in which to push through his plans for a modern defense system. He might be able to make it.

On June 13, 1933, he took time out to attend the 30th anniversary of his class at West Point, and to make the commencement address. It was a wonderful day for him. He was talking to his own people and at the place he loved more than any other spot in the world. To the graduating class he said in part:

Pacific habits do not insure peace nor immunity from national insult and aggression. Any nation that would keep its self-respect must keep alive its martial ardor and be prepared to defend itself. . . .

The unabashed and unsound propaganda of the peace cranks leads to muddled thinking.

As the necessity of national defense is sacrificed in the name of economy, the United States presents a tempting spectacle. . . .

Every reasonable man knows that war is cruel and destructive, and yet very little of the fever of war will melt the veneer of our civilization.

History has proved that nations once great, that neglected their national defense, are dust and ashes. Where are Rome and Carthage? Where Byzantium? Where Egypt, once so great a state?

Where Korea, whose death cries were unheard by the world? Let us be prepared lest we, too, perish.

His voice was hardly more than a whisper as he spoke these final words. Then the mood changed, and he was once again the old soldier pronouncing his blessings on his juniors.

Good luck, my dear young comrades-in-arms; happy landings, and God be with you.

The cadets and officers and their friends who heard the short address were never to forget his solemn and prophetic words.

This day MacArthur was stirred by his ever-present conviction of the dangers his country faced and how tragically unprepared she was. Nothing mattered to him but to awaken Congress and the citizenry to the true situation. He approached this great task with a devotion that had the quality of battle ardor and sacrifice.

In a very real way he was thoroughly enjoying the job of Chief of Staff, with its wide authority and its vast responsibilities. No previous Chief of Staff had possessed his peculiarly persuasive talents for winning over a critical Congressional Appropriations or Armed Services committee. In defending his requests, or in presenting new requisitions, his sincere and magnetic personality was utterly convincing in the impression it gave of insight and fairness. He exuded a feeling of

154

his own superb patriotism so that the things he asked for appeared in that light and consequently had to be granted.

He had his own way of dealing with visiting Congressmen and those seeking favors. If the requests could be granted without harming the Army, he was inclined to give way to them. If they were unreasonable or impossible, he was able to make his refusal sound just and fair.

Officers going off on special missions or to distant assignments would often drop in at his office for possible last-minute instructions. Following this custom, Major Truman Smith, who had just been appointed military attaché at Berlin, reported to General MacArthur. It was the first time they had met.

MacArthur received him most cordially and asked a few questions regarding his highly important assignment to Germany at this moment when Hitler was embarking on his menacing rearmament program. At the end of the short interview Smith rose to leave.

"Just one little point," MacArthur concluded, his eyes twinkling. "Don't take the British too seriously. Remember that no one likes to sleep with a corpse."

Certainly he had his own quiet sense of humor, and with the little crowd of officers who made up his official family he exhibited a warm, human side that the general public seldom encountered. There was, for instance, the time that he and his aide, Captain T. J. Davis, travelled in civilian clothes, on a late afternoon train to New York. When the second call for dinner was announced, Davis sent the porter back to the dining-car steward with the request to let them know when a table was available. When the word came and they entered the car, the steward somehow mistook T.J. for MacArthur. With elaborate courtesy he addressed the aide as General and led him to the reserved table. MacArthur took the cue and showed marked deference to his subordinate, addressing him as General and sirring him at every opportunity. And when the meal was over, he complimented the steward, thanking him for taking such good care of "my General."

His office hours were still of the same unusual pattern that he adopted when he became superintendent of West Point

Often he would remain in his office until 7 or 8 in the evening, and it was not uncommon at the end of a busy day for his aide, Captain Davis, Lt. Colonel Phillipson and his special aide, Major Ike Eisenhower, and possibly the Deputy Chief of Staff, to remain behind while he walked up and down in his office relating old stories told him by his father, or dipping into the rich memories of his own experiences in France and the Far East.

All during his life the lore and romantic details of the Army had seeped into his conscious and subconscious being. Fellow officers used to say that when he went to France in 1917 as chief of staff of the 42nd Infantry Division, he had already fought in two wars—the Civil War and the Spanish-American War. Certainly he knew intimately every battle and every leader of the great civil conflict that ended almost fifteen years before he was born.

And now in these early 1930s he was quietly preparing for what seemed to be the making of World War II. He spent most of his evenings poring over reports of American military attachés in foreign countries and studying the British and French military journals and the translations from service articles gleaned from publications of all the various European armies. Returning travelers who had found interesting details of foreign military matters were always welcome in his office.

One afternoon Brigadier General Henry J. Reilly, of the old Rainbow Division, steered into the General's office a former war correspondent [the author] who had known MacArthur since his brilliant days in France. The visitor had just returned from a tour of Manchuria and Siberia, and rumors of a possible Russo-Japanese war were still making headlines.

The correspondent, who had had considerable experience in various parts of Russia and Siberia during the early days of the Revolution, told what he had seen of troop movements and military activities in his latest visit to Siberia. He reported on the possible strength of garrisons in Vladivostok and along the Manchurian border and in other Far Eastern cities and key points, but somehow it didn't quite seem to jell. In disgust at his own failure to give accurate figures and details, the visitor finally blurted out that at least there was one thing that he was sure of—the morale of the Russian soldiers.

MacArthur pounded the table with his fist. "That's what I want to know!" he declared enthusiastically. "All this other makes no difference. It's the morale of the Red soldier I'm interested in. That's all that really counts. Go ahead!"

For an hour and a half the correspondent poured out the facts he had learned first-hand when he had covered the U. S. North Russian and Siberian Expeditions from 1918 to 1920, as well as the bitter revolutionary days in Moscow and Leningrad. He told of what he had learned on other trips, and on this latest study of Siberia. The Russian soldiers would fight, he swore. They were brave and ready to die if their country was invaded. And far more of them had been true converts to the Revolution than the outside world realized.

It was strong medicine for the American Chief of Staff, but he instinctively understood that inherent in the young Red soldier there was a stubborn love of Mother Russia, and that he would fight for this native land regardless of the type of flag she flew.

MacArthur, the realist, was not afraid to face new truths, no matter how harsh and distasteful they might be. His alert and far-seeing mind constantly searched for the things of the inner spirit, especially when they concerned the national dreams that help make up the imponderables of a country's military strength. He did not need to judge the merits of the Russian Revolution to understand the depth of the change that had taken place in millions of men there.

And he believed fully in Napoleon's dictum that morale is to all other factors as four is to one.

2

MacArthur was now well into his fourth year as head of the Army. He was making definite progress with his difficult and involved promotion bill and with other plans for the general improvement of the service and its fighting ability. He was again a welcome visitor at the White House, and every now and again the President would ask him over for a quiet, confidential chat. Roosevelt seemed to enjoy the range and independence of the soldier's mind and viewpoint. Now and again they would discuss some phase of the Roosevelt social programs, and MacArthur made no effort to conceal his opposition to certain of the ideas that were being put forward by such radical New Dealers as Harry Hopkins, Harold Ickes and Aubrey Williams.

What alarmed MacArthur was the definite turning away by the new administration from certain old concepts of strict constitutional government, with more and more power being concentrated in the hands of the Chief Executive. MacArthur had been brought up a strict constitutionalist, and he was deeply concerned over the somewhat radical turn of affairs resulting from the growing power of the leftist New Dealers. He made little effort to hide his alarm from the President.

Shortly before one of his informal meetings with the President, MacArthur had encountered a fresh outburst of extreme opposition to his promotion bill. A subsequent White House interview drifted into the matter of growing expenditures in the New Deal social program, and finally MacArthur spoke up rather sharply. He told the President that naturally he was honored the President should ask his opinion regarding the reforms and various socialization proposals under consideration, and he was flattered to find out that often Mr. Roosevelt accepted his views.

"You seem willing to ask my advice about almost everything except military matters," he continued rather tersely. "Why is this, Mr. President?"

The President, not the least disconcerted, replied after a pause, "Douglas, you are my American conscience."

But matters were not always so pleasant and amiable between the two men. Early in February 1934 there was considerable public comment on the graft revelations that had touched the commercial airplane lines carrying air mail. Suddenly and without consulting MacArthur, the President ordered that the air mail contracts be cancelled and that this highly specialized task be turned over to the Army Air Corps.

American army planes were not equipped for night or blind flying. Nor were army pilots familiar with the mail routes.

They had only one-way radio equipment, and from the very start of the assignment there were fatal accidents. So much criticism poured into the White House that within a month the President decided to rescind his order and return the mail contracts to the private firms under certain restrictions he would ask Congress to grant.

In endorsing the proposed legislation the President wrote a letter to the Chairman of the House Post Office Committee in which he said that before he had cancelled the private air-mail contracts he had received definite assurances from the General Staff that the Army could successfully carry the mails.

At once John Callan O'Laughlin, editor of the *Army & Navy Journal,* wrote out the details of a formal interview that he had had with ex-Senator Hiram Bingham, President of the National Aeronautical Society. Bingham demanded to know what army officer had given such assurances. Certainly, he insisted, General MacArthur, Chief of the General Staff, had not given them.

Immediately copies of the interview were handed out to various newspaper correspondents at the National Press Club, and one of them hurried to the White House with the damaging information. Secretary of War Dern, General MacArthur and General Benjamin D. Foulois, head of the Air Corps, were all at the Secretary's office in the War Department when the President contacted Dern on the phone. After a few minutes of conversation Dern turned to MacArthur and said: "The President says you phoned him the assurance that the Air Corps could carry the mails before he issued the cancellation orders."

MacArthur emphatically denied he had done so and asked permission to speak to the President.

"I'm glad to talk with you, Douglas," the President began in his most disarming manner. "I've been thinking about you and how well everything is going in the War Department. You remember you phoned me before I cancelled the air-mail contracts and said the Air Corps could carry the mails and would be glad to undertake it."

MacArthur replied: "Mr. President, I dislike intensely saying what I am going to say, but I never telephoned you. I knew nothing about your plan to have the Air Corps carry the mails."

"But you are mistaken, Douglas," replied the President. "You phoned me, as I have said."

"No, Mr. President. The only time I saw you about the matter was yesterday, when you called General Foulois and me to the White House and gave us a spanking."

"But Marvin McIntyre [the President's Secretary] put your call through to me," Roosevelt insisted.

"Will you put Mr. McIntyre on the phone?" MacArthur requested. Thereupon the President hung up the receiver.

A few minutes later McIntyre appeared at the War Department, and hurried into the Chief of Staff's office. "General, don't you remember you phoned me, I connected you with the President, and you said the Air Corps could carry the mails?"

MacArthur walked over to where McIntyre was standing and glared down at him. His face was white with anger. "Do you mean to say," he demanded, "that I phoned you and asked to talk to the President and then gave him the assurance you describe?"

McIntyre wilted. "No, I suppose I'm wrong," he replied. And then he added: "But Steve Early said you gave that message."

"Where is Early? Bring him down here," MacArthur almost shouted, striding up and down the room in an effort to restrain his temper.

"He is not available tonight," McIntyre finally answered. He realized that the jig was up, and reluctantly added: "I'm afraid what he actually said was that you would be a good sport and see that the mails were carried all right."

3

Some time before this episode MacArthur had found himself in an embarrassing situation regarding Colonel George C. Marshall. Pershing had suggested to MacArthur that his former aide, who had done fine staff work in France, be made a brigadier general. MacArthur had only recently set up a special promotion board to recommend colonels for the grade of general officer, and he assured his old commander that he would immediately present Marshall's name to the board.

Marshall, who had only recently reached the grade of full colonel, had been shifted from his post of assistant commandant of the Infantry School at Fort Benning, Georgia, to the command of the fine 8th Infantry at Fort Moultrie near Charlestown, South Carolina. Most of his past military career had been spent not in command posts but as student or instructor in service schools or on staff duty or as special aide to General Pershing. He knew it was important now to balance his one-sided record by this particular tour of duty with troops.

The 8th Infantry, which had long enjoyed an enviable reputation as a top regiment, consisted at the moment of two separate battalions with only a single battalion and headquarters at Fort Moultrie. The situation was a bit difficult for maintaining *esprit de corps,* and Marshall's activities were further complicated by the added job of superintending the numerous CCC camps that were being opened in his area. This latter task seemed to appeal to Marshall, and he spent a large part of his time on the project. So noticeable was his ardor and success in the camp work that it came to the attention of certain high politicians and Brain Trusters in Washington who were involved in the whole Roosevelt social program. Certain friendly connections which resulted, and which seemed far-fetched at the time, were subsequently to prove of great value to Colonel Marshall.

When he had been with his regiment less than a year, an Inspector General from Washington visited the post. His resultant official report stated that the training program of the regiment was not satisfactory and that the entire outfit had seriously deteriorated under Colonel Marshall's command. The report arrived at the very moment he was being considered for promotion, and it destroyed any immediate chance Marshall might have had of being chosen a brigadier general by the special promotion board.

It so happened that about this same time Major General Roy Keene of the National Guard of Illinois came to Washington to talk over with the Chief of Staff the idea of a new senior instructor for the 33rd National Guard Division. General Keene was a powerful figure in Guard circles, and MacArthur wanted to show him every courtesy. When Keene insisted that he wanted a top man to work with the Illinois division, MacArthur told him that he could have the best officer in the Army.

Calling in Major General Edward Croft, chief of infantry, MacArthur asked him who was the best colonel of infantry available for this type of special service.

"I'd say George Marshall," General Croft answered without hesitation.

"Send him to the Illinois Guard," General MacArthur promptly ordered.

The assignment carried a handsome special pay allowance, and although Colonel Marshall would definitely have preferred to remain in command of regular troops, he had no alternative. Years later in her book of army memoirs entitled *Together,* Mrs. Marshall wrote feelingly of the Colonel's disappointment regarding the orders, but added that later he grew to be genuinely fond of Chicago and his assignment there.

As a matter of fact, it all worked out in favor of Marshall. He became a close friend of the Judge Advocate of the 33rd Division, Scott Lucas, who later became a United States Senator. As a member of the powerful Senate Armed Services Committee, Senator Lucas was able to be of inestimable value in helping to push forward George Marshall's career.

In years to come there was much speculation why MacArthur, despite the set-back due to the unfortunate adverse report by the Inspector General, had not later, and while he was still Chief of Staff, recommended Marshall to be made a general officer. The facts were that at this time the army was small and promotion was so slow that Marshall was almost at the bottom of the list of colonels. But MacArthur, with his shrewd knowledge of army affairs, might have wangled the promotion, if he had been deeply concerned—which, obviously, he was not. [Three years later, when Malin Craig was Army Chief of Staff, Colonel Marshall was promoted to brigadier general of the line. It was army gossip that General Pershing had gone directly to the President and urged this action. On September 1, 1939, Marshall was made Chief of Staff. Robert E. Sherwood, in his book, *Roosevelt and Hopkins,* contributes a very significant note regarding the high appointment, when he describes General Marshall as a man "for whom Hopkins had profound respect and whose appointment as Chief of Staff he had strongly recommended."]

Just how much this MacArthur-Marshall episode had to do with later events may never be correctly appraised. It was only human that a number of officers, including Marshall, should have been envious of the rapid promotion and the fame that came to MacArthur during and after World War I. Many worthy officers in France failed to receive even the temporary promotions they deserved, because the orders to Pershing from Washington forbade additional promotions after the Armistice. MacArthur, himself, had been recommended for two stars, and a large number of temporary colonels, among them George Marshall, were on the verge of being made temporary brigadier generals when the Armistice had intervened. Once back in the United States, all but a handful of specially favored officers were reduced to their normal permanent rank. This ruling forced Colonel Marshall back to his rank of major, where slow promotion under the strict seniority rule kept him for some time before he became a lieutenant colonel. Yet professionally he was one of the better known officers in the Army. The war had been over 13 years before he reached the rank of full colonel.

Temporary Brigadier General MacArthur, however, had not been busted back to his permanent rank of lieutenant colonel in 1919, and in February 1920 during his first year as superintendent at West Point he had been made a permanent brigadier general. Five years later he was made a major general, and at 50 was chosen Chief of Staff. It is easy to understand how less fortunate men might nurse envy of this man of apparent destiny.

So it was that MacArthur never could quite cope with the all-too-human criticism often levelled against him. No matter how generous and painstaking he was regarding rank and assignment, there was often no way he could balance the inequalities and differences in rank. As Chief of Staff he was deeply concerned in doing everything he could to help individual officers, and there are innumerable stories told about his interest and regard for those under him and his eagerness to undo any injustice they may have suffered. One incident illustrates the nature of his personal concern.

Toward the end of his second year as Chief of Staff, a young West Point graduate and his wife, detailed to foreign service, had become involved in a very silly and unfortunate episode which although of an entirely innocent nature had put them in an extremely unfortunate light. Through a curious chain of circumstances, the young lieutenant had been tried on charges of "conduct unbecoming an officer and a gentleman," convicted and sentenced to be discharged from the service.

A West Point classmate of the unhappy officer, then on duty in the United States, was appealed to, and he hurried to Washington and the War Department. It was his first visit, and in despair over the fate of his brother officer he approached Captain T. J. Davis, General MacArthur's aide, and blurted out the story of his unfortunate classmate.

The sympathetic aide told him to calm down, that he would try to get him ten minutes with the Chief of Staff. The young officer was admitted to the General's office, made to feel at ease and asked to explain the nature of his visit.

He was to stay ten minutes; he stayed over an hour. MacArthur was appalled at the harshness of the court's verdict. He asked for the papers in the case and after studying them promptly disapproved the findings, declaring the evidence was insufficient to merit such severity, and he at once reinstated the officer.

4

MacArthur had yet to succeed in his constructive plan for an effective Army. His Third Annual Report carried the final outlines for this Four-Army Plan, bringing the 9 corps areas into four great tactical armies, each with its own field army organization set up in skeleton form, and each commanded by the senior corps commander in that particular army territory.

Each of the four army commanders was to organize the framework for an actual field army staff that could be expanded immediately in case of an emergency.

With this Four-Army Plan went a G.H.Q. Air Force, that comprised an actual striking air force of 1,000 planes or more under the direct responsibility and command of the Chief of Staff. No senior officer in the United States Army had previously so fully appreciated the enormous striking potential of airplanes or shown the courage and imagination to unshackle them from ground commanders. America was now on the road that led toward at least some degree of national security.

Time was running out for MacArthur, for his term as Chief of Staff would end November 21, 1934. But on November 14 the President announced at a press conference that MacArthur would be continued as Chief of Staff for an indefinite period, and later Roosevelt directed Secretary of War Dern to keep MacArthur on until the War Department had completed its legislative program with the coming Congress. It seems that Pershing had personally recommended this move to the President.

MacArthur dramatically put forth his final requests. The Public Works Administration had already allotted $90,000,000 to the Army, with $54,000,000 earmarked for an army construction program. MacArthur now asked for $405,000,000 for new army housing, mechanization and motorization, anti-aircraft equipment and aircraft and modernization of field artillery. He pointed out that the enlisted strength of the regular army must be increased to 165,000 men, the Officers' Reserve Corps strengthened and the National Guard enlarged. In addition, he requested that the number of cadets at West Point be increased from 1,371 to 1,960.

Long before this he had suggested that the boys in the hundreds of CCC camps be given some army training and discipline. But the radical planners around the White House quickly squelched this idea. The fact that the CCC boys were receiving $30 a month, while the pay of the soldiers of the Regular Army was $21 monthly, did not strike them as at all unfair.

As late as February 20, 1935, MacArthur made a new proposal to the House Military Affairs Committee regarding a small amount of army training in the camps:

> I think there would be nothing finer than that the men in the CCC camps should be used as a nucleus for an Enlisted Reserve.
>
> I think no method could be sounder than to take these CCC men who have had six months in camp and give them perhaps two months more, in which they would receive military training. We could enroll them in the Enlisted Reserve for a certain number of years, with, perhaps a small stipend—say one dollar a month.

If he had been guilty of a crime against his country, MacArthur could not have brought down on his head more bitter criticism from the pacifist-minded advisors of the President.

Early in March 1935 MacArthur was forced to take another definite stand against the President. This time it was in direct opposition to the expanding powers of the Chief Executive.

In the $375,000,000 Army Appropriations Bill presented to the Senate Appropriations Committee was a promise that the enlisted strength of the Regular Army would be increased from 118,000 men to a maximum of 165,000, but it was provided that the President should have absolute control over the size of the Army. MacArthur—whose passion had long been the Constitution—immediately addressed the Congressional committee on this vital precedent:

> It has never been done before in the history of our country. We have the most complete confidence the President would immediately order the increase, but this places a burden upon the Executive Branch.
>
> Army strength questions have always been decided by Congress. If Congress should leave such an authority to the President, we should have to go before him and in effect have these hearings all over again.
>
> The President, splendid soldier as he is, and understanding the problems of National defense as he does, cannot be expected to make decisions which have not only involved the professional thought of the Army for years, but have engaged the attention of the Congressional Committees for weeks and months at a time.
>
> If you multiply such instances and continue to load on the

President the technical details, not only of the War Department but of other departments, you are going to break down the Government.

It was a smooth and politic way of presenting his violent objections. It seems certain that he was prepared to go to any limit in opposing the measure that would have advanced immeasurably the growing concentration of power in the hands of the President. Fortunately the committee was won over, and the raid was checked.

There were no reprisals from the White House. MacArthur apparently was to be kept on until the end of his fifth year. On September 7, the day before Secretary of War Dern left for Manila to witness the inauguration of the Philippine Commonwealth, Dern called MacArthur into his office and in a surprise ceremony pinned an Oak Leaf cluster on his Distinguished Service Medal. At the same time Dern made the formal announcement that he would make no recommendation regarding MacArthur's successor until he returned from Manila in mid-December 1935.

During MacArthur's last two tours of duty in the Islands he and Manuel Quezón, then speaker of the House of Representatives and leader of the independence movement, had often discussed the problem of Philippine security. In the summer of 1935, while Quezón was in Washington arranging for the formal establishment of the Commonwealth, he suddenly appeared in the Chief of Staff's office. Bluntly he asked MacArthur if he thought the Islands could defend themselves once they gained their full independence in 1946.

"I don't only *think* they can be defended," MacArthur answered; "I *know* they can."

Quezón immediately asked if he would be willing to come to the Philippines and act as military advisor during the coming six years of his presidency. MacArthur agreed, if Quezón could secure the approval of the Secretary of War and the President.

MacArthur still had almost 9 years of active army service in front of him, but to accept a subordinate assignment in the Army after being Chief of Staff would be difficult. The Quezón proposal seemed to offer an ideal solution to the problem of his own professional career if it could be so arranged with his two superiors. Half the battle already was won, thanks to a law recently passed by Congress authorizing the detailing of Army and Navy officers for special duty with certain foreign powers, which later included service in the new Commonwealth.

Quezón had no difficulty gaining the full approval of both the Secretary of War and the President. The formal press release regarding the appointment, however, was held up until the news of Quezón's actual election as President of the Commonwealth government, which occurred the day before Secretary Dern's departure for Manila. MacArthur would leave Washington September 30. The press release concluded with the positive statement that he would not be relieved as Chief of Staff until December 15.

This would give him a little more than a month after his arrival in Manila to lay out his detailed plans, which included the utilization of U. S. Army forces of the Department of the Philippines in the training and equipping of the native draftees. His objective was the ultimate use of the Islands' forces as an integral part of a great Philippine defensive system to be built during the ten years before 1946, when full independence would come. It was a matter of major importance to MacArthur that for a full month he would possess all the authority of Chief of Staff to project his ideas without obstruction or delay.

A formal but confidential letter was sent to MacArthur by the Adjutant General giving a secret special ruling that he was to be permitted to remain undisturbed on the assignment for a six-year period. It seemed that every possibility of error or slip-up had now been covered.

Two weeks before he was to leave Washington, MacArthur was invited to Hyde Park for a private luncheon with the President. When the two were alone, Roosevelt explained that the Governor General of the Philippines, Frank Murphy, was not interested in becoming first high commissioner to the Commonwealth government. Would Douglas be interested in having the important post?

MacArthur replied that he was deeply honored, but he could not leave the Army. He had pledged Quezón that he would help him build his defense system, and he could hardly go back on this solemn promise.

"Maybe you could do both," the President suggested.

MacArthur answered that if it could be arranged so that he could still remain in the Army and advise Quezón, he'd be proud to be the first high commissioner to the Philippines.

The President told him to get a special ruling from the judge advocate whether he could fill the two appointments. As soon as MacArthur returned to Washington, he put the matter in the judge advocate's hands. A day or two later he received the verdict: It was illegal for an officer to hold two government positions at the same time.

MacArthur immediately wrote a personal note to the President and gave him the negative decision. A little later Frank Murphy, hearing that MacArthur had been approached by the President, changed his mind and agreed to accept the post of high commissioner.

5

During the years MacArthur had served as Chief of Staff his mother had lived with him in the Number 1 Quarters at Fort Myer, across the Potomac in Virginia. Her health had steadily declined to such an extent that she had been able to act as hostess at only one or two of the few official dinners the General had been obliged to give. His widowed sister-in-law, Mary McCulla MacArthur, had not only graciously taken his mother's place but throughout these five years had spent a great deal of time in helping to care for her. The General had removed himself from all personal contact with social Washington, save only for the half-dozen official dinners and receptions that his position required him to attend each year.

From the very beginning of his discussions with Quezón, the General had made one stipulation concerning his appointment to Manila; he would accept the proposal only if his mother were well enough to go with him.

When he tentatively brought up the subject with her, Mrs.

169

MacArthur insisted that the sea voyage and the bright warm days in Manila would do her good. Mary was appealed to, and she agreed to accompany them. Whatever happened, the mother insisted, Douglas must not be deprived of this golden opportunity to do a great and lasting thing for his country and for himself.

The General called in Major Howard Hutter of the Army Medical Corps, who had long been a devoted physician to Mrs. MacArthur. The doctor described fully to him the exact condition of his 83-year-old mother. She was suffering from a chronic heart trouble, and there was absolutely nothing medically that could be done for her. The journey to Manila would make no change in her general condition, and life could be as gentle for her there as anywhere else. He had no professional objections to her going.

The last obstacle had now been removed. The General thanked him and then explained the great work that could be accomplished by the mission. Would Major Hutter come along as general medical advisor in such matters as passing on the sanitary side of the training camps and the health of the recruits in the new Philippine Army? The doctor, devoted as he was to the General's mother, and thrilled by the prospects of the imaginative and important work ahead, promptly accepted.

So it was that final plans were concluded for the great undertaking. With MacArthur would go a small official staff, consisting of Majors Dwight D. Eisenhower and James Ord, both of the West Point Class of 1915, Dr. Howard Hutter, the personal aide Captain T. J. Davis and one or two enlisted clerks.

Major Eisenhower would be chief of staff of the military mission, with Major Ord as his deputy. Eisenhower had just turned 45 and though he had not seen active service in France in the World War, he had won for himself a place as one of the outstanding younger army officers. Major General Fox Conner, G-3 of the A.E.F., who furnished much of the driving power of Pershing's war machine, had taken a great interest in Eisenhower when the latter had served under him in the Canal Zone. Somewhere along the line Ike had acquired a canny and unique ability; he was graduated at the top of his class in the gruelling two-year course at the Command and

General Staff School in Leavenworth; he had served under Pershing in post-war France and prepared a commendable brochure on the American Battle Monuments; his talent for writing speeches and reports had brought him the post of special aide to the assistant secretary of war; and he had added to his general qualifications by attending the Industrial War College.

MacArthur had brought him into the Chief of Staff's office late in 1932, and here he had quickly made himself all but indispensable. He had the rare faculty of being able to put down on paper the exact shade of meaning that his superior desired. "Ike got so he could write more like MacArthur talked than the General did himself," was the way one officer who served on the General Staff at the time explained it. His mind was sharp and keen, and he had been perfectly trained in staff work. He was to serve seven years in the closest contact with General MacArthur.

A few days before the departure of the mission from Washington MacArthur phoned the White House for an appointment to pay his final respects to Roosevelt.

The President received him with even more than his ordinary kindness. He was generous in his appreciation of the magnificent work the soldier had done for his country and for him personally. Finally the General arose to say good-bye.

The President looked up at him, and his voice sounded strong and warm with emotion.

"Douglas," he said slowly, "if war should suddenly come, don't wait for orders to return home. Grab the first transportation you can find. I want you to command my armies."

It seemed a gracious thing for Roosevelt to say. It was the final nod of professional approval, and no words could have meant more to the officer who was about to relinquish his high command.

Obviously MacArthur had a great deal for which to be proud and thankful. Ahead of him lay a difficult task that might some day prove to be of supreme importance to his own country as well as to the Islands he loved so deeply. It was fortunate that he had the official sanction and orders to continue as Chief of Staff until several weeks after he arrived in

Manila. This would give him time to lay out a plan whereby eventually the U. S. Regular Army forces in the Islands could be used in a variety of ways to help build and train the new Philippine army reserve. It was of considerable importance, too, that Secretary of War Dern was to be with him in Manila at the start.

Captain Davis secured for the party a private Pullman car that went straight through from Washington to San Francisco. When the Union Pacific train pulled into Cheyenne, the group was joined by Major Eisenhower, whose wife and small son were temporarily remaining in Denver. MacArthur stepped down from the car for a short walk on the station platform. He had made only one or two turns alongside the train when a young man approached in the dim light and asked him if he was General MacArthur.

"I'm a reporter from the paper here, and we just got news you were on this train," he explained, when he had been assured that he had found the right man. "What do you think of the appointment of General Craig as the new Chief of Staff?"

MacArthur smiled down at the young man and never batted an eye. Obviously the solemn pledge approved by the President had been broken.

"There couldn't have been a better appointment," he answered. "General Craig is a splendid officer and a fine gentleman."

At this moment the station agent hurried up with a yellow envelope in his hand. He recognized the General and handed him the telegram.

The bell was ringing on ahead and the porter was motioning him to board his car. He walked slowly back to his apartment and opened the envelope, that had been sent care of the ticket agent at Cheyenne. The message read:

The following telegram just received and since it conveys a message to you I am transmitting the same herewith quote I have detailed today Major General Malin Craig effective this date, to succeed General Douglas MacArthur, relieved this date as Chief of Staff of the United States Army, with rank of General. I have also signed the recess commission appointing General

Craig to the office of Chief of Staff. Please instruct the Adjutant General to issue the orders necessary to conform with the action I have taken. I have decided to make this appointment before I sail today on the Houston. Please extend to General MacArthur an expression of my gratitude and appreciation of his excellent service so exceptional that I called upon him to continue to per-form the duties of that office almost a year after the regular four-year detail had been completed. I am forwarding to you the order with the commission signed Franklin D. Roosevelt unquote. As acting Secretary of War I want again to express my deep regard of your unexcelled service to the nation, the National Defense and the Army in the high position you are relinquishing.

Harry H. Woodring
Acting Secretary of War

So the President had gone back on the agreement that Mac-Arthur was not to be relieved until December 15. And now it would be infinitely more difficult to do the job of creating an efficient Philippine Army that would act as a priceless reserve in trained manpower for America when it was needed. Mac-Arthur had counted heavily on his first month in Manila when he would still have had all the power and prestige of the Chief of Staff of the United States Army to back him up. Now he would have to do the best he could without it.

It was some time later that he learned the details of his sudden and mysterious relief by the President. Roosevelt had left Washington by special train for California a day before the MacArthur party. Accompanying him was Hugh Johnson, WPA administrator, who at the moment was in high favor with President Roosevelt. As a shavetail officer and classmate of MacArthur's, Lieutenant Johnson was assigned to a cavalry troop commanded by Malin Craig, West Point 1898. Later Craig had been looked upon with favor by Pershing's Chaumont clique. He had been chief of staff of a corps in France, and had been made a brigadier general of the Regular Army in 1921—two years after MacArthur, who was younger, got his permanent promotion to that grade.

Hugh Johnson had always kept in close contact with his old company commander, and now here on a special train California-bound, with world conditions in a precarious condition, the WPA administrator went to great lengths to convince the President that it was unsafe for both the Chief of Staff and the Secretary of War to be out of the country at the same time. Why not relieve MacArthur at once? He knew the very man for Chief of Staff—Major General Malin Craig.

And so it was that the energetic and pushing Hugh Johnson—who had been a sort of self-delegated rival of MacArthur's at West Point—talked President Roosevelt into summarily relieving MacArthur, regardless of the official orders that he was not to be replaced until mid-December. This conscienceless double-cross was in the end to deal a damaging blow to the building of America's strength in the Far East.

6

It might be a slight exaggeration to refer to MacArthur's assignment to the Philippines as a deliberately planned exile. But in many ways it proved to be exactly that.

Once in Manila he would no longer be a constant thorn in the side of the radical Brain Trusters who were moving Roosevelt more and more to the left and toward a semi-socialist state. These men were aware of the unusually strange relationship that existed between the President and General MacArthur. Roosevelt in all the years to come never quite lost his initial admiration for the extraordinary intelligence and pure patriotic motives of MacArthur, despite the President's frequent bitter words of criticism. The General might often oppose him and refuse to bend to his whims and wishes, but there could never be any serious doubt in Roosevelt's mind concerning his honor and his unique abilities. (Long after the President's death, and when he had finally returned home, MacArthur was to say, "Roosevelt was not my nemesis.")

To the White House hangers-on who were primarily interested in their hold on the President, the soldier had often stood as a roadblock to their designs. Once he was planted in the Philippines, he could be cut off and isolated from the President, and his strong influence could end. He could be given the silent treatment—as heartbreaking and deadly as the silence that had a few times been given to unethical army officers at West Point by the Corps of Cadets.

But his exile was by no means as simple or innocuous as all this. Already there were ominous portents and influences at work in Washington which had been spawned with President Roosevelt's 1933 recognition of the Soviet Union. At once secret groups friendly or actually subservient to the Soviets began to exert pressure on the government in behalf of the Kremlin. Apparently it was important for them to have MacArthur and his definitely patriotic authority over the Army far removed from Washington.

The extent and true purpose of the slowly expanding Red-sponsored intrigues in Washington were still concealed, but time was to bring to light certain parts of the subversive plots within America and elsewhere. The Soviets' interference with other countries had long been serious.

Back in the early '20's the Soviet Union had failed in her attempt to win over Chiang Kai-shek and his Kuomintang party, and the Russian political-military mission was driven out of China. But it left behind a vigorous and determined Communist-Chinese group, which Chiang was never quite able fully to eliminate.

Eventually, when World War II had been going on for some months in Europe, Russia effected a 5-year non-aggression pact with Japan. This guaranteed that Russia would not have to fight a two-front war if, and when, Germany attacked her. So far as the Soviets were concerned, it gave Japan a free hand in China, enabling the Japs to turn south and drive down the China Sea and through the Philippines to the fabulous wealth of Southeast Asia and the Dutch East Indies.

As a part of this Communist plan was the need of keeping the Philippines weak, so that Japan would be encouraged to turn her back on Siberia and someday plunge into a great adventure to the southward.

America, traditional friend of China and Chiang Kai-shek, opposed Japan's expanding invasion of the Asiatic mainland and her eventual turn southward, but failed to build up the military power in the Philippines that could have been a natural deterrent.

175

In very simple terms, it had for years been to Russia's advantage to keep Japan interested in her southern march so that Russia need have little fear for her own Far Eastern frontier in case Germany suddenly struck. To keep the Philippines weak—while secretly turning Japan to southern conquests— was part of her plot. MacArthur had no way of knowing all the sources of opposition to him and his patriotic efforts in the Philippines. What passed for years as little more than a deliberate personal unconcern and a refusal on the part of certain high officials in the General Staff and in the government to aid MacArthur may have had behind it secret and unrecognized forces of foreign and home intrigue.

7

There seems no doubt that MacArthur fully realized how final and conclusive his present assignment to the Far Pacific would be. Unless war came, his plan was to remain there six years, although actually the entire Philippine military program would involve ten years. He seemed now to be tied for good and all into the destinies of these Islands and of the Far East.

Japan was obviously the immediate potential enemy in the highly explosive period of the middle 1930s. Her march into the heart of China seemed relentless and irresistible. Her militarists apparently had a death grip on the government and to all practical purposes were in control though the Emperor often offered a sturdy resistance to them.

Japan's appeal to great portions of the brown races of the vast southeastern areas of Asia was genuine and incontestable. Her gradually maturing Greater Asia Co-Prosperity Sphere was pleasant bait to many native peoples in contrast to the exploitation of the old European conquerors. She promised a far less cruel exploitation, along with a complete lack of racial distinctions.

Communist Russia had just gone through her bitterest purge, liquidating thousands of old-line Bolsheviks who had once been leading civil and military officials. Stalin was absorbed in his struggle for his own complete domination within the Red borders. But intelligence reports that MacArthur had carefully studied revealed that Stalin was slowly building up his military might in Eastern Siberia, and at the same time he was developing great steel plants and factories far east of the Volga in the remote Urals and within the ancient boundaries of Siberia. Clearly he had not relinquished the old Russian dreams for warm-water ports on the Pacific.

Unaware of the depth of Red intrigues in Washington, MacArthur considered the loyal Philippines as America's key to the whole Western Pacific and to the control of the strategic sea lanes that paralleled the coasts of East Asia. From this friendly base America might some day have to fight the conqueror— possibly a succession of conquerors—of Asia and the Western Pacific.

It seemed at the moment of MacArthur's arrival in 1935 that Japan might be the first to strike. So he considered supremely important his plan for building a mighty pool of trained manpower in the Philippines, ready for America to use in some future hour of peril.

Douglas MacArthur, now 55 and at the height of his strength and powers, was risking his fate in this absorbing drama of the Western Pacific. It was a magnificent challenge and he met it head on. The challenge assumed a score of different faces, filling his mind and recalling to his memory the priceless truths he had learned in the years when as a young officer he had travelled with his wise father over the vast areas of the Far East.

During his many long nights of reading and study MacArthur had come across a strange prophecy made in 1855 by Commodore Matthew C. Perry, four years after his little fleet opened the sealed doors of Japan. It was in a remarkable paper that had been read before a meeting of the American Geographical and Statistical Society at Harvard and later published by D. Appleton & Co. Two long paragraphs deserve careful study.

It requires no sage to predict events so strongly foreshadowed to us all; still "Westward will the course of empire take its way." But the last act of the drama is yet to be unfolded; and not withstanding the reasoning of political empirics, Westward, Northward and Southward, to me it seems that the people of America will, in some form or other, extend their dominion and their power, until they shall have brought within their mighty embrace the multitudes of the Islands of the great Pacific, and placed the Saxon race upon the eastern shores of Asia. And I think, too, that eastward and southward will her great rival in future aggrandisement (Russia) stretch forth her power to the coasts of China and Siam; and thus the Saxon and the Cossack will meet once more, in strife or in friendship, on another field.

Will it be in friendship? I fear not! The antagonistic exponents of freedom and absolutism must thus meet at last, and then will be fought this mighty battle on which the world will look with breathless interest; for on its issue will depend the freedom or the slavery of the world—despotism or rational liberty must be the fate of civilized men. I think I see in the distance the giants that are growing up for this fierce and final encounter; in the progress of events that battle must sooner or later inevitably be fought.

And in MacArthur's mind were the words uttered by the young Senator Beveridge of Indiana in 1900: "The power that rules the Pacific . . . is the power that rules the world."

8

In a very definite way the five years he had served as Army Chief of Staff under two presidents had helped prepare him for the great and uncertain task he faced. He had become a prominent national figure, and his reputation for brilliance had made his name known in every capital in the world.

To most of his friends and intimates he still appeared decidedly complex. Despite all his personal magnetism, charm and definite superiority of intellect, he was beginning to be looked upon as more or less of an enigma, touched possibly by mysticism. His swift decisions drawn from the vast reservoir of his knowledge seemed only to add to his reputation for possessing an exceptional gift of intuition and insight.

Few seemed to have understood the singleness of his purpose, the over-all simplicity and directness of his mind and background. His moral sense clearly distinguished right from wrong, justice from unfairness. Above all, his impassioned love of country had long ago absorbed the strong personal ambitions of his youth.

These fundamentally important characteristics often were ignored by those whose myopic vision could see only his normal human weaknesses. Friends, constantly pouring out to him their full measure of devotion, could not at times understand why he apparently gave them so little in return. They confused his self-discipline and need for concentration with selfishness and unconcern. It was difficult for them to understand how fully he had consecrated his mind and heart to his country's service.

During most of his adult life he had sacrificed what would normally have been happy hours of companionship for the solitude and study that developed his mind in knowledge and judgment. But even though he seemingly pushed aside his natural gifts for human affection and friendship, nothing could dim his personal charm and magnetism.

11

THE LONG YEARS OF EXILE

Even before the ship touched at Honolulu the General's mother began to fail in a way that caused alarm. She was in her 84th year, but, as Doctor Hutter had assured the General, the long journey had nothing to do with her present condition.

The faithful Mary MacArthur was almost constantly with her in her cabin. Only once did the mother attempt to sit on deck. It proved far easier for her to remain propped up in bed.

For long periods during each day and evening her son would sit by her side and talk to her of his plans, as he had done all his life. He drew some solace from the fact that no matter what happened to her, he would be close by her. It was evident that she was probably facing her last illness.

An official party headed by Vice-President Garner, bound for the inaugural ceremonies in Manila, was on board, and there was considerable gaiety. MacArthur took no share in the festivities during the voyage, but the captain of the *President Hoover* did introduce him to a vivacious young lady from Murfreesboro, Tennessee, who had a quick smile and a ready wit. It was pleasant to walk the deck with her and to lean over the rail by her side and watch the sea.

Shortly before the ship pulled out of Honolulu two large boxes of flowers were put on board. One found its way to the cabin of Mrs. Arthur MacArthur, Sr.; the other was opened by Miss Jean Faircloth.

The General would have liked very much to have his mother meet the gay, attractive young lady, but it was not to be. Neither on board the ship, nor during the few short weeks she lived at the Manila Hotel before her death on December 14, 1935, did the mother set eyes on the slender, gracious woman who was to mean so much to her son in the years ahead.

She suffered from a cerebral thrombosis, a blood clot in the arteries of the brain. During her last days she rallied now and again, but finally sank into a coma. On the morning of her death she spoke to her son before she drifted off into her last sleep.

Thus ended the beautiful and lasting comradeship of mother and son throughout the years. Each had the highest respect for the intelligence and character of the other. And the households they had shared were filled with gracious, old-fashioned living.

In February 1937 the General brought her remains to Washington, where she was buried in the National Cemetery by the side of her distinguished husband. Acting Secretary of War Harry Woodring and a little group of intimate friends attended the simple rites.

2

The first bill that President Quezón presented to the Assembly of his new Commonwealth government was the National Defense Act that had been formulated by General MacArthur.

The hard core of the land defense rested on a small, profes-sional Philippine regular army of some 350 officers and 5,000 enlisted men, with a permanent army headquarters and staff. The real defense would ultimately lie in the troops of the reserve divisions, to be drafted and trained at the rate of some 40,000 recruits each year. Half of this number would enter the training camps for 5½ months' training each 6-month pe-riod.

In all, 128 camps were constructed at an individual cost of approximately $8,250, U. S. currency, each housing around 150 trainees. Each camp's permanent instructional force—the training cadre—consisted of three or four officers and eight to twelve enlisted men. Trainees were assigned to the camps nearest their homes, and eventually they were to become a part of the reserve division posted in their immediate locality.

When the Philippines should receive their full inde-pendence in 1946, the Philippine government would have a trained and organized militia of about 400,000 men, formed into some 40 divisions, strategically placed on all the important islands and ready for prompt mobilization to defend the landing beaches and oppose ground attacks in the particular area assigned to each unit. For training equipment and weapons, MacArthur was forced to be content with World War I Amer-ican stocks on loan. At the end of the ten-year training period—1946—he trusted that modern weapons would be supplied in part or wholly by the United States, depending, of course, on the world situation.

It was broadly formed after the plan of the citizens' army, based on the principles of universal selective service, which had proved so successful in Switzerland. In addition to the ground forces, there would be a fleet of 50 small, high-speed torpedo-throwing craft to oppose hostile landings and an air force of 250 planes.

MacArthur quickly established a splendid military academy, built on the model of West Point and under the superintend-ency of Colonel Pastor Martelino, a Filipino officer who had graduated from West Point in the class of 1920. An imagina-tive and energetic young American officer, Captain Bonner Fellers, who joined MacArthur's staff in February 1936, was assigned the job of creating almost overnight a Reserve Officers' Training School at Baguio.

Majors Eisenhower and Ord put in long hours organizing the first series of small cantonments, borrowing the initial training cadres from the Philippine constabulary, which eventually was to be incorporated into the regular Philippine Army. Besides the purely military side of the camps, there was a broad and humane effort to build up the health and economic well-being of the trainees, 80% of whom were from backward rural homes and surroundings.

Things progressed rapidly, but there was no question about the handicap imposed on MacArthur by his relief as Chief of Staff. One of the ideas that he had hoped to incorporate into his over-all plan was for the American Army in the Islands to school a number of enlisted Filipinos for use in the training program. It would have improved the quality of training given the Filipino selectees; and it would have been of enormous training value to the American Army itself. His sudden relief as Chief of Staff shattered these high hopes.

The Philippine Commonwealth, limited in funds as it was, was paying the full bill totalling $8,000,000 gold annually. U. S. Regular Army officers, both in Manila and Washington, were rather skeptical of the whole proposition. General Craig and his staff were too busy implementing MacArthur's Four-Army plan, as well as fighting to get additional troops and equipment, to be genuinely concerned about the fate of the great experiment on the other side of the world. The Philippine Department commander, taking his cue from Washington, sat idly by.

But despite this lack of interest in Washington and Manila, the alert and impetuous Manuel Quezón was delighted with the early progress made. His enthusiasm took the form of insisting that MacArthur accept the rank of field marshal of the then almost non-existent Philippine Army. At an elaborate ceremony at Malacañan Palace on August 24, 1936, President Quezón presented him with the commission, and Mrs. Quezón handed him the gold baton of a field marshal.

To the skeptical habitués of Manila clubs this was an event inviting sly comment. Probably at the moment the high rank

182

was hardly worth the gold that went into the baton. MacArthur, however, knew what the friendly gesture meant to millions of humble and patient Filipinos who had so much faith in him.

Almost from the beginning of his new duties he had to face hidden but effective civilian and governmental opposition, both in Manila and in Washington. Shortly after the new Philippine government came into being, High Commissioner Murphy intimated to Roosevelt that the Islands were not big enough for both MacArthur and himself. He insisted that MacArthur, as President Quezón's Military Advisor, should be directly under his own office.

The subsequent actions and reactions of Murphy form a somewhat curious pattern. A bachelor, he seemingly placed considerable store in the friendship of both President and Mrs. Quezón. As a matter of fact, he may have been envious of the long intimacy of MacArthur with the Quezón family. Once when he was rather petulantly chiding Mrs. Quezón regarding the General's close family relationship, she answered: "But, Frank, you don't seem to understand: Douglas is our brother."

After MacArthur had been in Manila a little more than a year, Murphy, who had returned to the States and been succeeded by the former Governor of Indiana, Paul V. McNutt, wired Quezón that President Roosevelt was anxious to see the Commonwealth President sometime during February 1937. As a result of this apparently friendly invitation, the Quezóns with MacArthur and a small group embarked for the States on January 23, 1937.

When they arrived in New York they found Murphy on vacation in Florida, and no word of welcome from the White House. It was a most embarrassing situation for the proud and sensitive President of the Commonwealth. MacArthur went straight to Washington to find out what was wrong.

He called Ross McIntyre, the President's secretary, and asked for an appointment with Roosevelt. He made it clear that he wanted to talk over the visit of the Commonwealth's President, and to explain that the invitation had come from Frank Murphy, and how important it was—especially to the Far East—that Quezón receive every courtesy and consideration. McIntyre replied that President Roosevelt had no idea what Quezón was doing in the United States, that he had sent no invitation for him to come to Washington either through Murphy or anyone else, and that he had no intention of seeing the Philippine Chief Executive.

MacArthur continued to urge the importance of Quezón being properly received, but McIntyre refused to be moved. The General then asked for an appointment to pay his own respects to the President. This was reluctantly granted, with the stipulation that it was not to be for more than five or ten minutes.

Less than two years before MacArthur had been accorded every courtesy in the White House; now he was grudgingly allowed a short courtesy call, only after he had insisted upon it.

The following day MacArthur kept the appointment, but instead of a few minutes he stayed for almost two hours. Once again there were hot words and a frankness that few ever dared to use with the President of the United States. MacArthur insisted that at the very least Roosevelt must invite Quezón to lunch. The whole Far Eastern world was watching the unprecedented experiment of this voluntary creation of the Philippine Commonwealth; the consequences of a snub to the President of the Philippines could have dangerous repercussions throughout the Asiatic world. MacArthur pointed out that the Japanese Army was again on the loose and if the United States should become involved in a Pacific war, it was absolutely necessary to have the enthusiastic loyalty of Quezón and the Islands.

Roosevelt finally agreed to invite Quezón alone to a private lunch, but that very same evening of the MacArthur interview Secretary McIntyre phoned that the President had changed his mind and the luncheon was off. MacArthur requested that he be switched to the President's phone, and so determined was his demand that McIntyre said he would himself talk to the President again and would call back the General. This time the secretary announced that Roosevelt had reconsidered the matter and would see Quezón at lunch.

In order to soften the appearance of the White House snub,

Acting Secretary of War Woodring gave Quezón and his group a large official tea party at the Mayflower. Both MacArthur and the new High Commissioner McNutt were present.

It was clear that certain men close to the President were in opposition to the Quezón-MacArthur team. And some commercial interests probably had both sincere and selfish motives in their desire to see the Philippines give up the idea of full independence and remain permanently as a commonwealth with free trade with the United States and with the great naval base in Manila Bay remaining securely in American hands. Powerful and conservative Spanish elements within the Catholic Church were definitely opposed to complete independence. But of even greater importance were secret influences managed by Soviet Russia that were concerned with prejudicing the Far East against the United States.

MacArthur, busy as he was in advising Quezón on many items, had certain affairs of his own to look after. On Friday morning, April 30, he appeared at the marriage chapel of the Municipal Building in New York with Major Howard J. Hutter and Captain T. J. Davis, his aides—and Miss Jean Marie Faircloth. At 10 o'clock Deputy City Clerk Philip A. Hines performed the civil marriage ceremony, and the party repaired to the Astor Hotel for a wedding breakfast.

It had been an unusual courtship. Until shortly before the ship carrying the MacArthur party and Miss Faircloth docked at Hong Kong, on the trip out to Manila in October 1935, Miss Faircloth had planned to leave the ship for a visit with British friends in the Crown Colony. But there was gentle pressure from all sides for her to continue to Manila and witness the colorful inaugural ceremonies.

She found it easy and pleasant to stay on at the Manila Hotel. She was a very youthful 35, and there were many attractive young bachelor officers and American civilians to keep her days bright and full. As time went on she dined rather often with the General and one or two of his aides in the public dining room of the hotel. Often the two would attend a movie together.

Shortly after the Quezón-MacArthur party had left for the States in January 1937, Miss Jean quietly departed from

Manila by plane. It was a rough voyage to Honolulu both for her on her plane, and for the official party on their ship. Quite by coincidence they all shifted at Hawaii to a steamer bound for San Diego. The marriage was to be kept a secret until the actual ceremony was over.

Back in Manila the MacArthurs lived in quiet contentment in a specially built penthouse atop the Manila Hotel. As he had done for the past 20 years, the General shunned all but a very few official gatherings, and spent most of his evenings in his library. His one relaxation continued to be the movies, and particularly when a Western was shown.

Toward the middle of August a letter was handed to him marked "Personal and Confidential." It read as follows:

WAR DEPARTMENT
OFFICE OF THE CHIEF OF STAFF
WASHINGTON, D. C.

August 6, 1937

PERSONAL AND CONFIDENTIAL

General Douglas MacArthur
Military Advisor to the
President of the Philippine Commonwealth
Manila, Philippine Islands.
My dear Douglas:

I am letting you know in this personal and confidential way that it has been decided that your services are needed in the United States and that upon completion by you of two years of absence on foreign service you are to be brought home for duty in the United States, and the directive in a confidential letter of September 18, 1935, from the Adjutant General to you extending the limits of your tour, will be revoked.

There will be made available to you if practicable any command for which you may express a preference, even though this will probably involve the arbitrary change of station and duties of the incumbent whose command will be desired by you. . . .

The return of your Assistants is not contemplated right now, in order that the work you are doing may continue as planned and until the Commonwealth President makes other arrangements for a Military Advisor who, after installation, will make such changes as he may desire.

I am suggesting that you communicate with me in code as,

aside from the Secretary of War, no one in the War Department knows the foregoing . . .

Please believe me, with kind regards and best wishes

Sincerely your friend,
(sgd.) *Malin Craig*

MacArthur studied the astounding document. At first he felt that some sudden fear of war had gripped the White House and that he was being called home to take over the building of a field army. But the more he considered the strange letter, the more he was convinced that such a possibility was not the reason for his recall. It might even be that he was being forced from his close association with Quezón in order to embarrass the whole Philippine independence movement and to deny the Philippine President the constant use of his help and advice.

Finally he ended by sending in code a cautiously worded reply to Craig:

I am naturally sorry to go. Particularly do I regret leaving unfinished a work which I regard as of transcendent importance and which represents to me an opportunity for service in the Philippines, to my own government, and to the Filipino people, for whom I have an abiding affection and esteem. I look forward with anticipation to whatever duty the War Department may have decided I should now undertake in the service of my country.

MacArthur

Quezón was distraught at the prospect of losing the advice and counsel of his trusted friend. He had constantly leaned on the General during many dark hours in these early days of the young commonwealth. To assure the swift and sure delivery of his protest, President Quezón now sent through the new High Commissioner Paul V. McNutt a long cable to President Roosevelt. It began:

I am deeply disturbed by the persistent rumors which have come to me both in the States and since my return to Manila, that the War Department contemplates the early relief of General MacArthur as military advisor to this government. While reluctant to impose upon your time with a subject that may have no foundation in fact, I am so upset by the consequences of

187

such a contingency that I have decided to present my own earnest convictions to you personally. . . .

From the inception of the defense undertaking, it was manifest that the individual selected to devise such a program in all its technical details . . . should be permitted to carry the program to its practical fruition. In my original conferences with the late Secretary of War Dern, looking towards the detail of General MacArthur on this task, this point was particularly stressed. I was then definitely assured that only in the event of war would General MacArthur be relieved from his position before the expiration of the six year period of my administration. . . .

But the American President did not bother even to acknowledge this cable—if he ever saw it. Quezón, now frantic over the prospect of losing his mainstay, appealed to MacArthur to ask for retirement from the U. S. Army in order that he might continue on as his Military Advisor.

Conscious of the growing opposition that had developed against him, MacArthur felt that his duty left him no alternative but to write Craig asking for retirement on December 31, 1937. There was some question whether this request would be granted. In the end, he was to feel grateful to Craig for taking his request directly to the White House and securing the personal approval of the President.

A curious sidelight on the situation is contained in a long letter to Mrs. Roosevelt at the White House from a trusted old friend, Fred Howe, who at this time was a newly arrived special advisor to the Philippine President on the problem of rural rehabilitation. It was the first report that Howe made indirectly to the White House. Certain passages seem to throw a degree of light on the character of the recent opposition there to MacArthur. The letter dated September 7, 1937, read in part:

. . . When I came out here I had been loaded with statements regarding President Quezón, about the American Army, about a 2,000,000 Philippine Army that was being created by General MacArthur, until I hesitated about coming. Much of this came from *The Nation* and other friends of a radical sort with whom I have long been associated.

And now to my mental amazement I find the same propaganda

being made by the imperialists that is being made by portions of the press and my friends back home. I am wondering if our friends are not being used, as they have been used before, to pull the chestnuts out of the fire, for those who want the United States to hold on to the Islands, to scuttle President Quezón and discredit General MacArthur, who has won my confidence as have few men I have met in the Islands. Instead of an army of 2,000,000 I find successive militia groups of 20,000 men being given six months training, largely with the ultimate objective of an army of 400,000 militia in ten years. Also that the training that they get is in hygiene, in agriculture, in handicraft, and in making them ready to take up homesteads and establish themselves as self-respecting citizens. . . .

But it is the success of President Quezón as an administrator, and of General MacArthur in building a citizen army, designed as a defensive army only, that stands in the way of an imperialistic policy. If President Quezón can be discredited and the trainee system, similar to the Swiss army, be halted, almost the only alternative is American military and naval protection of the Islands. And judging by what I hear from home and the attitude of the imperialistic interests in Manila, that would seem to be the present insidious line of attack; a line of attack in which the pacific minded persons are working hand in glove with the very forces they most fear. . . .

Almost certainly the Howe letter was read by President Roosevelt, but it made no difference. On October 11, 1937, Secretary of War Woodring released to the press a cable the President had just sent to MacArthur. Parts of it might almost have been copied from the telegram from Roosevelt that had been delivered to the General two years before, when he had suddenly relieved him as Chief of Staff. This latest message read:

Dear Douglas: With great reluctance and deep regret I have approved your application for retirement, effective December 31. Personally, as well as officially, I wish to thank you for your outstanding services to your country. Your record in war and in peace is a brilliant chapter of American history. Please accept my best wishes for a well-earned rest and for abundant happiness. I count on seeing you as soon as you get back.

Franklin D. Roosevelt.

One other phase of his virtually forced retirement from the Army at this time in 1937 is worthy of note: MacArthur was officially notified by the War Department that he would be raised to the rank of full general when he retired—which was the identical promise that had been made when his relief as Chief of Staff had been announced in 1935. But somewhere up the line, once again, the word given was ignored, for he was officially retired as a major general.

3

On November 21, 1937, the A.P. correspondent in Manila dispatched a cable stating that there was again talk in the Islands of the possibility of Filipino leaders asking that the full independence provision be changed to a permanent dominion form of government within the framework of the United States. Even Quezón was indicated as having seriously entertained the startling proposition.

The cable further went on to say that at the last moment before adjourning, the session of the National Assembly voted a resolution of thanks to MacArthur for his aid in organizing the Philippine Army, "but the Assembly deleted a section which would have authorized and empowered Quezón to retain MacArthur as his Military Advisor and to keep his name on the army roll for life."

MacArthur kept his own counsel. Meanwhile other cables were being sent from Manila. The day after Christmas *The New York Times* carried a dispatch that certain Commonwealth officials were critical of the burden of MacArthur's special salary.

It had been a well-kept secret that in addition to the then $6,000 retired pay of a major general, he was receiving from the Philippine government an annual salary of $15,000 gold as Military Advisor to the President, and the same amount for civil representation.

Officers on MacArthur's staff, who were still on active status in the United States Army but on assignment to the office of Military Advisor, also received a special *per diem* allowance of $10 gold from the Philippine government. Toward the end of Lt. Colonel Eisenhower's first extra year of duty, he took up with President Quezón the matter of an additional emolument for himself and he was granted an increase that amounted to $500 a month rather than the original $10 a day. Few questioned that for chief of staff to the military mission it was a just and fully earned increase in pay.

On Christmas day, President Quezón was scheduled to make a radio speech to America in the form of a fireside talk. But he was half sick and harassed, having been under terrific pressure from various church and business interests to back down from his commitments for complete independence for the commonwealth government in 1946, and to ask, instead, for a long-range dominion status, under the protection of the United States with free trade.

When MacArthur heard of the proposed speech he immediately protested and persuaded Quezón to cancel the broadcast.

But if Quezón wavered momentarily in his independence plans, he did not falter in his insistence that MacArthur stay on with him, regardless of everything else. On December 31 it was announced from Malacañan Palace that MacArthur was remaining as Military Advisor to the President.

MacArthur's only comment was: "This is a call of duty I cannot fail."

But in his own mind, there must have been considerable bitterness over being forced to retire from the American Army he had served so long. He was never to discover all the hidden reasons and secret ramifications that were responsible for the summary order for him to return home. To confuse the issue further there were groups around President Roosevelt and within the War Department that were well pleased to have him isolated and forgotten 10,000 miles from Washington.

4

Back in October of 1937 MacArthur disclosed confidentially to the senior members of the staff his pending recall to the United States. Neither Eisenhower nor Ord, both of whom had recently been promoted to the permanent rank of lieutenant colonel, could be criticized for wondering if the fat plum of Military Advisor might not fall in his lap. Each coveted the assignment. They had been fellow cadets at West Point and they were close friends.

From the start of the mission Lt. Colonel Ord, an accomplished Spanish scholar, handled personally the Philippine Army budget for both the Military Advisor's office and President Quezón. Ord and Eisenhower felt that the small permanent Philippine Regular Army, as distinct from the Reserve Army, should be substantially increased in size. With little help coming from the U. S. forces in the Islands, it was necessary to assign many of the Philippine regulars to the training camps and to the headquarters staff. The two senior planning officers of the mission felt keenly that there should be larger and more impressive regular units. But adding to the Philippine Regular Army strength would entail an enlarged budget, which was the one thing General MacArthur had promised Quezón he would never request.

Apparently Lt. Colonel Ord, knowing that MacArthur would soon be relieved as Military Advisor, and secure in the belief in the justice of his case, did construct a new budget and independently took it to Quezón, without clearing it through MacArthur, chief of the mission. President Quezón was aghast.

"Why, General MacArthur assured me that there would never have to be an enlarged budget," Quezón in effect explained. "I pledged the Assembly that I would never ask for an increase. I'd rather have an arm cut off than ask for it now."

Lt. Colonel Ord again carefully explained the need of the increases.

"Well, I'll do it if I have to," Quezón finally agreed, "but I have the most serious misgivings."

Quezón was so upset at the proposal that he held up certain routine matters that regularly passed between himself and MacArthur's office. Finally MacArthur, aware that there was something wrong along the line, called in his two senior assistants to find out what the trouble was. It was then that he discovered Ord's plan to get the budget increased.

When he demanded an immediate explanation from Ord, Eisenhower came to his classmate's defense. MacArthur justly resented the fact that he had not been consulted, even though he was shortly to be relieved and returned home. The interview was fiery, and deep scars were left. The close and intimate relation that had heretofore existed between the General and Eisenhower was forever destroyed.

Ord was killed shortly after this when a training plane in which he was a passenger crashed near Baguio. MacArthur in announcing the tragic death stressed his professional and personal regard for the talented officer.

In the fall of 1937, when Eisenhower's regular two-year assignment was drawing to a close, MacArthur had asked that Eisenhower's tour of duty on the military mission be extended for a third year. When that period was ending, he requested that he be kept on for a fourth year. It is an army tradition that on all Eisenhower's efficiency reports MacArthur had given him the highest possible rating, "Superior."

Sometime after the tragic death of Ord a major of infantry, Richard Sutherland, whose father was a Senator from West Virginia, and who had in 1916 been commissioned in the Regular Army directly from Yale, was assigned to the mission as deputy chief of staff. In the late summer of 1938 when Eisenhower left Manila to be gone four months, Sutherland filled in as chief of staff.

After Eisenhower's return he and Sutherland, with their widely different military and family backgrounds, developed certain cross-purposes. Sutherland gradually began to assume more and more power in the inner circle of the mission.

On October 25, 1938, MacArthur wrote to an old army friend regarding the general Manila situation:

> In the Army all goes well. The Constabulary has been separated from the Army proper and General Francisco has been named its Chief. It will have an appropriation of five million pesos of its own and will consist of 350 officers and 5,000 men. As there is to be no diminution in the Army budget it has eased up the financial situation considerably. Sutherland has proven himself a real find. Concise, energetic and able, he has been invaluable in helping me clarify and crystallize the situation.

Late in 1939, after Eisenhower had served 4 full years, Sutherland replaced him as chief of staff of the mission. The Mac-

Arthurs joined in the gay *despedido* to the Eisenhowers when they sailed. A day or two before their departure Dr. Howard Hutter gave a farewell dinner for them, and the General and Mrs. MacArthur attended. (It was the last time the two soldiers would see one another until a day in May 1946 when General of the Army Eisenhower, newly appointed Chief of Staff of the U. S. Army, arrived in his plane at the Tokyo airfield, where he was met by General of the Army Douglas MacArthur, Supreme Commander of the Japanese Occupation. Their next meeting after Tokyo was seven years later, when the newly designated Republican Secretary of State, John Foster Dulles, brought them together at a luncheon in New York City. Eisenhower was then President elect.)

5

It was obvious to MacArthur during these uncertain days that he had no real friends at court in Washington—save possibly Brigadier General Edwin M. (Pa) Watson, President Roosevelt's highly placed personal aide, and Steve Early, press secretary, both MacArthur's devoted admirers.

He realized how definitely and unmistakably he was being left alone. The men running the War Department were no longer his intimates. They were all fully occupied trying to make what little they had stretch out to cover the hundred and one items that called for help in the threatening world situation. And step by step they were being forced to accept the White House point of view that America must back up Britain in her growing conflict with Hitler's Nazi dictatorship.

MacArthur's Philippine Reserve Army was slowly increasing in numbers, but lack of properly trained officers, arms, equipment, and money for conducting even limited field exercises seriously handicapped his efforts. It was impossible in the original short 5½-month training periods, complicated by schooling in hygiene and physical and moral improvement, to give the draftees more than the most rudimentary instruction in soldiering. In most cases there was no training possible for units larger than a company.

Yet with proper aid from the White House and the War

Department and with full cooperation from the U. S. Army in the Philippines, there could have been added each year to the Philippine Reserve Army a competent force of 40,000 well-armed and trained soldiers, ready for any emergency. It seemed almost incredible that the men running affairs in Washington, regardless of any personal animosity they might have had against MacArthur, did not help in the building up of this priceless reserve of manpower in the spot where it might be so badly needed. It was not until some years later that the facts regarding Red and anti-American influences in the government in Washington brought new light on the failures.

6

Fortunately there was to be for MacArthur a very definite compensation for these years when professionally he had so little with which to accomplish his vast military dream, and when so many roadblocks were being erected against him. On February 21, 1938, he was presented with a son and heir.

Once again there was an Arthur MacArthur. The oldest son of his brother, Arthur, held the family given name until his death at the Naval Academy at Annapolis aged 17. The General's brother had died in 1924, so that the proud name was lost, until now when this little baby appeared to carry it on.

To MacArthur, recently turned 58, this was by far the happiest day of his life. Early that afternoon President Quezón and Captain Bonner Fellers, personal liaison officer between the Philippine President and General MacArthur, called to offer their congratulations.

The General was in fine fettle. He explained that some years before this when his two young nephews were married, he wrote each of them a half-serious, half-humorous letter explaining that since it was absolutely essential to perpetuate the name of their distinguished great-grandfather, their soldier grandfather and their own beloved father, he ordered and directed them to produce a son to be duly named Arthur Mac-Arthur. But as time went on, only girls had appeared.

And now on this fine day of February 21, 1938, he had again written his nephews. Since they had failed completely to carry out his orders he had decided he must take over the assignment personally—and he was now reporting to them that the mission had been completed most satisfactorily, and that there was once again an Arthur MacArthur.

When the baby was a few weeks old, the christening was held in the library of the penthouse atop the Manila Hotel. Only Dr. Hutter and one or two on the General's staff and Brigadier General Creed F. Cox, former chief of the Bureau of Insular Affairs were present. The local Bishop of the Episcopal Church officiated, and when the simple ceremony was ended, the General in measured tones so low they barely carried to the walls of the room proved again his great gift for words and deep sentiment.

It was a moment of supreme happiness for him, he said. Now the name Arthur MacArthur could live on. He hoped that a compassionate God would protect this little boy, so that he might long enjoy the superb inheritance that had been handed down to him.

All in all, these years in Manila were by no means marked exclusively by defeat or frustration. He faced his problems dispassionately, giving each its proper place and weight. He had no illusions about how he stood in Washington. But he realized that the men around the President and in the War and Navy departments were subject to terrific pressure during this period just before World War II.

MacArthur knew that Brigadier General George Marshall would shortly relieve Malin Craig as Army Chief of Staff. In the fall of 1936, Colonel Marshall, at the urgent request of General Pershing, had been made a brigadier general. After commanding a brigade of infantry in Washington state for a year, he was brought to the General Staff and assigned head of war planning. In 1938 he was detailed as Deputy Chief of Staff, and in the summer of 1939, when General Craig went on terminal leave, he became Acting Chief of Staff. On September 1, the day Germany invaded Poland, Roosevelt appointed him Chief of Staff of the Army.

General Craig would not have been MacArthur's choice as his successor. Craig was not always cooperative in helping along MacArthur's Philippine program. It is possible that Craig was pliable to the pressures from the White House and certain other sources, but he had no personal animosity toward MacArthur.

George Marshall, however, might very well allow a personal feeling of hostility to influence his attitude. MacArthur had no reason at this time to harbor the slightest feeling of ill-will toward the new Chief of Staff. How much Marshall may have held against MacArthur can never be positively known. In their army associations, from the days when they had been young lieutenants, there had always been a rather far-fetched conscious or unconscious rivalry between them. MacArthur's spectacular rise in rank, culminating in being made the 4-star Chief of Staff while Marshall was still a lieutenant colonel, could hardly have failed to arouse a certain jealousy. Nor was it quite human to expect that Marshall could forget the fact that MacArthur had not insisted that he be made a general officer. [Early in the war Marshall said to a militarily minded visitor (the author) in his office: "I'm interested in making young generals. You know I wasn't made a general officer myself until a bare two years before I would have reached the age limit for promotion. I never forgot it." He might have added that he never forgave the man whom he thought responsible for this delay.]

From the start of the mission back in October 1935 the cards had obviously been stacked against MacArthur by the men in power in Washington. Great events shaping up in Europe and Asia also were working against him and his dream of creating an adequate defensive Philippine Army. On his short visit stateside in the spring of 1937, he saw how the winds were blowing. Certain powerful groups were busy in their efforts to hypnotize America into a violent hate campaign against Hitler. By 1937 most of the important elements in the administration had joined up in creating a vast war propaganda machine.

Despite 1936 campaign pledges and forecasts, it was evident that there had been little substantial economic recovery and that unemployment figures were again advancing. Both Germany and Japan were casting dark war shadows, and it seemed easy and practical to build up a psychosis of fear against these twin threats to peace. And hate against Hitler was being carefully propagandized.

197

So it was that President Roosevelt and the groups that were urging him on found a valid reason for launching a rearmament program at home that coincided with a steady collusion with Britain's defense against the Nazis. Apparent concern over the new Japanese war against China, which started with the Marco Polo Bridge incident in Peiping in mid-1937, gave a strong argument in favor of much-needed preparedness.

As early as December 1937 there were informal exchanges and oral agreements made in London between the American and British navies, "in the event of the two fleets being required to work together in a war against Japan." Other moves followed this pattern of close coordination and mutual responsibilities of the U. S. and Britain.

In the spring of 1939 the U. S. Joint Board Planning Committee—the Army and Navy in Washington—made studies based on the prospect of America becoming involved in a World War. By May the talks reached the stage where the Joint Board discarded the old Orange Plan, replacing it with a new strategy called Rainbow Plan 1. This was rapidly expanded until there were five Rainbow Plans. They were laid before the President six weeks before the European war started. The old Orange Plan had contemplated war with only one nation and in one area—Japan—but the new strategy squarely faced the proposition of a war fought simultaneously against more than one enemy and in several theatres. Eventually Rainbow 5 was chosen as the working plan that would best meet the enlarged possibility. By this time it had the secret cooperation of the British.

Almost four years had now slipped by since MacArthur's arrival in Manila yet no single move of consequence had been made by Washington to assist him in building a great reservoir of manpower. Since the summer of 1937 the Japanese had been openly at war with Chiang Kai-shek, and the invading armies had slowly overrun most of the coastal areas and captured many important cities of China. A puppet government was established at Nanking on the Yangtze.

But a strongly conservative and pacifist group in Japan opposed the war party. Joseph C. Grew, the American ambassador in Tokyo, likewise exercised a steadying influence for

198

a peaceful settlement of the Japanese invasion of China, and for an avoidance of war between the United States and Japan. America's strong protective arm still remained around Chiang Kai-shek's shoulder, but Washington apparently was so steamed up in its hate of Hitler, and in its fervor to preserve Britain's empire, that there was neither time nor mood for any real attempt at conciliation with Japan.

MacArthur could do nothing more than to watch the darkening war clouds gather over both Europe and the China Seas. He was fully alert to the possible consequences of the Russian-German Treaty of August 23, 1939, which left both Germany and Russia free of the handicap of having immediately to fight a two-front war. Russia in her own time could attack her helpless western neighbors.

Hitler's attack on Poland came September 1, 1939, the day that George Marshall became Chief of Staff. At once he and his War Planning Board were faced with the problem of swiftly enlarging the American Army, building up war production and vastly increasing the size of the Air Corps. But there was still a strong isolationist sentiment throughout the country and it was consistently reflected in the Congress.

A progressive change of sentiment came after May 10, when the German Army swiftly overran Belgium and France and drove the British Army in complete rout to the beaches of Dunkirk. Immediately the President and his military advisors faced the possibility of the French fleet going over to the Germans. And an even more startling hazard to consider was that Britain might be invaded, and the great British fleet either neutralized or forced to leave its home bases.

On August 6, 1940, a group consisting of Admiral Robert L. Ghormley of the Navy, Major General George V. Strong of the Army and Major General Delos C. Emmons, Commanding General of the Army's G.H.Q. Air Force, departed secretly for London. It was the direct forerunner of the historic staff conversations which began in Washington on January 29, 1941, and lasted until March 27.

The summer and fall of 1940 were filled with a series of disturbing events: the air *blitz* on England; the uncertainty of the Soviet moves after her sharing the spoils of Poland at the start of the war; the transfer of 50 over-age but reconditioned destroyers to Britain; and the growing threat of Japan. After the military disaster of May 1940 both France and Britain pleaded for immediate shipment of surplus war supplies. President Roosevelt even urged the sending to Britain of every other B-17 bomber that was produced, but both Chief of Staff Marshall and General H. H. Arnold, chief of the Air Corps, succeeded in having the ratio reduced.

The matter of turning over army surplus to the British was placed in the hands of Secretary of the Treasury Henry Morgenthau, Jr., whose subsequent actions were opposed by Secretary of War Woodring. Some 550 75-mm. guns had already been declared surplus and assigned to Britain, when on June 11, 1940, a second lot of 500 cannon being requested, the order for their delivery was issued by Secretary Morgenthau. There were requests, too, for large amounts of small-arms ammunition.

About this time the Secretary of War received a message from the White House asking him to pass upon a proposal for additional aid to Great Britain. Woodring considered the fulfillment of the request inadvisable, and without stating his own opinions he asked General Marshall to study the problem and advise him promptly.

General Marshall took up the pressing matter with his G-4, whose answer was brief and to the point: "No guns should be declared surplus, obsolete, or placed in any other category that would render them available for sale. . . . It would take two years for production to catch up with requirements."

This was a part of the study Marshall handed to the harassed Secretary of War, which the latter marked "Approved, Harry H. Woodring," and sent post haste to the White House. A copy was dispatched to the Secretary of the Treasury, who was still handling Allied war purchases.

A few hours later a letter came from the President saying that since Woodring's refusal to approve the arms proposal for Britain showed that he was not in sympathy with the administration's policies, he desired his resignation. Woodring replied with an angry letter in which he indicted the national defense and the financial policies of the administration. He insisted that he had always been willing to help the Allies and had done so up to the point where such action jeopardized his own country's security.

Woodring recited the history of his consistent efforts to obtain adequate funds for preparedness and how always there had been sharp cuts made in his estimates, although the President had asked and received heavy grants for many WPA programs. He insisted that the billions now being spent would not mean adequate defense tomorrow, and that since it would take two years to be ready for war, prudence dictated that the government should avoid being drawn into a conflict until America was ready. The Secretary ended by saying that his resignation would take place at the close of office hours that afternoon.

When Woodring told General Marshall of his resignation, the Chief of Staff is said to have replied: "I am stunned. But I want you to know that you have been made the victim in place of the General Staff, which you have constantly supported and protected."

President Roosevelt subsequently tried to smooth out Woodring's bitterness but failed, even with the offer of an ambassadorship. A few days later, on June 19, 1940, Henry L. Stimson, ardent Republican interventionist and anti-Japanese extremist, was appointed Secretary of War. General Marshall saw that either he himself must ask for immediate relief as Chief of Staff or comply with the Commander-in-Chief in the White House and with the new Secretary of War now embarked on the road to certain war. He chose the latter course.

Almost simultaneously with the coming to the War Department of Stimson, who had been Mr. Hoover's Secretary of State, it was announced that the Republican vice-presidential nominee in the 1936 campaign, Frank Knox, had accepted the appointment as Secretary of the Navy. Both appointments were shrewd and disturbing political moves.

Into the advancing maelstrom of war there was now injected Roosevelt's fight for a third term. The isolationist groups were joined by a considerable element opposed to the idea of a third term, and still others were bitterly against the New Deal policies both at home and abroad. Roosevelt met the anti-war voters head on with the unequivocal pledge, made in a final speech in Boston, that no American boy would be sent to fight abroad, adding the famous refrain "I say it again, and again and again."

Meanwhile General MacArthur, absorbed in the problems that confronted him in the Philippines, almost 10,000 miles away, had long had his own definite ideas about New Deal policies. He was now retired from the Army and free to comment. On December 29, 1939, he wrote to an army friend in the States that he considered that the greatest disaster that could possibly visit the world would be Roosevelt's re-election as President of the United States.

MacArthur realized fully the dangers of the President's war policy. For America, it was not so much a matter of drifting into intervention in Europe as being definitely pushed toward that end by the administration itself. Here in Manila, lying athwart the sea roads leading from Japan to the rich war resources of Malaya and the Dutch East Indies, he could not help realizing the oblivion that awaited him. No single move had been made in his behalf. He had been completely abandoned and neglected. Already Europe and Hitler were marked as the No. 1 concern of the administration, and the far Pacific and American obligations there were pushed to the rear.

7

By the latter part of 1940, General Marshall and his War Plans Division (WPD) with White House pressure behind them were deep in the problem of hurriedly increasing the armed strength of the nation. On August 27 the National Guard was voted into federal service for one year, and on September 16 a Selective Service Act of a single year's duration was passed by Congress. Both were subject to the definite commitment that no troops would be sent to foreign countries outside the continental limits of the United States. War factories were beginning to turn out quantities of arms and equipment, training camps were springing up, and considerable progress toward a real defense was being made.

In October 1940 Churchill dispatched a message to Roosevelt requesting that an American naval squadron be sent to

Singapore. Both Admiral H. R. Stark and General Marshall opposed the request on the ground that it might provoke action by Japan. But the dictum by Stark that "the vital theatre is the Eastern Atlantic, and the Western Pacific a secondary one" met the avowed approval of Marshall. The British conception that Germany was "the principal foe, with Japan as the one to be fully disposed of at a later date" had been accepted by the American chiefs of the armed services. There was no place in the high councils of power in Washington for anyone who opposed this fiat. The order had come straight down from the White House, and behind it stood the tremendous influence that Churchill already wielded on the President and on Harry Hopkins and others of the Inner Circle.

MacArthur's role apparently had been reduced to little more than that of a trainer of Philippine draftees. Militarily starved as he was, his deepest concern was for his country's preparedness.

In answer to a cable sent by William Allen White, chairman of the group called Defend America by Aiding the Allies, he emphasized the two fatal words that ran like a dark thread of doom through the pattern of all American military history:

> You have asked my military opinion as to whether the time has come for America to give continued and further aid to England, in the fight for civilization. The history of failure in war can almost always be summed up in two words—too late. Too late in comprehending the deadly power of the potential enemy. Too late in preparedness. Too late in uniting all possible forces for resistance. Too late in standing by one's friends.
>
> The greatest strategic mistake in all history will be made if America fails to recognize this vital moment, if she permits again the writing of that fatal epitaph—too late.

In June 1940 Major General George Grunert was sent to command the Department of the Philippines. He immediately began forwarding requests for more personnel, anti-aircraft defense, ammunition and war equipment. In the months of July and August alone he dispatched to Washington eight separate warnings and urgent recommendations. On September 1 he wrote personally to General Marshall explaining that a defeatist attitude was growing in the Philippines to the point where it was strongly believed that the United States had actually abandoned the idea of defending the Islands.

General Grunert, an old friend of General MacArthur, was in full sympathy with the broad conception of the Philippine Army that MacArthur had been building under such trying handicaps. With Grunert's early recommendations that a strong air force and submarine fleet be based in the Philippines, he suggested that 500 American officers be assigned to help train the Philippine Army units. After some delay 75 officers came.

As for actual help for the Islands, General Marshall and the White House now lagged far behind the War Plans Division of the General Staff. As early as March 1940 the WPD recommended that the Philippine force be augmented by a composite air wing, a regular army infantry division, an anti-aircraft regiment and additional harbor defense troops. Disinterest, confusion, lack of trained men and equipment, and the fear of Hitler overrunning Britain cancelled out these recommendations.

It was not until December 26, 1940, that Army Chief of Staff Marshall approved a War Plans Division recommendation that the Philippine Scouts, an integral part of the U. S. regular forces, be increased from 6,000 to 12,000, along with additions to the old 31st Infantry Regiment and the two Coast Artillery regiments, and a small increase in anti-aircraft guns.

Early in February 1941 Marshall ordered that some 60 officers due to return home after their regular tour of duty in the Islands be held there, and that the wives and families of Army personnel be sent back to the States. Since MacArthur had long been retired from active service the order did not affect the residence there of Mrs. MacArthur and little Arthur.

Shortly before this, MacArthur decided to address a personal letter to the Chief of Staff. It was in the nature of an opening wedge, and fully outlined his plans for a Philippine Army and what he hoped to do with it. But the immediate result of this was nil.

Along about April of 1941 MacArthur could no longer stand the ambiguous state of his abandonment. With complete humility he wrote a letter to Steve Early, press secretary and trusted advisor to the President. Early had been an old friend of MacArthur's from the days before America's entry into World War I, when his newspaper beat had been the War Department. He had been one of the reporters who in 1917 had signed the letter to Secretary of War Baker praising the work of Major Douglas MacArthur, then press censor.

MacArthur asked Early to take up with the President the idea of recalling MacArthur to active service. The General would be glad to undertake any assignment that might be given him, but he pointed out that all the Army forces in the Far East should be consolidated into a single command. In this his concern was for his country and for the fate of the Islands, and not for any petty personal ambition. To him the situation was desperate. Yet he got no direct reply.

On May 29 he addressed a letter to Marshall. Three weeks went by before Marshall answered. The vagueness of his letter could hardly have satisfied MacArthur. The Marshall letter read in part:

> Both the Secretary of War and I are much concerned about the situation in the Far East. During one of our discussions about three months ago it was decided that your outstanding qualifications and vast experience in the Philippines make you the logical choice for the Army Commander in the Far East should the situation approach a crisis. The Secretary has delayed recommending your appointment as he does not feel the time has arrived for such action. However, he has authorized me to tell you that, at the proper time, he will recommend to the President that you be so appointed. It is my impression that the President will approve his recommendation.

It was probably shortly before he received this letter that MacArthur wrote his second letter to Steve Early. The tenor of this note expressed a conviction that he was not to be recalled. Consequently he had decided shortly to leave the Islands and go to San Antonio, Texas. Apparently his usefulness was ended.

When there was no immediate reply, he actually ordered Dick Marshall, his deputy chief of staff on the mission, to secure transportation on the first available steamer. But matters of far greater significance were in the making.

On June 22, 1941, Hitler, against the advice of his best

generals, plunged into the limitless reaches of Russia. Fear and hate of the Nazis left little room for cool appraisal of the situation by the civil and military leaders in Washington. Even professional military opinion was that the Soviets would collapse in from three to six weeks.

So it was that the Russian invasion, instead of bringing a release from pressure sounding Britain's early doom, created a panic-stricken belief that in a matter of weeks Russia would be knocked out, and the triumphant Hitler would turn either westward and attempt the invasion of England, or southward to the Middle East and cut the life lines of the British Empire. The fall of the Empire would then be assured.

On July 13 Harry Hopkins flew to London on a secret mission for President Roosevelt that was certain to involve America still more deeply in European intervention. A few days later, while Hitler's tank divisions were rolling toward Moscow and Leningrad, Hopkins started a hazardous air journey to Moscow and immediately began making plans with the Red leaders to include them in the Lend-Lease program, backed by a promise of every possible aid from the United States. As a consequence of this new commitment, and of Hopkins' later optimistic report that Russia might hold out, the situation soon became even less favorable for substantial reinforcing of the Philippines. Russia would now share the American largesse with Britain.

As part of the sequence of events that were to affect the Philippine situation, Harry Hopkins on his return by air from his Moscow trip joined Prime Minister Churchill on the battleship *Prince of Wales*. Together they crossed the Atlantic to the sea conference with Roosevelt and his military and naval advisors. It was the first time that the "former naval person" and the President were face to face.

In this secret sea meeting in August 1941, Roosevelt made definite mutual commitments with Churchill that either would go to the help of the other if Japan attacked the United States, Britain or a third country (the Netherlands) in the Pacific.

It had long been certain that America's entrance into the struggle against Germany would cause Japan to declare war against the United States, since the island empire had publicly announced such a course of action on April 21, 1941, shortly after she signed a non-aggression pact with Russia.

Previous to this on September 28, 1940, Japan had signed a Tripartite Treaty with Germany and Italy, in which it was agreed that the three nations would go to war against any nation not then a participant in the European war or the Sino-Japanese war that attacked any one of the three. Obviously this was aimed directly against America. If the United States engaged in war against Japan, America would automatically be involved in war against Germany and Italy.

At this time there were still strong peace elements active in Tokyo that tried consistently throughout most of 1941 to find some way to conciliate Washington and avoid war. But what Washington wanted was not conciliation but some means of getting into the war against Hitler. The interventionists were doing their level best. Germany was offered insult and repeated provocations but she refused to press any retaliation.

On July 25, 1941, apparently in answer to Japan's intrusion into Indo-China, an executive order from President Roosevelt broke off all trade relations with Japan, and Great Britain and the Netherlands concurred in the stringent restrictions that meant the virtual economic strangling of Japan.

The fact that Russia was now cast as an ally of Great Britain immediately changed the status of Stalin in the eyes of the administration. Overnight the official propaganda shifted its slant on the Russian dictator and his American Communists and fellow travelers. The official Communist line turned squarely from urging the country to stay out of the European war at all costs to strong pleas that America must now enter this great fight to save democracy.

Russia had shrewdly played her cards in the great war game, particularly in the way she had used her Red agents and their accomplices in molding and directing Washington opinion. She had helped to turn Japan's ambitions southward toward the priceless loot of Southeastern Asia and the lower Pacific. She had tried to pit embittered America against Japan rather than against Hitler, but now with her former Nazi ally charging across her own European borders, she was desperately concerned in her attempt to get America into the world struggle by bringing about a Japanese-American war.

The spade work had long been under way. The pro-British, pro-internationalist, anti-Hitler groups were all ready to accept Stalin. Back from his costly mission to Moscow, Harry Hopkins, the President's most intimate advisor, is reported to have said: "It is ridiculous to think of Stalin as a Communist. He is a Russian nationalist."

8

Sometime in the middle of July 1941 a two-line cable was brought to MacArthur. It was signed by Major General Watson, the President's military aide and confidant but still devoted to MacArthur. The gist of it was that MacArthur was to take no steps to leave the Philippines until he heard further from Watson.

A few days later, as MacArthur was eating breakfast on the Sunday morning of July 27, Manila time, he noted a small box in the lower left-hand corner of the Manila *Tribune,* announcing that the native Philippine Army was being called to the colors under the command of a lieutenant general.

A second item of exciting news was a cabled report that 30,000 Japanese troops had landed in Saigon, the capital of French Indo-China.

An hour or two later a wire was brought to him with the single word "Congratulations." It was signed Lehrbas, an old newspaper friend from the Washington days.

Then two more cables arrived. One was an open message stating the President of the United States had ordered the Philippine Army mobilized under MacArthur, who was to assume the rank of lieutenant general, as soon as Congress could grant the authority. Later MacArthur learned that the President had waited until he left for Hyde Park and was well away from the War Department and General Marshall before he had personally directed the sending of the cables.

The second cable was signed *Marshall.* It spelled out the details of the new assignment:

Effective this date there is hereby constituted a command designated as the United States Army Forces in the Far East. This command will include the Philippine Department, forces of the Government of the Commonwealth of the Philippines called into the service of the armed forces of the United States for the period of the existing emergency, and such other forces as may be designated to it. Headquarters of the United States Army Forces in the Far East will be established in Manila, Philippine Islands. You are hereby designated as Commanding General, United States Army Forces in the Far East. . . .

So uncertainty was over. MacArthur would do his best to make up for lost time and for the neglect and indecision that had been meted out to him by Washington. It would not be easy.

As yet he could have had no inkling of any possible Washington-London plan that would eventually lead to abandoning the Philippines to their fate, while the U. S. Far Eastern Fleet pulled out of Manila Bay and attempted to save British interests in Malaya, Burma and India, along with the Dutch East Indies. MacArthur had no full reports of the secret talks and agreements arrived at between Britain and America during the Atlantic Charter meeting at sea or at the several earlier top secret sessions of the armed services of the two countries held in London. Not for a moment could he conceive the idea that his country might turn her back on her sacred obligations in the Pacific.

12

THE RACE AGAINST TIME

MacArthur lost no time in starting the ball rolling on that Sunday morning of July 27, 1941. He put in a call for Dick Sutherland, and when he found that he had left for the golf course, he telephoned Deputy Chief of Staff Dick Marshall to round up Sutherland and bring him over as quickly as possible.

As soon as the two officers arrived at the penthouse of the Manila Hotel, they went to work. To start with, there would have to be a greatly enlarged staff. Then there must be worked out the hundred and one problems of constructing large training centers, forming the platoon and company units of the Philippine Army into battalions, then regiments and finally into divisions. MacArthur's plan for the defense of the Philippines had not yet reached a 50% fruition. Immediately requisitions must be sent to the War Department for guns, ammunition, equipment, specialist troops, officers and money.

Within an hour President Quezón telephoned that he was leaving for the hotel, and MacArthur and his two senior officers hurried to meet him at the entrance. Quezón, his eyes bright with courage and hope, impulsively put his arm around his old comrade.

"All we have, all that we are, is yours," he said dramatically.

MacArthur and his assistants got an additional lift when they read in the Manila papers of August 13 that the American Congress had finally passed the Extension of the Draft Act that kept the draftees, as well as the National Guard outfits, in federal service for an additional year. The bill had squeezed through the Lower House by a vote of 203 to 202.

There were now 27 infantry, 6 armored and 2 cavalry divisions in various degrees of training in the States, of which 4 infantry and 2 armored were fully trained and ready to be shipped anywhere. Certainly there would no longer be any question of lack of trained men and special units for reinforcements for the Islands. Surely MacArthur's pleadings for more troops would be answered now.

Early in August the War Plans Division of the Army recommended sending out a National Guard anti-aircraft regiment and a complete infantry division and increasing the several American units already in the Philippines. There were suggestions for 50 pursuit planes and some 31 light bombers and a number of items of special equipment. General Marshall's office promptly disapproved sending the infantry division but substituted an additional tank battalion and a maintenance company.

War supplies were actually beginning to flow westward, but only the most enthusiastic would have called them more than a trickle as compared with the lend-lease shipments going to Britain, and those that soon would be en route for Murmansk on the dangerous sea voyage to North Russia. But some help was on the way, and hope returned that if war with Japan could be held off for as little as six months, MacArthur would have some 125,000 Filipino trainees armed, fairly well trained and incorporated into divisions and in position to oppose Japanese landings. From the start of the mission MacArthur's plan had revolved around the theory that his task was to provide manpower capable of assisting in defense during the period of transition from commonwealth to republic. Until that date the main responsibility for the defense of the Islands was definitely American. But Washington had failed to honor this obligation, refusing MacArthur real help of any kind.

Throughout August of 1941 there was no hour of rest for MacArthur's harassed staff. On the 15th of the month the small Philippine air force was inducted into the U. S. service by General MacArthur personally. "Only those are fit to live who are not afraid to die," he told the little group of Filipino pilots and ground men.

By September 1 a number of enlarged training camps were ready, and on that day twelve Filipino regiments were inducted into federal service. Reinforcements and supplies, now arriving from the United States, included 425 reserve officers, who were immediately assigned to the new units. Requisitions had already been made for 246 additional officers from the rank of major to general.

It was evident that the Army War Plans Division in Washington had a keener appreciation of the Philippine situation and its needs than the Chief of Staff and his office: at least it was less inhibited by secret plans and commitments to Britain and Russia. A number of times its urgent recommendations were pushed aside by General Marshall or at best only partially adopted. On October 13 the WPD submitted to the Chief

211

of Staff a memorandum on Command in the Pacific, in which it compared the growing strength of MacArthur army forces with the weakness of American naval units. The War Plans Division recommended that all U. S. forces there be put under command of General MacArthur, and that the Navy be asked to accept the plan. The only result of that memorandum was a skeptical comment written on it by Colonel Walter Bedell Smith, Marshall's special aide, and one word added by the Chief of Staff, "Hold!"

2

Even before MacArthur had been called back into active service he had sent suggestions to the War Department showing how the old Orange Plan, which considered only the holding of the Manila Bay area, could be enlarged into an over-all plan that would include the protection of the principal Philippine Islands from an invader. He now proposed a daring air idea which, with sufficient time and will to carry it out, would not only make the Philippines practically invulnerable to invasion but would change the whole strategic conception from one of defense to one of offense. Heavy B-17 bombers, based on the Islands and properly supported, could present an assault threat to Japan and her sea lanes to the southward that could actually stymie her war dreams.

This was an imaginative plan that undoubtedly caught the fancy of President Roosevelt, as well as General H. H. (Hap) Arnold of the Army Air Corps. It called for building a complete air arm, with heavy and light bombardment, augmented by ample dive bombers and protective fighters, and based on a string of air fields stretching the 700 or 800 miles from lower Mindanao to upper Luzon, with shops, supply depots, air-warning devices and all the accessories of a completely modern and efficient air arm.

Time was the all-important factor; time to build both the necessary ground defenses, and the air force itself; time to consolidate an air route from Australia, northward through the Dutch Islands and Malaya to Mindanao and then on to Manila; time and planes and weapons—and above all else, the will-to-win here in the Western Pacific. No one doubted that MacArthur had this last qualification. There was still little proof that it had been matched, as far as the Western Pacific was concerned, anywhere in the War Department or in the Chief of Staff's office in Washington.

At least the whole picture of help for the Philippines underwent a great change for the better by the end of September. MacArthur was informed of the approval of his plan to close the narrow straits that led to the Visayan Sea in the central area of the Islands by mounting heavy guns at the several entrances. He was to go ahead with his plans to integrate the air defenses of the Philippines with Australia, the Dutch East Indies and Singapore. But there was still a reckless disregard for dates and timing. One particular War Department plan for aid ended its proposals with the completely unrealistic suggestion that: "This augmentation to be commenced about April 1942 and to be completed about October 1943."

The Army Air Corps threw itself into the perilous task with high enthusiasm. The first nine of the new B-17s landed at Clark Field, 65 miles north of Manila, early in October 1941. Shortly afterwards 50 P-40E pursuit planes were unloaded at Manila, and Air Corps ground personnel disembarked.

But still no driving will-to-win had appeared in Washington in army ground force circles when it came to help for MacArthur. In the United States there were now 1,400,000 soldiers in various degrees of training. The Louisiana exercises alone had given final polish to some 400,000 soldiers. And there were vast quantities of tanks and guns and equipment of all kinds rolling out of the factories. Lack of Pacific shipping still offered a definite sea roadblock, since Britain and Russia had highest priorities. Yet the threat of war with Japan was constant, and nothing of a realistic nature was being done to discourage her.

On October 5 Major General Lewis H. Brereton of the Army Air Corps was brought to Washington from Florida and was informed by General Arnold that MacArthur had asked for him to command the Far Eastern air force, now being organized. He was told that ultimately there would be four bombardment groups and five fighter groups—which would give

213

him by the middle of 1942, 170 heavy bombers, 86 dive bombers and a total of 195 pursuit planes. In time he would have the necessary air-warning installations and the various ground units, mobile air depots and other special services. Brereton was skeptical when he left General Arnold's office and reported to General Marshall. The Chief of Staff gave him a fill-in, emphasizing the new strategic concept for the Islands. Marshall showed him prepared studies and had him read the report by MacArthur that gave him the big picture. Later Brereton was handed a secret sealed letter marked "For General MacArthur's eyes only."

Brereton was still skeptical. He pointed out to the Chief of Staff that if the situation in the Far East became critical the presence of a strong and unprotected force of B-17s might so aggravate the tension that this air threat, instead of acting as a deterrent to war, might actually spark a Japanese decision to attack. There had been little or no effort in Washington at secrecy in this sudden decision to build up the American air and ground power in the Philippines. It was a peculiar and unaccountable procedure thus blatantly to advertise the reinforcements now being hurried to the Manila Bay area. It was almost as if Washington were actually inviting Japan to attack the Philippines before the Islands could be made strong enough to resist invasion. Common sense seemingly would have dictated that utmost secrecy be used in this dangerous enterprise.

Brereton asked Marshall how much time he would have and what was the War Department's estimate when Japan might be expected to attack. He was told that it was the opinion of the High Command that hostilities would probably not begin before April 1, 1942. By that time the required air reinforcements and auxiliaries would be in place, and MacArthur's army ground requirements would be completed.

It was now early October of 1941; but April 1, 1942, when MacArthur would be fully prepared, was still almost six months off. Even six months was little enough to do the job.

On November 3 Brereton arrived in Manila on the Clipper from Guam. He reported at once to MacArthur's headquarters and then with Chief of Staff Sutherland was driven to the Manila Hotel where MacArthur lived. His welcome was most cordial. Brereton turned over the confidential letter from General Marshall. MacArthur read it and his eyes sparkled.

"Dick," he exclaimed to Sutherland, pounding his desk in a characteristic gesture, "they are going to give us everything we have asked for."

Once again came up that fatal date of April 1, 1942. It had at least been partially sold to MacArthur, too. It was a convenient target day to use here in the far-away Islands, where the threat of war was so near at hand and the chances of defeat so strong. Yet it seems incomprehensible that MacArthur, the realist, could actually have believed that Japan would accommodate her future enemies by giving them five more peaceful months to build a great air and ground force for both defense and potential assault against her. But it can be assumed that he knew almost nothing of the underlying machinations in Washington. Morale here in the Islands was already shaky and this promise of time was priceless in helping him to instill a mood of confidence and a fighting spirit.

MacArthur, clearly, was thinking how air bases in Australia and the Dutch Indies and Malaya must be integrated into Philippine defense for the coming war. Three days after Brereton's arrival MacArthur sent him on a swift survey of friendly fields as far south as Rabaul, Lae and Port Moresby in New Guinea. When Brereton returned, MacArthur was far less optimistic about the time element than before. The startling sequence of events indicated clearly that instead of any attempt at conciliation, Washington was laying down terms that Japan could accept only by withdrawing completely from her conquests in China and in the Far East.

On October 17 the bitter, uncompromising War Minister Tojo had replaced the far more reasonable Prince Konoye as Japanese Premier. On November 18 Special Envoy Kurusu caught the China Clipper at Manila, en route for Washington.

That night MacArthur, still the realist, said to his intimate staff: "I know this fellow Kurusu. He's been completely discredited in Tokyo, and his being sent to Washington now means he is to take part in some dirty job. This may be *it*."

November 4 had considerable local significance for the worried people of Manila; early in the afternoon the 4th Marine Regiment arrived straight from the Japanese hotbed of Shanghai. As Commander-in-Chief of the Army forces, MacArthur could not help but wish that the fine regiment could be under him instead of being a part of Admiral Hart's command.

On this same November 4 Secretary of State Cordell Hull, himself an interventionist, told the Cabinet in Washington that the conversations with the Japanese representatives were going badly. On November 7 he reiterated that there seemed every possibility of early war with Japan.

November 7 was to assume the greatest importance. At a Cabinet meeting that day President Roosevelt solemnly polled the several secretaries as to whether they believed the American people would follow him into a war if Japan attacked. The vote was unanimously in the affirmative.

The fate of Russia hung largely on the fact that Hitler's forces besieging both Moscow and Leningrad were shortly to face what turned out to be the hardest Russian winter in many years. Britain was incessant in her pleas for America's active participation in the European war. Hitler must come first, she insisted: then she would throw her full weight in the Pacific war. But all the propaganda forces of the administration, coupled with those of the interventionists, who now ranged from Communist agents and their Red sympathizers to the intensely pro-British, Republican Cabinet members Stimson and Knox, still could not arouse the American people to accepting a war with Germany. This left an attack by Japan as the only possible and sure-fire way to draw America into the war in Europe.

For some time a fairly large proportion of the American fleet had been stationed in the Atlantic. The remainder, save the small Far Eastern squadron, had been directed personally by the President to base in Pearl Harbor. Admiral James Otto Richardson had protested violently, stating that the fleet was vul-

nerable at Pearl Harbor and besides was undermanned and unprepared for war and should be pulled back to the Pacific
Coast until it was brought up to battle strength. For this protest he was relieved of command in January 1941. Admiral
Husband E. Kimmel replaced Richardson, and in March he was
forced to send to the Atlantic three battleships, one aircraft
carrier, four light cruisers and eighteen destroyers. Of Kimmel's
three remaining carriers, one was sent to a Pacific Coast drydock
for overhauling in the fall of 1941.

The Washington policy played directly into the hands of
Japanese militarists. Japan's military intrusion in China and
subsequently into Indo-China had made her the whipping boy
for the men around the White House who wanted war. Apparently no offers by Japan, even the pledge to withdraw from
the Tripartite Treaty with Germany and Italy and a virtual
withdrawal from all southern China, had any effect on the
Washington crowd. The voices of Churchill, Stalin and Roosevelt and the great propaganda machine insistently demanding
America's entry into the war were apparently too powerful to
overcome.

On November 13 MacArthur read the report of Navy Secretary Knox's speech, warning of the grave national peril ahead.
That same day a meeting of the operations chiefs of the various armed services in Washington decided on the necessity—or
at least the gesture—of pushing forward by a full month the
troop movement scheduled for the Philippines. Reinforcements that were to be sent to Manila in January were ordered
to be shipped in December. Certain anti-aircraft guns and ammunition earmarked for Hawaii and Panama were directed to
be re-routed to Manila.

MacArthur felt now that there had finally come to the
Washington leaders a new sense of their responsibility to the
Philippines. It seemed apparent that Washington was genuinely concerned in pushing reinforcements across the Pacific.
Shipping was still a problem, but the guns, planes, men and
supplies were at last rolling westward. MacArthur had been
cabled that on December 1 alone 19,000 troops were scheduled
to leave San Francisco for Manila.

Some weird sense of unreality seemed still to affect General

Marshall. How much he was influenced by secret White House orders and commitments may never be known. Certain of his actions were unexplainable. At an important staff meeting on November 26 the official notes of the conference, reporting an over-all statement by the Chief of Staff, read:

> While the President and Mr. Hull anticipate a possible assault on the Philippines, General Marshall said that he did not see this as a probability because the hazards would be too great for the Japanese. . . .

The War Plans Division's recommendation for a unified Philippine command under General MacArthur, which had been shoved aside and marked "Hold" by the Chief of Staff, now assumed a certain significance. The order to delay the decision not only went against every modern conception of the need for unity of command in a field of operation, but it forced MacArthur openly to oppose the demands of Admiral Thomas C. Hart in Manila Bay that tactical command by the Navy was necessary over Army Air Corps elements when they were operating in conjunction with the Navy. In plain words, this meant that in any joint Navy-Air action the Navy would be in over-all command. The proposal was forwarded to Washington with MacArthur's comment that it was "entirely objectionable" to him.

The Army War Plans Division supported MacArthur, and there was a lively exchange of cables and hurried conferences in Washington. Strangely enough General Marshall seemed far more disturbed over the Navy's unfavorable reaction than over MacArthur's. As late as November 28 Marshall tersely cabled MacArthur:

> I was disturbed to receive your note of November 7 transmitting correspondence between Hart and yourself. I was more disturbed when Stark sent over to me your letter to him of October 18. However, your cable of November 28 stating "intimate liaison and cooperation and cordial relations exist between Army and Navy" was reassuring. . . .

4

In Washington the diplomatic crisis was moving toward a final showdown. On November 20 the Japanese envoys presented what was virtually their last attempt at conciliation.

Six days later Secretary Hull answered with his Ten Points, which if accepted would mean the total eclipse of Japan in Asia. War was certain from this key date of November 26, 1941. On the following morning a report of "hostile action possible at any moment" was sent to MacArthur. It was the first of several war warnings dispatched from Washington, and MacArthur acted upon them at once.

He had at that moment as the hard core of his defense a total of 2,504 officers and 28,591 enlisted men in the United States Regular Army establishment. Of this last figure, 16,634 were Americans and 11,957 were finely trained Filipino Scouts, who years before had been incorporated into the regular U. S. forces. Of the enlisted total of 16,634 Americans, 4,940 belonged to the air force. The only Regular Army infantry regiment on the Islands was the reliable 31st Infantry, which had seen service in the Siberian Expedition toward the end of World War I and during the Japanese occupation there. The remainder of the Americans, outside the National Guard antiaircraft tank and special artillery units, were assigned to the harbor defense, based for the most part on Corregidor.

The 31st, with two Scout regiments and artillery units, comprised the Philippine Division. The Philippine Division with the 26th Cavalry and the small First Regular Division of the Philippine Army, built around former constabulary troops, made up the only seasoned holding forces MacArthur had with which to meet a determined invasion.

Besides these few well-armed and well-trained troops he had a total of something more than 110,000 men of the Philippine National Army. One regiment of each native division had had three months' regimental training; another had two months; and the third regiment less than a month. These native divisions had little or no artillery, and to the outfits on Luzon artillery and tank battalions were to be assigned from the headquarters pool as needed.

All the ground forces under General MacArthur were grouped into five major commands. The most important, the North Luzon force, was assigned to Major General Jonathan M. (Skinny) Wainwright, and while it consisted of three Philippine Army Reserve divisions its only seasoned troops were the 26th Cavalry and certain other small Scout outfits and a magnificent demolition group of engineers under Colonel Hugh J. Casey. This North force was assigned positions that would cover the landing beaches at Aparri and Vigan in the north, and the vulnerable shores of Lingayen Gulf, some 110 miles above Manila.

5

It was evident to MacArthur that the first effort of the Japanese would be to attack his small, quarter-built air force. From the days of the Billy Mitchell trial, almost fifteen years before this, he had held high the potential role of air power. But now he was fearful that his tiny force could not last long under the smothering attacks that the overwhelmingly larger Japanese air forces would lay down.

As a precautionary measure he directed his chief of staff to base the 35 long-range bombers at Del Monte Field in the southern island of Mindanao. He was conscious of how small the protecting force of fighters was and how helpless the practically undefended Clark Field, with no dispersal areas, would be against heavy air attack.

A record of MacArthur's exact air strength shows that he had 194 modern aircraft on hand, of which 107 were operational, or ready for combat. Only Clark Field could be considered modern, with a runway long enough to accommodate the B-17s. At Del Monte there were two crude strips on which the Fortresses could land and take off, and the start had been made to build repair shops and supply depots, and within two or three months they would have a fairly modern bomber field. Up and down the almost 1,000-mile-long chain of islands, sites for a score and more of fighter fields had been laid out, only Nichols Field outside Manila was near completion, and four or five others were far enough along to be classed as serviceable for fighters only.

On the morning of December 7 there were eight U. S. troop ships bound for Manila with reinforcements that would have more than doubled the entire American-born forces there. They were bringing badly needed guns, ammunition, dive bombers and pursuit planes. In the sky lanes an entire additional bomber group of 30 B-17s was starting on the Pacific bomber route that led to the Islands.

But even though the twin threat of "too little and too late" now thundered down on him, MacArthur was determined that he would still not be lost. If the Japanese suddenly struck these Islands, MacArthur, even with the little he had, could hold Corregidor and the entrance to Manila Bay for at least four months, time enough for American air power and the fleet to come to his relief.

In Hawaii there were 57,000 ground and anti-aircraft troops and the finest planes America possessed, with complete warning installations and well-guarded fields. Here, too, the great Pacific fleet was based. It seemed only reasonable that if the Philippines were suddenly attacked, there would sooner or later start from this Pacific Gibraltar an avenging sea and air armada that would be able to penetrate any Japanese blockade and bring MacArthur the tools of war and victory.

With the ample warning sent him on November 27, MacArthur calmly went about his final preparation. Every necessary disposition was made. Every man and gun and plane was on the alert. Apparently there was nothing more that he could do.

It was late on the Sunday night of December 7 (Manila time) when he turned out the light in his bedroom in the penthouse of the Manila Hotel.

Tomorrow might well be the day. The Navy's communication center in the great tunnel on Corregidor had been furnishing him with decoded Japanese intercepts that had been picked up between Tokyo and its Embassy in Washington. The messages were in the most secret of the Japanese codes and even without subsequent warnings from Washington it was

221

clear to both General MacArthur and Admiral Hart that war was certain and would come at any moment.

Both officers were well aware of the fact that Japan had started all three of her modern wars with surprise attacks: against China's helpless fleet in 1894; against Russia's Asiatic fleet at Port Arthur ten years later; and against the German stronghold at Tsingtao in Shantung province on the mainland of China in 1914. Each attack synchronized almost to a minute with a formal declaration of war. It was recognized that a sudden surprise attack against a key spot was a fully understood part of her war strategy. The only real uncertainty was where it would come.

The ground forces in the Philippines might be assailed and forced back into their final prepared defenses, but certainly they would not be surprised. They were as ready as they could be with their inadequate defenses on this night of December 7, Manila time.

[Thirteen years after the events occurred a remarkable book by Rear Admiral Robert A. Theobald, U.S.N. Ret., published by Devin-Adair, shed considerable new light on the highly controversial question of just how America got into the war against Japan. It is titled *The Final Secret of Pearl Harbor*, and bears the sub-title, *The Washington Contribution to the Japanese Attack*. In a carefully documented defense of Admiral Kimmel, the naval commander at Pearl Harbor, Theobald piles up a vast amount of evidence that points to the assumption that not only did President Roosevelt plot the war but it seems he must have been assisted in the secret plans of leaving Pearl Harbor open for surprise attack by both Admiral Stark and General Marshall. Much of Theobald's case is based on the fact that of the eight U. S.-made Japanese Purple Machines that could decode the most secret of the Japanese codes styled Magic, none had been sent to Pearl Harbor, although there was one in the Navy Communication center on Corregidor and one in London. Thus Hart and MacArthur themselves could follow all the most secret messages between Tokyo and the Japanese Embassy in Washington and analyze the growing menace of a Japanese attack. Among the messages decoded were the series from Tokyo directing Japanese agents in Hawaii to report constantly on the exact locations of the American warships in Pearl Harbor. The book points out that while the American commanders in Manila Bay were thus alert to the chances of war, the unfortunate commanders in Hawaii were denied the same opportunity to read and evaluate the full messages and to draw their own conclusions regarding possible attack. Subsequently they were smeared and ruined in order to clear General Marshall, Admiral Stark and President Roosevelt of responsibility.]

13

"I SHALL RETURN!"

It was 3:40 on Sunday morning, December 8, Manila time, when General MacArthur was awakened by the ringing of the special telephone on his night table. It was connected by direct wire to Dick Sutherland's office at 1 Victoria Street, where the chief of staff had been sleeping on an army cot for several nights.

"Jap planes are attacking Pearl Harbor," Sutherland tersely announced.

"Pearl Harbor?" MacArthur questioned incredulously. "Why that should be our strongest point!"

He was assured that a commercial cable had substantiated the official report. Yet he could hardly believe that the vast sea- and air-screen around Hawaii could have been successfully penetrated by enemy bombers.

The defenses at Pearl Harbor were far different from his own inadequate air, sea and ground makeshifts. For the past five days his single radar functioning in northwestern Luzon had each dawn been picking up approaching Japanese aircraft,

223

and he had approved sending up fighter squadrons to try to intercept them. The attempts were unsuccessful, but the air forces had been on full alert.

The tactical handling of the air forces was completely in the hands of General Brereton and his staff. Several days before this tragic morning, MacArthur had ordered the 35 B-17 Flying Fortresses 500 miles south to the safety of Del Monte Field on Mindanao. After some delay half the great ships were sent on below, but for some reason 17 still remained at Clark Field above Manila.

An explanation that has some validity is that the partially completed Del Monte Field had room for only four squadrons of bombers. When the two squadrons from Clark Field arrived, there was still room for two more squadrons, which could have included the remaining B-17s in Luzon. But the 7th Bombardment Group comprising four squadrons was shortly expected from the Pacific. It is possible that it was for this reason that the two remaining squadrons at Clark Field were not dispatched before hostilities opened, as MacArthur had instructed.

At 9:30 A.M. a large force of enemy bombers was reported over Lingayen Gulf heading toward Manila. Pursuit squadrons were immediately sent up to intercept them. At the same time, as a safety measure, the 17 B-17s at Clark Field were ordered into the air. But the enemy bombers suddenly shifted their course, turned northward and bombed the summer capital at Baguio.

The *all clear* was now sounded at Clark Field, and the fighters returned for refueling. The 17 Fortresses had gas enough to stay in the air for a full 10 hours, but instead of being allowed to take advantage of this safety of the limitless skies, the commander of Clark Field ordered them to return to the field.

At 11:45 a report came in of an enemy formation over Lingayen Gulf less than 100 miles away and moving southward. The fighter planes were being gassed while the pilots grabbed a bit of lunch. A half hour later four of the squadrons were in the air and the last of the P-40 fighters were starting to take off when high in the sky appeared an enemy bombardment force, together with dive bombers, escorted by fighters flown from carriers somewhere in the China Sea. In a matter of minutes 15 of the priceless B-17s on the ground were completely destroyed and the other two were seriously damaged. Clark Field's anti-aircraft defenses proved totally inadequate; the enemy attackers systematically wrecked and burned planes, supply depots, installations and every vestige of the one modern airfield in all the Islands.

It was a catastrophe of the first magnitude. From the moment that the news reached MacArthur, he spoke no single word of official censure against the air commanders who had failed to move their bombers to Mindanao as he had directed. Instead of obeying this instruction they had ordered the bombers to return to the landing field from the safety of the skies after the first enemy bombers flew inland. The Fortresses had been caught like sitting ducks. It was an irreparable loss, but it was the fortune of war.

At once confusing and conflicting reports were made by General Brereton and certain members of his staff. The stark facts were clear enough in themselves: MacArthur had lost by noon of the first day of the war roughly half of his bombers and modern fighters.

His air force was simply too small to survive the attacking Japanese air armada. Had it survived this first day, in a very short time its entire destruction would have been inevitable. There was almost a total lack of dispersal areas, and the ground defenses were all but nonexistent. Had every fighter been in the air that fatal noon their almost certain destruction would have come either in aerial combat or when gas shortage forced them to land. It seems certain that most of them would have been destroyed within a day or two by sheer enemy superiority of numbers.

Very soon there were issued in Washington sponsored versions that were little less than veiled charges against the lack of foresight and the bad judgment of General MacArthur and his chief of staff. MacArthur personally became the target of the bitter accusations that were never quite to stop.

So angry was the continued criticism heaped upon both himself and Brereton that on June 25, 1943—a full year and a half after the occurrence—he issued from Brisbane a formal statement that should have closed the account. It is a direct and simple recital of events:

25 June 43

My attention has been called to a number of statements implying criticism of the handling of the Air Forces by their Commander, Major General Lewis H. Brereton, in the Philippines at the beginning of the war, the implication being that through neglect or faulty judgment he failed to take proper security measures resulting in the destruction of his Air Force on the Ground. Such statements do grave injustice to this officer and his gallant subordinates. General Brereton had in the Philippines only a token force which, excluding trainers and hopelessly obsolete planes, comprised but 35 heavy bombers and 72 fighters. He was further greatly handicapped by lack of airdromes, there being only one in Luzon, Clark Field, that was usable by heavy bombers and only five usable by fighters. Many airdromes were under construction in the Philippines, but they were not completed and available on December 7. The entire command had been placed on a full war basis two weeks before the outbreak and had taken up defensive dispositions. Security and reconnaissance patrols had been flown regularly. Two of the 4 squadrons of heavy bombers were dispatched to Mindanao out of reach of enemy bombers but from where they would attack any target in the Philippine area and, by topping off at Clark Field, reach the limit of their range to the north. Forty-eight hours before the attack, the command was alerted. General Brereton, on December 6, informed his subordinate commanders that war was imminent and ordered all officers and combat crews to be ready for duty at all times. . . .

His tiny air force was crushed by sheer weight of numbers. Its combat crews fought valiantly but were hopelessly outnumbered. Due to the shortage of fighters and to the lack of dispersal fields, the bombers, the famous 19th Group, were withdrawn to Mindanao, and later, to Australia and Java where they were soon engrossed in the struggle for the Dutch East Indies and Australia. Back in the Philippines, our fighters, under the brilliant leadership of the late General H. H. George, maintained the unequal struggle with the greatest persistency and success, finally succumbing to inevitable attrition, their last memorable attack being on Subic Bay, March 2, when only four were available to strike.

The Air Forces in the Philippines planned carefully and executed valiantly. Any attempt to decry their record can spring only from a complete lack of knowledge of the facts involved.

The MacArthur detractors never ceased their attacks and continued pounding away on the charge that he had been guilty of some terrible neglect in command.

[A number of years after the events occurred General MacArthur was asked by Dr. Lewis Morton, distinguished army historian, to comment on certain decisions reached in regard to the Pacific strategy. One of these questions was: "Did Hq. USAFFE believe on 8 December, after it was learned that Pearl Harbor had been attacked but before the attack on Clark Field, that it had authority under existing directives and war plans to attack (by air) Japanese territory or was it believed that action should be deferred until the Japanese made the first 'overt' move?" General MacArthur wrote out the following answer:

My orders were explicit not to initiate hostilities against the Japanese. The Philippines while a possession of the U. S. had, so far as war was concerned, a somewhat indeterminate international position in many minds, especially the Filipinos and their government. While I personally had not the slightest doubt we would be attacked great local hope existed that this would not be the case. Instructions from Washington were very definite to wait until the Japanese made the first 'overt' move. Even without such a directive, practical limitations made it unfeasible to take the offensive. The only possibility lay in striking from the air but the relative weakness of our air force precluded any chance of success for such an operation. Our only aggressive potential consisted of about thirty-six B-17s. Their only possible target was the enemy's fields on Formosa. Our advance fields in Luzon were still incomplete and our fighters from our other fields in Luzon were too far away from Formosa to protect our bombers in a Formosa attack. They did not have the necessary radius of action. The enemy's air force based on excellent fields outnumbered ours many times. In addition, he had a mobile force on carriers which we entirely lacked. Our basic mission directive had confined our operations to our own national waters so no outside reconnaissance had been possible. The exact location of enemy targets was therefore not known. Our air force was in process of integration, radar defenses not yet operative and personnel raw and inexperienced. An attack under such conditions would have been doomed to total failure. As a matter of fact, I had for safety reasons ordered the bombers to withdraw from Luzon to Mindanao to be out of enemy range. This was in process of accomplishment when the enemy's air attacked. I did not know it at the time, but later understood that General Brereton had suggested to the Chief of Staff, General Sutherland, that we should initiate operations by an attempted "strike" at Formosa. Had such a suggestion been made to me, I would have unequivocally disapproved. In my opinion it would have been suicidal as well as in direct defiance of my basic directive.]

2

With ruthless efficiency the Japanese war machine drove southward through the South China Sea. The concentrations of planes, ships and ground forces in the ports of Formosa, lower China and Indo-China that had been steadily growing now turned into deadly fighting outfits. Proud Hong Kong was the first point to fall, the British garrison crumpling before the enemy attacks and surrendering within one week after war began. Five hours before the Japanese bombers first cut through the Philippine skies, a heavy aerial offensive struck at British dromes on Singapore Island, with serious damages to planes and installations. The sun had barely come up when another strong force attacked British airfields in North Malaya. Everywhere the results were the same; planes were destroyed on the fields, and installations were ruined. Within three days British air strength in Upper Malaya was a thing of the past; 80% of the defending planes had been destroyed, many of them burned on the ground—proving once more that there can be no second-best air force.

MacArthur followed the disastrous news as it trickled in to him. There was cause for grimness in the report of the sinking of the battleships *Prince of Wales* and *Repulse* 50 miles off the Malayan coast on December 10. Within two hours the only two Allied battleships in the whole Western Pacific and in the seas of Southeastern Asia had gone to the bottom.

Meanwhile the Japanese continued the systematic bombing

of the naval installations at Cavite and Manila Bay and the deliberate destruction of what still remained of MacArthur's tiny air force. Admiral Hart had kept back in Manila Bay 3 of his 14 over-age destroyers, a small number of his 37 submarines, and all 6 of his swift PT boats. A number of merchant ships were still in the bay, but so eager were the Japanese to eliminate the few fighter planes that had survived their initial assaults that they did not bother to bomb the vessels, and only one or two did not escape. Within a few days only a handful of pursuit planes remained on Luzon. In order to prevent the overwhelming Jap Air Force from destroying the remaining 15 B-17 bombers and the dozen long-range naval patrol planes still on Mindanao, they were ordered on December 15 to Australia and the Dutch East Indies.

Two days after the war began successful Japanese landings were made at Aparri in the extreme north in Luzon and at Vigan on the northwestern shoreline. Soon Jap fighters were operating out of the Aparri area. On December 12, landings were made at Legaspi at the southeastern end of Luzon. MacArthur recognized all these as only preliminary moves and not the real invasion.

He refused to be drawn into the trap of being thrown off balance and disrupting his plans by sending the bulk of his ground forces to the far northern coastal points and thus weakening his defenses along Lingayen Gulf. Both he and General Wainwright were confident the main landings would take place there. Ten days later some 80 Japanese ships of all kinds dropped anchor in the gulf. The landings were bitterly opposed, but there could be no doubt about the outcome.

MacArthur's air force by this time had been almost completely destroyed. All but a token force of the Navy had been dispatched to other waters and to other distant causes. Fewer submarines than you could count on one hand, and little more than that number of planes were left to face the mighty Japanese landing force, covered by carrier-based fighter planes and a fleet of warships. No real attempt at landing was made until the enemy had been assured that virtually no air or sea force was left to oppose him.

General Wainwright at Lingayen Gulf had his orders. He

was to fight a stubborn delaying action, but he was to take no chances of having his forces enveloped and destroyed. Quickly the pattern of defense developed, once it was evident that he was unable to deny the landing beaches to the Japanese at Lingayen. Already the enemy forces from Vigan had marched south and, joining up with the main invasion group at Lingayen, begun the great drive down the 40-mile-wide Central Valley toward Manila.

Numerous streams cut across the main north-south roads, and before each river crossing the bridge roadblocks were set up by Hugh Casey's band of engineers and demolition teams. When the advancing Japanese patrols were checked, enemy tanks and guns would be brought up to blast out the defenders, Wainwright's men would slowly give way, and Casey's dynamiters would blow the bridges.

Five well-placed lines of defense were laid out across the Central Valley long before the actual landings. Here strong efforts were made to hold up the enemy advances. The delaying operations would be repeated again and again. Stand and fight; slip back and dynamite. Each main withdrawal required an exactness of timing that ordinarily would not have been attempted with other than experienced troops. Full regiments and even larger bodies were at times engaged, but the fundamental defense tactics were to hold until the last possible hour, never permit the advancing enemy to infiltrate through the flanks and then double-envelop. For the most part it produced effective delay, despite the stark fact that the Philippine National Army was made up of poorly armed and only partially trained troops. MacArthur and his officers and men were now paying a terrible price for the neglect and unconcern that had long been handed out to them by a Washington absorbed with European affairs.

Far to the south below Manila the attenuated Philippine-American groups were forced to give way quickly behind the landing beaches on Lamon Bay. Sudden panic was thrown into the defenders when a fairly heavy landing was made to the north of Legaspi. Using his two well-trained constabulary regiments and self-propelled guns as the core of his resistance, Major General George M. Parker fought hard to stem the tide of

230

The fighting on Luzon and the side-slip into Bataan.

Japanese, while the rest of his three southern divisions withdrew northward through Manila. These included his forces on the western shore of Batangas on the China Sea. To avoid capture they must race through Manila, then try to cross the twin Calumpit bridges. Once over the bridges they could side-slip westward into the rugged fastness of Bataan peninsula. At best it was a desperate gamble.

But it proved to be a perfectly executed withdrawal by these southern divisions. Above the city and the key bridges the North Luzon forces under Wainwright fought a stubborn holding operation which gave the soldiers southward the days and hours they needed. The national Filipino troops, poorly trained and armed, battled valiantly beside their more experienced comrades.

The British forces in Malaya were facing the same problem, but their judgment in dealing with it was an entirely different story. In their desire to block the Japanese drive southward toward the impregnable base of Singapore, the British commanders became victims of a hopeful philosophy of jungle security which was disastrous for them.

The British had relied on the adverse weather. No enemy landings on Malaya, they reasoned, could be made during the monsoon season. And if the Japanese did land, they insisted, they could not penetrate the jungle in force.

But the specially trained and equipped Japanese battalions infiltrated the tropical forests and deadly swamps, slipped and slithered around the British strong points and finally overwhelmed them in a deadly double envelopment. Thus the jungle-and-monsoon complex proved as costly to the British as their Singapore complex which considered the island bastion invulnerable. When the terrible test came Singapore's great guns pointed helplessly toward the sea, while the air above it immediately became Japanese territory, and soon the ground approaches from the north fell into enemy hands.

The over-all Japanese strategy was now clear. The Philippines were surrounded on three sides by strong enemy air and sea bases; to the north lay Formosa; on the west across the South China Sea were enemy concentrations in Indo-China

232

and on the Chinese mainland; and to the east in the Pacific were the Palau Islands, the Marianas and the great island fortress of Truk in the Carolines, all in Japanese hands. Below lay the loot worthy of a war.

No longer was there any reality in the former hopes of MacArthur or of the imaginative minds in the War Plans Division in Washington that bombers based in the Philippines and aided by submarines could cut the water route through the South China Sea and deny the Japanese the oil and supplies that could power their war machine.

Everywhere MacArthur was on the defensive and fighting for his life. The news that all eight of the heavy battleships, with two cruisers and several destroyers of the U. S. Pacific fleet, had either been sunk in the shallow, muddy bottom of Pearl Harbor or put out of action in the first hour or two of the attack gave the Washington crowd the excuse to maintain secretly that the Philippines must now be left to their fate. In the Pacific there were still three great aircraft carriers and their accompanying swift cruisers and destroyers and submarines. In the Atlantic there were three more American carriers and a fleet of battleships, with two of the newest and most powerful battleships in the world. As late as March 1941 this Atlantic fleet had been augmented by three battleships, four light cruisers and eighteen destroyers from the Pacific fleet based at Pearl Harbor.

Yet no amount of realism or common sense could keep MacArthur, Quezón and the men around them from feeling that, by some magic, real help might still be sent the 20,000 and more American soldiers, marines and naval personnel and their 100,000 Filipino comrades fighting with their backs to the wall. Britain was not in immediate danger. Germany and Russia were locked in a death struggle. Only here in the Philippines were Americans fighting, and only here was there a definite pledged national obligation backed by more than 40 years of mutual trust and endeavor.

3

One of the first steps taken by General George Marshall in response to the challenging situation came five days after the Pearl Harbor disaster, when he ordered Brigadier General Eisenhower to report immediately to Washington from San Antonio, Texas. During the Texas-Louisiana maneuvers, Eisenhower had made a brilliant record as chief of staff of General Walter Krueger's Third Army. And now in a twenty-minute talk Marshall laid out the broad background of the American war plans as they fitted into the disastrous upset resulting from Japan's attack on Pearl.

Long before this tragic debacle of December 7 Marshall had been won over completely to Roosevelt's philosophy that the first and commanding demand on America was to help check Hitler's drive in Russia, thus keeping the Soviets in the war, and at the same time to go to the aid of Britain and her endangered empire. It was immediately necessary, however, to try to convince the American public that everything possible was being done for the relief of their own soldiers and their Filipino comrades in the Philippines.

The administration and the armed services consequently must at least go through the motions of trying to get help to MacArthur, whose brave stand against great odds had almost overnight made him a world hero. At the same time it was expedient for them to build up this fighting figure, if for no other reason than to shift the growing criticism away from the Pearl Harbor disaster.

Eisenhower was sent for because his four years as chief of staff of the Philippine military mission had presumably given him a background of the entire Far Eastern situation. Marshall ended his short conference with the blunt question, "What should be our general line of action?"

Eisenhower asked for a few hours to ponder the problem. Ten thousand miles away doom was closing down on the chief under whom he had served seven years. Here at hand, however, was General Marshall, who probably would be the dominant military figure in the global struggle that lay ahead, and who, as Army Chief of Staff, held a position of almost unlimited authority. To fathom precisely just what lay in his senior officer's mind was a rare ability possessed by temporary Brigadier General Eisenhower. In this particular case he had only to translate into a plausible military plan his surmises of what General Marshall wanted. This was a fairly simple task for the experienced staff officer, who knew that the accepted over-all strategy was to bend every immediate effort to defeat Hitler, and later to settle with Japan.

No such harsh word as "abandonment" was used by Eisenhower when he reported back to the Chief of Staff. Since the Navy refused to sponsor any sea or air guarantee, obviously no real rescue or relief could be attempted. At present there could be little more done than to hire adventurous old tramp ships in Australia and the East Indies to try to run the Japanese blockade and land supplies.

Australia, he held, must quickly be built up as a great base of operations for the future, and the sea lane from the States protected by swiftly built Southern Pacific island bases. MacArthur and his American and Filipino soldiers, with thousands of American civilians and a nation of 17,000,000 still under the legal and moral protection of the United States, must for the present be sacrificed to what was accepted in Washington as the larger needs of Europe and North Africa, the Middle East and India and the demands of Russia. In a gesture of complete agreement Marshall turned from Eisenhower's verbal report with the order, "Do your best to save them."

No one will ever be quite able to estimate accurately how much could have been done in aiding the Philippines if there had been a stubborn will-to-win. Formal cables signed by Marshall indicate that there was much urging from the Chief of Staff's office to American army officers in Australia and the Dutch Islands to bribe and bully ship captains and crews to undertake the perilous attempt to run the Japanese blockade and take supply ships to the Philippines. The able and driving Patrick J. Hurley, one-time Secretary of War, now commissioned a reserve brigadier general, flew to Australia to attempt to push through the blockade-running; and Colonel John A. Robenson was sent on north to Java with a suitcase full of American currency. But it was too late.

No words by Marshall could change the basic responsibility for the tragedy of unpreparedness that he had allowed to develop in the Philippines. The very hectic and extravagant effort now being made obviously came when it was too late for anything but the most desperate and all-out attempt at relief. Even a real effort might have failed to do much more than hearten and build up the morale of the helpless and beleaguered force, but that at least would have been important in offsetting the mood of abandonment that had captured the men.

MacArthur on Corregidor repeatedly argued with Washington that the enemy's sea blockade was thin and penetrable, and that a supreme effort should be made to push blockade-runners directly across the Pacific. All that might have been attempted by Washington certainly was not being done, granted that the risks were very great.

All told, six submarines were to reach Corregidor, the first, the *Seawolf,* appearing at dawn of January 30, 1942, with 27 tons of much-needed .50-caliber and 75-mm. ammunition. Later two more subs brought in ammunition and two others carried food supplies—but only one of the two was able to land its cargo.

In all only three cargo ships ever reached the Philippines. The *Coast Farmer* left Brisbane in middle February and landed its 3,000 tons of rations and a large amount of ammunition at Anakan in Gingoog Bay on the north coast of Mindanao. On March 6 the *Dona Nati* arrived at Cebu in the central islands with 5,000 tons of rations and considerable ammunition and medical supplies. Eleven days later the *Anhui,* a smaller ship, docked at Cebu with supplies, and four crated P-40s lashed on her deck. These P-40s were to fly and to fight in the last wild days of resistance.

Of the grand total of 10,500 tons unloaded from the three ships, only 1,100 tons were ever to reach Corregidor or Bataan.

Even before MacArthur realized how insignificant the amount of supplies to reach him would actually be, he dispatched a message to Washington pleading that help be sent him directly from the West Coast of America. His message to the Chief of Staff on February 22, 1942, proved how desperate was the need for help. One paragraph read:

> Nowhere is the situation more desperate and dangerous than here. . . . The quantities [of supplies] involved are not great but it is imperative that they be made instantly available in the United States and that the entire impulse and organization be reenergized and controlled directly by you. If it is left as a subsidiary effort it will never be accomplished.

The last sentence of this dispatch hinted at the truth behind the failure.

Everything that had to do with the official Washington attitude regarding any serious and determined aid for the Americans and their comrades in the Islands was "a subsidiary effort."

No one probably will ever be able to judge accurately what the result would have been had the swift new American battleships and the three great air carriers and their cruiser and destroyer escorts in the Atlantic joined with the four carriers and their escorts and the numerous submarines remaining in the Pacific and sallied forth at the proper moment and under the right conditions to challenge the Japanese fleet and clear the way to Manila Bay.

The best naval advice available was that even the combined fleets, fired with the unconquerable fighting spirit of the U. S. Navy, would have been taking the greatest possible risks in boldly facing the Japanese fleet in a battle area of Japan's own choosing, and with the American armada 5,000 and more miles away from its bases. Even with the advantage of having cracked the Japanese codes, the result might have been utterly disastrous to the Americans.

But it is probable that the top-level decision against making any such brave effort at relief had long before been reached by the White House, with little regard for purely naval or military advice. The Atlantic war came first in every consideration. The pleas and pressure by Churchill far outweighed those by MacArthur. Hitler must be defeated first, even if it were necessary to abandon all the pledges and the honor involved in protecting the Philippines and the doomed men trapped there. It had been so resolved for almost a year before the actual shooting war began. The easing of the conscience of those American leaders responsible had long ago been accomplished. Only the public had yet to be fooled.

On April 23, 1944, Admiral Ernest J. King, who succeeded Admiral Stark as Commander-in-Chief, United States Fleet, wrote in his First Report to the Secretary of the Navy the following comment:

> The sudden treacherous attack by Japan, which resulted in heavy losses to us, made our unfavorable strategic position at the outbreak of the war even worse than we had anticipated. Had we not suffered those losses, however, our fleet could not have proceeded to Manila as many people supposed and there relieved our hard pressed forces. Such an undertaking at that time, with the means at hand to carry it out and support it, would have been disastrous.

4

During the late December days the swiftly moving drama that centered at the two key Calumpit bridges over the Pampanga river north of Manila absorbed the energy and the hours, day and night, of MacArthur and his field commanders. The retreating Filipino regiments in lower Luzon, using their commandeered motor transport and their rolling trains and guns, streamed through Manila and on to the north. By sturdy delaying tactics they had held back the enemy columns coming up from the south below Manila, while Wainwright's troops blocked the Japanese advancing down the Central Valley. On several occasions near panic seized the partially trained units in the north, but skillful leadership kept the half-armed and inexperienced defenders from being enveloped and the whole plan of withdrawal from collapsing.

Only a few of the South Luzon force remained below the twin bridges over the Pampanga river when on December 30 orders came to block an enemy breakthrough on the right flank and above the key structures at all cost. Swampy ground gave a certain protection, and with the self-propelled artillery and a battalion of tanks that MacArthur ordered up a day or two before, the Japanese were held.

All during the early part of the night of New Year's Eve final truckloads of troops and supplies from the south rumbled across the bridges and moved along the jammed highways toward the green doorway into Bataan. Quietly the last defending battalion slipped back over the long steel structures. Dawn was just breaking on the new year of 1942, and the Japanese outpost was cautiously feeling its way forward, when Casey's dynamiters slammed down their electric switches and the great friendly bridges were no more.

MacArthur's split-second timing had won. But there was still the terrifying threat that the Japanese would bomb the crowded roads that led to Bataan and that a fresh holocaust would scream down on the columns of men and supplies. It seemed almost unbelievable that the prowling enemy air force, complete masters of the sky, had not long before bombed the Calumpit bridges and the roads from Manila, but so absorbed had they been in destroying the last few planes MacArthur had that they had missed this chance to cripple him irreparably.

On the first day of the new year MacArthur at least had the satisfaction of knowing that his great side-slip into Bataan would be successful. For one reason or another, he had been unable to concentrate all his military and medical supplies and all the food that was available into the mountain fastness; but he had largely kept his troops intact and there had been time for him to construct trenches and strong points in the upper end of the heavy wooded and mountainous area. The fact that he was short in certain types of ammunition, particularly for his anti-aircraft guns, was not his fault. Washington simply had failed to supply him. This was even more seriously true in regard to Corregidor. It was long kept a whispered secret that months before Pearl Harbor MacArthur had been forced to ship the greater part of his .50-caliber ammunition to the British at Singapore. Most of it, however, had been replaced.

One disturbing fact was apparent to him. Along with the Philippine soldiers and their American comrades, who numbered a total of 80,000, there had slipped through the Bataan entrance 26,000 Filipino civilians. This meant that he now would have a certain amount of local supplies used up in feeding civilians whom he had not figured on. Long before the agonizing end of the Bataan campaign this would prove an important factor contributing to the final disaster.

5

The retreating troops of the South Luzon force were just beginning to withdraw northward through Manila when MacArthur, with the approval of President Quezón, decided that he should officially abandon Manila, declare it an open city and thus save it from almost certain aerial destruction. On December 24 he sent Lt. Colonel Sidney Huff, his former naval advisor on the staff of the military mission and now his senior aide, to inform the president and High Commissioner Sayre that it was time to move the official government to Corregidor.

Jean MacArthur hurriedly packed a few necessities for the four members of her immediate household. On Christmas Eve as she prepared to leave the penthouse with all its treasures in books and trophies his father and mother had left the General, she passed a tall, beautifully carved cabinet that contained the many decorations awarded her husband during the 45 years since the first little gold medal had been given him as a lad of 17 at the Texas Military Academy in San Antonio. Quickly she opened one of her suitcases, discarded one or two garments and then, spreading a bath towel on the floor, removed the medals from their cases and wrapped them in a tight bundle. In one of the General's suitcases were two or three photographs of his father and mother. Nothing else in the apartment was taken with them.

The swift twilight of the tropics had fallen over Manila when the party gathered at the landing dock and slipped aboard the little boat that would undertake the 30-mile trip to Corregidor. That afternoon the General had his final talk with Admiral Hart, who had come in on a submarine for this last conference. The two men had not seen eye to eye; there had been many differences between them.

All communications with Washington were in the hands of

240

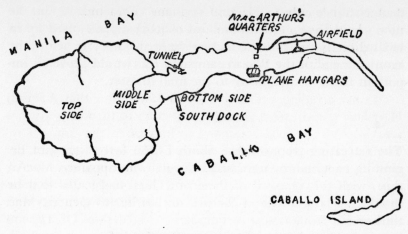

Corregidor Island—last to fall in Luzon.

the Navy and its wireless station on Corregidor. Rear Admiral Francis Rockwell was to remain in command of such naval forces and installations as were not removed or destroyed. These included the experienced 4th Regiment of Marines and some hundreds of enlisted naval men who had been at Cavite and would soon arrive on Corregidor. Hart left on Christmas Day, leaving behind 3 gunboats, 3 minesweepers, 6 motor torpedo boats and a few odds and ends of tugs and yachts. By January 31 all the few remaining submarines had left Philippine waters.

It was a bitter realization for MacArthur that even in the narrow confines of Manila Bay and the fortress of Corregidor and the battlefields of Bataan, he had not the authority of a unified command. He had no formal jurisdiction whatever over the badly needed Marines or the ground naval force. Apparently he was dependent upon the friendship and good will of Admiral Rockwell. Fortunately Rockwell was younger and far more amenable and cooperative than the critical and exacting Hart.

As the two men stood to say good-bye on the day before Christmas, Admiral Hart made no mention of any change in the chain of command regarding his naval and marine forces still in the Philippines. As days and weeks went on and the desperate struggle to hold Manila Bay grew in intensity, Mac-

241

Arthur felt keenly the lack of supreme command, so that he might have the considerable naval contingent and the 4th Marines directly under his orders. Finally in late January he remonstrated with the War Department on the unreasonable situation.

At once a radiogram came back to MacArthur that Admiral Hart had been instructed on December 17 to turn over all that remained of his naval command to him when the Admiral relinquished personal control. General MacArthur showed the new instructions to Admiral Rockwell, who apparently either was completely ignorant of them or at least had made no mention of any knowledge of the previous orders to General MacArthur.

When Hart left on Christmas Eve he informed the commander of the 4th Marines, Colonel Samuel L. Howard, whose outfit was then at Olongapo at the northern end of the Bataan peninsula, that he was now under the tactical employment of the Army. Colonel Howard at once reported to MacArthur and Sutherland and was requested to take his regiment to Corregidor and integrate it into the beach defenses of the fortress. On December 29 he was officially designated as commander of all shore defenses. Eventually Howard's total beach force numbered more than 4,000 men, of whom 1,352 were marines.

Both the 4th Marines and the ground naval forces had their own independent supply and medical setups on Corregidor. Not until sometime in February, when orders came from Washington making clear that MacArthur was in full command of all forces in the Philippines, was the Navy and Marine personnel subjected to the 50% reduction in rations that was the lot of the Army people. They had their own food, clothing and medical depots and rigidly controlled them. With unified command, however, MacArthur pooled all the resources, and from then on the Navy and Marine files shared equally with the Army men.

Never did MacArthur make an effort to try to discover who was actually to blame for the confused situation.

[In the list of questions asked General MacArthur some years after the war was one that read: "Upon what considera-

242

tion and on what contemporary information was the decision to withdraw to Bataan made on December 24, 1941, based?" MacArthur's formal reply was as follows:

My concept for the initial defense of the Philippine Islands was to defeat the enemy on the beaches where he would be at his weakest in any attempted amphibious landings. There were three possible areas in Luzon for such landings—north, south and of much lesser expanse, southeast. My forces were meager, poorly equipped and only partially trained. I deployed the I Corps in the north under General Wainwright, the II Corps to the south under General Jones and local Philippine forces to the southeast. The I Corps was unable to prevent the enemy from securing beachheads in the north and was being gradually forced back from one defensive line to another. No major attack had developed on the south line but reports reached me about midnight that a landing had been made in the southeast and our forces there were unable to hold the enemy who was driving rapidly west toward Manila. This would have split the II Corps from the I, divided my forces and subjected them to destruction in detail. I immediately ordered Jones to withdraw by forced marches from the south to Bataan through Manila, and Wainwright to temporarily stand in the north and at all cost to hold clear the road nets leading to Bataan until the II Corps could take position there and our base of supplies be moved from Manila to Mariveles and Corregidor. When these moves had been successfully accomplished, I evacuated Manila and declared it an open city to save it from destruction. This decision and its brilliant implementation by the field commanders involved made possible the months of delay to the Japanese advance caused by the sieges of Bataan and Corregidor. I have always regarded it as the not only most vital decision of the Philippine Campaign but in its corollary consequences one of the most decisive of the war. This view was confirmed later from the Japanese records. Imperial Japanese Headquarters stated, "It was a great strategic move. The Japanese 14th Army Headquarters . . . never planned for or expected a withdrawal to Bataan. The decisive battle had been expected in Manila. The Japanese commanders could not adjust to the new situation." And politically it stood as a symbol— there was a spiritual influence exerted by the American resistance on Bataan.]

6

While the MacArthur forces in the north of Luzon were fighting their great delaying action and the plan to leave doomed Manila for the Rock had been decided on, history-making events were occurring in Washington. On December 23 Prime Minister Churchill and a retinue of 87 of his highest naval, army and air advisors and war chiefs slipped into the Capital. Churchill was the guest of the President at the White House, and most of the officers were entertained at the British Embassy.

Long ago, even before Pearl Harbor, there had been general agreement that the first and commanding job was to win the war against Hitler. The coldest Russian winter in years had suddenly proved to be a sturdy ally of the Soviets. A million German soldiers already were bogged down in the heavy snows outside the Red capital, and there was now a growing hope that the Russians might hold on, certainly until the following spring. But to the south another conquering German force had already taken Odessa, and the Black Sea was no longer secure.

It took little effort apparently for the persuasive Churchill and his visiting staff to transfer many of their own most pressing problems of the global war, mainly including the exigencies of the British Empire, into the hands of the American war leaders. It was simple for them to prove that the Japanese war must wait, but the threat toward India must be met and checked by way of the Middle East and Europe rather than from the Pacific.

Sooner or later, they argued, the Japanese would overextend themselves. The farther from their home bases the outposts of their conquests extended, the more vulnerable they would ultimately become to a final combined attack by the victorious Allies—once Hitler was crushed. British arguments stressed the ideas to those sitting around the long conference table that there was no doubt that the Philippines were lost, in all probability Malaya, Singapore and the Dutch East Indies were doomed, and even Australia faced grave danger of invasion. But once Europe and Britain were saved, all that had fallen to the enemy in the Far East would be reclaimed and

Japan would be driven back to her tiny islands. American power and British cunning could easily turn the trick.

Then suddenly a release in Melbourne, Australia, shook the war planners almost off their comfortable seats in distant Washington. The morning of December 28 the powerful Melbourne *Herald* carried an article by the Labor Prime Minister, John Curtin.

> I make it clear that Australia looks to America, free from any pangs about our traditional links of friendship to Britain.
>
> We know Britain's problems. We know her constant threat of invasion. We know the dangers of dispersing strength—but we know that Australia can go and Britain still hang on.
>
> We are determined that Australia shall not go. We shall exert our energy towards shaping a plan, with the United States as its keystone, giving our country confidence and ability to hold out until the tide of battle swings against the enemy.
>
> We refuse to accept the dictum that the Pacific struggle is a subordinate segment of the general conflict. The Government regards the Pacific struggle as primarily one in which the United States and Australia should have the fullest say in the direction of the fighting plan.

So at last the disheartened men drawing back into Bataan and Corregidor, the abandoned troops, sailors and airmen in Malaya and at Singapore and through the Dutch Islands and on below to Australia and New Zealand had a champion who dared to oppose the complacent planners in Washington. Obviously these experts were too concerned with Hitler to be able to see clearly beyond the Urals or the eastern shores of the Arabian Sea or on to the west of Pearl Harbor. John Curtin along with Richard Casey, the Australian Minister to the United States, suddenly became men to be reckoned with.

Churchill and Roosevelt immediately took time out from their European and Middle East war games to lower their sights toward the discouraged victims of Japanese aggression. The British Premier sent a friendly and encouraging message to Curtin, and then at a White House press conference asserted that, while a military alliance between Australia and the United States was inevitable because of their geographic situation, he looked for no weakening of the Dominion's link with Britain.

President Roosevelt at once dispatched a long message to Quezón in which he said:

> The people of the United States will never forget what the people of the Philippine Islands are doing this day and will do in days to come. I give to the people of the Philippines my solemn pledge that their freedom will be redeemed and their independence established and protected.
>
> The entire resources, in men and materiél, of the United States stand behind that pledge.

7

Working on MacArthur's staff as a member of the press section was an energetic and patriotic Filipino newspaper editor, Carlos Romulo. Once MacArthur was established on Corregidor, engineers managed to set up a small broadcasting station called The Voice of Freedom, and daily Major Romulo poured out inspiring messages to the troops on Bataan and the people over Luzon.

This latest pledge from the President of the United States was broadcast more than once, but somehow its vague implication of help was translated into signs and portents that had no basis in reality. Together with a later statement by President Roosevelt, it became the basis for a mythical assurance that shortly aid would come by sky and sea.

Meanwhile on Bataan the long ordeal of hunger and fever, of wounds and death, gripped the beleaguered peninsula. The thousands of civilian refugees complicated more and more the food situation and almost at once the garrison was put on half rations. Later this amount was again cut, so that instead of receiving even 1,500 calories daily the amount was reduced to little more than half. Somehow the supplies must be made to hold out over a period of four to six months, by which time relief would surely come.

Cutting north and south through the center of Bataan ran an irregular chain of wooded mountains dividing the 25-by-15 mile defense area in the peninsula into east and west zones. A

246

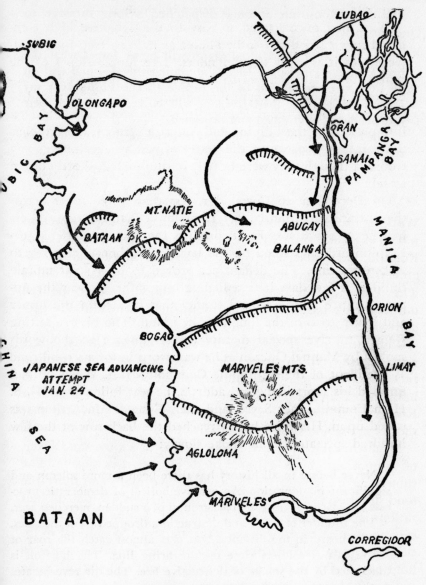

The defense lines on Bataan.

corps command was established on each flank of the central chain, and the General Headquarters reserve was placed so that help could be hurried to either battlefield.

What had once looked so easy to the Japanese high command now turned out to be almost as much a trap for the attackers as it was for the defenders. The jungle slopes of the central mountains offered to the Japanese a prospect for infiltration, but time and again those enemy units that managed to penetrate behind the defensive lines were stopped and driven into pockets by the Filipino and American troops. Nevertheless the constant pressure of the better armed and trained enemy troops, although they were heavily outnumbered, shortly began to tell.

On December 26 Corregidor, less than three miles across the entrance to Manila Bay from lower Bataan, received its first heavy air attack. For two hours the General and his two Filipino orderlies stood on the lawn of his house, refusing to seek protection. The defiant act proved to be a great morale builder. A few days later a little group gathered near the upper entrance to the central tunnel that connected the upper and lower areas of the long narrow island. The bizarre setting seemed to give special dignity and eloquence to the words spoken by Manuel Quezón as he was sworn in for a second time as President of the Philippine Commonwealth. When he had finished his short inaugural address, he was followed by U. S. High Commissioner Sayre, and then General MacArthur was called upon. His voice barely reached the back row of the few hundred spectators as he spoke slowly:

> Never before in all history has there been a more solemn and significant inauguration. An act, symbolical of democratic processes, is placed against the background of a sudden, merciless war.
>
> The thunder of death and destruction, dropped from the skies, can be heard in the distance. Our ears almost catch the roar of battle as our soldiers close on the firing line. The horizon is blackened by the smoke of destructive fire. The air reverberates to the roar of exploding bombs.
>
> Such is the bed of birth of this new government, of this new nation. For four hundred years the Philippines have struggled upward towards self-government. Just at the end of its tuitionary

period, just on the threshold of independence, came the great hour of decision. There was no hesitation, no vacillation, no moment of doubt. The whole country followed its great leader in choosing the side of freedom against the side of slavery.

We have just inaugurated him, we have just thereby confirmed his momentous decision. Hand in hand with the United States and the other free nations of the world, this basic and fundamental issue will be fought through to victory. Come what may, ultimate triumph will be its reward.

Through this its gasping agony of travail, through what Winston Churchill called "blood and sweat and tears," from the grim shadow of the Valley of Death, oh merciful God, preserve this noble race.

8

The month of January seemed interminable to the men on Bataan and Corregidor. In the green jungles of the peninsula malaria and tropical diseases accounted for the death and incapacity of far more men than the fire of the Japanese. With rations reduced more than one-half, most of the troops on the Rock suffered the same disability from lack of food as those on Bataan, and there were frequent and sustained bombings of the fortress.

One of MacArthur's constant chores was to help sustain the ailing President Quezón. The foul air of the tunnel had brought on a recurrence of active tuberculosis, and he grew so weak that he could barely walk.

Back home the name of MacArthur was assuming tremendous popularity. Both the United States and the Allied world were in desperate need of a symbol of courage and stubborn fighting ability, and MacArthur filled the bill. Only in his military area were native forces doing their full share in a common defense, and only around Manila Bay were the Japanese invaders being checked and actually pushed back on their heels.

Despite the fact that Marshall and his associates were too absorbed in planning the destruction of Hitler to make any serious attempt to answer MacArthur's call for help, there were many reasons why the only senior American general who was actually fighting should not be sacrificed. On February 2 a radiogram signed by Marshall, but probably written by Eisenhower, inquired about MacArthur's plans for his wife and young son. Two days later a second wireless from Washington announced that serious study was being made regarding the removal of civilian officials from the Rock.

For the first time Marshall outlined the possibility of MacArthur being sent to Australia to assume command of army forces being gathered there. The other alternative was that he might be ordered to Mindanao, where the length of his service would depend on the success of cargo ships in running the Japanese blockade and the efficiency of the guerilla operations. His views were requested.

MacArthur's resentment at his suggested removal from his troops at the moment of their greatest need for him was far from placated by a paragraph in the Marshall cable that read:

> It is understood that in case your withdrawal from immediate leadership of your beleaguered forces is to be carried out, it will be by direct order of the President to you.

[MacArthur had no way of knowing that the phrase "by direct order of the President to you" had been included in the cable at the suggestion of Colonel J. Munroe Johnson, former commander of the 117th Engineers, of the Rainbow Division of World War I, and an old friend of the General's. The colonel had explained to Roosevelt that he was positive that MacArthur would not obey orders for his withdrawal if they came from the War Department alone, but that it would take a direct command from the President as Commander-in-Chief.]

A few days before the last messages were sent to MacArthur, Quezón on Corregidor, plagued by statements made by General Aguinaldo in Manila and by an offer of the Japanese Prime Minister to grant the Philippines their full independence, formally transmitted a message to General MacArthur which was, of course, intended ultimately for President Roosevelt. The questions Quezón asked showed the desperate mood that now gripped him:

> We decided to fight by your side and we have done our best and we are still doing as much as could be expected from us under the circumstances. But how long are we going to be left

250

alone? Has it already been decided in Washington that the Philippine front is of no importance as far as the final result of the war is concerned and that, therefore, no help can be expected here in the immediate future, or at least before the power of resistance is exhausted? If so, I want to know because I have my own responsibility to my countrymen whom, as President of the Commonwealth, I have led into a complete war effort. . . . It seems that Washington does not fully realize our situation nor the feelings which the apparent neglect of our safety and welfare have engendered in the hearts of our people here. . . .

The Roosevelt reply could hardly have deceived even the sick and distressed Quezón. One portion read:

Although I cannot at this time state the day that help will arrive in the Philippines, I can assure you that every vessel available is bearing to the Southwest Pacific the strength that will eventually crush the enemy and liberate your native land. . . .

A week went by and then in complete frustration Quezón evolved a fantastic plan of action that would have been completely foreign to him in anything bordering on normal times. On February 8 he called his Cabinet together on the Rock and read them a long dispatch that he contemplated sending the President of the United States through General MacArthur. Then he talked the matter over with High Commissioner Sayre and finally with the General. The result was that a radiogram was sent to the President, with attending remarks by both the High Commissioner and General MacArthur.

Quezón's proposal was no less than that the Philippines be immediately granted full independence by the United States, and that they then be neutralized by a formal agreement between Japan and the United States. All Filipino troops would be disbanded, and all fighting on the Islands would end.

The accompanying report of High Commissioner Sayre approved the proposal, "if the premise of President Quezón is correct that American help cannot or will not arrive here in time to be availing."

In forwarding the two messages General MacArthur added his own interpretation:

Since I have no air or sea protection you must be prepared at any time to figure on the complete destruction of this command. You must determine whether the mission of delay would be better furthered by the temporizing plan of Quezón's or by my continued battle effort. The temper of the Filipinos is one of almost violent resentment against the United States. Every one of them expected help and when it was not forthcoming they believe they have been betrayed in favor of others. . . . So far as the military angle is concerned, the problem presents itself as to whether the plan of President Quezón might offer the best possible solution of what is about to be a disastrous debacle. It would not affect the ultimate situation in the Philippines, for that would be determined by the results in other theatres. If the Japanese Government rejects President Quezón's proposition it would psychologically strengthen our hold because of their Prime Minister's statement offering independence. If it accepts it, we lose no military advantage because we would still secure at least equal delay. Please instruct me.

It was a desperate gamble that MacArthur was taking. He was certain that only some such shock as the messages from Quezón, Sayre and himself could shake the administration out of its mood of abandonment. His innate realism made clear to him the impracticability of the whole scheme, but he was willing to pay the cost of this final attempt to awaken Washington and possibly gain even slight help.

Certainly the President, Secretary of War Stimson and Chief of Staff Marshall were genuinely disturbed by the proposal. All three understood the delicacy of the situation, and they could not help but know the anguish and despair of the exhausted leaders on Corregidor and Bataan. Many hours of work went into President Roosevelt's cautious answer to Mac-Arthur:

My reply must emphatically deny the possibility of this Government's agreement to the political aspects of President Quezón's proposal. I authorize you to arrange for the capitulation of the Filipino elements of the defending forces, when and if in your opinion that course appears necessary and always having in mind that the Filipino troops are in the service of the United States. Details of all necessary arrangements will be left in your hands, including plans for segregation of forces and the withdrawal, if your judgment so dictates, of American elements to Fort Mills [Corregidor]. The timing also will be left to you.

American forces will continue to keep our flag flying in the Philippines so long as there remains any possibility of resistance. I have made these decisions in complete understanding of your military estimate that accompanied President Quezón's message to me. The duty and the necessity of resisting Japanese aggression to the last transcends in importance any other obligation now facing us in the Philippines. . . .

I therefore give you this most difficult mission in full understanding of the desperate nature to which you may shortly be reduced. The service that you and the American members of your command can render to your country in the titanic struggle now developing is beyond all possibility of appraisement. . . .

There then followed the suggestion that Mrs. Sayre and the MacArthur family be given the privilege of accompanying Quezón's official party to Australia by submarine and then on to the United States. Quezón tried to soften the blow to MacArthur's pride, but no words could ease his sense of humiliation. Then Quezón turned to the subject of Jean and Arthur accompanying him and his family, if and when they left.

The General sought Jean, and quietly they talked it over. The military situation was rapidly deteriorating, and there might not be another such favorable chance of escape for the two he loved so deeply. Jean must make the decision herself.

In a very real way it was the final test, the culmination of the oddly beautiful love story of this lonely man and this gracious and spirited woman, 20 years his junior. She must consider the little boy who in two weeks would be 4 years old.

"We have drunk from the same cup," she finally said. "We three shall stay together."

The General now reported back to the Filipino President, his own dear and loyal friend. When he had heard the decision, Quezón slowly shook his head. He was almost speechless from the impact of MacArthur's words.

"You are signing their death warrant, General," he whispered. But he sensed that this was neither the time nor the place for argument.

MacArthur wrote out his joint answer to Marshall's personal

inquiry of four days before and to this latest suggestion that his family leave. They would remain on Corregidor with him and "share the fate of the garrison." He would fight to destruction on Bataan, and then do the same on Corregidor.

"I have not the slightest intention in the world of surrendering or capitulating the Filipino forces of my command," he continued. "There has never been the slightest wavering among my troops."

The following day Marshall answered that he was concerned over the sentence that read that he and his family would "share the fate of the garrison." There was even a hint that there might be another assignment that would necessitate his being separated from his family under increased peril and great embarrassment.

In the same message was included an inquiry about anti-aircraft ammunition, and when MacArthur replied on February 15, he answered this specific inquiry but made no mention of the personal part of the communication.

It was a day of anxiety on the Rock and in the wooded hills of Bataan. On this day of February 15 the "impregnable" fortress of Singapore fell, and now the Japanese held Malaya and most of Borneo and the Celebes. The way was open to Sumatra and Java, and on to the south lay the prize of Australia.

Boldly MacArthur cabled Washington that there was still a chance for an attack on the extended Japanese sea lines of communication. The desperate situation still could be reversed if the Navy, with its powerful carrier force, was willing to take the risk.

At the moment MacArthur was not aware of the growing magic of his name. As early as February 5 the House of Representatives rang with speeches in his praise.

The professional politicians around the White House took note. With the Presidential elections still two and a half years away could it be that the far-sighted Republicans were grooming the new military hero as a candidate?

MacArthur, totally unaware of these happenings, kept a tight rein on the desperate fighting on Bataan. Returning from an inspection that took him to the forward command posts, he

254

found President Quezón worried over MacArthur's safety. He laughed off the President's words of caution and announced that he proposed soon to set up his own advance headquarters on Bataan.

Quezón was shocked. He earnestly cautioned MacArthur that should anything happen to him the whole defense would immediately collapse. The morale of the command, particularly of the Filipino troops, depended upon his well-being. Even the General, the President insisted, could not realize the depth of the devotion felt for him by the officers and soldiers of the Philippine Army. No longer did they look to America or even to President Roosevelt to save them and their country. It was to MacArthur alone that they turned.

MacArthur did his best to relieve the ailing leader of his concern, insisting in a light vein that the Japanese had not yet made the bullet with his name on it. But Quezón was not to be dissuaded. MacArthur's serious response that at times even the supreme commander must bolster morale by his own personal display of courage failed to win over the Filipino leader. Largely as a result of this pressure MacArthur made no more trips to Bataan, although its wooded areas were less open to accurate heavy bombing than the small and exposed Rock. As a result of this deference to the wishes of the weak and failing Quezón, MacArthur was subjected to endless attacks on his courage, some even by officers and men in sister services. The high point in calumny was reached in the coining of the bitter phrase "Dug-out Doug," so often to be repeated in Washington by the anti-MacArthur groups.

At the time and during the years to follow it has been difficult for his countrymen to understand the peculiar hold that MacArthur had not only on the people of the Philippines but on all the native races of Asia and the Western Pacific. Possibly it had to do with his inherent sympathy for their aspirations toward new national and social freedoms and for their revolt against the ancient imperialism of their former overlords. Such leaders as Quezón and Romulo were to give it expression in these perilous days of the invasion, and it was their confidence and urgings that inspired him to use his famous statement, "I shall return!"

The Quezón family and several high officials of his government left Corregidor by submarine late on the night of February 20. For several days there had been conferences going on in Washington between Richard Casey, the Australian Minister, and the British, Dutch and U. S. officials, with the result that the United States finally agreed to accept the major responsibility for the eastern half of the American-British-Dutch-Chinese areas. This included in particular the Dutch East Indies, Australia and her island approaches and, of course, the Philippines. The western portion of the vast area would still remain the responsibility of the British.

On February 21 an important Cabinet meeting was held in Canberra, Australia, at which it was decided to ask formally that General MacArthur be ordered to Australia at once and be given command of the area newly assigned to the United States. The same day General Marshall radioed MacArthur that President Roosevelt was considering the proposition of ordering him to Mindanao, where a base of operations for a relief force for Luzon might be set up if a successful allied air and naval counterattack from the Dutch East Indies materialized. Marshall's wire continued:

> The foregone considerations underlie the tentative decision of the President, but we are not sufficiently informed as to the situation and circumstances to be certain that the proposal meets the actual situation.

Prime Minister Curtin's spectacular demand for MacArthur had now reached the White House. Without waiting for MacArthur's answer to Marshall's message of the previous day, the President sent a personal radio message ordering him to proceed to Mindanao as quickly as possible, and as soon as he had stabilized defenses there, to go on to Australia.

It was the final blow that MacArthur's realism had felt must come sooner or later. He was now summarily ordered to leave his comrades in arms for a far more important assignment. He was not to be permitted the honor of sharing their fate.

He walked from his desk in the tunnel and slowly made his

256

way to the little house where Jean and Arthur stayed between bombing raids.

He felt physically exhausted from the helplessness of his situation. For the first time in his life it seemed that he must disobey a formal order, even though it be from the President of the United States. He would demand the right to stay with his troops and share their fate.

His quiet determination grew as he laid bare his thoughts to Jean. She had no word of admonition or advice. She could only steel his resolve.

Finally he sent his orderly for Dick Sutherland, his chief of staff.

[Some years later MacArthur described (to the author) the tragic decision he had to make: "I fully expected to be killed. I would never have surrendered. If necessary I would have sought the end in some final charge." He hesitated before he spoke again: "I suppose the law of averages was against my lasting much longer under any circumstances. I would probably have been killed in a bombing raid or by artillery fire. . . . And Jean and the boy might have been destroyed in some final general debacle."]

He showed Sutherland the decoded message from the President and bluntly explained that he could not leave his men. He started to write out his refusal to obey the order from his Commander-in-Chief.

But the impossibility of any such action was made clear to him. Had he not been assured that a great American force was rapidly being built up in Australia—a concentration of planes, tanks, ships and men? With this he could hurriedly mount a rescue command and return to the Islands. And there was the immediate alternative that he might ask for a postponement of his departure from Corregidor.

He delayed his final decision for two days. When it was evident that there was no other way out, he sent the President a reserved message of acceptance. He insisted that the failure to support the Philippines properly had created the difficult situation which he had been able to meet only because of the very special confidence the Filipino people and Army had in him. He explained frankly that his sudden departure might result in the collapse of the Filipino lines, and he asked that his departure be delayed until the psychological moment.

"Please be guided by me in this matter," he concluded. "I know the situation here in the Philippines and unless the right moment is chosen for the delicate operation a sudden collapse might result. . . . These people are depending upon me now; any idea that might develop in their minds that I was being withdrawn for any other reason than to bring them immediate relief could not be explained."

Two days later he received a message bearing Marshall's name: "Your No. 358 has been carefully considered by the President. He has directed that full decision as to timing of your departure and details of method be left in your hands."

MacArthur radioed that the arrangements were satisfactory. For some reason not understood at the time, Japanese pressure on the battle lines in Bataan had lessened, and probing efforts by American and Filipino troops had disclosed that portions of a crack division of Japanese troops had been withdrawn from the Islands, and that the enemy line at the moment was only thinly held. This might mean that the enemy was pulling back in preparation for a major attack. But if such an attack did not materialize, MacArthur radioed that "we may be approaching the stalemate of positional warfare."

[After the war was over the facts came out: The enemy was re-grouping his forces and waiting for siege guns to arrive from the Hong Kong area. During this time of temporizing, MacArthur even considered the possibility of a break-through from Bataan to the Zambales mountains of western Luzon, where his liberated forces might continue an intensive guerilla operation.]

Ten days after the message ordering his withdrawal, Marshall jogged him with the word that conditions in Australia made urgent his early arrival there. In a previous radio he had been informed that the British-American Combined Chiefs of Staff had ordered Field Marshall Wavell to dissolve his staff and turn the command of operations over to the Netherlands authorities. But MacArthur would not be under this jurisdiction, and he was to continue to communicate directly with the War Department.

258

[A sidelight of some importance appeared a number of years later when the forceful Patrick J. Hurley told of a singular talk he had had with Field Marshall Wavell shortly before MacArthur's relief and during the most desperate days of the Java campaign. The fine old British soldier explained that for some time he had been watching MacArthur in the newsreels and releases and studying his background and record. "He is a superb battle commander, but I think he demands personal publicity," Wavell went on. "If he were theatre commander, I fear he might wake up some morning and find he had lost one of his armies." Hurley at once made an elaborate defense of MacArthur, explaining how it was necessary for an American commander to take careful stock of the public's reactions to him and his actions. "At heart MacArthur is most conservative," Hurley remarked. "He is really a Highland Scotsman and watches every possible enemy. He is experienced and can be completely trusted in every emergency." The following morning Wavell, himself a Scots Highlander, read to General Hurley a cable he was dispatching to Churchill, recommending MacArthur in the highest terms as a theatre commander. . . . It is interesting to note that in May of this same year of 1942, Chief of Staff Marshall's orders sending Hurley to Egypt and then to Russia contained the definite order that he was not to see Field Marshall Wavell again.]

On March 10 MacArthur felt that the situation on Bataan would permit him to leave, and he so cabled Washington. Two evenings later he and a party of 20 boarded four swift PT boats. A submarine of the same type that had carried the Quezón and Sayre parties was available, but MacArthur insisted on going out by what seemed to many the more precarious way.

9

A week before his departure from Corregidor MacArthur began formulating his final plans for the forces and command setup he would leave behind him. First, he split the Visayan-Mindanao force, comprising all the troops on the islands south of Luzon, into two commands: Brigadier General Wm. F. Sharp, previously in full command, would now have only the great island of Mindanao, which MacArthur planned to use as a base for the counterattack he hoped to make from Australia; the middle islands of the Visayan group would fall to Brigadier General Bradford G. Chynoweth, now at Cebu. An independent force called Harbor Defense, comprising Corregidor and the three small island forts in Manila Bay, would be under Brigadier General George F. Moore. Major General Wainwright, II Corps commander on Bataan, would be relieved of his corps and would lead the Luzon Force, comprising both corps on Bataan and all troops scattered over Luzon.

The over-all command of the whole Philippine forces would remain under control of the United States Army Forces Far East, which would still function on Corregidor, with promoted Brigadier General Lewis C. Beebe in direct charge as Deputy Chief of Staff of USAFFE. Thus MacArthur, although 3,000 miles away in Australia, would still be in supreme command of the Philippines through his deputy chief of staff on Corregidor. Apparently the plan was not explained to General Marshall, in Washington, for almost immediately after MacArthur had arrived in Australia Wainwright was promoted to the grade of lieutenant general and dispatches began to arrive from Washington addressed to the Commanding General of Philippine Forces and obviously intended for him. General Beebe, ordered by MacArthur to keep command as deputy chief of staff, was confused and shortly a most embarrassing situation arose as to who was actually in command—Wainwright or MacArthur's deputy chief of staff. So apparently Marshall had moved without consulting MacArthur, and MacArthur, in turn, had neglected to inform Marshall of the new chain of command, which was well within his province to make.

It is obvious that MacArthur had his own reasons for arranging the separate commands as he did; eventual defeat was only a matter of time, and it may well be that he realized that as long as he held tight to the actual over-all command the Japanese could force no single American commander to order the surrender of all the American-Philippine forces scattered throughout the many islands. MacArthur was particularly interested in holding as much as he could in Mindanao (even though it be only jungle and mountain hide-outs) in the hope he would be able to use the island as a staging area for some future rescue force.

On the other hand, the split command was distasteful to Wainwright, who at the start had no authority over Corregidor and the supply base there. But the eventual cost of the single command, authorized by Marshall and the President, became painfully evident when Wainwright was forced to surrender all his scattered commands.

Occupied and harassed as MacArthur was during his first weeks in Australia, his anguish regarding the plight of his comrades on Bataan apparently never left his mind. Sometime before he left Corregidor he had evolved a plan for some possible future action conceived around the idea of a break-out from Bataan. It was based on the desperate chance that he might be able to fight his way to the Japanese base at Olongapo, in the northwest corner of the Bataan peninsula, capture supplies there and then dissolve into the Zambales mountains to carry on a determined guerilla warfare. In a message he sent to General Marshall on April 1, he said that he had not explained this to Wainwright for fear it might tend to influence his decisions.

In this same message to the Chief of Staff in Washington MacArthur made a suggestion that showed clearly the desperation of his thinking, and the simple courage that gripped him. He had urged Wainwright never to surrender but to fight on until death. He now cabled that he was ready to fly back to Bataan and personally lead this last forlorn hope. In his own words, he would "rejoin this command temporarily and take charge of this movement."

Marshall's reply was noncommittal. But to MacArthur there was an urgency that was inspired by a deep sense of duty and honor that called for the right of a commander who advised death rather than surrender to share in the fate of his men. From the far-removed safety of Washington—under quiet suggestion from London to abandon the Philippines and concentrate everything on the victory over Hitler—this passionate concern of MacArthur's for the trapped men around Manila

261

Bay and his willingness to die with them must have seemed rather unrealistic and bizarre.

The collapse of the starved, beaten and demoralized troops on Bataan came exactly 29 days after MacArthur left Corregidor. On April 7 Major General Edward J. King, commander on Bataan, sent his chief of staff to Wainwright with the painful news that his collapse was imminent. He was ordered to counterattack. Two days later the brave and able King, exhausted and overrun, had the moral courage to disobey his oral orders from Wainwright and to accept the full responsibility of asking the Japanese for surrender terms. The Jap conquerors demanded that King surrender Corregidor, as well as Bataan, which, of course, he had no authority to do.

MacArthur was fully aware of the impending disaster, but the actual news of the collapse came to him as a shock. He immediately wrote out in pencil a brief message to be radioed in the clear to Wainwright, which showed the depth of his emotion:

> The Bataan Force went out as it would have wished, fighting to the end its flickering forlorn hope. No army has ever done so much with so little, and nothing became it more than its last hour of trial and agony. To the weeping mothers of its dead, I can only say that the sacrifice and halo of Jesus of Nazareth has descended upon their sons, and that God will take them unto Himself.

MacArthur knew that only a few short weeks now separated Corregidor from its doom. And he was conscious, too, of the unspeakable ordeal that these ten thousand men and the handful of brave women were going through. There was bitterness in his heart when he heard that the Japanese had placed heavy bombardment artillery in the immediate vicinity of the hospital area in lower Bataan and were shelling the Rock, night and day, from this sanctuary.

Wainwright resisted with all the courage and determination of a fine old soldier, but the noose had been pulled tight, and finally there was nothing he could do but surrender. He tried desperately to gain the best possible terms, but he was helpless. On May 6 he was forced to bend before complete enemy dictation. Immediately before he entered into the capitulation he radioed General Sharp on Mindanao that Sharp was no longer under his (Wainwright's) orders and was now exclusively under MacArthur's command.

When Wainwright told General Homma that he had no authority over any troops outside Luzon, the surrender negotiations were broken off. The severest pressure was now brought on the American commander, and finally in utter desperation he agreed to complete surrender of the Rock and to order all commanders everywhere to give up. A rumor was spread that if any resistance took place anywhere in the Islands, the 10,000 troops on Corregidor would be destroyed.

When word of the disaster arrived in Australia, MacArthur wrote out his final comment on the courage and resistance of the men who had held the Rock and the entrance to Manila Bay inviolate for five months lacking only a day. The bitter memories and heartaches would never leave him.

> Corregidor needs no comment from me. It has sounded its own story at the mouth of its guns. It has scrolled its own epitaph on enemy tablets. But through the bloody haze of its last reverberating shot, I shall always seem to see a vision of grim, gaunt, ghastly men, still unafraid.

10

And now came one of those strange and almost unaccountable bits of history that often touch war with moments of high drama. Wainwright, trapped and helpless, had been understandably intimidated into broadcasting the order directing all his subordinate commanders, everywhere in the archipelago, to surrender immediately. Scattered throughout all the larger islands were considerable forces of Filipino and American troops and guerillas, who had plenty of munitions cached in mountain hide-outs and had every intention of fighting on. With Wainwright's broadcast at midnight on May 7, informing all officers to surrender at once, Major General Wm. F. Sharp, in Mindanao, wirelessed MacArthur for instructions. MacArthur, in Australia, answered that Wainwright's order had no validity and ordered Sharp to break up his forces into small guerilla groups and take to the hills. He added, however, "You have full authority to make any decision that may be required in this emergency."

General Sharp broke up his command, but on May 9 Colonel Traywick, Wainwright's representative, arrived by plane with a Japanese officer. Traywick carried a letter from Wainwright explaining the circumstances. With it went the threat that if Sharp's entire force did not capitulate at once, the Japs might open fire on the helpless Corregidor garrison. A second rumor had it that for every day of delay ten American officers on Corregidor would be shot.

General Sharp decided that he had no other course but to radio all commanders in the Mindanao-Visayan group to surrender. One officer, Brigadier General Bradford G. Chynoweth, commander of Cebu, definitely refused and made his plans to transfer his command to Leyte, where he would organize a large guerilla band. He was clearly under the impression that only MacArthur could order a general surrender of all the forces in the Philippines, and he was prepared to fight on. May 15, an envoy arrived from Sharp, and at the same time there came an announcement, apparently from Stateside, that MacArthur was no longer "in communication" with the Philippines. The following day the gallant Chynoweth had to march his men down from the hills.

On nearby Panay, where there was a force of some 7,000 Philippine and American troops, Colonel Ralph W. Christie, commanding officer, bluntly questioned General Sharp's latest orders. In desperation he wirelessed that without MacArthur's orders he felt his surrender might be treason. He asked Sharp simply to give him a free hand and stated: "I strongly urge you to have the approval of the War Department through MacArthur." Hard-pressed Sharp wirelessed back: "No further comments from you are desired. Acknowledge this message and state action taken at once."

And so it was that the bravest of the brave were forced to surrender under the rumored threat of ghastly reprisals on Corregidor. Had General Marshall permitted MacArthur to continue to handle the whole Philippine situation from his command post in Australia and not interfere with MacArthur's arrangements, it is possible that guerilla resistance in the central and lower islands would have long continued. It would have taken thousands of Japanese troops, needed elsewhere, to clean out the organized forces that the American officers, scattered throughout the Islands, were forced to surrender at this time.

The real difficulty lay in Marshall's early wireless that the full authority and command of the Islands rested in Wainwright alone. This had been picked up by the Japanese, and when Wainwright tried to deny to the enemy that he had authority to order the scattered units to the south to surrender, he was confronted with orders from Marshall.

Wainwright had done his best, and he was in no way to blame for the unfortunate circumstances in which Marshall's hurried action had placed him. Had there been no interference from Washington, there would at least have been validity to Wainwright's contention that he had no authority to order general surrender throughout the Islands. If MacArthur erred at all, it was only in his failure to notify Washington of his new setup in the chain of command. Certainly it was MacArthur's right and duty to make such dispositions as he chose, because the Philippines were still completely under his over-all command.

The Japanese conquerors were so bitter and angry at their failure to overrun Luzon and Corregidor in the two months that had been allotted them that they were prepared to go to the cruelest possible ends to force the surrender of all organized resistance in the Islands.

So deadly would this threat of reprisal against the helpless Corregidor garrison have been, that it is to be seriously doubted if the scattered American commanders could have long stood against the terrible pressure. Most of them would have been forced to give way before some appalling ultimatum, involving the lives of their comrades on the Rock. Even if Wainwright's authority had not been increased, and MacArthur, now in Australia, had continued to hold actual command, the grim reality of the Japanese threats might still have succeeded in bringing about surrender.

MacArthur himself might have been forced to adopt with

265

all the scattered American commanders the same course that he followed in his cabled instructions to General Sharp on Mindanao: "You have full authority to make any decision that may be required in this emergency." Thus the net result might have been the same—ultimate surrender of the various units under the threat of deadly reprisals.

In MacArthur's eyes the fundamental error had been made months and even years before war came, when there had been ample time to build up an adequate defense in the Islands— had the *will* been there, and had British and later the Russian influence been less powerful.

11

During the days immediately before MacArthur had boarded his PT boat he had been concerned with the problem of the make-up of the personnel of the party to accompany him to Australia. He hesitated to strip his experienced USAFFE staff on Corregidor, but he knew that immediately on his arrival in Australia he would have urgent need of the men who had long been working closely with him. He studied the list made out by his chief of staff, and finally settled on 18 service men: 16 other officers, his sergeant secretary, and himself.

Besides Chief of Staff Sutherland and his deputy, Brigadier General Richard Marshall, the list included Admiral Rockwell and Captain H. G. Ray of the Navy; Brigadier Generals Spencer B. Akin, William F. Marquat, Hugh J. Casey and Harold H. George; Colonels Charles A. Willoughby and Charles P. Stivers; Lt. Colonels Sidney L. Huff, L. A. Diller, Francis H. Wilson and Joe R. Sherr; Major Charles H. Morehouse, Captain Joseph McMicking and Master Sergeant Paul P. Rogers. They were all indispensable to MacArthur in forming his new staff.

The MacArthur detractors found a new opportunity for renewing their criticism of the General. There now was whispered a particularly vicious story that had not the slightest basis of fact: By word of mouth and by letter and print the story was spread that desperately ill American nurses were denied transportation from Bataan while the furniture and even the piano from the General's apartment atop the Manila Hotel were loaded in the four PT boats that made the trip to Mindanao, and then transferred to planes carrying the little party to Australia.

The actual fact was quite different: Each of the 21 people taken off the Rock, including the General and the three members of his immediate family, was permitted a single suitcase. There was no other luggage of any kind.

A second endlessly recurring charge centered on the fact that the Cantonese nurse, Ah Cheu, was taken out in preference to some American. Ever since young Arthur was a few days old this amah had been an intimate member of the family. If and when Corregidor finally succumbed, it was almost certain that this Chinese woman would be singled out for special torture and probable death. The Far Eastern Commander took it for granted that it remained his unquestioned and sole prerogative to make his own decision regarding this devoted and adopted member of his family.

The continued smears and bitter personal digs that revolved around this perilous voyage were not allowed to die out completely. Never once did the General bother to attempt to answer them or to justify his actions.

During the dangerous sea and air trip the General's spirits were constantly revived by the thought that once he reached his new assignment he would find a sufficient force awaiting him so that he could immediately organize a great relief expedition for the Philippines. If he was fortunate enough to survive the coming ordeal of the hazardous voyage to Australia, Colonel Carlos Romulo on Corregidor was to announce over the Voice of Freedom radio MacArthur's solemn pledge, "I shall return!"

MacArthur's word alone still carried weight and promise. The Filipino soldiers and civilians believed in him. "Even '*We* shall return!' would have lacked the magic that rested in the simple pledge 'I shall return!'" Romulo explained some years later.

Rarely did the General refer to the long and dangerous journey that started from the Rock on March 11. The subsequent fate of Corregidor and Bataan weighed too heavily on his heart.

To an old friend [the author] staying at his headquarters almost two years later, he relived the great adventure. So simple were his words and so accurate the sequence he unfolded, that it is repeated here from an account written at the time for a book called *MacArthur and the War Against Japan,* published by Charles Scribner's Sons:

> It was seven fifteen when the General walked across his porch to where his wife was seated. "Jean," he said gently, "it is time to mount up." Quietly they went down to the South Dock where Bulkeley waited with his PT-41. Shelling had been intermittent all day in the dock area. They boarded the vessel—all but the General. He had stopped and turned to bid Corregidor his farewell.
>
> The men on the dock stared at the lone motionless figure they knew so well. In his war-worn clothes he loomed gaunt and forlorn. His eyes roved the desperate scene before him in all its naked bleakness. Almost every building, every shed, every tree had been burned and blasted. The great fires that had raged had left their black streaks from one end of the Rock to the other. Great crevasses were torn everywhere. Corregidor looked like a tortured body that had been ripped and gouged and twisted into something no longer human.
>
> His eyes seemed to search through the broken, shattered ruins up to the top where he could still catch the gleam of the barrels of the big guns. Up there in command of the Top Side was his classmate, Paul Bunker. Forty years ago they had been associated together on one of West Point's most famous football teams— Bunker, the star, a double All-American—MacArthur in the more humble role of team manager!
>
> It was just dusk and the faint night breeze was beginning to ripple the waters. A strange silence had fallen as though death were passing by. Even the firing had ceased.
>
> Slowly the General raised his cap—that famous cap. Even through his tan he looked white and ashen, and there was the suspicion of a twitch at the muscles of his mouth. One could have heard a pin drop.
>
> He looked around as he stepped aboard. Every man on the dock stood bareheaded. They all knew he had not more than one chance in ten.

Then came the General's quiet voice—"Cast off, Buck."

At 8:30 the four boats rendezvoused at the opening to the mine field. They crept through, led by a navy mine layer. At 9:15 they opened up the throttles and roared away.

Very shortly they began to pick up Japanese signal fires. All along the coast the enemy had established a system of signalling by fire that might have been old Indian signals. The warning signals could now clearly be seen, but the sound of the PT engines was like the sound of bombers, and the watchers mistook it.

The PT boats ran in a diamond formation, and the orders were to attack anything that blocked the way. Each of the boats carried torpedoes and .50-caliber machine guns, and the General felt they could break through any ordinary blockading line. If they were attacked from the air they were to hold together, put up a curtain of fire, and depend on their high speed maneuverability.

Off to the left they soon made out Japanese blockading ships. Immediately they changed course to pass to the west and north. All night long similar alarms took place, but with great skill and good luck the Japanese craft were by-passed. In the diamond pattern Bulkeley's boat led off. Admiral Rockwell in the fourth boat closed up the rear.

The seas became increasingly heavy, and the little boats pounded and rolled. It was difficult to hold formation, and about 3:30 in the morning, the pattern was broken despite every effort to hold it. They had planned to rendezvous that morning at a deserted island. When they lost formation, the lead boat tried for several hours to collect the other boats, but was unsuccessful. When day broke it headed for another deserted island, three sailing hours north of the rendezvous. Here they hoped to find cover to hide during the day.

In a distant cove they made out a small craft which was identified as one of their own ships. But those aboard failed to recognize the General's boat and prepared for conflict, dumping their spare gas drums and manning their guns. At the point of opening fire General Akin fortunately identified MacArthur's PT-boat and shouted "Hold fire!" His keen eyesight prevented a horrible catastrophe.

They remained in the cove until about 2:30 in the afternoon, anxiously scanning the skies for the enemy's inevitable searching planes. To be spotted would be to be lost. Little Arthur was prostrated and was running a high fever. The amah was deathly sick. The General and his wife were good sailors and had weathered it well. The General ordered the vessel to try to make the original rendezvous point, a wild and uninhabited island.

The seas were running high and dangerous. The second boat had dumped its spare drums when it had mistaken MacArthur's craft for an enemy ship and its gas was running low. They found Admiral Rockwell at the rendezvous, and took on the passengers from the boat that was out of running for lack of fuel. Around 6:30, they set out to cross the Mindanao Sea for Cagayan. Rockwell's boat led and Buck's followed. The fourth boat arrived at the rendezvous about one hour after they left, and immediately followed them into the Mindanao Sea alone.

Before darkness closed in they ran into enemy destroyers, but these apparently failed to pick them up, for they slipped by them. They were getting all they could out of the old engines now. The Mindanao Sea was choppy and they were taking heavy punishment. It was like being in a cement mixer, which buffeted them from one side to the other. The next day most of the passengers were black and blue from head to foot.

It had just turned daybreak when they arrived at Cagayan in north central Mindanao. The General turned to Buck and his officers and men of the two boats. "It was done in true naval style," he gratefully pronounced. "I take great honor in awarding the boats' crews the Silver Star for gallantry and fortitude in the face of heavy odds."

General Sharp met them at the dock. He was General MacArthur's Commander in Mindanao and had a force of about 25,000 men. In the Visayas, General Chynoweth had about 20,000 men. These were units of the Philippine Army in those sectors which had been mobilized when the war broke. It had been General MacArthur's plan to use these troops in guerilla warfare, if the defense of Bataan failed.

Four bombers had been ordered from Australia to meet the party. Two failed to arrive and the third crashed in the Bay. The fourth was so old and dilapidated that General Sharp had started it back to Australia without passengers before MacArthur's arrival.

Three replacement planes were at once started from Australia and two of them finally arrived. In the meantime the Japanese had word that the MacArthur staff had reached Mindanao and they rapidly pushed forces north from Davao to seize the field.

The planes arrived just before midnight, and took off shortly afterwards. They were flying over enemy-held country patrolled by enemy planes, but under cover of the night they managed to evade all contacts. At 9 that morning they arrived at Batchelor Field, forty miles south of Port Darwin. "It was close," said the General on landing: "but that's the way it is in war. You win or lose, live or die—and the difference is just an eyelash."

But they still faced danger. The Japanese evidently had spotted the two planes, for in less than three hours after the Forts had landed on Batchelor Field, a heavy air attack was launched. The General's party had left for Alice Springs by a scant ten minutes when the dive bombers and fighters roared in. But the priceless quarry was gone.

12

On March 17, when his plane from Mindanao came down at Batchelor Field near Darwin in Northern Australia, MacArthur turned to an American officer standing by and asked how many American troops were now in Australia.

The officer was a little dumbfounded at the question. "As far as I know, sir, there are very few troops here," he answered.

MacArthur could not believe the words. He spoke in an aside to his chief of staff, Dick Sutherland: "Surely he is wrong."

Following a three-hour flight to Alice Springs, there came a long rail trip across the endless Australian desert. Late on the afternoon of the third day he reached the junction of the wide-gauge above Adelaide and found a luxurious private car awaiting. On it was Dick Marshall, his deputy chief of staff, who had been dispatched by air to Melbourne ahead of the rest of the party in order to find the true state of affairs.

To the General's first question Marshall gravely shook his head. Instead of a great American troop concentration there was practically nothing with which to build a relief force; no infantry or tanks; only two National Guard Coast Artillery anti-aircraft regiments, a regiment or two of field artillery and two regiments of Engineers and some scattered Air Corps personnel, with 250 planes in various states of efficiency; a grand total of 25,364 U. S. Army and Air personnel. MacArthur had left in Bataan and on Corregidor almost three times that number of fighting men.

With this alarming news, came the report that except for one brigade of the 6th Division that had just arrived in Perth, every experienced unit of the splendid Imperial Australian Expeditionary Force of three divisions was still concentrated in the Egyptian desert and the Middle East. Yet their own homelands were in imminent danger of actual invasion.

All that night the broken MacArthur walked the darkened corridor of his railroad car.

But when dawn came he had recovered his calm purpose and decision.

PART THREE

Enemies on
Two Fronts

1942-1945

Outline of the continental United States superimposed on the area of the early counteroffensive in the Southwest Pacific theatre.

14

1942—WAR ON A SHOESTRING

MacArthur was seated on the rear platform of his observation car when the train pulled into the great station at Melbourne at 9 o'clock the following morning. It was some moments before he realized that the cheering thousands crowding into the station and overflowing the streets were there to welcome him.

An official party greeted him and escorted him through the station. Outside he inspected a small guard of honor of American soldiers. Since no U. S. infantrymen were available, a platoon of engineers had been brought in. If they had been West Point cadets, the old soldier could hardly have been more proud of them.

He was brought over to a little group of Australian and American reporters and radio men. While at breakfast in his car that morning it was suggested that he might be called upon to make some statement on arrival at Melbourne, and he had written out by pencil a few notes on a folded sheet of paper. But when an announcer from the Australian Broadcasting Company held up his hand microphone and asked that he say a few words the General spoke extemporaneously and straight from his heart:

I am glad indeed to be in immediate cooperation with the Australian soldier. I know him well from World War days and admire him greatly. I have every confidence in the ultimate success of our joint cause; but success in modern war requires something more than courage and a willingness to die; it requires careful preparation. This means the furnishing of sufficient troops and sufficient material to meet the known strength of the potential enemy. No general can make something out of nothing. My success or failure will depend primarily upon the resources which the respective governments place at my disposal. In any event I shall do my best. I shall keep the soldier's faith.

2

Within 48 hours after his heartening welcome he learned many disturbing facts. It was immediately clear to him that a dangerous sense of defeatism had settled down over a large part of the seven million people of Australia. Civilians and military men alike talked freely of the Brisbane Line, a purely imaginary line drawn from Brisbane on the central-east coast to Adelaide in the south, on which the fight for the true heart of Australia would be made. Below this line were the four or five most important cities and the larger proportion of the population. The vast empty areas comprising three-quarters of the continent to the north and west seemed undefendable and after a token resistance would be abandoned to the Japanese.

In MacArthur's opinion his first problem was to replace this psychosis of defeat with the challenging attitude that reflected the real character of these brave and stubborn people. Despite Churchill's violent disapproval, the three battle-proved Imperial divisions were starting on their long and dangerous journey home from Egypt and the Middle East. Their arrival would help stimulate confidence, but what was immediately needed was a bold concept of a new strategy that would break the mood of fear and despair.

Four days after he reached Melbourne MacArthur drove the two hundred miles through rolling grasslands and groves of eucalyptus trees to the capital at Canberra. There he was closeted alone with the Prime Minister, John Curtin, who had been responsible to a considerable degree for his assignment to Australia.

In a matter of minutes the two men came to an understanding that was never once broken in letter or spirit. When they arose to go to the meeting of the Australian War Council, Mac-Arthur put his arm around the shoulder of the sturdy labor leader.

"Mr. Prime Minister," he said with obvious fervor and sincerity, "you and I will see this thing through together."

That evening he was the guest of honor at a banquet given by the Prime Minister and members of the Parliament, and the words he spoke there sped by press and radio to the last lonely ranch station in the distant Back of Beyond. Australia was not to be abandoned and lost. It was a short speech to carry such hope and promise:

Mr. Prime Minister, Distinguished Members of the Commonwealth Government:

I am deeply moved by the warmth of greeting extended to me by all of Australia. The hospitality of your country is proverbial throughout the world, but your reception has far exceeded anything that I could have anticipated.

Although this is my first trip to Australia I already feel at home. There is a link that binds our countries together which does not depend upon written protocol, upon treaties of alliance or upon diplomatic doctrine. It goes deeper than that. It is that indescribable consanguinity of race which causes us to have the same aspirations, the same hopes and desires, the same ideals and the same dreams of future destiny.

My presence here is tangible evidence of our unity. I have come as a soldier in a great crusade of personal liberty as opposed to perpetual slavery. My faith in our ultimate victory is invincible, and I bring to you tonight the unbreakable spirit of the free man's military code in support of our just cause. That code has come down to us from even before the days of knighthood and chivalry. It will stand the test of any ethics or philosophies the world has ever known. It embraces the things that are right and condemns the things that are wrong. Under its banner the free men of the world are united today.

There can be no compromise. We shall win or we shall die, and to this end I pledge the full resources of all the mighty power of my country and all the blood of my countrymen.

Mr. Prime Minister, tonight will be an unforgettable memory for me. Your inspiring words and those of your compatriots will be emblazoned always in my memory as though they had been carved on stone or bronze. Under their inspiration I am taking the liberty of assuming the high honor of raising my glass in salute to your great country and its great leaders.

To the millions of discouraged Australians it was as if a bright torch of hope had suddenly been lit. Shortly they were to be lifted again by MacArthur's words, "We shall make the fight for Australia in New Guinea!"

3

For the moment he had neither a defined theatre nor a directive. The vague terms and promises made by President Roosevelt in his radiograms to Corregidor had left the general impression in MacArthur's mind that he would replace Wavell at least in the eastern half of the sprawling area of command that had once been the responsibility of the British Field Marshal. But indecision and bickering had gripped the Pacific Council sitting in Washington, and MacArthur's immediate position was still nothing more than commander of the United States Army Forces in Australia, which he automatically assumed as senior U. S. officer present.

New Zealand demanded that it retain control of its own home defenses, and the U. S. Navy insisted that it be allotted a large South Pacific area that had once been included in Wavell's theatre. The British still claimed control over the western portion of Wavell's limitless area. So it was not until April 18, one month and a day after he arrived in northern Australia, that MacArthur could announce the boundaries of his Southwest Pacific theatre and his broad directives.

He was shocked when he had discovered that an American Army division which had arrived on the Australian continent in the middle of February had been reloaded and shipped

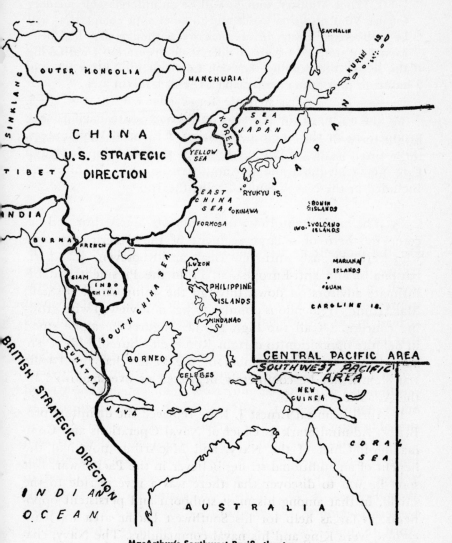

MacArthur's Southwest Pacific theatre.

some 750 miles eastward to the French Island of New Caledonia. This Patch Force had left Australia 12 days before MacArthur's plane had landed at Batchelor Field. The "Americal" division at New Caledonia had been rapidly reinforced and shortly the Patch Force alone had more American ground fighting troops than there were in the whole of the American command in Australia. With it went a considerable air force and a far larger navy than remained in the Australian area.

In the inter-service struggle for Pacific control the U. S. Navy had acquired the North, Central and South Pacific areas, grouped under the single designation of Central Pacific areas. The lower western dividing line was the 160° longitude, so that New Caledonia and the Southern Solomon Islands were included in the Navy's South Pacific theatre.

Even before these military developments MacArthur had become the hero of a large segment of the American people who were variously anti-New Deal, anti-Roosevelt, anti-internationalist and anti-Europe-first. From the President and his intimate advisors on down through the Joint Chiefs of Staff, MacArthur's tremendous popularity was now viewed with growing concern. Of all the high military figures he alone stood in definite opposition to certain Roosevelt-Churchill ideas. He had already become a symbol of the belief that the Pacific war should not be completely neglected or overshadowed by the Atlantic war.

In April Admiral Ernest J. King replaced the definitely pro-British Admiral Stark as Chief of Naval Operations and Commander-in-Chief of the Navy, and MacArthur now had the benefit of an additional strong believer in the Pacific war. But soon he was to discover that there was a reverse side to the shield, in that among his most stubborn and persistent opponents, as far as help for his Southwest Pacific area was concerned, were King and his naval commanders. The Navy, chagrined and humiliated over its share in the disgraceful tragedy at Pearl Harbor, insisted on taking over control of the Pacific war. Both MacArthur and the Army, it stubbornly insisted, must accept a secondary role in the Navy's private war: in the eyes of the Navy men it was a large ocean, with small land areas,

280

which committed the U. S. to amphibious tactics and "island-hopping"—and final assault over water.

It was the natural conclusion that General Marshall would automatically oppose Admiral King and his demands for more and more control in the Pacific. As a matter of fact the records of the Army War Planning Board prove that at times there was sturdy opposition to the endless Navy requests. But nothing short of a complete and all-out Army resistance to King's demands for enlarged control could have given MacArthur and his theatre the protection they needed against submergence by the ambitious and influential Navy.

Meanwhile a strange incident occurred in Congress that was further to widen MacArthur's already somewhat strained relations with the White House. On March 25 a resolution was introduced in the Lower House that MacArthur be voted a Congressional Medal of Honor. It was passed with applause, and three days later the President duly bestowed the highest decoration the nation possessed. The significance of the incident lay in the fact that, despite its name, the medal is actually proposed and given by the President and not by Congress. Rarely had Congress openly prodded a President to bestow the Congressional Medal of Honor.

But this was of slight significance compared to events that started two months later when the New York Legislature requested that June 13, the day General MacArthur had graduated from West Point, be designated as MacArthur Day. Governor Lehman duly proclaimed the anniversary. At about the same time a joint resolution was passed by Congress and on June 12 signed by the President designating the same date as MacArthur Day.

When a press conference reporter asked the President what he thought of honoring living heroes by thus setting aside special days in their honor, the President replied that occasionally he thought it was a good thing. He added that fifteen war heroes were coming to see him tomorrow, and he did not think tribute to them should be delayed until they were dead.

But Roosevelt's possible cynicism was by no means reflected in the warm-hearted tributes John Curtin paid to the American General at the start of a three-day celebration in Australia.

MacArthur Day opened the long week end on June 13, with Sunday as American Flag Day, and Monday as the official birthday of King George VI.

Despite the first call that Britain and Russia had on the American war effort, and the fact that Admiral King and his Pacific areas came next, MacArthur finally did begin to get reinforcements and supplies. On April 6 the 41st National Guard Infantry Division arrived, and on May 14 the 32nd Division disembarked. Of equal importance was the arrival of brigades of the Imperial Australian divisions from the Middle East.

MacArthur now felt certain that the potentially fine naval and air base at Rabaul, New Britain, at the northern end of the Solomon Seas, was the key take-off spot for further Japanese advances southward. They had seized it on January 2, but were slow in building it up. Yet it obviously would be the staging area for enemy drives either southward toward the lower New Guinea area or southeastward down the Solomons to the American-Australian line of communications. In early March 1942, the Japanese had captured the airdrome at Lae and its sister port of Salamaua on the eastern shore of lower New Guinea.

One hundred and seventy-five miles to the south of Lae, across the high Owen Stanley Mountains, lay Port Moresby, the strategic advance stronghold that must be captured by the enemy before he could hope to invade eastern and northern Australia. Port Moresby was 45 minutes by bomber from the Japanese air strips at Lae.

On May 3 a Japanese task force with aircraft carriers, heading for Milne Bay, attempted to swing around the lower tail of New Guinea. It was intercepted by a U.S. task force with two aircraft carriers. The Battle of the Coral Sea that ensued was the first sea battle in history in which no surface ship fired a single round. The American force turned back this vanguard of a probable amphibious invasion of Port Moresby, but it was an expensive victory. The giant carrier *Lexington* was lost, and the Japanese had only a small escort carrier sunk. But Moresby was saved.

To the east, across the wide Solomon Sea, the Japanese

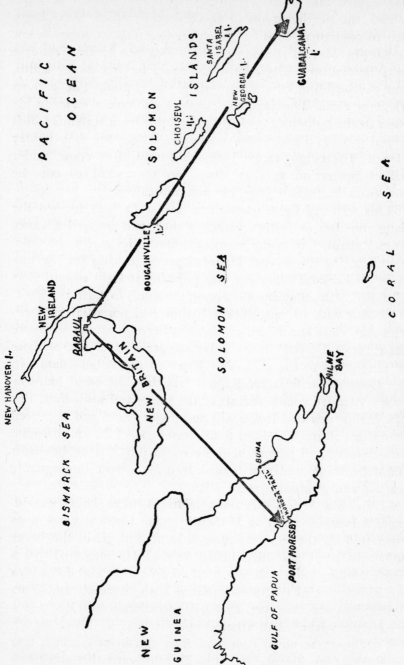

Importance of the Japanese stronghold of Rabaul.

had landed and built a fighter strip below Rabaul at Buka Island, the northernmost of the Solomons. Their next move was to construct strips on Bougainville, 100-odd miles below Buka. On May 3, the day of the Coral Sea battle, Japanese were landed on Tulagi, some 200 miles further to the south, and the building of a fighter strip was started. The pattern was now clear. The Japanese would soon have a series of air bases in the Solomons operating southeast from Rabaul, which would serve as a succession of stepping stones for their fighter planes. Their long-range bombers would thus come under fighter protection as they drove on southward to cut the American-Australian line of communication.

This series of fighter bases and utility harbors formed the dangerous left or eastern prong of their two-pronged advance from Rabaul. On to the westward, 600 miles across the Solomon Sea, lay the second Japanese prong, resting for the moment on Lae and Salamaua, but pointing straight toward Port Moresby, Milne Bay and then on to the south to Australia itself.

Rabaul with its magnificent harbor and potential air facilities was thus the heart of the southern Japanese offensive possibilities. Directly above it lay the great naval and air base of Truk, and to the northwest Yap and the Palau Islands in the Central Pacific area. Rabaul was thus the ideal half-way base for future enemy thrusts to the south and southwest. But MacArthur saw that it was still only lightly held and suggested that if the Joint Chiefs of Staff would give him an adequate carrier force and proper help, he could pinch it off before it could be reinforced and turned into an almost impregnable sea, air and ground fortress.

While MacArthur's recommendations were being considered, Admiral Nimitz at Honolulu came forward with plans for a raid on the new Japanese base at Tulagi, in the lower Solomons, some 500 miles below Rabaul. He suggested that a single Marine raider battalion could do the job, and his idea met the approval of Admiral King. Both Marshall and MacArthur insisted, however, that the operation would demand a much larger force than a battalion.

The Japanese naval code had long ago been cracked, and U. S. naval intelligence was thus able to learn that since two big American air carriers were still in the Coral Sea, the Japanese now planned to send their own carrier force to the Central Pacific in a move to crush Midway and then capture key islands in the Aleutians. Nimitz immediately rendezvoused his carrier forces close to Midway—one flat-top coming 3,000 miles at full speed from the Coral Sea—and on June 3 and 4 their planes located and sank four of the Japanese flat-tops. Overnight the entire naval ratio in the Pacific was changed to America's advantage. It was a master stroke.

Four days after the brilliant Naval Air victory at Midway MacArthur again urged that an all-out surprise attack be launched at the earliest possible moment against Rabaul. He now had two full U. S. divisions and the experienced Imperial Australian 7th Division that could be used as occupying troops after an amphibious force had won the beachheads. He would need the loan of a specially trained Marine amphibious division to make the initial landing. And until fighter strips could be captured or built, he would need carrier-based fighter planes to support his bombers attacking from their home air fields at Port Moresby.

The one requirement that was absolutely necessary was unity of command. Since the fighting would be in MacArthur's theatre, it was obvious to the army planners that he must be in command. But as the initial action would be of a naval nature, a naval officer, temporarily serving under MacArthur, should head the sea task force.

General Marshall personally presented the bold idea on June 25, but Admiral King and his navy advisors insisted that MacArthur might lose the carriers operating in range of the land-based bombers and naval flying-boats at Rabaul and at other bases in the Solomons. MacArthur explained that he had no idea of rushing blindly in to attack Rabaul; that he would feel his way, and secure enough bases on the Guinea coast and near enough to Rabaul to assure him ultimate air protection.

But Admiral King still refused, arguing that an attack might be mounted about August 1 but that the first objective should be the inferior Japanese positions in the Solomons below Rabaul and the Santa Cruz Islands. Rabaul, the ultimate objective of the Allied counterattack, must come later. Not only must the operations be under the South Pacific naval commander, but MacArthur must contribute his surface ships and submarines and his long-range land-based bombers.

Once the Navy had completed the Tulagi operation, King insisted, then MacArthur could continue with the island-hopping operation on up the Solomon chain to Rabaul. Since the initial phase, called Task One, would cover Guadalcanal, part of which lay in the Southwest Pacific theatre, MacArthur's eastern demarcation line must be conveniently moved west from 160° East to 159°.

Task Two included capturing the Japanese bases in the remainder of the Solomons, and at Lae and Salamaua on the northeast coast of New Guinea. Task Three indicated the seizure and occupation of Rabaul and the other enemy positions in the New Britain-New Ireland area. These would come under MacArthur, but naval task commanders would always be in command of all amphibious landings. It was a Presidential directive.

By July 2 Marshall gave way to King's demands, and any chance of a unified command in the South and Southwest Pacific areas was lost. Five days after the Marshall-King decision it was discovered that the Japanese had moved on from Tulagi and were starting an air strip on Guadalcanal Island. Naval planners felt the emergency of the new situation, and Vice Admiral Robert L. Ghormley, in command of the South Pacific theatre, was immediately ordered to fly to Melbourne from New Zealand and confer with General MacArthur.

The two commanders saw eye-to-eye as they studied the vast unfolding picture of the two-pronged Japanese drive southeastward and southwestward from Rabaul, down the Solomons and the New Guinea coast. To turn it back there must be a single strategic plan, utilizing in perfect harmony all the resources of the two far-Pacific areas, the two services and their air forces.

Since the time and chance to move swiftly against Rabaul had now gone, the three tasks must be synchronized, and the whole vast operation must move ahead as one. Consequently MacArthur and Ghormley recommended that the Tulagi-

Guadalcanal action be delayed until more ships, planes and troops were available, and until MacArthur was able to organize sufficient forces to present an offensive power.

The Joint Chiefs of Staff promptly rejected the suggestion, and Ghormley was directed to attack Guadalcanal on August 7, one week after the original date set. The 1st Marines landed unopposed. But enemy forces were soon brought in by sea from the north, and a desperate battle for the unfinished airfield began. On the night of August 10 three U. S. cruisers and an Australian cruiser were sunk off Savo island, in the first of a series of deadly sea encounters, in which the Allies were by no means always successful.

Vice Admiral Ghormley was relieved of command of the South Pacific area on October 18 and was replaced by Admiral William F. Halsey. But it was February 9, 1943, before the Guadalcanal campaign officially ended. It had taken six months and two days to do the job that had at first seemed such an easy chore.

4

From the earliest days of his arrival in Australia the menace of the Japanese-held base of Rabaul was as clear to MacArthur as was the need to hold fast to the Port Moresby base in lower New Guinea. Some 200 miles southeast of Moresby, at the very tip of New Guinea's tail, lay Milne Bay, which was almost as valuable a key spot for Allied defense and offense as Moresby itself.

As his first move in putting into effect his decision to make the fight for Australia in New Guinea, MacArthur dispatched to Port Moresby two of the ablest members of his staff, Brigadier Generals "Hal" George—who was soon to meet a tragic death on the airfield at Port Darwin—and "Pat" Casey, his chief engineer officer. They reported that conditions in Moresby were deplorable from every possible military angle.

MacArthur immediately ordered the construction of airfields and a base in this strategic stronghold at Milne Bay that could handle his bombers, fighters and transport aircraft. Casey collected such bulldozers, scrapers and road-making machinery as he could get together and hurried north with the colored 96th U. S. Engineer Battalion. Along with him went a tall, lean, Norwegian-born Missouri engineer, Colonel Jack Sverdrup, who had a way with native workers that was shortly to pay off in big dividends.

Stretching down the lower centre of the great island of New Guinea, lay, like the dorsal vertebrae of some prehistoric monster, the high mountains of the Owen Stanley range, their peaks often hidden for days at a time by low-hanging clouds. Rain forests covered their sides, and eternal danger hung over the green, treacherous jungle of their eastern slopes that stretched on to the shore lines of the Solomon Sea.

From the western foothills of the range, some 30 miles inland from Port Moresby, a trail or trace zig-zagged for 70 miles eastward over the high Kokoda Pass and on down the long slopes to the swampy tropical country. It led to the coconut plantations and missionary establishments, built around the clusters of huts called Gona and Buna on the eastern coast.

On July 22 an intelligence report of a most alarming nature came from Brigadier General Willoughby's G-2 office. The Japanese had suddenly landed large forces at both Gona and Buna on this eastern Guinea coast, almost directly across the mountains from Moresby. A day or two later even more disturbing news filtered in; a considerable enemy force, using several hundred natives from New Britain as food and ammunition bearers, was advancing along the jungle trail that led up the long mountain slopes toward Kokoda Pass, and then across the hump of the range down to key Port Moresby on the west.

A small Australian force had shortly before this landed by barges at Gona, and although outnumbered 10 to 1, it was attempting to block the advancing Japanese column. The Aussies could do little more than give way. Shortly other militia men from the misty heights of the pass joined in the bitter resistance, but it was a losing fight from the start.

MacArthur reviewed the situation. Even if the tireless enemy soldiers won the Kokoda Pass and started down the western slopes of the Owen Stanley range toward Port Moresby, it

How the Japs tried to double-envelope Port Moresby in New Guinea.

did not seem humanly possible that they would have enough strength left to exploit their incredible march. There was nothing to be immediately alarmed over, although it did signify the determination of the enemy to capture Moresby.

The day that the Japanese started toward Kokoda Pass, Major General George C. Kenney arrived in Brisbane, where Allied headquarters had recently been established. MacArthur

289

had asked for him to relieve Major General George H. Brett, and when the stubby, dynamic air commander with the crew haircut and an overwhelming sense of accomplishment reported the following morning, it didn't take MacArthur long to give him his orders. He was to re-vamp and re-inspire the 5th Air Force. Things looked alarming at Port Moresby. It was Kenney's first job to decide what was needed to build up air power there in the quickest possible time. He left at dawn the next morning. It was the way Kenney did things. In the long list of brilliant air commanders he had a unique reputation. In 1934 when the G.H.Q. Air Force had been established by MacArthur as an integral part of the Four-Army Plan, Kenney had been made G-3 in the air setup. And now, eight years later, MacArthur sent for him to help in the great task that lay ahead.

It was evident now that the incredible Japanese advance over the Kokoda Pass toward Port Moresby was no wild raid. Five jungle-trained Japanese battalions were leap-frogging one another, taking terrible losses as they first won the high pass and then started down the western slopes toward the prize harbor. Exactly 31 days after they had landed on the Buna-Gona shoreline they fought their way into Kokoda Pass village, 55 miles from their starting point. Below them lay the slopes of the Owen Stanleys. They pushed on without a moment's rest.

Fully aware of the possibility of some other daring and co-ordinated Japanese move, MacArthur saw to it that the Australian General Thomas A. Blamey, Allied Ground Commander, placed two brigades of Australian militiamen and regulars at Milne Bay southeast from Moresby. A company or two of U. S. engineers were hurriedly trying to finish three air strips, of which only one was serviceable.

Early in the morning of August 26, before dawn broke, heavy Japanese forces landed at Milne Bay, and for twelve days a desperate jungle battle followed. When the fighting ended with the total annihilation of these forces (whose mission had been to gain a foothold here at Milne Bay and then move by barge up the Guinea coast to Moresby), their brothers on the Kokoda Pass, almost 200 miles to the north, had reached a defended ridge a scant 35 miles from their prize. The incredible plan had been for the two attacking forces, one from the east and the other from the south, to form a giant pincer that would crush the key Port Moresby between them. The enemy group that landed at Milne Bay had now been completely destroyed, and the other on the Pass was turned back when only 22 miles from its goal, after it had performed deeds of valor and endurance that were magnificent.

And now these plagued and defeated Japanese must fight their way back up the deadly trail to Kokoda Pass, and then on down the dangerous eastern slopes to their future burial grounds at Buna, Gona and Sanananda. Xenephon's Ten Thousand might have had a worthier cause, but they have no greater claim to the harsh immortality of arms than does this band of two or three thousand ragged, stubborn, hard little men, writing their own deathless Odyssey on the Kokoda Pass.

5

Save for American airmen and the contribution of the U. S. engineers at Milne Bay, the fighting so far in Guinea had been done by the Australians. But soon the 32nd and 41st U. S. Divisions, now finishing their final jungle training north of Brisbane in the Rockhampton area, would be fighting alongside the Aussies. At last MacArthur had sufficient manpower to attempt the annihilation of the Japanese strongholds at Buna and Gona on the upper coast of southern New Guinea.

But he had little in the way of a balanced offensive force. His Seventh Fleet was a fleet in name only. It had no shore bombardment warships, supply ships or special landing craft. It had no transports or sea-lift, save of a token and shadowy nature.

But MacArthur did have George Kenney. And faced with the task of taking out Buna and Gona, with their 11,000 Japanese troops, protected by the sea on one side and by almost impenetrable swamps on the other, he found that his apparently unsolvable problem of logistics was so much grist to the mind and imagination of this extraordinary airman.

Already the Aussies had rolled the stubborn Japanese back

down the eastern end of the Kokoda Pass and across the flooded rivers and the swampy plains to the coast. Kenney quickly flew most of the U. S. 32nd Division the 1,000 miles from Rockhampton to Port Moresby. While this was going on Colonel Jack Sverdrup started up the Kapa Kapa trail, below the Kokoda Pass, with a force of 297 "Fuzzie Wuzzies," armed with shovels, axes, picks and machetes. The 2nd Battalion of the U. S. 126th Infantry slogged on ahead of him. Sverdrup was travelling light. In sixteen days he followed the trail on foot over the lower Owen Stanleys he hacked four temporary air strips out of the tall native grass. The following day Kenney's transports brought in 1,000 Aussies.

Sverdrup moved his grass cutters on to a spot called Dobodura, which was ten miles from the Japanese fortress of Buna. Quietly they cut out parallel strips in the tall grass corridors. And now out of the murky Guinea skies the big transport ships could slide in and unload men and food and supplies. In a single day Kenney's fliers brought in an entire army field hospital, operating tables and all. On their return trip the transports were filled with sick and wounded men. The vicious tropical diseases were knocking out four or five soldiers for every one an enemy bullet cut down.

In many ways it was a one-sided fight that the Aussies and the Americans were forced to make in this terrible Papuan jungle along the east coast. Lack of sea power denied MacArthur the warships that might have shelled the rear of the strong points and thick bunkers and the tough defensive positions the Japanese had built. For all of MacArthur's hatred of frontal attacks, he had no alternative for his Aussies and Yanks, already weakened by malaria and poor food and sleepless days and nights. Every advance had to be made through swamps and deadly jungle straight in the face of an enemy hidden in thick-walled, low-roofed and expertly camouflaged bunkers that seemed impervious to bombs and cannon fire.

As a matter of fact things were going far from well with the units of the 32nd American Division now stalled in front of Buna. One day in late November MacArthur ordered Lt. General Robert L. Eichelberger, I Corps Commander at Rockhampton, to fly at once to advance G.H.Q. at Port

MacArthur prepares to take the offensive in New Guinea.

Moresby. Eichelberger and his chief of staff, Brigadier General Clovis Byers, reported in at the wide corridor of Government House. MacArthur's information from Dobodura had him deeply worried.

He told Eichelberger that he was putting him in command at Buna. His first job would be to relieve the commander of the 32nd Division, and he was to go right on down the line and replace every unsatisfactory officer. He was to put sergeants in charge of battalions if he found it necessary.

MacArthur made no attempt to disguise his deep concern. Suddenly he stopped in front of Eichelberger and his voice took on an almost terrifying tone.

"Bob, get me Buna—or don't come back alive!" It was a definite order.

A moment later the harsh mood was displaced by one of quiet despair as he spoke of the long series of disappointments and failures that had followed him. "Why must I always lead a forlorn hope?" he almost pleaded.

Eichelberger flew to Dobodura early that next morning. Few soldiers ever faced a more desperate task than was his. First, he must relieve his own West Point classmate and use his pruning knife as far down as battalion commanders. Then he had to rebuild morale and spirit by showing himself in every wavering front-line post and on every dangerous trail. In less than a week he had turned a discouraged, emotionally upset and exhausted division into a fighting outfit.

To the north of the American sector across a roadless swamp were the tough 7th Australian Imperial Forces, with parts of the U. S. 126th Infantry, later relieved by the 163rd Regiment of the U. S. 41st Division. The nature of the fighting became clear with the relief of the 2nd Battalion of this 126th Infantry. Of 1,100 men who had foot-slogged their way to the Aussie sector, exactly 95 gaunt and utterly exhausted doughboys were able to walk out to awaiting planes that flew them back to the rest areas at Rockhampton.

Eichelberger took Buna village on December 14. Five days before this the Aussies overran Gona, but they still faced days of hard fighting.

In the nine and a half months since he arrived in Australia

MacArthur had checked the Japanese drive southward, saved Port Moresby and Milne Bay and destroyed the enemy's forward bases at Buna and Gona. Short-handed though he was, he could finally take the offensive. He was sure now that nothing could stop him from ultimately fulfilling the vow, "I shall return," that he had made on the grim rock of Corregidor.

[Three years after this, MacArthur's then military secretary, Brigadier General Bonner Fellers, unearthed in Tokyo a curious bit of information; when the word of the capture of Buna was brought to the Emperor at his palace in Tokyo, he solemnly shook his head. He sensed the skill of MacArthur and the power that lay behind the Allied effort. Deep in his heart he knew that Japan was doomed. He, as well as the American commander far to the south, understood the deadly nature of the advancing bomber line.]

MacArthur was glad that the terrible year of 1942 was ended. The bitter memories of Bataan and Corregidor still haunted him. And the road ahead was long and rugged.

He continued to be at the bottom of the global priority list, and he could expect little help from Washington. His own political friends back home had probably harmed him more than they had helped him. The constant intrusion of his name as a possible Presidential candidate in 1944 infuriated the New Deal politicians, and the resentment of the White House was reflected down through the War and Navy departments.

Early in October MacArthur felt compelled to repudiate publicly any but purely military interests. His statement read:

> I have no political ambitions whatsoever. Any suggestion to the contrary may be regarded as merely amiable gestures of goodwill dictated by friendship. I started as a soldier and I shall finish as one. The only hope and ambition I have in the world is for victory for our cause in the war. If I survive the campaign, I shall return to that retirement from which this great struggle called me.

He could only trust that 1943 would prove less harsh for him both on the Japanese war front and the Washington political battlefront.

[To the question of how the system of by-passing or leap-frogging was subsequently developed in the Pacific, MacArthur answered in late 1952:

The system is as old as war itself. It is merely a new name, dictated by new conditions, given to the ancient principle of envelopment. It was the first time that the area of combat embraced land and water in such relative proportions. Heretofore, either the one or the other was predominant in the campaign. But in this area the presence of great land masses separated by large sea expanses with the medium of transportation of ground troops by ships as well as land transport seemed to conceal the fact that the system was merely that of envelopment applied to a new type of battle area. It has always proved the ideal method for success by inferior in number but faster moving forces. Immediately upon my arrival in Australia and learning the resources at my command, I determined that such a plan of action offered the sole chance for aggressive action. For its application it demanded a secure base from which to anchor all operations. Australia was plainly the only possible base—but the enemy still held the initiative and was advancing. The plan of the Australian Chiefs of Staff was to give up New Guinea and northern Australia and defend on the so-called Brisbane Line. Such a concept was fatal to every possibility of ever assuming the offensive and even if tactically successful would have bottled us up on the Australian Continent probably permanently. I determined to completely abandon the plan and to stop the enemy advances along the Owen Stanley Range in New Guinea. It was one of the most decisive as well as one of the most radical and difficult decisions of the war. Its success came through the Buna-Gona-Milne Bay-Coral Sea battles. From this point on I never doubted our full success. The first actual physical by-pass was probably when I had Halsey's forces, which had been placed under my operational control, by-pass the lines of Guadalcanal along the west coast of Bougainville.]

15

1943—THE BITTER YEAR

The American ground forces under MacArthur's command at
the beginning of 1943 consisted of two National Guard infantry divisions, a few thousand special troops and the 1st Marine Division, which was at Melbourne recuperating from
the costly Guadalcanal battle; at best MacArthur could consider its use in his theatre as only of a shifting and temporary
nature.

Official War Department figures eventually released, showed
the paucity of MacArthur's ground and air command in com-
parison with the Army as a whole. On January 1, 1943, the total
strength of the U. S. Army, including the Air Corps, was
5,391,033.

MacArthur's total of 106,663 was 3,316 less than the army
and air personnel in Admiral Halsey's South Pacific theatre,
and 24,494 less than Nimitz had in the Central Pacific, which
included posts in Hawaii and the Canton and Christmas Islands. The three Australian Imperial divisions and the Aussie
militia and air force are not included in the figures of the Southwest theatre. Likewise Marine strength is not counted in with
the Army strength in the South and Central Pacific. Roughly
speaking, one balanced the other.

So MacArthur, at the turn of 1943, had slightly less than
2% of the total U. S. Army and air force. His allocation of
106,663 gave him almost exactly 10% of the 1,057,454 Army
and air force personnel then stationed outside of the Continental limits of the United States. His share of the total
U. S. naval forces, in both men and ships, was even smaller
than his percentage of Army troops.

Fortunately the global war situation, save here in the distant
Pacific and Southeastern Asia, had started to turn definitely

in favor of the Allies. General Montgomery's ponderous superiority in men, tanks and air at El Alamein had enabled him to rout Rommel and drive his famous Afrika Corps across the deserts of North Africa. Lt. General Eisenhower had landed in French North Africa on November 8, 1942. His units were pushing eastward to face the remnants of Rommel's armor at Kasserine Pass and a final victory in Bizerte and Tunis on the coming 13th of May.

Russia was still deep in her second winter of war, and Hitler's forces were breaking their back against Stalingrad. Russia was now receiving 30% of the total lend-lease, and spring would see her start back on the long trail that would eventually lead to Berlin and the annihilation of the Eastern German armies.

In the air the British and Americans had shifted the comparative air strength over Europe from a 2 to 3 ratio in favor of Germany, to a 3 to 2 ratio in favor of the Allies. Germany had received her death wounds on the bloody fields of Russia and in the skies over her own homeland.

But the picture was very different with regard to Japan. In the vast periphery of her conquests, only at Midway and in the Coral Sea, at two tiny spots on New Guinea and in the lower Solomons and on the western borders of Burma had she been seriously challenged. She had been allowed the time to consolidate her gains and her priceless war loot.

General George C. Marshall, dominant figure of the U. S. Joint Chiefs of Staff, diligently seeking ways to expand America's might in the European theatre, was determined to carry out the Roosevelt-Hopkins pledge to Stalin for a second front. In the late summer of 1942 he had pushed plans for an Allied invasion across the English channel and had almost broken with Churchill because the British leader insisted that it would be folly to attempt any such movement at this time. But Marshall now returned to his determination to launch a great second front in France by early summer of 1943.

Such was the global picture when on February 6, 1943, Roosevelt and Churchill with their senior military chiefs and civilian advisors met at Casablanca in North Africa. Four days before the conference opened the Russians announced the liquidation of the German Army before Stalingrad. Complete victory over Germany now appeared so certain that it seemed but a small task to decide in advance the broad terms of surrender. At a press conference the President launched the proposition of *unconditional surrender*. It was to prove the most costly phrase in the entire course of the war.

Secretary of the Treasury Henry Morgenthau, Jr., was already evolving the plan to turn Germany, once it was broken, into a pastoral state by destroying her heavy industries and prohibiting their reestablishment. Roosevelt's idea of unconditional surrender fitted perfectly into the pattern of hate and revenge then prevalent among a large group of Americans. A brilliant young brigadier general, Albert C. Wedemeyer, head of the War Plans section of the General Staff, accompanied General Marshall to the conference and tried to warn his immediate superior of the eventual danger and disaster that lay in the Morgenthau and Roosevelt theories of utterly crushing Germany.

Events of great secrecy and questionable design were already under way in Washington. It was some time later before the almost unbelievable sequence of the hidden plans and devious actions finally came to light; even a full ten years after the events occurred there were still great breaks in the continuing story of Communist intrigue and conspiracy that had been developed and were functioning at high levels in Washington.

As early as 1934 a small but expertly organized Red cell, called the Silvermaster Spy Ring, was planted deep into one of the most sensitive posts of the Treasury Department, with Harry Dexter White, chief assistant to Mr. Morgenthau, as an important member. Shortly after this other cells were formed with members settled in key spots in the White House, in offices in the State Department, and in other top posts. This was the beginning of a sordid conspiracy against the interests of America and in favor of Communist Russia which did irremediable harm to America, the effects of which are still felt.

At this period centering in 1943 the principal and immediate result was the plan written by Harry Dexter White and backed by Morgenthau for the pastoralization of Germany. Without the knowledge or approval of either Secretary of State Hull or Secretary of War Stimson, Roosevelt presented it as a fully accredited doctrine at the later Quebec Conference, where it was duly accepted by Churchill.

In Washington the American Communists, who had kept well under cover during the 22 months of the Hitler-Stalin peace, were no longer official outcasts. Agents direct from the Kremlin plotted the work to be done by their American agents, and it was not long before spies planted in the very heart of the government were stealing such priceless possessions as the atomic bomb secrets and the designs for proximity fuses. Other Red spies soon began to influence highly important policy-making decisions in the State Department. Alger Hiss was eventually to become the best known of these traitors.

Aliens in America and certain religio-political zealots whose principal concern was to make sure of crushing Hitler and to take revenge on the whole German nation found it easy and natural to espouse the same general line as that put out by the secret Communist plotters and their dupes, fellow travelers and sentimental followers. These two large groups, along with the millions of pro-British interventionists and internationalists, under the active leadership of the administration completely dominated all channels of American propaganda. No microphone or typewriter could long stand against these men and groups, who seemed often to be far more concerned with revenge and with saving the Soviet and British empires than with the ultimate fate of America. From the very start of the war they had largely been against giving adequate support for MacArthur and his area—6,000 miles from San Francisco.

MacArthur, fighting his far-away war in the Southwest Pacific, had no part in the great decisions, and his advice was not asked. Roosevelt and Churchill, and now Stalin, agreed that the war against Japan must be kept in its distinctly secondary place. Stalin had readily concurred as long as it was certain that Japan was sufficiently engaged to prevent her attacking Siberia and forcing Russia into a two-front war.

A new element now brought into the slightly confused picture was the whispered suggestion that Stalin might withdraw from the global war and make peace with Germany unless the United States and Britain hurriedly established a second front against Germany. The threat, completely unrealistic though it was, apparently continued to carry great weight, particularly in the minds of the President, Harry Hopkins and General Marshall; but somehow it was held less important by Winston Churchill.

The war against Japan must drag along. Germany must first be driven to her knees and accept unconditional surrender, before the men fighting in the air and jungles and on the dangerous seas in the distant Pacific would get help.

As early as 1943 the Asiatic dreamers in the Kremlin visioned the possibility that great elements of the Japanese Army, particularly in Manchuria and Korea, might eventually be won to Communism. If at the end of the war Russia could have an important hand in the making of the Pacific peace, not only China but Japan might be drawn into the Red orbit and thus become partners in the Communist conquest of the world.

2

MacArthur's immediate problem in New Guinea was to push the forward fighter strips further and further ahead in the rugged country back from the coastal regions and thus furnish air cover for his advancing long-range bomber line. He never lost sight of the fact that his principal target was Rabaul, so that he could break out through the Vitiaz Strait into the Bismarck Sea and start on the long trip back to the Philippines.

He still had little or no fleet or even adequate sea-lift for troops and supplies, but he did have Kenney and the American and Australian air forces. The bitter campaign against Buna and Gona proved what the transport plane could do as a packhorse and sea carrier. By gaining air supremacy MacArthur could control the sky and make the ground and waters below it safe from enemy air and sea attacks.

The reduction of the minor Japanese shore base at Salamaua, and the far more important concentration some twenty miles on to the north at Lae, came first on his schedule. Toward the end of February 1943, Brigadier General Charles A. Willoughby's intelligence discovered that a large convoy was being prepared to transport the equivalent of a Japanese army division from Rabaul to the New Guinea port of Lae.

MacArthur called in Kenney, who took off for New Guinea to work out the job with his deputy, Brigadier General Ennis Whitehead. Playing the influence of the weather and a lot of hunches, they decided to gamble on the Japanese convoy coming through the Vitiaz Strait at 10:15 on the morning of March 3. That would put the ships in range of the whole 137 aircraft that Kenney had in New Guinea at that time. The gamble paid off. At 10:15 A.M. the Yank and Aussie aviators opened the almost fabulous engagement known as the Battle of the Bismarck Sea.

When it was over, six Japanese destroyers and from eleven to fourteen merchant vessels lay at the bottom of the strait, somewhere around 10,000 Japanese personnel were destroyed, and at least 60 aircraft were shot down. The Allied losses were 13 men killed and 12 injured, with 4 airplanes shot down and 2 crash-landed at their home bases.

Kenney took off immediately for Washington in company with Major General Sutherland, MacArthur's chief of staff; the Southwest Pacific's G-3, Brigadier General Stephen J. Chamberlain, and Captain H. J. Roy, the naval representative. It was a combined begging and selling mission.

In Washington animosity against MacArthur was reaching the boiling point by the time Sutherland and Kenney started back for Australia and New Guinea. There were definite rumors that Roosevelt was about to relieve him of his Southwest Pacific command. But it was certain that MacArthur would demand an Army court of inquiry, and his friends would insist on a Congressional hearing. It might be best to let his deputies get back to their stations before taking any drastic steps.

Then a strange public-relations consideration entered the picture. From Switzerland on March 12, came confidential news that the two American crews who had been shot down in the Doolittle raid over Tokyo in April 1942 had been brutally executed. For ten days the report had been held back in the fear that the public reaction might call for immediate and increased action against Japan. Certainly it was not the appropriate time to relieve MacArthur.

3

Dividing his time between Brisbane and Port Moresby, Mac-Arthur laid out his plans to pinch off Lae, Salamaua and then Finchhafen with the least possible loss of American and Australian lives. As the hot tropical days and weeks slipped by, MacArthur was ceaseless in his demands upon Kenney and Whitehead—now aided by an imaginative and experienced air operator, Colonel Merian C. Cooper—to continue blasting Rabaul and a great new enemy base on up the Guinea coast at Wewak. Nothing could induce MacArthur to move until he had complete mastery of the air. With that assured, he could use his advance landing fields exactly as more conventional commanders used their expensive coastal beachheads and sea bases to move ahead.

It was already August 1943 when Rear Admiral Daniel E. Barbey, now assigned to the Southwest Pacific theatre, for the first time was able to assemble sufficient landing craft and sea-lift—and secure enough equipment for the newly organized army amphibian force—to undertake and sustain a fair-sized coastal operation. Early on September 4 Barbey landed General Ralph M. Wooten's AIF 9th Division—the splendid Rats of Tobruk—at Hopoi Bay, east of Lae.

At 9:00 the next morning 305 Allied planes rose from nine fields in lower Guinea and took their place in a formation that was as perfect as a sky parade on Air Force Day in peace time. It headed for a spot called Nadzab in the high and almost inaccessible Markham Valley, a scant 20 miles northwest of enemy-held Lae. In front rode five squadrons of deadly B-25s. They came sixteen abreast like spanking circus horses. Each carried eight .50-caliber guns in its nose, and they cut the tall grass as clean as Sverdrup's natives could have done. Behind them sailed a dozen A-20s that laid in even ribbons the three lanes of smoke. In the open columns between the smoke lanes came 96 C-47 transport planes, spaced in three rows of 32 planes each. At their head rode a B-17 Flying Fortress, with Douglas MacArthur as its star passenger. Before noon the entire U. S. 503rd Parachute Regiment had hit the silk, along with a full battery of Aussie 25-pounders.

It was America's first effort at a large scale air-drop and it was perfectly executed. Lae and Salamaua were now surrounded and helpless—triple-enveloped, as a matter of fact.

Within 18 days both enemy strongholds on New Guinea had fallen, along with Finchhafen—and here at hand lay the waters of the key Vitiaz Strait. To clean out the scattered Japanese bases still remaining on New Britain Island on the east side of the narrow strait, would be practice work for the small but well-oiled MacArthur machine.

Gloucester, at the west tip of New Britain, fell to the 1st Marine Division on December 26. The Vitiaz Strait was now clear. Ahead lay the remainder of the great land bridge of Dutch New Guinea. Admiral Barbey had landed these marines in a highly skillful blind night maneuver through dangerous coral reefs with MacArthur's shoestring Navy.

4

Back in July of 1943 the decision was made in Washington that Admiral Halsey would have tactical charge of the actual operations in the drive on northwestward up the Solomon chain of islands, and MacArthur would have the strategic command.

From their first meeting Halsey and MacArthur formed a strong personal liking for each other. More than once the soldier declared that the fighting spirit of Nelson had descended on the pugnacious old sea bull. In return Halsey recognized the uncanny talents that MacArthur exercised in his twin formulae: "All there is to know is when and where to fight" and "Always hit 'em where they ain't."

The entire vast Solomon-Bismarck seas area was in the nature of a double horseshoe, with the two backs of their "U's" resting on New Britain Island—one horseshoe pointing south and enclosing the Solomon Sea; the other pointing north, encompassing the Bismarck Sea. In other terms, each arm might be described as one arm of a gigantic bear hug.

Briefly stated, the MacArthur-Halsey plan was for Halsey to advance up the east side while MacArthur moved up the west arm of the lower horseshoe, with the 600-mile wide Solomon

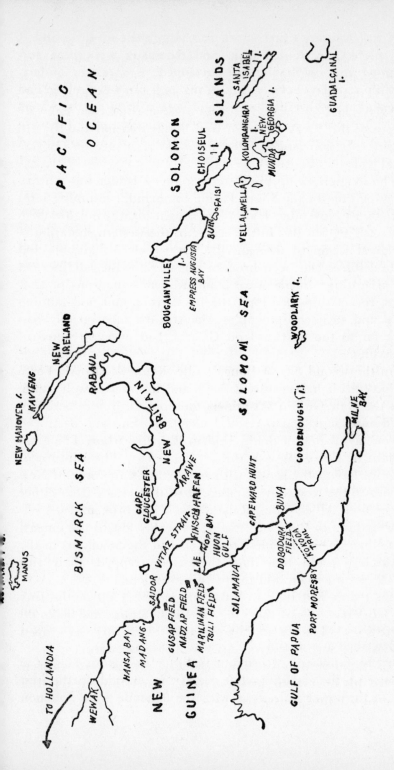

The offensive in the Solomon and Bismarck seas.

Sea between. From the start Admiral King had seen to it that Halsey's people lacked little in their prolonged struggle to hold Guadalcanal and finally to drive out the Japanese reinforcements. Before the desperate six months of fighting ended, the Navy had fed in two Marine divisions and two Army divisions of the XXIV Corps. A fresh Army division and the 3rd Marine Division landed after organized resistance on Guadalcanal ended on February 9, 1943.

The long climb up the eastern Solomon ladder was a heartbreaking task for the South Pacific command, consuming most of 1943. By November Halsey had fought his way northward to Princess Augusta Bay in the center of the western shoreline of the great island of Bougainville. Overwhelming air, sea and ground forces had been brought together for the landings. In the assaulting armada were bombardment squadrons of warships, rocket ships, flat-tops, the latest troop and tank-landing ships and such equipment as MacArthur's men, grimly battling far to the westward on Guinea, had never dreamed of possessing.

On the second day of Bougainville, Kenney's 5th Air Force let loose all it had against Rabaul, and in exactly twelve minutes the New Guinea sky-raiders took out airdromes and supply dumps, sank destroyers and merchant ships and destroyed 100 enemy planes on the ground in Rabaul harbor. The great menace of Rabaul was a thing of the past. The capture of Augusta Bay to the south, with MacArthur's air force in New Guinea to the west, now exposed Rabaul to attack from either one or both Allied bases. Rabaul's back was broken.

Everything to the south was irretrievably lost to the enemy. More than 50,000 Japanese troops still in the Solomons to the southward would now find themselves trapped, their rice and bullet lines cut, and themselves abandoned.

MacArthur had only to finish his mopping up of the tiny Jap bases on the east shore of the Vitiaz Strait, and he could call it a year. The sea and air roads northward were now open to him. He was at last on his way home to Manila.

[To the question of how seriously the lack of carriers affected his operations in the SWPA, MacArthur, years after the events, bluntly answered:

Most seriously. The very essense of our so-called "by-passing" method of advance depended upon securing air control over the area covered in each forward step. In the present state of development of the art of war no movement can safely be made of forces on sea or land without adequate air protection. The limit of such protection in our case was the possible radius of operation of our fighter planes. This radius had to be measured from the actual location of our ground air bases. This required the seizing or construction of such new bases at each forward movement. The presence of carriers with their inherent movability would have immeasurably increased the scope and speed of our operations. I know of no other area and no other theatre where they could have been used to such advantage. The enemy's diversion of his air forces on many different islands and fields was peculiarly adapted to his piecemeal destruction which would have been drastically assisted if we could have utilized the mobility of carriers in surprise concentrations. For instance, with our overall inferior air strength, in order to neutralize the enemy's superior combined air strength at Rabaul and Aitape, being limited to ground air strength, I had to locate a temporary air base in New Guinea between these two enemy air garrisons to operate by surprise, with my entire force concentrated first on the one and then on the other. Their combined force could have beaten me but divided I destroyed them unilaterally. The presence of carriers would have entirely altered our potential. Prime Minister Curtin did his best to persuade Prime Minister Churchill to let us have carriers, and I did the same with Washington but without success. To this day I cannot understand why the decision was in the negative.]

5

General MacArthur's reaction at the time to this exact period of the war is expressed in a letter he wrote on June 13 to an old Army friend who had been on his staff in Manila in 1936 and '37. It read:

I was so glad to receive your letter of April 30, and to know where and how you were. Little or no news reaches me and I have lost all touch with my old friends. Your estimate of the situation is substantially correct. It is too bad that so few of

307

those who control would agree with you. It has been a desperate time for me since the war started, always the underdog, and always fighting with destruction just around the corner. I could have held Bataan if I had not been so completely deserted. I take some comfort from Stonewall Jackson's creed, "that if necessary, we will fight them with sticks and stone." But I find that sticks break in our hands and stones can't go very far. A merciful God has miraculously brought me through so far, but I am sick at heart at the mistakes and lost opportunities that are so prevalent.

To MacArthur it was evident that this year the Washington front had been almost as difficult for him as the Japanese front. He had barely escaped the angry storm of reproof that blew up in the Capital as a result of his demands expressed jointly with Prime Minister John Curtin in March and April that more attention and help be given the Southwest Pacific theatre.

His friends, however, had not for a moment let up on their bitter harangues against the White House and the Joint Chiefs of Staff for what they considered the unfair treatment of Mac-Arthur and his area. This fight had for the most part been in the hands of a little group of politicians and publishers and a few embattled columnists and radio commentators who might be called the anti-Roosevelt crowd. These kindred spirits were using every method they could find to support Mac-Arthur, to discredit the administration and its conduct of the war and to oppose the ambition of the President for a fourth term.

In middle May of 1943 the pro-MacArthur faction gained a vociferous champion from the Democratic ranks. Senator A. B. (Happy) Chandler of Kentucky suddenly broke out on the Senate floor with the statement that the recent Allied successes in North Africa, in an area that had been considered British responsibilities, had so changed the whole global picture that more attention should now be given the Pacific, and it should be done before Japan could consolidate her gains.

"I am one citizen of this country," the Senator went on, "who believes sincerely that the Pacific cannot wait, and that if anything comes of the conference now being held by Mr. Roosevelt and Mr. Churchill a major decision should be made to give the Pacific war the consideration which facts justify it having in the general scheme of world affairs."

The following day the President vigorously repudiated Chandler's suggestion. A day later Churchill, addressing a joint session of Congress, pledged that Britain would in the proper time wage the war against Japan "while there is breath in our bodies and while white blood flows through our veins."

From August 17 to 24, 1943, Churchill and Roosevelt met in their first conference at Quebec. The Pacific was low on the agenda, and while the meeting was mainly in preparation for possible later conferences in which Stalin would be present, there were important decisions made regarding the Atlantic theatre. Eisenhower was to be in charge of the Mediterranean area. Marshall's ambitions to command the European theatre and the great cross-channel invasion was left for later decision.

Within a month this command problem created a violent storm both in inner circles and in Congress. Those behind Marshall suddenly presented the idea that he be made global commander in chief, with the title of General of the Armies. Either Lt. General Somervell or Lt. General Eisenhower would then become Army Chief of Staff. Senator Chandler countered with the suggestion that there be a single Pacific and East Asia Command under General MacArthur. Even the name of Lord Louis Mountbatten was tossed into the controversy.

The American and British press carried reports that MacArthur's "part in the war is to be progressively curtailed and his command reduced to a secondary and subsidiary role." In a desperate attempt to neutralize the criticism against him and his strategic conceptions, MacArthur released on September 21 a carefully worded reply. He had just completed double envelopment of Salamaua and Lae with extremely small losses, and the following day he would capture Finchhafen. His statement read:

> It makes little difference whether I or others wield the weapons, just so the cause for which our beloved country fights is victorious. However subordinate may be my role I hope to play it manfully.

My strategic conception for the Pacific Theatre, which I outlined after the Papuan Campaign and have since consistently advocated, contemplates massive strokes against only main strategic objectives, utilizing surprise and air-ground striking power, supported and assisted by the fleet. This is the very opposite of what is termed "island hopping" which is the gradual pushing back of the enemy by direct frontal pressure, with the consequent heavy casualties which will certainly be involved. Key points must of course be taken but a wise choice of such will obviate the need for storming the mass of islands now in enemy possession. "Island hopping" with extravagant losses and slow progress —some press reports indicating victory postponed as late as 1949—is not my idea of how to end the war as soon and as cheaply as possible. New conditions require solution, and new weapons require maximum application and imaginative methods. Wars are never won in the past.

I have no personal military ambitions and am perfectly content in such role as may be prescribed for me.

The remarks by no means lessened the bitter conflict. Proponents of the strategy recommended by the Joint Chiefs of Staff to send large American air and ground forces to the Burma-Chinese area now smarted under new attacks by Senator Chandler. Chandler insisted that if and when the Burma Road was opened, it would be of little real consequence.

Either by direct letter or by other means Chandler succeeded in securing a rough outline of MacArthur's strategic conception, and he openly laid it out on the Senate floor: Once the Solomon-Bismarck seas were cleared, he claimed that Mac-Arthur would move upon the great southern Philippine island of Mindanao, and from there probably advance to Luzon and eventually on to Formosa. From the Philippine bases American submarines and bombers could cut the Japanese life-line that led from her rich loot in Malaya and the Dutch East Indies to her home islands. Deprived of oil, rubber, tin, rice, quinine and other vital necessities, she would see her war potential ruined.

Again Chandler and his Congressional friends insisted that MacArthur be put in supreme command of the entire Pacific. Roosevelt made no effort to hide his violent opposition, while the Army high command concentrated on trying to find out just how Chandler had obtained his secret information.

It had now become everybody's fight in Washington, and

the Navy did not miss the opportunity to get in its licks. Early in November Rear Admiral W. H. Young stated that "American supplies are reaching the Southwest Pacific in quantities sufficient for large scale operations against the Japanese."

Once again MacArthur answered, and on November 13 released a formal statement;

> I am reluctant to discuss such a subject. The Southwest Pacific has something less than 5% of American military resources, and is now receiving something less than 10% of what America is shipping overseas. This is much more than formerly. The percent of air resources is somewhat lower. Without complaint, the area is doing everything it can with what it has.

On the strictly political side of the Washington controversy, the unauthorized campaign to project MacArthur's name into the coming Presidential campaign was beginning to assume greater importance. In the early summer of 1943 Governor Thomas E. Dewey of New York was the leading Republican candidate, but Wendell Willkie, who had made the unsuccessful fight in 1940, was still being seriously considered. MacArthur's name was now definitely injected into the contest.

In Chicago plans for nation-wide MacArthur-for-President clubs were pushed, although it was admitted that the General had not been consulted regarding the action. On July 9 a local club formally opened its headquarters.

A few days later Colonel Robert R. McCormick, editor of the *Chicago Tribune,* said in an interview in New York City: "Roosevelt is in a hell of a position. If MacArthur wins a great victory, he will be President. If he doesn't win one, it will be because Roosevelt has not given him sufficient support."

That same day Senator Arthur H. Vandenberg remarked at his home in Grand Rapids, Michigan, that "at present MacArthur would be the best choice for the Republicans for next fall."

Obviously MacArthur was becoming involved in a situation that might well get beyond his control. On August 25 Representative Hamilton Fish gave out a statement in Goshen,

New York, that indicated how a number of professional politicians were thinking:

> Republicans and anti-New Deal Democrats are united in opposing the 4th term for President Roosevelt and the power-hungry bureaucrats and left-wing New Dealers in Washington.
>
> I am in favor of drafting General MacArthur as the Republican candidate for President and Commander-in-Chief of our armed forces on a win-the-war platform and on a one-term plank, as opposed to a fourth term and military dictatorship.

Two weeks later Senator Arthur Capper of Kansas injected a new note into the picture by the statement that he believed that either General Eisenhower or General MacArthur would be the Republican Presidential candidate in 1944. He continued:

> Either of them would make a fine President. The people of Kansas lean towards Eisenhower because he comes from Kansas, but they consider that MacArthur would make an excellent choice, too.

On September 17 the Gallup poll announced the result of its question: "If the Presidential election were being held today, and Roosevelt were running for President on the Democratic ticket and MacArthur on the Republican ticket, how do you think you would vote?" The nation-wide result was: Roosevelt 58%; MacArthur 42%.

In the farm areas, particularly in the anti-internationalist Middle West, however, the result was almost the exact reverse: Roosevelt 44%; MacArthur 56%.

6

Across the Atlantic and at the eastern end of the Mediterranean and deep in the Middle East, events that would help shape the political world for possibly a hundred years or more were in the making. At Cairo from November 22 to the 26th, 1943, Roosevelt and Churchill conferred with Chiang Kai-shek. China was definitely promised by Roosevelt that she was to have Formosa and Manchuria and all Japanese interests therein, once a Pacific victory was secured.

312

Two days later the President and the British Prime Minister met at Tehran for a three-day conference with Dictator Stalin. Already it was evident that Roosevelt was beginning to weaken in energy and mental coordination. His own certainty that he could win Stalin to the Roosevelt design for a peaceful world was quietly being fostered by the shrewd and calculating Red dictator.

Eisenhower, who was present at the Casablanca conference and was a member of the American delegation at Cairo, did not go to Tehran. MacArthur had not been invited even to the Cairo conference, where important decisions involving China and the Pacific areas were decided.

In addition to Eisenhower at Cairo, the President's top group of advisors, both at the conference on the Nile and at Tehran, included Harry Hopkins, Admirals Leahy and King, and General Marshall. Not one of them seemed willing or able to warn the President effectively that Stalin was swiftly becoming the master of the situation. Marshall especially was an ardent spokesman for Russia to enter the Pacific war, apparently without regard to the price the dictator might ask. Yet there could be little doubt that neither Germany nor Japan could possibly win against the war machines they were now facing.

General Marshall decided to return to Washington via the Indian Ocean and the Pacific. The news of the impending visit of the Army Chief of Staff reached MacArthur at his advance headquarters in Port Moresby as he was taking off for a conference with Lt. General Krueger at his headquarters on Goodenough Island. Only the landings at Port Gloucester remained unfinished in his long campaign to win both sides of the Solomon Sea and clear the way through the Vitiaz Strait for advanced bases in New Guinea on the road back to the Philippines.

He was of the opinion that as a result of both the present and the past differences between himself and Marshall, their meeting might be somewhat embarrassing to his distinguished visitor. MacArthur seriously considered conducting the Gloucester operations in person, thus relieving Marshall of his presence.

"No, I'll stay," he finally remarked to one of his senior staff officers. "But I'll make the prophecy that he'll never see me alone. He'll always find a way to have someone else present."

Kenney met General Marshall at Port Moresby and flew him to Goodenough Island, where the visitor had a long conference with General MacArthur and his senior commanders. At their meeting MacArthur and Marshall called each other by his given name and there was every evidence of friendly cordiality. At the pep talk and general survey made by Marshall it turned out that MacArthur was the complete listener.

Marshall went on his way the next day. MacArthur was right; never for a moment had Marshall sought to be alone with him. Nor did he evince any desire to confide in MacArthur or to give him his own inner thoughts and ideas on the global struggle.

16

MACARTHUR ESCAPES THE TRAP

MacArthur had long been convinced that the least expensive and quickest way to win against Japan was to pool all the resources of the various Pacific areas under one supreme Pacific commander. This would make conclusively overwhelming concentrations of land, sea and air forces for the successive steps essential to the ultimate defeat of Japan.

There were two possible approaches to the Japanese home islands, and the enemy had succeeded in setting up island roadblocks in each of these great sea-and-land avenues of attack. In choosing either route for the main effort against Japan the first essential was to pool all resources under a united command.

314

The Navy under King preferred the approach that led almost straight across the central Pacific, in a ponderous movement westward, building bases on the captured enemy islands as it drove ahead.

MacArthur with insufficient sea forces to challenge even a small part of the Japanese fleet was fortunate in having the great buzzard-shaped island of New Guinea as a land-bridge that offered a road of nearly 1500 miles toward the Philippines, his prize objective. Kenney's New Guinea-based planes, clearing out enemy air bases and concentrations ahead of the advancing ground forces, could cover the march as far as the extreme upper tip of New Guinea. But from there on the great Central Pacific fleet would have to be borrowed for strategic and tactical support.

Once bases were secured in the Philippines, the sea lanes between Japan and Southeast Asia and Indonesia could be cut by submarines and bombers. The numerous enemy air and sea bases that lay to the east in the lower Central Pacific route would likewise be flanked and thus by-passed and left "to die on the vine." Most of the fighting, under this conception, would take place in MacArthur's Southwest Pacific area and consequently would largely be under his command.

In an attempt to sell this idea to the South and Central Pacific naval, air and ground commanders, MacArthur sent Generals Sutherland, Chamberlain and Kenney and Vice Admiral Thomas C. Kinkaid on an exploration trip. On January 24, 1944, the group arrived in Hawaii and started their missionary work. Their first convert was army Lt. General Robert C. Richardson; next came Admiral Jack Towers, the oldest airman on Nimitz's staff and one of the most experienced and wisest flyers living. Admiral Forrest Sherman, the Central Pacific chief of operations, was apparently already convinced, and Admiral "Mick" Carney, Halsey's chief of staff, now agreed to the general strategy. Admiral Charles H. McMorris, Nimitz's chief of staff, argued that the enemy-held Marshall and Caroline Islands should first be captured before any final decision was reached.

On the third day of the conference Admiral Sherman and General Sutherland took off for Washington in the hope of winning over the Joint Chiefs of Staff. General Kenney hurried back to Brisbane with the good news that everything seemed propitious. MacArthur complimented his airman on the progress made, but reserved judgment as to the outcome.

The Joint Chiefs of Staff in Washington listened quietly while Sherman and Sutherland presented their arguments for a single unified axis. But Admiral King was too navy-minded, and apparently General Marshall and possibly General Arnold were averse to any strategic plan in which the Southwest theatre would become the primary area of Pacific combat, and which would result in making of MacArthur the supreme commander of the main Japanese war effort.

Bitter repercussions regarding proposed new military ranks and titles were already rampant in Washington. Early in January 1944 the President publicly backed the idea of giving Marshall and Arnold the rank of General of the Armies, a rank that had been voted Pershing at the end of World War I. As for the Navy, King and Leahy would be rewarded with a new rank of Admiral of the Fleet. MacArthur and Nimitz, who were actually in command of the fighting in the Pacific war, were left completely out of the picture.

Bills were drawn up and sent to Congressional committees, but friends of both Pershing and MacArthur made such violent protests that the whole idea was dropped. General Malin Craig, who succeeded MacArthur as Army Chief of Staff and who had been recalled to active duty as head of the Promotion and Retirement Board, called the whole business "disgraceful."

Preparations for the Presidential election of the coming fall, involving as it did the dispute over a fourth term for Roosevelt, suddenly developed a new angle: the definite suggestion that General Marshall be the running mate of the President in order to insure for the Democrats the soldier vote. The Roosevelt boom, too, was given decided impetus by the highly questionable statement of the President's own physician, Vice Admiral Ross McIntyre, who publicly guaranteed the good health of the President, although those who saw him at close range knew that he was probably dying.

Meanwhile ardent groups continued to build up the

candidacy of MacArthur for the Republican Presidential nomination. Raymond Clapper, a distinguished newspaper columnist, visited MacArthur's headquarters and cabled home that in his opinion the General would take the Republican nomination if it was offered him. MacArthur issued no denial.

In Washington the President approved a carefully drawn policy agreement that would settle the bitter argument whether a Regular Army officer had the right to enter politics. The decision held that an officer in the regular establishments could become a candidate *only* if the nomination were tendered to him "without direct or indirect activity or solicitation on his part."

But MacArthur had little time at the moment to ponder over the new ruling. On February 27 he slipped out of Brisbane, and flying to Milne Bay, at the lower tip of New Guinea, boarded the U.S.S. *Phoenix* as the guest of Vice Admiral Kinkaid. Two mornings later under a murky sky a little group of swift destroyers, with a single reinforced squadron of the 5th Cavalry tucked on board four of the tin cans, dropped anchor in the bay of Los Negros, in the Admiralty Islands. After a short preliminary bombardment the men went ashore. MacArthur went with them.

A few days before this, Kenney's reconnaissance planes had brought back pictures showing that there was no real enemy strength on the island of Los Negros, which had the only good airfield in the group. Willoughby's intelligence insisted that there were 4,000 troops, mostly on the main island of Manus, which proved to be substantially correct. The isolated Admiralty group, with the magnificent harbor of Manus, was on the extreme eastern flank of the enemy-held Bismarck Sea, and MacArthur immediately decided that if he grabbed it in a surprise attack and was able to hold it and gain its airfields, his own right flank would be fully protected for his coming advance up the coast of Dutch New Guinea. The little force he took with him could handle an initial landing and reconnaissance on Los Negros, and he personally would make the decision whether to pull out or hold on until reinforcements from the 1st Cavalry Division, already loaded and waiting, could be hurried forward.

Sniper bullets were still whistling from the edge of the air strip when MacArthur shoved forward from the beach to look over the situation. Finally he turned to Brigadier General William C. Chase, commander of the 800 dismounted cavalrymen, and said, "You've got your teeth in him now. Don't let go!" Chase grinned and nodded his head in approval. He knew that his men here on Los Negros could beat off the dribbling attacks from nearby islands.

[A curious incident occurred on the warship going toward the uncertain adventure, when MacArthur's aide, Colonel Larry Lehrbas, casually mentioned to the General that the few troops he would be sending ashore had had no actual battle experience. MacArthur replied slowly: "I have known this 5th Cavalry for almost 60 years. When I was a little boy of four my father was a captain in the 13th Infantry at Fort Selden, in the Indian frontier country of New Mexico. Geronimo, the Apache scourge, was loose, and our small infantry garrison was to guard the middle fords of the Rio Grande. A troop of this same 5th Cavalry under Captain Henry Lawton, who was later killed as a major general in the Philippines, with Charles King, an old friend of my father's, as his lieutenant, rode through to help us. I can still remember how I felt when I watched them clatter into the little post, their tired horses gray with desert dust. . . . They'd fight then—and they'll fight now. Don't worry about them, Larry."]

[When asked long after the war as to the background of the decision to by-pass Rabaul and strike at the Admiralties, MacArthur answered:

The potential value militarily of Rabaul to our arms was to furnish an advance naval base. In the progress of the campaign its value to the enemy had been practically neutralized as an air or naval base for further enemy advances and was largely reduced to a stronghold of defense—but its harbor facilities were good and lacking such an advanced naval base for ourselves it represented an appreciable prize. When our intelligence detected that the Admiralties, with a fine naval haven at Manus, was lightly held the picture changed. The base at Manus was superior in every way and farther advanced. If it could be taken

318

with little loss it would save our relatively weak forces the heavy penalty necessary to reduce Rabaul. When General Kenney reported to me that Whitehead's reconnaissance confirmed no heavy concentration of enemy forces at Manus I determined to attack and if successful leave Rabaul "to die on the vine." The surprise was complete, the Admiralties were taken with minor loss and Manus became our great intermediate naval base.]

The brilliant move to the Admiralties brought a fresh avalanche of favorable publicity for MacArthur. But the States were eight or ten thousand miles away and in Australia and New Guinea there was more than enough to occupy the General's mind. For one thing he faced the task of flying to the Australian capital at Canberra to be the guest of honor at a banquet given by Prime Minister Curtin and the Australian Parliament celebrating the second anniversary of his arrival at Port Darwin. Only once before, in March of 1942, when he had first journeyed to Canberra, had he left his immediate war duties for a single day or night.

At the close of the great dinner the Prime Minister and the opposition leader made gracious speeches, and then John Curtin introduced the General. Deeply touched by the solemn moment and by memories of the anguish and defeat that had surrounded his initial arrival, MacArthur arose, stern and white-faced. He used no notes. In cold type much of the warmth and quiet emotion of his talk this night is lost:

Mr. Prime Minister: I cannot tell you the sense of distinction I feel in being Australia's guest tonight. It adds another link to the long chain of friendship which binds together our peoples and our countries. It is a symbol of that unity of effort that recognizes but one indomitable purpose—victory.

The last two years have been momentous ones for Australia. You have faced the greatest peril in your history. With your very life at stake, you have met and overcome the challenge. It was here the tide of war turned in the Pacific, and the mighty wave of invasion broke and rolled back.

Two years ago when I landed on your soil I said to the people of the Philippines whence I came, "I shall return." Tonight I repeat these words, "I *shall* return." Nothing is more certain than our ultimate reconquest and liberation from the enemy of those and adjacent islands. One of the great offensives of the

319

war will at the appropriate time be launched for that purpose. With God's help it should be decisive, not only of redemption but of Japanese isolation from southern conquests and of Chinese restoration of Pacific Ocean communication.

On such an occasion as this my thoughts go back to those men who were sent on their last crusade in the jungle thickness to the north where they made the fight that saved this continent. With faith in their hearts and hope on their lips they passed beyond the mists that blind us here. Their yesterday makes possible our tomorrow. They came from the four quarters of the world, but whatever the land that gave them birth, under their stark white crosses they belong now to Australia forever.

I thank you, sir, for the high honor and hospitality of tonight in their and their comrades' names. I shall always recall it as joined with their immortal memory.

Rough-handed men, who had come up from the mines and ranches and factories of this isolated continent, made no effort to hide the tears in their eyes as they cheered this leader from a distant land.

2

That night the Prime Minister told General MacArthur an amusing story about his visit to Washington. At least once MacArthur repeated it [to the author]. Curtin had finished his official farewells and was ready to fly back to Australia, when he decided to drop in at the White House for a purely informal call on the President. Roosevelt received him graciously, and Curtin explained that he had come only because he wanted to thank him again for his many courtesies and personal kindnesses.

Just as he was getting ready to leave the Prime Minister suddenly said: "Mr. President, certainly it's none of my business and probably I shouldn't say this, but I can assure you in utter honesty and sincerity that General MacArthur has no more idea of running against you for the Presidency than I have. He has told me that a dozen times."

According to Curtin's story there were a number of papers on the President's desk, and as Roosevelt reared back in his chair he threw up his arms and the papers were scattered in all directions.

"Steve! Steve!" the President yelled gleefully.

The understanding press secretary, who had just left the room, stuck his head back into the study and the President shouted the news.

He was as happy as a boy with a new toy, Curtin told MacArthur. Then he added: "I'm sure that every night when he turned in, the President had been looking under the bed to make dead sure you weren't there."

But shortly the entire political atmosphere of MacArthur's unsolicited candidacy was to be blackened by a cloud that was of a most embarrassing nature. On Friday morning, April 14, papers over the country carried the text of two letters that a freshman Representative, Dr. A. L. Miller of Nebraska, had written MacArthur, and his replies. On his own responsibility the Congressman had released both his own letter and Mac-Arthur's, which had been marked *Personal*.

The first letter read in part:

Sept. 18, 1943

My dear General:

. . . There is a tremendous ground swell in this country against the New Deal. They have crucified themselves on the cross of too many unnecessary rules and regulations.

You should not be a candidate for the Presidency, but should permit the people to draft you. When drafted you should accept the nomination by saying "I accept the nomination as a candidate for the Commander-in-Chief of our armed forces." I am convinced that you will carry every state in the Union and this includes the solid South.

Let your friends in this country nail to the cross the many vicious underhanded moves which will be started to smear and destroy you as a citizen and commander in the Pacific.

Undoubtedly this letter will be read and perhaps censored. The New Deal, including President Roosevelt, is scared to death of the movement in the country for you. Roosevelt will probably not even be a candidate if you are nominated.

I hope you will not consider that these ideas are conceived with any thought of personal gain to myself or party. I am suggesting them because I am certain that unless this New Deal can be stopped our American way of life is forever doomed.

You owe it to civilization and to the children yet unborn to

321

accept the nomination, which I am most certain is just as sure as the sun will rise tomorrow. You will be our next President.

With kindest personal regards,

Sincerely yours,

A. L. Miller, M.C.

Fourth District, Neb.

MacArthur's answer of October 2 obviously was intended only for the Congressman's eyes:

I thank you so sincerely for your fine letter. . . . I do not anticipate in any way your flattering predictions, but I do unreservedly agree with the complete wisdom and statesmanship of your comments.

I knew your state well in the days of used-to-be. I have enjoyed many a delightful hunting excursion there and shall always remember with so much gratefulness the whole-hearted hospitality and warm comradeship extended to me on such occasions. Those days seem singularly carefree and happy compared to the sinister drama of our present chaos and confusion.

On January 27, 1944, Dr. Miller wrote a second letter to the General that read:

. . . During the holidays I had an opportunity to visit through Texas, California and Nebraska. I again want to tell you there is a tremendous revolution on in this country. It is more than a political revolution. It is a mass movement by the citizens who are displeased with the many domestic mistakes now being made by the Administration. They are also convinced that the events leading up to Pearl Harbor and since Pearl Harbor in the allocation of war supplies are not above critical examination.

. . . A great many people in the country are seriously concerned about the wave of communism and nationalism which seems bound to engulf the European countries, Asia and South America. It is that system of government generally in which government is no longer the servant of the people but their master.

If this system of left-wingers and New Dealism is continued another four years, I am certain that this Monarchy which is being established in America will destroy the rights of the common people.

There is no movement which attracts so much attention and so little criticism as the one that is labelled MacArthur for Commander-in-Chief and President of a free America. . . . It

322

is going to take an individual who is fearless and willing to make political sacrifices to cut out the underbrush and help destroy this monstrosity . . . which is engulfing the nation and destroying free enterprise and every right of the individual.

MacArthur answered on February 11, 1944, and it was addressed as follows:

PERSONAL:

Dear Congressman Miller:

I appreciate very much your scholarly letter of January 27. Your description of conditions in the United States is a sobering one indeed and is calculated to arouse the thoughtful consideration of every true patriot.

We must not inadvertently slip into the same condition internally as the one which we fight externally. Like Abraham Lincoln, I am a firm believer in the people, and, if given the truth, they can be depended upon to meet any national crisis. The great point is to bring before them the real facts.

Out here we are doing what we can with what we have. I will be glad, however, when more substantial forces are placed at my disposition.

With cordial regards and best wishes,

Douglas MacArthur

When the letters were published a barrage of bitter recrimination descended on MacArthur, now in the midst of preparations for the great Hollandia operation. He had no other recourse but to issue a statement in his own defense. At best it was a most awkward situation, with a possibility of dire consequences. His public answer, dated April 17, 1944, was the third time that he had repudiated all political ambitions:

My attention has been called to the publication by Congressman Miller of a personal correspondence with him. In so far as my letters are concerned they were never intended for publication. Their perusal will show any fair-minded person that they were neither politically inspired nor intended to convey blanket approval of the Congressman's views. I entirely repudiate the sinister interpretation that they were intended as criticism of any political philosophy or any personages in high office. They were written merely as amiable acknowledgments, to a member of

323

our highest law-making body, of letters containing flattering and friendly remarks to me personally. To construe them otherwise is to misrepresent my intent. I have not received Congressman Miller's third letter in which he is reported to advise me to announce candidacy for the office of President of the U. S.

The high Constitutional processes of our representative and republican form of government, in which there resides with the people the sacred duty of choosing and electing their Chief Executive, are of so imposing a nature as to be beyond the sphere of any individual's coercion or decision. I can only say as I have said before, I am not a candidate for the office nor do I seek it. I have devoted myself exclusively to the conduct of war. My sole ambition is to assist my beloved country to win this vital struggle by the fulfillment of such duty as has been or may be assigned to me.

But even this formal disavowal failed to pacify the angry critics who sprang to the defense of the President and his administration. So great was the chorus of disapproval that on April 30, shortly after his return from the unprecedented Hollandia by-pass, he felt it necessary to issue a follow-up statement. This time his remarks were so pointed and conclusive that they removed all possibility of Roosevelt having to face him in his fight for a fourth-term election in November. Also, the Dewey forces no longer had to consider the threat of Mac-Arthur as a condidate for the Republican nomination. His statement read:

> Since my return from the Hollandia operation I have had brought to my attention a number of newspaper articles professing in strongest terms a widespread public opinion that it is detrimental to our war effort to have an officer in high position on active service at the front, considered for nomination for the office of President. I have on several occasions announced I was not a candidate for the position. Nevertheless, in view of these circumstances, in order to make my position entirely unequivocal, I request that no action be taken that would link my name in any way with the nomination. I do not covet it nor would I accept it.

Apparently this was a definite enough avowal to satisfy the most skeptical critic or the worried professional politicians.

324

On January 2, 1944, MacArthur's people swooped down on the small Japanese base of Saidor on the Guinea coast a short distance above the mouth of Vitiaz Strait. It advanced Kenney's fighter line so that his bombers could penetrate under fighter cover northwestward to the great enemy base at Wewak. In the country between Saidor and Wewak were 5,500 Japanese at Madang and an additional 10,000 at Hansa Bay. At Wewak were 16,000 enemy troops, and at all three bases were air strips and fighter craft.

By-passing Madang and Hansa Bay, MacArthur might strike directly at Wewak, but it would be contrary to his dictum of "Hit 'em where they ain't." Wewak was apparently as far as his fighter planes could protect his bombers. Two hundred miles on up the Guinea coast was the beautiful harbor of Hollandia on Humbolt Bay. Willoughby's G-2 had been reporting for some time that the Japanese were building the Hollandia area into a great supply base; its three fields, tucked well behind the Cyclops Mountains, were swiftly being turned into an important air center.

While preliminary work was going ahead on plans for the landing at Hansa Bay, Brigadier General Bonner Fellers, the able and imaginative head of G-3's Planning Board, conceived the idea of an alternative move, embracing a great 500-mile by-pass directly to Hollandia. However, it was frowned on, and Fellers was directed by his immediate superior, Major General Steve Chamberlain, to forget his bold dream and complete plans for the Hansa Bay operations. But MacArthur, upon being advised of the daring Hollandia suggestion, quietly sent word to go ahead with drawing up the plan for the big jump. Kenney was consulted, and both he and the Navy representative, Captain Ray Tarbuck, were confident that the great by-pass could be successfully accomplished.

The day that orders for the half-way Hansa Bay landings were actually being mimeographed, MacArthur called a conference of all his commanders and bluntly announced Hollandia as the next operation. Brigadier General Fellers, who had originally conceived the idea, was called on to make "the dry run" before the group. The brilliant plan would by-pass 60,000 enemy troops and leave them for mosquitoes and crocodiles and hunger and disease to finish off.

Kenney, who enjoyed the prospect of the impossible, gave ample assurance that he could take out all enemy airfields at Hollandia and in the intervening 500 miles of coastal country. By March he would receive a batch of new, long-range P-39 fighters, and by installing extra belly-tanks in his old models he would actually have fighters that could accompany the bombers all the way to Hollandia and return.

MacArthur immediately asked the Navy in the Central and South Pacific for landing craft and escort carriers, with the additional loan of the beautiful new flat-tops of the main Pacific fleet to give protection immediately before and during the actual Hollandia landings. Admiral Nimitz flew out to Brisbane to draw up the final integration of his naval and air forces with those of the Southwest Pacific.

Manus Harbor in the Admiralties was chosen as the base for the joint rendezvous, with Admiral Dan Barbey in charge of the amphibious force. Lt. General Walter Krueger, commander of the Sixth Army, accompanied the expedition, but Lt. General Eichelberger, with his I Corps, comprising the 24th and 41st U. S. Infantry Divisions, would have actual command of the landings at Hollandia and Tanahmerah and the capture of the airfields to their rear. A third landing would be made at Aitape, 120 miles to the east of Hollandia, with Brigadier General Jens Doe in charge. MacArthur sailed with Admiral Kinkaid on the cruiser *Nashville*. As air-coordinator of Nimitz' flat-tops and the ground army the fabulous Colonel Ralph J. Erickson was aboard Lt. General Eichelberger's destroyer.

During the night of April 19-20 the 300 ships secretly assembled outside Manus, and at dawn there spread out before the excited eyes of the thousands of ship-borne soldiers a sight no words can quite describe. In a circle some ten miles across, the mighty armada moved northwestward as though bound straight for the great Japanese base at Palau. Swift destroyers rode the outer circles. Each of the three groups that were to make the landings sailed in columns, with American and

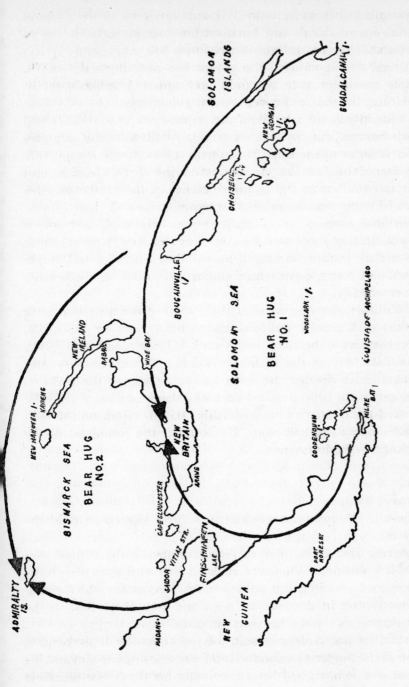

The great "bear hug" that won the strategic seas.

Australian cruisers in between. Escort carriers sent their planes aloft to scan the distant horizons for enemy snoopers. Far to the northwest a task force of swift new battleships and carriers blocked the approach of any Japanese fleet from the north. They would provide the final preliminary bombardment of the three beaches and cover the actual landings.

Suddenly during the night the armada swung to the left and each column cut back to its target. At 6:20 in the morning the warships opened up. Most of the 4,000 enemy troops were quartered behind the mountains on the three airfields, and the few soldiers at the landing beaches in the Hollandia area fled in terror and surprise. Vast stores, guns and thousands of tons of equipment and supplies were abandoned, and only a few scattering shots met the Americans as they stepped ashore from their landing craft and amphibious alligators and amphtracs. Not a single American soldier was killed on the beaches by enemy fire.

Within a day or two after their capture the air strips were hosts to Kenney's fighters, and within another week the bombers were heading northward up the doomed Guinea coast. By May 17 the island of Wakde fell, and ten days later Eichelberger opened the desperate battle among the connecting caves and deep bunkers on Biak Island; and once again he proved the quality of his leadership. His fine work on the Hollandia operation had won "Uncle Bob" the command of the brand new Eighth Army.

4

MacArthur's headquarters had now been located in Brisbane for two years. In the late summer of 1942 his advance headquarters were established in Port Moresby, in the Papuan end of New Guinea. Whenever such severe fighting as the Buna and Lae operations was going on, he lived at the old Government House in the tropical port, and from here flew to the battle areas to make his own first-hand surveys.

At Brisbane a double suite of rooms in the housekeeping end of the modern Lennon's Hotel was set aside for him and his family. The hotel had been taken over for the senior members of his headquarters staff, and a few rooms were reserved for Very Important People, many of whom never got a glimpse of the Supreme Commander.

The usual maid service was supplied by the hotel for the family quarters, but almost all the simple meals were prepared either by the energetic and devoted Jean MacArthur or by Ah Cheu. The General's taste in food ran to unpretentious dishes, and when his aide would telephone Jean that he was about to leave his office a few blocks away, she would busy herself with the late lunch or supper. Regardless of the time, she sat down and shared the meal with him.

His schedule was similar to what he had been following for the quarter-century since he had been appointed superintendent at West Point when he wore the single star of a brigadier general. He would get to his office somewhere around 9:30 or 10:00 and not leave until nearly 1:30 or 2 o'clock. After lunch he would ordinarily take a short nap, and once he returned to headquarters he seldom left until 8 or 9 o'clock. Often he would be awakened in the night to receive important cables or intelligence reports.

There was usually time for official military and civilian visitors from home, but he was unimpressed by names alone or by missions. There were no formal dinner parties, public receptions or official nonsense of any kind. He kept his mind and his time free for important business only. About the only variation in his old formula was that he no longer spent late hours at night in reading.

Along in this spring of 1944 news came from the fighting front that a Japanese junior officer had been captured, and in a pocket of his tunic had been found his diary with proof that he had taken part in beheading one of the Doolittle fliers who had been shot down in the Tokyo raid. An old writing friend attached to headquarters in a very personal way happened to be with the General when he received the report.

He read it aloud [to the author], and slowly a fire of anger began to blaze deep within him. He rose to his feet and as he paced back and forth a solemn resolve fused into words.

"I shall assign the finest lawyer in my command to this man's defense," he vowed, his eyes flashing with rage. "I shall see to

329

it that he is given a fair and just trial. And if he is found guilty I shall hang him to the tallest tree in New Guinea, so help me God!"

5

While MacArthur was clearing the way through the Vitiaz Strait in December 1943, and then in late April conducting his great 500-mile Hollandia jump and the subsequent operations against Wakde and Biak, Nimitz' navy had not been idle in its vast Central Pacific area.

Back in November of 1943 it had captured Tarawa in the Gilbert Islands, but due largely to faulty intelligence work regarding the shore approaches and the enemy's guns, this was a costly victory. The price paid was 985 brave marines killed and 2,193 wounded. The island had been defended by 2,700 troops and 2,000 civilian laborers.

But the terrible mistakes were not repeated when, on the last day of January, triple landings were made on the Kwajalein atoll by the 2nd Marine Division and the Army's 7th Infantry Division.

Eniwetok came next on the Navy schedule, and then on June 15, 1944, landings were made on the well-defended island of Saipan in the Marianas. The hard battle continued until July 9, and mopping-up operations by the 27th Infantry Division continued for nearly two months. All but 2,068 of the 29,000 in the Japanese garrison were killed. The American casualties were 3,126 killed, 326 missing, and 13,160 wounded, a total of 16,612.

Planes from the aircraft carriers of the great Central Pacific Fleet had begun pounding away at the enemy's 500 land-based planes in the Marianas for four days before the assault landings began. An additional 500 Japanese carrier-based planes had been assigned to the defense of the island group, but most of them were suddenly shifted to oppose MacArthur's operation against Biak far to the southwest. By the time the Saipan landings began Admiral Marc A. Mitscher's brilliant task force had virtually wiped out all this enemy air.

Four days after the beachheads had been established on

Saipan, a Japanese carrier force let loose a major air action that immediately brought on the Battle of the Philippine Sea. During the opening day 402 enemy carrier planes were destroyed at a cost of 26 American Navy planes: and American submarines sunk two enemy carriers. On the second day four more Japanese air carriers, one battleship, one cruiser and one tanker were sunk. With six of her air carriers gone to the bottom, Japan's air strength on the sea was never to regain its potency. The result of this great American naval triumph was made clear four months later in the three key battles of Leyte Gulf.

Shortly after this a victory over nearby Tinian, in the Marianas, was won by the Navy at a bargain price. But the same could hardly be said for Guam, where the 3rd Marine Division, with the 1st Provisional Marine Brigade and the 77th Infantry Division in support, suffered 1,919 killed and 7,122 wounded—a total casualty list of 9,041. The Japanese lost some 17,000 killed and 485 taken prisoner.

These bloody and prolonged battles for the Marianas were still in progress when MacArthur landed by his private plane, *Bataan,* at Pearl Harbor on July 26. Two weeks before this he had received a cable from General Marshall ordering him to attend a coming conference with a Mr. BIG in Hawaii. It was a fair guess that the Mr. BIG was the President of the United States.

As no mention of bringing staff officers with him had been made, MacArthur left on his plane with only his personal aide, Colonel Larry Lehrbas, who was enroute to the United States; a medical aide, Lt. Colonel Chambers, and Brigadier General Bonner Fellers, G-1, who a short time before had been in charge of the planning section of his staff. MacArthur paced up and down the narrow aisle of the *Bataan,* disgruntled and angry at the idea of being called away from his war duties.

Now and again he would stop his endless walking to give vent to his feelings. The words fairly crackled out between his lips during one particular outburst: "The humiliation of forcing me to leave my command to fly to Honolulu for a political picture-taking junket! In the First War I never for a moment left my division, even when wounded by gas and ordered to the hospital. In all my fighting days I've never before had to turn my back on my assignment."

When his plane taxied in at the landing field he was driven at once to the quarters of Lt. General Robert Richardson, the commander of all army training in the Central Pacific and an old friend from West Point days. Soon Richardson arrived with an invitation from the President asking MacArthur to board his ship immediately.

MacArthur was still in his flying clothes when the President enthusiastically greeted him and seated him to his right. The movie cameras began clicking. MacArthur had not seen the President for almost seven years, and he was shocked to note how obviously his health had failed.

Back at Richardson's quarters later that afternoon Mac-Arthur angrily reiterated that he felt convinced that the President's purpose in the trip was just as he had surmised—that Roosevelt, having been nominated in Chicago for a fourth term, felt it would be good politics to show himself intent on winning the Pacific war and conferring in complete harmony with MacArthur.

Just before dinner that evening MacArthur was handed a highly confidential letter from Admiral King, who had left Pearl Harbor only a day or two before. Obviously it was King's friendly idea to put MacArthur on his guard regarding the proposed intrusion of the British into the Far Pacific battle area. Such differences as there were between the two men had always been solely professional and not personal. Certainly they shared the same views regarding what was best for their country when it came to the neglect of the Pacific in favor of the European and Mediterranean theatres.

In June 1944 the British and American Combined Chiefs of Staffs had met in London. The British advanced the idea of their taking over the operations against the Japanese-held Dutch East Indies, using the western and northern ports and installations in Australia as their base. This included the suggestion that as soon as MacArthur's forces were established in the Philippines, Mountbatten would take command of Australia and the rich Dutch islands.

The letter only added to the resentment MacArthur must

332

have had over being pulled away from his own theatre and responsibilities for this present meeting with Roosevelt. Nor were matters helped when after dinner at Richardson's quarters he received a message from the President inviting him to ride with him on a tour of inspection the following morning. MacArthur was scheduled to have dinner with Roosevelt that next evening, to be followed by a final conference on the second morning.

That night MacArthur felt almost as depressed and frustrated as he had on Corregidor on the day, more than two years before, when he fought against the black mood of despair that came with the President's personal orders that he leave his doomed garrison and proceed to Australia. As he walked the floor of his bedroom here in Richardson's quarters this late July night of 1944, he talked without restraint to a trusted member of his staff regarding his long years of struggle and his many defeats and frustrations: and he spoke of his country's inadequate leadership, the terrible mistakes made in the war and America's uncertain future. He seemed to unburden himself in a way he had seldom if ever done before in all his life.

The following morning he sat with the President and Admiral Nimitz in a motor car that was driven slowly through an avenue of smartly dressed soldiers, lined up shoulder to shoulder on both sides of the highway. General Richardson put on a magnificent spectacle, with more than 25,000 troops snapping their rifles to "Present Arms" as the President rode by.

During the lengthy inspection MacArthur turned to Roosevelt and asked if he, the President, believed he could defeat Dewey as easily as he had defeated Willkie four years previously. Roosevelt replied that he was so busy with the war that he was paying little attention to practical politics. Gently MacArthur prodded him, and finally Roosevelt observed that Dewey was a nice little man but inexperienced. He left the impression that he had no fear of the New York governor as Republican candidate.

When the dinner was over at the President's house that evening, the three guests, Admirals Leahy and Nimitz and General MacArthur, pulled up their chairs in front of a great wall map. Admiral Nimitz was asked to present the Navy's plan for Pacific victory. Quietly the Admiral explained that once MacArthur was well planted on Mindanao, he was to be left there with two or three army divisions and part of his 5th Air Force. He would be relieved of the remainder of his troops and air and assigned to the task of cleaning up the Japanese garrisons in the lower Philippines and the Dutch East Indies. Such part of the 5th Air Force that remained under his command would have the job of neutralizing the enemy air in Luzon, which, in turn, would be by-passed by the Central Pacific Forces, despite its quarter-million Japanese troops and the great naval and air bases still functioning there.

In the meantime the Navy would continue its drive across the Central Pacific, building strong bases as it pushed westward. By the early summer of 1945 it would be ready to invade Formosa, if necessary. MacArthur's air would continue to be held responsible for the neutralization of the Japanese air on Luzon.

MacArthur was astounded. So this was the reason for the conference! He was to be forced to go back on his solemn pledge to the thousands of tortured and starving American prisoners of war and internees and to the millions on the Islands who had believed in him and in America. His own vow to liberate the Philippines, as well as Roosevelt's pledges and his country's American national honor, were all to be betrayed!

George Marshall's name was not mentioned, but MacArthur could hardly help concluding that he must at least tacitly have given his consent to this disturbing plan to abandon the liberation of 7,000 emaciated American war prisoners and civilian internees and 17 million enslaved Filipinos. But, obviously, even the Joint Chiefs of Staff would not dare sponsor such a radical undertaking as this unless the President himself could be influenced to make the final decision.

MacArthur, aroused and alert, kept his composure and quietly began his arguments. He had not prepared himself to face any such shocking change in his over-all war plans, but he rose to the challenge. He explained that he could not guarantee to neutralize the net of Japanese air bases on Luzon from either Mindanao or Leyte. He could accept the assignment only if he occupied the lower end of the long, narrow island of Luzon itself.

If he were permitted to take Manila Bay, American sea, submarine and air power could then cut the life-line of enemy merchant shipping from the conquered areas of Indo-China, Malaya, Siam, Burma and the Dutch East Indies. From the Manila Bay district and from air bases in the northern part of Luzon, the enemy air forces on Formosa could be smothered and its landing beaches neutralized.

Later that night MacArthur managed a few moments alone with the President. He warned him of the political consequences of the move.

"You cannot abandon 17 million loyal Filipino Christians to the Japanese in favor of first liberating Formosa and returning it to China," he passionately argued. "American public opinion will condemn you, Mr. President. And it would be justified."

Nimitz and the President's personal chief of staff, Admiral Leahy, returned to the room, and the talk went on until midnight. Months before this MacArthur had figured out his resultant plan of operation, once he had sufficient sea, air and ground forces, and when the time had come to land at Lingayen Gulf in Luzon and then advance southward to Manila. He declared now that he could be in Manila in five weeks from the day his troops stepped ashore on the landing beaches, 120 miles above the Philippine capital.

Admiral Leahy challenged the statement. MacArthur answered that all that he could do was to give his honest professional estimate. Leahy graciously answered that the General was in a position to know, but that he could not conscientiously approve of the estimate. Time was to prove how right MacArthur was, for six months later he completed the almost unbelievable task of entering Manila in exactly 26 days from the initial landings at Lingayen Gulf.

The President made no final decision. They would talk it over the following morning at 10:30. The President planned to board his cruiser after lunch, and MacArthur would then return to Brisbane by air.

After this session had ended, the navy strategists among themselves had outlined additional arguments which Nimitz now presented. Again MacArthur made it clear how necessary for winning the war was the capture of Luzon, and how easy it would be to cut Japan off from the oil and rubber, rice and tin that she was getting from her conquests along and below the South China Sea, once Manila Bay and northern Luzon were in American hands.

The President interrupted: "But, Douglas, to take Luzon would demand heavier losses than we can stand. It seems to me we must by-pass it."

There was neither bitterness nor excitement in MacArthur's studied reply.

"Mr. President," he began, "my losses would not be heavy, any more than they have been in the past. The days of the frontal attack are over. Modern infantry weapons are too deadly, and direct assault is no longer feasible. Only mediocre commanders still use it. Your good commanders do not turn in heavy losses."

Then he outlined his whole conception of future operations in the various areas of the Southwest Pacific. Once he held the whole of the Philippines, he would begin the reconquest of the Dutch East Indies, using mostly Australian troops for the ground operations. He would move down on these Dutch islands from his bases in the north, attacking them from their rear.

For a moment he referred to the items in the confidential letter he had received from Admiral King, which had briefed him on the British plans to establish Mountbatten in Eastern Australia. MacArthur warned the President that both Australia and the Netherlands would be suspicious of imported British leadership.

The President replied that he had not the slightest intention of making it possible for the British to take over any part of the Dutch possessions.

And then with all the passion of his being MacArthur reiterated his plea for America not to abandon her pledge to the Filipinos that we would rescue them and restore their

336

liberties. When he had finished, he bowed to the President and quietly left the conference.

As he passed around the end chair Admiral Leahy plucked at his sleeve.

"I'll go along with you, Douglas," he said in a stage whisper.

When MacArthur flew back to his battlefront that afternoon, he took with him no positive assurance from the President that he had escaped the trap set for him. But never again was the Navy's plan of by-passing Luzon officially referred to, and MacArthur went ahead with his program to move straight on north to lower Mindanao.

His was the long view as against those who were concerned primarily in hurrying along unconditional surrender and gaining complete victory at any cost in both the Atlantic and Pacific wars. Tragic and inevitable were the results of America's failure to have a well thought-out and continuing national and global policy.

It was this lack of the long view that was playing such deadly havoc with American interests in the many important conferences that had been or were about to be held. Yet not once had there been a formal request for MacArthur's conclusions regarding the over-all problems of this Pacific world. Nor, save here at Pearl Harbor, had he been invited to attend a single conference anywhere throughout the war.

17

1944—THE MAGIC TOUCH
AT LEYTE

With the President's personal refusal to sanction the Navy plan to by-pass MacArthur and Luzon, there came an easy working agreement between the actual commanders within the two great areas to get on with the war. But it was yet to be seen how much Admiral King personally was willing to abandon the last of his hopes to make the Japanese war primarily Navy-controlled.

Certainly King had no idea of slacking off his drives straight across the Central Pacific. He had a wary eye on Iwo Jima and then possibly either Okinawa or Formosa. Four months after the capture of Saipan in July 1944 the new long-range B-29 bombers were blasting Tokyo, while other groups of these superb aircraft were being based in Allied fields in lower China.

Kenney had been given control of the 13th Air Force from the South Pacific, in addition to his own 5th Air Force, but never was he given a single B-29, which could double the range and could carry twice the load of his outmoded B-17s. General "Hap" Arnold was made the exclusive control agent of the Joint Chiefs of Staff for these deadly B-29s, now being turned out by the hundreds. This provision made it certain that MacArthur's Southwest theatre would have none of these magnificent new weapons, despite their usefulness in covering the tremendous distances involved. It was a very specific illustration of how MacArthur was constantly being starved.

On September 15, 1944, simultaneous landings were made by the Navy on the Island of Peleliu of the Palau group, in the southwest corner of Nimitz's Central Pacific Area, and by MacArthur on the island of Morotai. Morotai is only a little more than 300 miles south of lower Mindanao. The right flank of MacArthur's drive on north to the Philippines would now be secure.

Morotai was the last of a long series of landings that were made by MacArthur during the 1500-mile advance along the shores of New Guinea. Below Morotai, some 200,000 Japanese troops were now by-passed. There were possibly 20,000 on nearby Halmahera, which was by-passed in favor of Morotai.

In preparation for the twin landings on Peleliu and Morotai, Kenney's two air forces and the carrier force of Halsey's great Third Fleet proved once again the importance of taking out not only the enemy air on and near the actual landings but all air within 500 miles of the beaches which were to be assaulted. There were 250 Japanese planes on Halmahera, close to Morotai, and these were destroyed or driven off, and the fields on Mindanao and all threatening enemy bases were bombed to their death.

As a consequence, MacArthur, now aboard the cruiser *Nashville,* could see his men wading ashore *standing up,* with a resultant casualty list of only 44 Americans. The Navy, however, had been less fortunate on Peleliu, where the 1st Marine Division and the 81st Army Division eventually killed and buried 11,968 enemy troops and captured 468, but the American losses were 1,097 killed, 242 missing and 6,792 wounded.

Shortly after the first waves hit the shores at Morotai, MacArthur made a talk to the men on the beachhead. It was written down at the time and later given out as a formal statement, containing the essence of his thoughts about the war and the fate that awaited Japan. It was obvious that he was already thinking deeply on the post-war problems that would face both Japan and her victors. His words to his troops were:

> Our position here is now secure and the immediate operation has achieved its purpose. We now dominate the Moluccas. I rejoice that it has been done with so little loss. Our campaign is entering upon its decisive stage. Jap ground troops still fight with the greatest tenacity. The military quality of the rank and file remains of the highest. Their officer corps, however, deteriorates as you go up the scale; it is fundamentally based upon a caste and feudal system and does not represent strict professional merit. Therein lies Japan's weakness. Her sons are strong of limb and stout of heart but weak in leadership. Gripped inexorably by a military hierarchy, that hierarchy is now failing the nation. It has neither the imagination nor the foresighted ability to organize Jap resources for a total war.
>
> Defeat now stares Japan in the face. Its barbaric codes have dominated Japanese character and culture for centuries and have practiced a type of national savagery at strange variance with many basic impulses of the Jap people. Its successful domination has been based largely on the people's belief in its infallibility. When public opinion realizes that its generals and admirals have failed in the field of actual combat and campaign, the revulsion produced in Japanese thought will be terrific.

Therein lies a basis for ultimate hope that the Japanese citizen will ease his almost idolatrous worship of the military, and readjust his thoughts along more rational lines. No sophistry can disguise the fact from him that the military has failed him in this, his greatest hour of need. That failure may mark the beginning of a new and ultimately happier era for him. His hour of decision is close at hand.

The spell of war was on MacArthur. Walking along the busy beachhead, where men and supplies were still pouring ashore, he stopped now and again to talk to little groups of soldiers. Later he stood with a few officers and for a long moment he gazed northward toward the enemy-occupied Philippines. Deep emotion gripped him as he said in a low voice, as if speaking only to himself: "They are waiting for me there. It has been a long time."

2

Back in the new G.H.Q. at Hollandia, Captain Ray Tarbuck, U.S.N., assigned to MacArthur as a naval representative, was detailed to write out the general sea plan for the Philippine invasion. The original idea of securing bases in Mindanao had been abandoned because Kenney's air would be too far from the Manila Bay area and because Nimitz refused to send units of the great Pacific Fleet into the restricted inland seas. Tarbuck's orders now were to draw up detailed plans for the naval side of the invasion of Leyte.

While Tarbuck was busy with this task, a navy flier from the Central Pacific carrier force, which was engaged in bombing Manila Bay installations, was downed on Leyte as he was returning to his ship. By luck he landed safely and fell into the hands of friendly Filipino guerillas, who managed to signal a submarine that returned him to his carrier. His report that Leyte was lightly held was forwarded by Halsey to Nimitz, who in turn relayed it to the Joint Chiefs of Staff attending the Roosevelt–Churchill conference in Quebec. Nimitz added the suggestion that if the Leyte invasion were to be pushed forward, he would abandon the invasion of Yap and offer Mac-

Arthur the use of a Central Pacific Army Corps now enroute to Yap. The Joint Chiefs immediately agreed to the suggestion if MacArthur approved.

The U.S.S. *Nashville,* with MacArthur on board, was observing radio silence off Morotai, so that the decision had to be made by the senior staff officers then at the new G.H.Q. at Hollandia in New Guinea. Kenney happened to be on hand, and he added his weight to the suggestion by Sutherland and Steve Chamberlain, chief of the operations section, that the plan not only be accepted but that the date of the invasion be advanced from December 20 to October 20. This new date left only one month and five days to complete new plans. When MacArthur returned, he was delighted with the decision and the swift turn of events.

While Tarbuck hurried along his naval plans to meet the new invasion date he developed an uncanny seafarer's hunch that the Japanese must soon commit their battle-line or run the risk of its being bombed out of Singapore or destroyed before the final assault on the home islands. Through various channels he went about collecting every grain of information regarding the available enemy warships, their auxiliaries and their movements. A close track showed a gradual but positive build-up of sea power in the Philippine area, with the possibility that the enemy was working out a decoy system that might be termed a "scattered concentration."

While the Japanese fleet was spread over a great area, a careful checking showed that the entire fleet could appear *simultaneously* in self-supporting task forces at strategic sea channels, where they might first destroy piecemeal elements of the protecting American sea power or lure them away. They could then swiftly annihilate the American amphibious force at the moment it was engaged in the landings and consequently was utterly powerless to defend itself. Time was to prove the correctness of Tarbuck's imaginative thinking.

General Tomoyoki Yamashita, conqueror of Singapore, was transferred from a top command in Manchuria to the defense of the northern Philippine group, including Luzon and Leyte. But the Army high command seemed to be in no great hurry. Certainly the Americans would strike first at the Davao area in Mindanao and would not attempt the invasion of Leyte and Luzon until early December.

It was due to this fatal miscalculation by the Japanese Army that MacArthur attained complete strategic surprise in his landings in Leyte Gulf on the morning of October 20, 1944. Most of the enemy troops were so completely thrown off balance that they abandoned their forward defense lines, fleeing to the hills in their rear. The four American divisions moved swiftly inland, and within ten days all organized resistance in the rich eastern Leyte Valley was ended, and five airfields were captured.

Ordinarily the rainy season slackened off before the middle of October, but in this fall of 1944 Leyte was subject to almost continual rains. Toward the end of the month one of the severest typhoons in local history swept westward from the Pacific. It set back the American advances and gave the enemy time to bring in heavy troop reinforcements and to dig in in the rugged hills and narrow mountainous valleys that lay between the Leyte Valley and the ports and cities to the western and southern ends of the island.

The five airfields captured during the initial drive were soon little more than mud flats. Only one was usable, and it could handle only a few fighters at a time. For once Kenney was faced with almost complete frustration.

Halsey's great Third Fleet was assigned to provide strategic support for the landing operations on Leyte Gulf. In plain words, his job was to keep his fleet between the Japanese naval forces and the American landing in Leyte Gulf. On the fourth day, while the captured airfields were still covered with mud, the big carriers and swift battleships belonging to the Central Pacific Command moved north to intercept the Third Japanese Fleet, which was believed to be coming down the east coast of Luzon from its home waters. It was the purpose of this Japanese Third Fleet to lure Halsey's force away from the Leyte Gulf area, so that three other Japanese naval forces, moving from the Sulu Sea east through the narrow Straits of San Bernardino and Surigao could rendezvous off Leyte Gulf at dawn on October 25. After destroying Kinkaid's covering fleet the enemy could then annihilate the helpless American supply ships and landing craft that were still at the Leyte landing beaches. It was a bold and imaginative plan, but fortunately the keen Captain Tarbuck had called the turn, and Kinkaid had made the necessary dispositions.

The two southernmost Japanese forces were discovered on the morning of October 24 by American scouting submarines and reconnaissance planes, and that same day bombers from Halsey's flat-tops, now moving north, did some damage to one of the attacking groups known as the 1st Attack Force.

On the night of the 24th-25th a small enemy fleet called the C Force entered the Surigao Strait below Leyte and in the darkness was knocked off balance by a sudden PT and destroyer attack from Rear Admiral Jesse B. Oldendorf's force of cruisers and old battleships of the Seventh Fleet. Completely surprised, the enemy now faced the concentrated radar-controlled fire of the American heavy ships, and by dawn the Japanese had lost two battleships and three of their four destroyers, and a heavy cruiser was so damaged that it was later sunk by carrier planes. History may record that weird midnight engagement as the last naval battle between surface fleets where the great battlewagons slugged it out.

A second Japanese naval group, called the 2nd Attack Force, immediately followed C Force into Surigao Strait, but when it saw the disaster that had overwhelmed its sister C Force, it turned tail and fled. Two of its destroyers were sunk in the action, and a crippled light cruiser later was finished off by American land-based bombers. The total loss to Kinkaid's Seventh Fleet so far was one destroyer damaged and one PT boat sunk.

At almost the identical hour that the battle of Surigao Strait was taking place to the south, the Japanese 1st Attack Force was quietly steaming eastward through San Bernardino Strait to make its great try at the landings in Tacloban Bay in Leyte Gulf. Halsey, unaware of the new twin threats, had already sent his great fleet north to meet the Japanese naval force sent south to decoy him away from the waters where Japan would make her desperate efforts to get at the American landings.

Despite the loss of the mighty *Musashi*, the Jap 1st Attack

343

Force succeeded in passing through the San Bernardino Strait which Halsey was supposed to defend with his own swift new battleship. His critics point out that while he was fully justified in sending his great carriers and their escorts on north to meet the Japanese force moving southward, he should have planted his battlewagons here in San Bernardino Strait between lower Luzon and upper Samar. Halsey's air previously had trailed this force through the inland seas and bombed it heavily. In fact it was largely his crippling of the mighty *Musashi* with her 18-inch guns that led him to believe that this particular enemy force could no longer sortie into the Pacific through the San Bernardino Strait.

But Halsey's subsequent move northward opened the San Bernardino door into the Pacific to this Japanese 1st Attack Force, which swiftly passed through the Strait and then steamed south along the eastern shore of Samar and headed for Leyte Gulf and its deadly rendezvous with the 2nd Attack Force and C Force—with the vast American amphibious fleet lying helpless between them. This 1st Attack Force was still completely unaware of the disaster that during the night had befallen the two task forces of her sister fleets.

At daybreak the Japanese commander was first aware that he had been rediscovered when American carrier-based reconnaissance planes and then the small escort carriers themselves came into view. It was about all the naval force that Kinkaid could muster to oppose this new and terrible threat from the north. Fortunately the enemy had no carrier planes, but he boldly moved his sturdy surface ships against the out-gunned Americans.

Even though the U. S. escort carriers launched their attack planes, the Japanese managed to sink one light carrier and two destroyers, and the small American force finally had to give way before the withering Japanese fire, including that from the new *Yamato,* with its nine 18-inch guns and a range of 45,000 yards.

Suddenly the Japanese commander, Admiral Kurita, broke off the attack and turned back north toward San Bernardino Strait. He had lost three cruisers by air attack, and he was aware the Japanese C Force to the south had met disaster. An interception of open radio messages in English brought him the information that within two hours planes from carrier units of Halsey's great fleet to the north, now fully awake to the dangerous situation and steaming full speed to help in his destruction, would be attacking him.

Under the protection of darkness Admiral Kurita re-entered San Bernardino Strait and sped westward toward the protection of his home bases. Thanks to Tarbuck's planning and Kinkaid's alert seamen the desperate plan to sink Kinkaid's fleet piecemeal and then destroy the helpless armada of supply ships and landing boats at the beachheads had gone awry. But the margin of safety had been a narrow one.

On to the north off Cape Engaño in Luzon, where Halsey had been lured by the Japanese Third Fleet, the victory of the American carriers over the Japanese had been almost complete. In the nine-hour over-the-horizon engagement Halsey's air sank four carriers—almost completely devoid of planes —one light cruiser and three destroyers. None of Halsey's great battlewagons fired a shot, yet only two enemy battleships, two light cruisers and six destroyers, all damaged, escaped to the north.

MacArthur's post-war reactions as to the respects in which the absence of a unified command in the Pacific impaired the effectiveness of the American operations against the Japanese were frank and clear-cut:

> Of all the faulty decisions of the war perhaps the most unexplainable one was the failure to unify the command in the Pacific. The principle involved is perhaps the most fundamental one in the doctrine and tradition of command. In this instance it did not involve an international problem. It was accepted and entirely successful in the other great theatres. The failure to do so in the Pacific cannot be defended in logic, in theory or even in common sense. Other motives must be ascribed. It resulted in divided effort, the waste of diffusion and duplication of force and the consequent extension of the war with added casualties and cost. The generally excellent cooperation between the two commands in the Pacific, supported by the good will, good nature

345

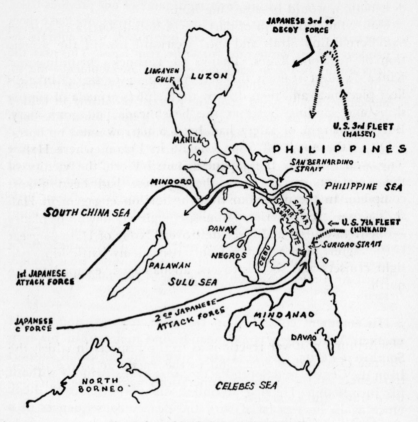

The vital naval battle that saved Leyte Gulf.

and high professional qualifications of the numerous personnel involved, was no substitute for the essential unity of direction of centralized authority. The handicaps and hazards unnecessarily resulting were numerous indeed, but by way of illustration I will elucidate the one which produced the greatest jeopardy. It developed in the course of the Leyte landing.

After Morotai, my next jump was tentatively to seize the islands off Davao Bay, to base our air to cover the following objective which was Leyte. It was necessary to make this intermediate move because of the approximately 300-mile limit of air coverage. Any landing had to be within covering distance of our previous bases, as it would take time to build or secure new bases and make them operative. Until this was done our beachheads were entirely dependent for air protection from the rear bases. This was the determining factor in each move of the envelopment—the so-called "hit-'em-where-they-ain't" and "leave-'em-die-on-the-vine" maneuver. It was based upon the concept of cutting in behind the enemy's bastions and severing his supply lines. The high command after Morotai expressed the desire to speed up operations in the belief that Leyte was lightly held, a report somewhat confirmed by naval air reconnaissance but which later proved not entirely accurate. It was suggested that if I moved direct on Leyte, naval air would cover me in landing, and sixteen little "flat-tops" would stay to cover the command until we could build local air fields and bring forward our own ground air. The hop was double the usual distance and violated my basic concept never to risk having my ground forces uncovered from ground-based air. Under the conditions, however, I decided on the movement.

His comment continued in the same reserved and concise manner. While he was Commander-in-Chief within his own Southwest Pacific theatre, Halsey's Fleet and all naval support from the Central and South Pacific areas were distinctly without his jurisdiction. He had absolutely no authority over them. Once again he was faced with the deadly consequences of a divided command. His quoted remarks of the action were made eight years after the great battle had ended and any personal bitterness had long ago disappeared. He went on:

I believe this was probably the first time a ground commander ever placed his complete trust so absolutely in naval hands. The 7th Fleet was reinforced with the old battleships and the little carriers, and Halsey's fleet containing the new battleships and big carriers under Nimitz's command was ordered to operate in the same general waters to the north. I was on the cruiser *Nashville* accompanying our convoys. It early became evident to me

347

that Halsey was too far to the north to properly cover the Gulf of Leyte, and I so radioed Nimitz asking him to drop Halsey back. This would not only insure my base but would insure that his fleet being in the action as the magnetic attraction of my point of landing would draw the enemy's fleet there. Three times as I remember I sent such dispatches but without result. Nimitz repeated to Halsey apparently without getting through and then finally authorized me to communicate directly with Halsey but it was then too late. In the meantime, the enemy's forces acted with great skill and cunning. A decoy drew Halsey further to the north, the Japanese attacked from the south in the Mindanao Sea and drew our battleships and cruisers there to match his force and then, evading our air reconnaissance, came through the San Bernardino Straits and moved on our base and rear naval echelons in the Bay of Tacloban.

Probably two hundred or more vessels were there exposed. We instantly threw in our little flat-tops which gallantly and successfully repulsed the attacking Japanese force. In doing so, however, the planes were practically destroyed and my potential air umbrella to protect my ground forces and operations disappeared. For the following month I was thereby in gravest danger, as the Japanese under General Yamashita regarded this as the crucial point of action. Actually, with the failure to hold the so-called "Yamashita Line," which collapsed with our Ormoc envelopment, the Emperor afterward told me, the Japanese admitted defeat and all their efforts were to accomplish an end without internal explosion. Leyte came out all right but the hazards would all have been avoided by unity of command.

3

Early in the afternoon of Leyte's D-Day, October 20, General MacArthur with President Osmeña and Brigadier General Carlos Romulo, Generals Krueger, Sutherland, Kenney and a little group climbed down from the cruiser *Nashville* to a landing barge and in the choppy sea headed for the beaches. It was the hour MacArthur had been dreaming of for two years, seven months and three days.

That afternoon he hurriedly issued a proclamation and 48 hours later, when the 1st Cavalry Division captured Tacloban, he broadcast the words written out under deep emotional pressure when he had first touched the good earth of these historic islands. The proclamation read:

To the People of the Philippines:

I have returned. By the grace of Almighty God our forces stand again on Philippine soil—soil consecrated by the blood of our two peoples. We have come, dedicated and committed, to the task of destroying every vestige of enemy control over your daily lives, and of restoring, upon a foundation of your indestructible strength, the liberties of your people.

At my side is your President Sergio Osmeña, worthy successor of that great patriot, Manuel Quezón, with members of his cabinet. The seat of your government is now therefore firmly reestablished on Philippine soil.

The hour of your redemption is here. Your patriots have demonstrated an unswerving and resolute devotion to the principles of freedom that challenges the best that is written on the pages of human history. I now call upon your supreme effort that the enemy may know from the temper of an aroused and outraged people within, that he has a force there to contend with, no less violent than is the force committed from without.

Rally to me! Let the indomitable spirit of Bataan and Corregidor lead on. As the lines of battle roll forward to bring you within the zone of operations, rise and strike! Strike at every favorable opportunity. For your homes and hearths, strike! For future generations of your sons and daughters, strike. In the name of your sacred dead, strike. Let no heart be faint. Let every arm be steeled. The guidance of divine God points the way. Follow in His name to the Holy Grail of righteous victory.

Time gives a certain unreality to the old-fashioned eloquence, but General MacArthur knew the deeply religious nature of the people he was addressing and what this day of national redemption meant to them.

4

For the first ten days or two weeks of the Leyte campaign, the 24th, 96th and 7th Infantry Divisions and the 1st Cavalry Division met no heavy opposition, and by November 7 they had reached the mountains and rugged hills that skirted the eastern fringe of the Central Leyte Valley. The Japanese High

Command had rushed parts of two divisions from Mindanao, Cebu and Panay, and it was evident that they intended to make the defense of Leyte the decisive action of the Philippine defense.

The unusual rainy weather persisted, and until well into November the only usable airfield was the one near Tacloban. Hardly more than a score of Kenney's fighters could operate from it at a time.

The great carriers of Vice Admiral John S. McCain's Task Force 38 of Halsey's Third Fleet continued now and again to blast at Manila and Luzon bases, while Kinkaid's little escort carriers gave some air protection nearer at home. Then suddenly a new and deadly menace presented itself—the Japanese suicide plane. Never before had it been tried out as a distinct and formal tactical weapon. During November alone 150 *kamakaze* sorties were flown, and serious damage was done to several American ships. It disclosed the desperate nature of Japanese determination and what might be expected in the future as American forces neared the Japanese homeland.

By Christmas General Walter Krueger's dogged Sixth Army had control of all the ports and main cities and highways, and the following day MacArthur issued a report that the Leyte campaign, save for mopping-up operations, could be considered ended. The task of cleaning up the heavy fortified pockets of Japanese, still in the hills and narrow valleys, was now in the capable hands of Lt. General Eichelberger and his recently organized Eighth Army.

In the two months and six days that had elapsed since Krueger's forces landed in Leyte, the enemy's counted dead totalled 56,263, the captured 359. The victory cost the Sixth Army 2,888 killed, 9,858 wounded and 161 missing. For each American casualty the Japanese had paid 4½ men.

There was still no letup in the mass suicide charges of the enemy or in his refusal to surrender until the last man was killed. It took several months more for Eichelberger's men to finish up the job. G.H.Q. estimated that probably not more than 6,000 Japanese were left on the island that Christmas Day when the Eighth Army took over. When Eichelberger had finished his distasteful job he accounted for 24,294 counted dead and 439 missing Japanese in Leyte and neighboring Samar alone. His own losses were 432 killed, 22 missing and 1,852 wounded.

In mid-February the three divisions of the borrowed XXIV Corps were removed from Eighth Army control and sent to rest-areas in eastern Leyte, in preparation for the coming Okinawa campaign under the Navy's command. There seemed to be no limit to the lavish stores put ashore for their re-fitting. The old jungle fighters of the Southwest Pacific had never seen such magnificence. From top to bottom the men of the visiting divisions were being issued brand-new clothing, equipment, guns, cannon, jeeps, trucks and tanks.

Yet never once in all the history of the Southwest theatre had a single full division of MacArthur's forces been completely re-equipped at one time. Even now the left-behind cast-offs of this borrowed XXIV Corps had to be salvaged and used to help equip some of the divisions of the new Eighth Army for the desperate campaigns that lay ahead.

Almost ten years later Admiral Ray Tarbuck, the regular naval officer long attached to MacArthur's staff, described without the slightest restraint how the Southwest Pacific had suffered from the very beginning of the war from a deliberate policy of discrimination by the Joint Chiefs of Staff and the Navy itself. His account began:

> One word about MacArthur's supplies. We got the minimum sustenance for modern war. On trips back to Washington I saw P-38s in great numbers on each coast as part of the home intercepter force. In New Guinea we were fighting Zeros with P-40s that were post-dated. In the 7th Amphibious Force we manufactured our own rocket launchers and converted our own LCIs to rocket ships. No Navy Yard for us. We made 56 combat amphibious landings, all successful, and were without carrier availability on 45 of them. We had seaborne air support on only 11. We got our blankets and mutton from Australia. We not only got what Europe couldn't use, but we got the leavings of the Trans-Pacific. The Central Pacific Navy had numberless supply ships, reefers and tankers, but the 7th Fleet rarely saw any, because some one drew a pencil line on a Pacific chart and said, "The Central Pacific Area ends here." The battle between the Army and the Navy was almost as tough as the Jap War.

In a very definite way this statement furnishes at least part of the answer to the disturbing question as to why it has so often been alleged that General MacArthur failed to capture the personal loyalty and affection of many of the men who served under him.

He and his Southwest Pacific were continuously handicapped by the designs and studied interferences of Washington, from the White House to the Joint Chiefs of Staff. He was constantly forced to pay the price for his opposition to the dreary mistakes, the endless jealousies, discriminations and bickerings of rival services, administration politicians and unfriendly brass. He could do little for the relief and comfort of his soldiers and airmen and sailors fighting in the deadly jungles and seas of New Guinea and neighboring islands.

Marines and army personnel attached to the South and Central Pacific under the Navy's command had the first and often the only call on rest camps, recreational areas, extra supplies, food and relief. Tens of thousands of MacArthur's men in the Southwest Pacific actually served as much as 18 months without a break in malarial and disease-infected tropical areas with no relief, simply because neither the Navy nor the administration would grant the ships to transport MacArthur's weary and battle-worn troops to pleasant rest areas. Again and again the Southwest was at the very tail-end of supply lines and relief.

Homesick, unhappy men, conscious of being by-passed, naturally blamed their commanding general for their neglect. MacArthur swiftly became the target of their censure for the conscienceless and deliberate restrictions put on him by rival services and by the office of the Army's Chief of Staff.

5

It was clear to MacArthur that the work of defeating the 235,000 Japanese soldiers estimated to be on Luzon should be assigned to his Sixth Army and its commander Lt. General Walter Krueger. Krueger would have the help of part of Eichelberger's smart Eighth Army until Manila was captured, and then MacArthur would divide the entire Philippine archipelago into two areas: Luzon would comprise the Northern Area, while all the islands to the south would constitute the Southern Area and would be placed under Eichelberger.

The Central Pacific carrier-based planes and the bombardment groups from the American bases on the China mainland, along with planes from the South and Southwest Pacific, began bombing the 70 airfields on Luzon. At the same time there were air strikes against enemy fields and bases as far away as Formosa and Okinawa and even the Japanese home islands. The daring Halsey raided the upper China Sea with his Third Fleet, and his carrier-based planes combed the area for targets.

MacArthur still was not satisfied until every enemy air assault potential was covered. Less than 200 miles southwest of Manila and a little west of southern Luzon lay the island of Mindoro. MacArthur now ordered this island seized and airfields quickly constructed that could give him additional air coverage in his final attack on Luzon.

Within MacArthur's own staff there was almost unanimous agreement in favor of postponing the attack date of January 9, 1945, which had been set for the initial landings on Lingayen Gulf, 110 miles to the north of Manila. MacArthur would not agree. Nor would he be swerved by a Navy demand that the invasion route be up the east coast of Luzon, around its northern tip and then down its western shores to Lingayen Gulf. The shorter way was south from Leyte Gulf through Surigao Strait and across the inland Philippine seas to the South China Sea. Then the route lay straight north to the invasion beaches of Lingayen Gulf. Since Halsey refused to risk the ships of his great Third Fleet in the dangerous coastal waters, MacArthur would now have to undertake this without any protective help from the Central Pacific Fleet. He would be on his own.

Once MacArthur's seaborne forces reached the landing beaches in Lingayen Gulf, then Halsey's great Third Fleet would guard them against any sea or air force attacking from the north, but his would still be an independent command, operating completely outside MacArthur's authority.

6

On December 15 MacArthur was made a 5-star general of the army, along with Marshall, Eisenhower and Arnold. Marshall's appointment was first by a matter of hours and carried seniority, and MacArthur ranked second in the top level grade. At the same time Admirals Leahy, King and Nimitz were made admirals of the fleet.

In no way did this settle the old and bitter controversy over unity of command in the Pacific, nor did it lessen the steady and determined opposition to MacArthur in Washington. He was definitely an outsider, denied the full knowledge of the secret settlements that had been made or were about to be made among Roosevelt, Churchill and Stalin in the series of global conferences. To only one, Cairo, was the stubborn and valiant fighter-leader Chiang Kai-shek asked to attend. MacArthur was not even invited to this Cairo meeting, where vital decisions regarding China and the Pacific were discussed. It had seemed fit, however, to ask the possibly overrated Lord Mountbatten to fly in from the Burma campaign in which he was hopelessly floundering.

The war against Hitler was obviously about to end. From early in 1940 fear and hate of the Nazi had absorbed most of the attention of the Roosevelt administration, and by 1943, when victory was almost certain, the dangerous desire for revenge on Germany began to blur the picture of a firm and lasting peace.

From now on hate and revenge dominated the final actions of both Roosevelt and Churchill. Their struggle for complete war victory apparently had used up their energies, so that they had little heart or imagination left to see to it that their war success was translated into lasting peace.

MacArthur, fighting his brilliant campaigns at the other side of the world, was left out of the inner circle and confined to concern for swift Philippine liberation and to his belief in the significance of the Western Pacific in the long years ahead. Shortly before he was made a general of the army he talked off the record to a group of correspondents who gathered on the porch of the former Japanese Club at Tacloban, Leyte, which he had taken over as his quarters. He was seriously worried over the deterioration of the Chinese situation and over the general failure of Washington to understand the great importance of the Pacific in the long view. He felt that neglecting the war against Japan in favor of the demand that Germany first be utterly crushed was a tragic mistake.

He explained to his listeners his belief that much of the future destiny of the human race lay in the lands adjoining the Pacific. "The history of the world for the next thousand years will be written in the Pacific," he prophesied.

Japan, he was sure, had long understood this, and it had become the logical basis for her doctrine before the war of the Greater Asia Co-Prosperity Sphere. Japan had seen that if she could establish domination over China, she was in a good position to control the Eastern world.

He pointed out that from his point of view Stalin, too, clearly saw the historic importance of the Pacific, and even while the Red dictator fought so desperately for survival in Europe, he was actually looking over his shoulder toward Asia. If Chiang Kai-shek was to be crushed, MacArthur argued that China would be thrown into confusion and her existence as a nation of the free world imperiled.

Communist Russia, he insisted, would sooner or later try to reverse the results of the Russo-Japanese War of 1904-5. She still dreamed of recovering Port Arthur, thus securing a warm-water port into the Pacific, and, as well, regaining her lost toe-hold in Manchuria.

It was several weeks before the Yalta Agreement, with its secret clauses, was signed. Months would slip by before MacArthur was told the details of the bargain Stalin made at Yalta, when the Russian dictator agreed to become a member of the planned United Nations and enter the war against Japan within three months after a victory over Hitler. For these doubtful pledges Roosevelt and his advisors, with Churchill's consent, promised the Communist leader the recovery of all that the Czar had lost in Manchuria 40 years before. It was fondly hoped that Chiang Kai-shek could be forced to accept this Roosevelt-Churchill bartering of his own lands for the recovery of which he had been fighting the Japanese for seven straight years.

Since his first voyage of discovery into India and the Far East in 1905-6, MacArthur realized that some day destiny would force America to take her rightful place in the vast struggle for power that was slowly developing in the Western Pacific. He had never for a day forgotten the prophecy of the brilliant young Senator Beveridge: "The power that rules the Pacific . . . is the power that rules the world."

MacArthur knew, too, that to the modern Kremlin mind a Russian-dominated Communist China was of supreme importance in her plan to absorb all Asia into her Red sphere. It had long been a Moscow theory that the shortest road to Paris and London ran through Peiping and Delhi.

18

1945: LUZON—THE BRILLIANT CAMPAIGN OF LIBERATION

The very act of setting foot on the shores of Leyte on October 20, 1944, fulfilled MacArthur's vow, "I shall return." But he still looked forward to the moment when he could announce to the world that he had wiped out the American humiliation of Bataan and Corregidor, and that Manila with its thousands of starving prisoners was liberated.

It was almost two and a half years since he had first taken the offensive in the green and deadly swamps and jungles protecting the tiny Japanese strongholds of Buna and Gona on the upper coast of the Papuan end of New Guinea. Then he had

had little compared with his present three-dimensional force, now poised to spring on the great prize of Luzon. In a way it was the last of the mighty roadblocks barring his way northward to the home islands of Japan. He believed implicitly that Luzon was the key to the ultimate defeat of Japan.

With few exceptions the senior members of his staff were the same men who checked and then turned back the Japanese from their southern drive toward Australia, thus protecting the lines of communication with America. Kenney, with his 5th Air Force, and Kinkaid with his enlarged Seventh Fleet were still his strong right and left arms. His experienced and ample Sixth Army remained under the same tough old Walter Krueger, who drove his own staff like a Prussian army group commander. MacArthur's new Eighth Army had the decidedly more versatile Bob Eichelberger as its inspirational spearhead.

But competent as were the planners at G.H.Q. and on the staffs of his two armies and the sea and air forces, it was the Old Man himself who really initiated the course of the strategic moves and passed on them during their various stages of development. The chief of staff at G.H.Q., for instance, might order certain future plans drawn up and presented to the Commander-in-Chief. MacArthur would listen quietly while the presentation was being made on the map. Then with uncanny skill he would point out the weak points. At times he would even demand an entirely new objective, because the one suggested might prove too costly in human lives.

Always he completely dominated the situation. The imaginative and tireless George Kenney had "more ideas than a dog has fleas"—as some ardent member of the staff said—and he sold many of them to his Chief. But the final decision with its priceless element of split-second timing and the perfection and precision of the entire operation always bore the personal hallmark of MacArthur.

Above all else was his intense aversion to frontal attacks, and his determination to save the lives of his own forces. Always he would find another way out when he was convinced that a given operation would cost more casualties than seemed absolutely necessary.

357

The series of naval battles that were fought to protect the supply fleet in Leyte Bay on the fourth and fifth days after the initial landings there, had destroyed the last of the real striking power of the Japanese Navy. In order to assist in the planning of the Luzon campaign for early January of 1945, Nimitz willingly flew to Leyte for a conference and assured MacArthur that Halsey's roving Third Fleet would clean out the South China Sea and thus eliminate all fear of an enemy sea force barging into his delicate landing operations at Lingayen Gulf. MacArthur now needed only the same guarantee regarding enemy air attacks.

During the final three months of 1944, while the air preliminaries and the subsequent heavy fighting were going on in Leyte, most of the enemy air potential in the Philippines had been destroyed. A total of 120 scattered air bases had suffered the full treatment, including 70 bases on Luzon alone. With January 9 set by MacArthur as D-Day—although actually called S-Day, and J-hour for this particular operation—there came a plastering of enemy air that blanketed every known drome for roughly 1,000 miles in all directions.

Although Kenney was never to have a single B-29 under him, the new XXI Bomber Command sent its Superfortresses from Saipan and the other fields in the Marianas to the Japanese home islands; the combined China-based XX Bomber Command and the Fourteenth Air Force pounded at targets in Formosa and along the China coast; and Kenney's newly organized Far East air forces smothered local Philippine and Dutch East Indies targets. MacArthur's precaution to establish air fields in Mindoro, 200 miles southwest of Manila, helped to neutralize the fields on Luzon and to protect the invasion fleets as they moved through the dangerous inland sea and passageways to Lingayen Gulf.

MacArthur's over-all strategic plan for the conquest of Luzon appears simple in the telling. For weeks before the actual landings the airfields on the long, narrow island were methodically bombed, and beginning January 1, 1945, deceptive measures were initiated against fake landing spots in the Bicol and Batangas areas of lower Luzon. Channels and harbors were swept of mines, and deceptive preliminary landing operations were started. There were even dummy parachute drops, and every evidence was planted for an invasion of lower Luzon.

The advance warships of the Luzon attack force left their anchorage in Leyte Gulf on January 2. As the fleet made its way through the dangerous narrow waters, the enemy brought out his hidden aircraft and Cebu-based submarines and attacked. A suicide plane sank an escort carrier, and much dammage was done to a number of vessels. Admiral "Uncle Dan" Barbey's escort sank a Japanese destroyer which attacked out of Manila Bay as the convoy passed Corregidor. On January 6 advance elements of the fleet reached Lingayen Gulf, harassed constantly by reckless air attacks of the enemy. MacArthur was urged to postpone the landings scheduled for the 9th, but his answer was to request Halsey's big carriers to help with the neutralization of the Luzon airfields. It was a touch-and-go decision he had to make.

The Japanese apparently had shot their bolt, and by January 8 the air offensive was limited to a few suicide missions. American warships and planes could now concentrate on the shore bombardment, in preparation for the actual landings the following day. All but 3 of the 30 American vessels put out of commission were sunk or damaged by suicide planes.

At 7:00 in the morning of January 9 the fire-support ships opened up on the Lingayen landing beaches, and then the naval gunfire lifted to the enemy targets in the rear. At 9:30, when the first assault waves hit the beaches, they were met by little opposition, save against the 43rd Division, which landed at the northern end of invasion shore line. Amphtracs rapidly pushed inland across rice paddies, fish ponds and swamps. Men, ammunition, bulldozers, artillery and supplies of every kind poured out on the beaches, and by nightfall 68,000 troops from the 6th and 43rd Divisions of Swift's I Corps and from the 40th and 37th Divisions of Griswold's XIV Corps were planted on a quarter-moon-shaped beachhead, 17 miles long and 4 miles deep.

The Central Plain of Luzon, with Lingayen Gulf at its northern end, runs southeastward between rugged mountain chains for a little more than a hundred miles. The plain is 30 or 40 miles wide; about 15 miles above Manila it is pinched off into a bottleneck between swamps, then widens out again as it approaches the capital city.

The rugged Caraballo mountains form the northeastern edge of this wide valley, and further on these stubborn mountains lose themselves in the great Sierra Madre range, which runs along the east side of the broad plain and extends south far below Manila. To the west lie the Zambales mountains, with Fort Stotsenburg and Clark Field nestling in the foothills, halfway down from Lingayen Gulf.

MacArthur's general plan was to drive swiftly down this Central Plain, and at the same time push the enemy back into the mountains to the northeast and on both east and west flanks. General Yamashita, thrown off balance and handicapped by the loss of his air, had chosen not to oppose the American landings on the beaches, although he had nearby a force of 36,000 men that could have counterattacked during the confusion of that first evening. By the time he realized the weight of the American forces, which on the initial day advanced 4 miles inland from the beaches and were occupying well-placed and powerful defensive positions, it was too late for him to re-organize his plans.

MacArthur came ashore early on the morning of the landings and after spending most of the day on the beaches, returned to his cruiser for the night. The following day, while Krueger's men drove down the Central Valley and against the Japanese pockets close to the mountains, MacArthur located his advance headquarters in an abandoned schoolhouse in the village of Santa Barbara.

From the start there was heavy fighting directly north of the beachhead, and to the east and northeast formidable cave defense-systems were encountered. General I. P. Swift, I Corps commander, immediately had his Corps reserve brought ashore, and the 25th Division belonging to the reserve of Griswold's XIV Corps also was landed in Swift's zone.

To the right or west of the Central Valley, Griswold's XIV Corps was meeting much less opposition. Quickly it seized the airfields outside the town of Lingayen, then crossed the Agno river and drove on south along the slopes of the Zambales mountains. Within ten days after landing, the 40th Division had pushed more than 50 miles to the southward, and the 37th Division, on its left, had advanced in line.

In the meanwhile Swift's I Corps was encountering the stiffest sort of fighting as it drove eastward and northeastward against the line of Japanese caves and dugouts in the foothills of the Caraballos. It was evident that the Japanese were fighting a purely defensive war, and that they would not compromise on their old no-surrender suicide tactics. With communication tunnels dug between their hillside caves and deep trenches, and with ample supplies of ammunition and food, they were fighting the type of war that best suited their fanatical bravery.

At dawn each day MacArthur and one or two of his staff would take off in an ordinary jeep to the spot where some advancing American unit was being held up. His headquarters in the schoolhouse at Santa Barbara was tentative. Actual plans for the running battles were drawn at the headquarters of Krueger's Sixth Army, and while MacArthur did not care to interfere in the tactical orders, he could not contain his restless insistence that the tempo of the attacks be increased.

There was no pity in his heart for this enemy who had slaughtered his men on the Bataan death march, had broken every rule of modern war and had committed tens of thousands of atrocities. He was ruthless and calculating, but compassionate and careful for his own people. He wanted from his commanders neither excuses nor heavy casualty lists. Count the enemy dead and give him the figures!

Krueger, experienced soldier as he was, often exasperated MacArthur with his overcaution. Constantly the Sixth Army commander protested that he must not neglect his flanks or overextend his lines of communication. He must take no chances. He must play it safe.

But it was not overcaution that MacArthur wanted. What he demanded now was speed, attack, surprise, power, daring, valor—and all tied into as much air support as Kenney could give him. He had the enemy off balance, and he proposed to keep him that way.

The wars he had fought or had studied until they were almost a part of his being now gave him a sense of battle conflict so sound and secure that it bordered on intuition. An intense sense of reality seemed to join with a sixth sense in a dynamic will-to-win that could not fail to inspire the commanders who came under the intensity of his leadership. The very sight of the calm figure, quietly encouraging and directing the actual leaders in the field, somehow counterbalanced Krueger's discretion and demand for more caution and security.

A bombed and abandoned sugar central was located a few miles from Clark Field, now within the American lines. Here, at Hacienda Lucita, MacArthur established his temporary headquarters. Krueger's Sixth Army H.Q. lay thirty miles or so behind him.

Several times previously he had quietly urged Krueger to drive harder and move faster. Finally he sent the message by one of his most trusted staff officers, explaining to him that if he, MacArthur, personally went again he was certain he would finally lose his temper and relieve this old comrade, who shared his birthday and was but a year his junior in age. He could not quite do that. But he could send word to his plans and operations officer to turn up the tempo.

[When MacArthur was questioned years later how soon after the Lingayen landing he had hoped to secure the Central Plain and the Manila Bay area, he answered:

There was no fixed timetable. I hoped to proceed as rapidly as possible especially as time was an element connected with the release of our prisoners. I have always felt, however, that to endeavor to formulate in advance details of a campaign is hazardous as it tends to warp the judgment of a commander when faced with unexpected conditions brought about by the uncertainties of enemy reaction or initiative. I therefore never attempted fixed dates for anything but the start of operations. The rate of progress in this operation was fast and more than fulfilled all hopes and expectations. The only place the enemy could hope to counterattack successfully, except locally on the battle line, was at Lingayen itself to cut my line of supply. My beachhead and harbor base were exposed to attack from Formosa and the north. The 7th Fleet had been reinforced from the Central Pacific by battle ships with accessories and as long as these defended the

Lingayen roadsteads my naval supply line was secure. Admiral Nimitz was preparing for the Okinawa attack, however, and felt these ships must be recalled as soon as possible. I then threw the XI Corps, under General Hall, by sea to the Zambales Coast so that if Lingayen in its weakened naval state became jeopardized I could shift my supply line to a more secure geographical position. The movement also placed Hall's forces so as to threaten the flank of the enemy's main line of resistance in the Manila Plains. No counterattack developed and the enemy's resistance in the Plains rapidly crumbled when I enveloped the other flank with the 1st Cavalry Division.]

2

Never for a day since he came ashore had his mind been free from thoughts of the half-starving and mistreated American prisoners of war who had served under him on Bataan and Corregidor. The Filipinos who survived the death march had been paroled, but there had been no such mercy for the Americans. MacArthur had always felt that these men, with the civilian American internees, were his special charge. Their rescue lay like a heavy weight on his heart.

His plan to enter Manila in some swift and almost reckless drive was based on the certain knowledge that only by surprise and great valor could the 3,500 American men, women and children at Santo Tomás and another 1,000 held in Bilibid prison, be saved from some horrible death. The same assumption was true for a half-thousand American and Allied prisoners of war held in a camp in the western foothills of the Sierra Madre mountains at Pangatian, a few miles northeast of Cabanatuan. It was at Cabanatuan that the north-south Highway 5 crossed the Pampanga river, half-way down the eastern side of the great central valley. This was all Japanese-held country, and only a wild and daring raid had the slightest chance of succeeding.

MacArthur gave his approval to a bold rescue plan which was evolved around the capture of this Pangatian camp. A force of 134 picked men from the highly trained 6th Ranger Battalion was chosen to carry out the desperate mission. Well-supported by tough Filipino guerilla fighters, the little group worked its way through the enemy territory and shortly after dark reached the prison camp and launched its surprise attack. The guards and some 200 enemy troops were killed, at a loss of only 2 Americans killed and 10 men wounded. Swiftly the 486 American prisoners and their 36 Allied comrades were brought together and all through that night the sick and emaciated men were helped back to liberated territory. At daybreak on January 31 they were met by Americans in jeeps and hurried on to the town of Guimba, where they were received with open arms and given hot food and medical care.

Early that morning MacArthur went among them, gripping their hands, patting their shoulders, calling a number of them by their first names and assuring them all that their worries were over.

The next mercy mission now became foremost in his mind.

3

The 1st Cavalry Division came ashore January 27, exactly 17 days after the first troops hit the beaches on Lingayen Gulf. The division's original commander, Major General Swift, now had I Corps, and its present C. O. was Major General Verne Mudge, a fearless and experienced leader.

Two days after its landing MacArthur jeeped to Guimba to talk over with Mudge the idea of cutting loose a flying column from his division and sending it hell-for-leather the 100 miles south to Santo Tomás University in Manila, in the hope that by the very daring of the wild drive he might rescue the 3,500 American internees there. Mudge was enthusiastic.

MacArthur carefully gave his final instructions. Mudge would be racing through enemy country, but he must disregard his own flanks and rely on speed and surprise. He was to engage in no unnecessary fights and to permit no delays that could possibly be avoided. Air attack squadrons from the 24th and 32nd Marine Air Groups, especially trained in close support of ground units, would help protect his flanks and provide reconnaissance. The rest of the division would follow the speeding column as fast as it could drive through. No matter

364

what happened, the mercy mission would be sustained, and the entire Sixth Army would stand by if necessary.

"Get to Manila!" MacArthur concluded. "Go around the Japs, bounce off the Japs, but get to Manila! Free the internees at Santo Tomás! Take Malacañan and the Legislative Buildings!"

Mudge grimly saluted and pledged that he would not sleep until he entered Manila. He would start at midnight this very night, February 1. To spearhead the 100-mile drive he chose what amounted to two composite squadrons that included troopers of field artillery, tank and medical units and a third outfit consisting of two tank companies and a reconnaissance troop. They were designated as 1st, 2nd and 3rd serials. Men, weapons, ammunition, water and four days' rations, with extra gas drums, were loaded for the headlong dash that would have delighted the fighting heart of Rommel. Mudge put Brigadier General Chase in direct charge of the flying column and relieved him of his divisional responsibilities.

In the darkness the three columns started across rice paddies, plowed fields and broken country toward Cabanatuan. Before daylight 5th Cavalry troopers under Lieutenant Colonel William E. Lobit waded and swam the Pampanga river and captured the Valdefuente bridge at the very moment the enemy was preparing its destruction. Major General Mudge personally picked up a handful of troopers and dashed for a cache of 3,000 pounds of dynamite that had been placed on the structure to be detonated by mortar shells. Under fire and with only a split-second to spare, Mudge and his men dumped the dynamite in the river and saved the bridge. This sort of reckless valor showed itself in scores of incidents.

Late that second afternoon MacArthur visited a squadron of the 5th Cavalry that was halted by a broken bridge just north of Angat below Bulacan. He had faith now that the great gamble would pay off.

By midnight, 48 hours after the columns had set out on their magnificent adventure, they had reached a point only 15 miles from their goal. There was little sleep or rest. The three columns often fought individual battles, and they lunged down steep embankments and across streams and around roadblocks in the face of murderous fire.

By 6:30 on the evening of the third day, the leading elements of the flying column crossed the city line. Luck rode in the forward trucks of this serial of the 8th Cavalry, as they rolled by the Chinese Cemetery, two miles within Manila limits. Lt. Colonel Haskett L. Connor, Jr., alert and suspicious, picked up two Filipinos who formerly had been with the Philippine Scouts of the American Army. Darkness had settled down, but they offered to show the way to the gates of Santo Tomás.

At 8:30 this night of February 3 a light tank, the Battling Basic, belonging to the 44th Tank Battalion, crashed through the front gate of the University compound. All lights within the walls had been ordered out, and Japanese guards were firing from their prepared stations.

In a matter of minutes the rest of the American column pushed inside, overwhelming and killing most of the guards. Only one group of 63 Japanese soldiers, barricaded in the well-built Education Building along with 267 American internees held as hostages, escaped the avenging fire. At dawn on the 5th they were permitted to march out with their weapons, after it had been made certain their hostages were untouched.

Late on that afternoon previous to the rescue, an American plane buzzed the prison camp, and a number of the internees saw something drop from the cockpit. Quickly the object was retrieved; it was a pair of aviator's goggles attached to a note that read: "Roll out the barrel. Santa Claus will be coming Sunday or Monday."

It was around 8:30 Sunday night when *he* actually got there.

4

It was time now for MacArthur to begin his great double-envelopment movement which would extend its steel arms around the entire southwestern quarter of Luzon and close the trap on Bataan, Manila Bay and Batangas. Thousands of Yamashita's confused troops would be crushed to death in the surprise sweeps.

The days immediately before Verne Mudge led his flying column down Highway 5 in its dash for Santo Tomás, Major General Charles P. Hall's XI Corps made surprise landings on the west coast above Subic Bay, and in the northwestern corner of Bataan peninsula. The next day the one-time American naval base of Olongapo fell unopposed to the Americans. The swiftly moving columns now started their drives eastward across the twisting dirt trails and enemy roadblocks, to cut off Bataan from the Zambales mountains and deny it to the bewildered Japanese. A few days later the 151st Regimental Combat Team boarded a swift convoy, which slipped out of Subic Bay and landed at Mariveles on the lower shore of Bataan, only three miles from the grim rock of Corregidor in the mouth of Manila Bay.

One battalion drove on around the lower point of Bataan, then straight up the road along the eastern shore. Three days later it joined up at Limay with the 1st Regimental Combat Team of the 6th Division, which had broken through from the Central Valley and had then rapidly driven down the east coast of Bataan. The double envelopment of the woods and battlegrounds of the peninsula was now complete. Bataan had fallen 20 days from the time General Hall's forces first stepped ashore at Subic Bay, and then turned eastward to seal off the northern entrances into the escape haven.

That same day when the enveloping forces met at Limay on the Manila Bay side, MacArthur paid his tribute to the men, Americans and Filipinos alike, who had fought and died here. There was a ring to his words as he referred to the long-ago days when his troops had been starved and neglected:

> Bataan, with Corregidor the citadel of its integral defense, made possible all ·that has happened since. History, I am sure, will record it as one of the decisive battles of the world. Its long protracted struggle enabled the united nations to gather strength to resist in the Pacific. Had it not held out Australia would have fallen with incalculable disastrous results.
>
> Our triumphs of today belong equally to that dead army. Its

367

heroism and sacrifice have been fully acclaimed but the great strategic results of that mighty defense are only becoming fully apparent. The Bataan garrison was destroyed due to its dreadful handicaps, but no army in history more thoroughly accomplished its mission. Let no man henceforth speak of it other than as of magnificent victory.

But there still remained one savage task that was possibly even closer to MacArthur's heart than had been this recovery of Bataan. Corregidor must be retaken, but there must be no reckless expenditures of American life. He studied the plans for its envelopment until he was satisfied.

A single battalion of the 151st Regimental Combat Team boarded landing craft at Mariveles, crossed the three miles of open water and fought its way to a beachhead on the lower tip of the Rock. For three weeks Kenney had been giving Corregidor almost around-the-clock bombing, and two hours before the sea landing was made the 503rd Parachute Regimental Combat Team was flown up from Mindoro and dropped on the topside of the once great fortress. Late that afternoon the two invading American outfits joined up, and by dawn the island was split into halves.

The garrison, confused and half-senseless from the terrible bombings and the three-day naval bombardments, took to their mortar pits and tunnels, and fought on until all but 19 of the 4,516 defenders were killed. It took eleven days and a total of 209 American dead, 19 missing and 725 wounded to wipe out the bitter score of Corregidor.

Three days later MacArthur crossed from Manila to the Rock. It seemed almost a religious rite to him. No other spot in the world held such bitter and lasting memories. The group that accompanied him, sensing his emotion, drew back, and he stood alone gazing into the black and unspeakable charnelhouse that had been the Middle Tunnel. It had held the hospital and storerooms and bomb shelters and his own G.H.Q. In those long-ago days it withstood a half-hundred bombings and weeks of heavy shell fire. Here he had been forced to suffer the anguish and humiliation of leaving his doomed comrades.

A little later that day he attended the brief ceremonies that formally marked the return to the historic Rock. Finally he addressed the 34-year-old Colonel George Madison Jones, West Point '35, whose paratroopers had fought so valiantly alongside their comrades of the infantry battalion that had landed on the beachhead. The stream of his emotion was running deep:

Colonel Jones:

The capture of Corregidor is one of the most brilliant operations in military history. Outnumbered two to one, your command by its unfaltering courage, its invincible determination and its professional skill, overcame all obstacles and annihilated the enemy. I have cited to the order of the day all units involved, and I take great pride in awarding you as their commander the Distinguished Service Cross as a symbol of the fortitude, the devotion and the bravery with which you have fought.

I see the old flagpole still stands. Have your troops hoist the colors to its peak, and let no enemy ever haul them down.

5

This classic seizing of Bataan and Corregidor and the clearing of the entrance to Manila Bay had all been part of the great upper arm of the enveloping movement whose ultimate mission was the liberation of southern Luzon. Meanwhile a second arm to the south under Lt. General Eichelberger drove deep into the heart of Batangas province from a beachhead at Nasugbu, 70 miles southwest of Manila. The brilliant 11th Airborne Division advanced 19 miles on foot in the first 28 hours after it hit the beaches. Ahead of them now rose the high Tagaytau ridge. It blocked the way on to the north and the back door to Manila.

Eichelberger ordered the entire 511th Regimental Team, comprising three parachute battalions and a winged artillery battalion, to board their air transports at Mindoro Island below and to take off. The drop was perfect, and almost as if by magic Eichelberger now possessed the 2,490-foot ridge that commanded the country around it. Far to the north could be seen the roofs of Manila faintly shimmering in the bright afternoon sun. The swiftness and surprise of the moves had left the Japanese defenders of the strategic heights helpless and aghast.

Eichelberger loaded his paratroopers in trucks and pushed on. Toward evening he ran into heavy fighting at the river crossing at Imus, but nothing apparently could check for long the momentum of his advance. That night he and his troops caught an hour or two of sleep in Paranaque, the entrance gate to Manila. Here he faced 12,500 Japanese marines guarding this southern passageway stretching between Manila Bay and Fort McKinley. Within four days after his initial landings, he had driven a wedge 69 miles straight into northwestern Batangas. Finally its fine cutting edge was blunted and turned by an entrenched enemy that knew how to die but not how to surrender.

Eichelberger had missed out on the big prize of Manila, but he had done his level best.

Meanwhile, on the night of February 3, when the special squadron of the 8th Cavalry drove its steel mounts into Santo Tomás concentration camp on the north side of Manila, Troop F was detached from the leading column for a daring attempt to capture Malacañan Palace on the Pasig river. It succeeded in taking almost unscathed the beautiful old Spanish dwelling where General Arthur MacArthur had lived in 1901-2 when he was the first military governor of the Philippines. There were several counterattacks by Japanese during the night, but the troopers held on.

The following day the advance columns of the U. S. 37th Division fought their way to Bilibid prison, where they liberated 1,000 American prisoners and internees. Soon afterward elements of both divisions crossed the Pasig in their joint mission of enveloping the city. By the 11th of the month they had swung to the southwest through the outskirts and reached Manila Bay on ahead. One brigade of the 1st Cavalry fought its way to Fort McKinley, then turned east to engage the enemy in their caves and connecting dugouts in the Sierra Madre.

MacArthur hoped that the beautiful city of Manila might be won without being destroyed, but it was not to be. The Japanese had fortified public buildings and residences which were well located for tactical defense. Guns, ammunition and food were piled into these improvised forts. Here the Japanese made their suicide stands. Finally the ammunition was exploded and the buildings set on fire. The blazes spread and in the end almost four-fifths of this matchless city, the Pearl of the Orient, was razed to the ground.

On February 7 in the earliest days of the Manila fighting MacArthur toured the captured prison camps and for hours roamed among the rejoicing internees, greeting such beloved old friends as Theo Rogers whom he had known since he was a lieutenant more than 40 years before. Rogers had been defying his jailers for three years and was one of the unsung heroes of the terrible incarceration. Sniping was still going on along the University walls, and when MacArthur inspected Malacañan Palace a little later, there was still indiscriminate firing.

His troops were now well within the great city, and its doom was clear. But his thoughts were on the final victory over Japan as he made a short statement:

> The fall of Manila marks the end of one great phase of the Pacific struggle and sets the stage for another. We shall not rest until our enemy is completely overthrown. We do not count anything done as long as anything remains to be done.
>
> We are well on the way, but Japan itself is our final goal. With Australia saved, the Philippines liberated and the ultimate redemption of the East Indies and Malaya thereby made a certainty, our motto becomes "On to Tokyo!" We are ready in this veteran and proven command when called upon. May God speed the day!

Actually there still remained three full weeks of isolated fighting in Manila, for the Japanese had to be burned or blasted out of one modern structure after another. Finally the survivors sealed themselves up within the high stone walls of the picturesque old Walled City. For days they held out against artillery and mortars, flame throwers, hand grenades and gasoline poured through holes in roofs and ceilings and set afire. It was March 4 before the last fanatical defender was killed.

6

Even after the double relief of Santo Tomás and Bilibid prison, one more mercy mission remained to be fulfilled before MacArthur could feel that he had done his full duty to his old comrades.

On February 3, the very day that the flying column of the 1st Cavalry Division stormed its way into Santo Tomás University grounds, MacArthur sent word to Lt. General Eichelberger in Batangas province that at the earliest moment it was feasible he should attempt the rescue of the 2,000 American and Allied prisoners of war and civilian internees held in a prison camp at Los Baños, on the southern shore of Laguna de Bay. The stockade was 50 miles within the Japanese lines and across swampy and difficult country.

Eichelberger had just moved up with the men of the 511th Parachute Regiment, who had dropped on the strategic Tagaytay Ridge, and were preparing for their dash toward Manila. A few days later the units he had been leading were transferred to the Sixth Army and he flew back to his Eighth Army H.Q. in Leyte. He turned over to Major General Joseph M. Swing and his 11th Airborne Division the mission to rescue the prisoners at Los Baños.

As leader of the difficult venture Swing chose Colonel Robert Soule of the 188th Glider Regiment, who had been wounded at Tagaytay Ridge and had been recommended for promotion to brigadier general and for a Distinguished Service Cross. In some ways this Los Baños mission was even a more desperate assignment than either of the two previous rescue tasks. Besides the regular guards at the camp, there were several thousand enemy troops not more than three or four hours' march from the stockade.

Filipino guerillas, posing as friendly natives, were sent in to spy out the land. They returned with an American engineer, Peter Miles, who had recently escaped. He was able to draw maps of the exact location of the camp and the pill boxes, sentry posts and defensive measures.

A half-hundred amphtracs that were modernized versions of the old alligators and buffalos were collected and moved from the Fort McKinley area to Paranaque on Manila Bay below the city. Nichols Field was now in American hands, and nine C-47s were brought in and made ready for a company of paratroopers.

On February 20 a detachment of 32 Americans and 80 Filipino guerillas made their way to the northern shore of Laguna de Bay and quietly paddled their native *bancas* to the lower end of the shallow lake and went into hiding. When nightfall came, on Washington's birthday, the group slogged on foot for seven hours across rice paddies and through swamps. Early in the morning of February 23 they set up columns of phosphorous smoke as markers for both the paratroopers and the flotilla of amphtracs, which were loaded with picked men from the 1st Battalion of Soule's own regiment.

The leaders of the three converging outfits might have been using stop watches, so accurate was their coordinated timing. While the guerillas suddenly broke in through the gates and killed the sentries, the amphtracs walloped up the lake shore and rattled toward the firing. In a matter of minutes the paratroopers dropped from the sky and hurried into their agreed positions to meet any Japanese countercharge. Soon American air patrols appeared, ready to help if needed.

Swiftly the helpless litter cases were carried to the amphtracs and rushed to safety. The shuttle service went into action, and all the 2,000 prisoners were safely evacuated. Close to 250 Japanese guards were killed, at a total loss of 2 dead and 1 wounded American. The internees had a single casualty—one man slightly wounded.

MacArthur had had no personal share in the exact planning of this third miracle rescue, but it had his magic touch. Water, ground and air had all three contributed. To the technique of the double envelopment was now added the new contribution of vertical envelopment. In miniature that had been repeated here all the elements of surprise, speed and force, and the complete use of every type of weapon, communication and coordination that MacArthur had mastered.

It was a post-graduate school of war that he had been running these past three years.

7

In Washington the reaction to MacArthur's phrase, "On to Tokyo," made in his press release when the heart of Manila was captured, was resentment against him. Navy spokesmen quietly put out the word that "MacArthur will go to Japan only over their dead body." Even the reports now arriving of the heavy losses on Iwo Jima, fought under over-all Navy command, did not soften the criticism against MacArthur.

On February 10 John Callan O'Laughlin, publisher of the important *Army & Navy Journal,* and MacArthur's devoted friend, ran an editorial regarding the future invasion of the Japanese home islands that brought a storm of disapproval. In part it read:

> Reports are current that the plans for the invasion, which have been approved, contemplate his [MacArthur's] retention for the clean-up job in the Philippines, and the assignment of another officer as commander of the invading expedition.
>
> In view of MacArthur's superb leadership, the significant results that have been obtained by purely American forces and the low number of casualties his men have sustained, it would seem that there would be no question about his continued leadership of the military operations to be conducted in the homeland of the Far Eastern enemy.
>
> No one knows better than MacArthur that without the protection his command and communications have received from our incomparable fleets, an advance could not have been made into the Philippines. It follows that his realization of the debt he is under to the Navy and Fleet Admiral Nimitz's knowledge that land operations must complete Japan's defeat have facilitated the closest cooperation between the two commanders, and that this cooperation would unquestionably continue during the attack on the enemy's home islands.
>
> And because he knows them thoroughly and has profited by their use, General MacArthur is the military commander who should lead our forces into these islands. We hope the President and the War Department will so announce.

Making one of his regular calls on the Army Chief of Staff, O'Laughlin found Marshall very much disturbed by the editorial. A day or two later in a confidential letter to ex-President Hoover, O'Laughlin wrote of Marshall's pique:

> He spoke of MacArthur as obstinate and ambitious. . . . Apparently the only friend in the Navy the General has is Halsey, who has lauded the General as a great leader . . . Marshall declared he would have something to say as to who would be Supreme Commander in the Far East. He said that there must be organized for that region another Supreme Headquarters Allied Expeditionary Force, with British representation as in Europe. . . . One rumor is that Marshall or King, neither of whom have led troops nor fleets in battle, may be sent in Supreme Command. Marshall, a 5-star General, is senior to MacArthur of the same rank.

On March 14, Lt. General George Kenney arrived in Washington from Manila on a mission from MacArthur to get more planes. In a long talk with the Chief of Staff he insisted that Japan had lost her air power, her navy and merchant marine, and that there was no longer any necessity of holding back until Germany was defeated or the Russians came in. Marshall called in several members of his staff and asked Kenney to repeat his analysis. Marshall countered with the suggestion that he did not agree with Kenney's arguments that Japan was at the end of her rope. He insisted she still had a great army and was full of fight. Likewise, he made it clear that he had little faith in the Japanese overtures for peace.

Less than a week later Kenney called on President Roosevelt and gave him the same general optimistic picture regarding the rapid disintegration of Japan's sea and air power, and he assured the President that America could invade when and where she wished. When he was leaving, the President suggested that Kenney would probably like to know whether Nimitz or MacArthur was to run the invasion. The President's exact words that Kenney shortly reported to MacArthur were: "You might tell Douglas that I expect he will have a lot of work to do well to the north of the Philippines before very long."

But whether Roosevelt's memory was short, or he had merely been indulging in little pleasantries, or the pressure against MacArthur's appointment was suddenly too great for him to withstand, the fact soon became clear that there was no substance to the message he had sent through Kenney to Mac-Arthur, intimating that he was to be supreme commander.

On April 5 the Joint Chiefs of Staff announced a split command in the Pacific, Nimitz to be in charge of all naval forces, MacArthur to control all army forces.

Seven days later, April 12, the President was dead.

PART FOUR

No Substitute
for Victory

1945-1954

19

A SUNDAY MORNING
ON THE BATTLESHIP *MISSOURI*

While MacArthur was conducting his giant envelopment movement on Luzon, there were important developments elsewhere in the world.

From February 4 to 14, 1945, the Big Three met at Yalta. Roosevelt, who had been elected for a fourth term only three months before the conference, was obviously a dying man, and Churchill likewise had passed the peak of his powers.

Only one of the Big Three, Stalin, still possessed great vigor and the exact knowledge of what he wanted. Hatred of Hitler and Germany had worn out the other two, with the additional tragedy that neither they nor certain of their most trusted advisors had a long-range view of what was required for a lasting peace in Europe. The idea of *unconditional surrender* and revenge still largely dominated the American and British leaders, with General Marshall apparently obsessed by what he felt was the need of securing Russian help at any price to bring about an early war victory over Japan.

For some time there had been divided opinion among the U. S. Joint Chiefs of Staff regarding the necessity of an actual invasion of the Japanese home islands and whether Russia must be brought into the Pacific war. Marshall and his Army people in the Pentagon had favored both of these propositions. On the other hand, since early 1944 Admiral Leahy, the President's personal Chief of Staff, had felt that naval and air blockade coupled with air bombardment could eventually bring Japan to her knees, without actual invasion and without Russia's entering the Pacific war. Admiral King and his own staff had been less optimistic. They seemed to favor the idea that Japan would have to be destroyed before she would surrender, and that an invasion of the China coast might be necessary. Sixty-six cities were to be destroyed by bombing, which had already started. (Later King was to agree to a direct invasion of the Japanese home islands, without the use of bases on either Formosa or the China coast, but he still clung to his prejudice regarding navy domination over the army.)

Within the inner policy-making group of the American delegation at Yalta was a glib and attractive young man, who bore the highest possible recommendations from Assistant Secretary of State Dean Acheson. Long afterward it was discovered that Alger Hiss was a Communist spy who had been skillfully planted in the State Department. He had originally been brought to Washington by Supreme Court Justice Felix Frankfurter.

The sick and undependable Roosevelt, his already handicapped mind inflamed with grandiose ideas of a World State that he would head, obviously was in no shape to bargain with the calculating Stalin, who knew exactly what he wanted. Roosevelt's principal advisor, the equally exhausted and dying Harry Hopkins, offered little assistance to Roosevelt in exacting a practical long-range agreement with Stalin. Obviously what was needed was a settlement that at least would give America the benefit of a decent European peace and a future Asiatic pact that would carry out America's sacred obligations to her old ally, Chiang Kai-shek, and would guard her own great Pacific interests. Hopkins, who had got along so well with Stalin by the simple expedient of giving him everything he wanted, apparently backed the President in his unrealistic idea that by the sheer weight of his trust and his generosity to Stalin he could win over the tough dictator to a sense of honor and decency.

The net result, however, was that his support of Roosevelt's post-war U. N. views permitted Stalin to move ahead to the control of Poland, to the dismemberment of Germany and to the subsequent tragedies that befell Eastern Europe—with all hope for a permanent and decent peace grounded for long years to come. As to the Far East, the secret terms of the Yalta agreement betrayed Nationalist China and actually gave away lands and rights that belonged to her and to no one else. In return for this last dishonest act Stalin promised to enter the war against Japan within three months after victory over Germany and, in addition, to become a member of the future United Nations.

There was no possible way that MacArthur could know of these secret terms affecting China's integrity. As a matter of fact, even the Secretary of State and members of the American Cabinet—as well as Chiang Kai-shek—were kept in ignorance of them for some time. Stated briefly, the Yalta concessions included: the leasing to Russia of Port Arthur at the head of the Yellow Sea; making Dairen into a free international port; the return of the one-time Russian rights on the Manchurian railroad, and handing back to Russia the strategic lower half of Sakhalin Island and the Kuriles immediately north of Japan. Stalin promised as part payment his support of the Nationalist Government of Chiang in China.

At the final plenary session at Yalta the persuasive Stalin, according to Admiral Leahy, openly explained: "I want only to have returned to Russia what the Japanese have taken from my country." The fact that much of it had actually belonged to China apparently was overlooked when the President remarked: "That seems like a very reasonable suggestion from our ally—to get back that which has been taken from her."

Stalin agreed at the time that he would enter the war against Japan within three months after the German surrender. Marshall had won his point. Regardless of the price, America was to have Russian help against Japan.

MacArthur, of course, learned nothing of these disastrous secret agreements until months after they had been consummated. Never once had he been formally consulted by Washington regarding the need for bribing Stalin to enter the Pacific war.

As a professional soldier he could not help admiring the valor and fighting qualities of the Russian Army and the military resistance of the Kremlin dictatorship. On February 23, 1945, in the midst of the desperate fighting in Manila, he issued a statement that read:

> The anniversary of the Russian Army cannot fail to be a memorable event to every soldier of whatever nationality. Its extraordinary achievements represent in many respects the most magnificent war effort the world has ever seen. It epitomizes what so emotionally moves all fighting men—courage, sacrifice for country, steadfastness under stress, and that white flame of determination which burns but the fiercer when desperation is faced. These are fundamental military virtues which constitute greatness and produce immortality. God grant its complete victory in its just struggle.

Whether MacArthur wrote out this statement at the direct request of the War Department is not known. Three years previously on a hint from the War Department he had issued a highly complimentary salute to the gallantry of the Red soldiers.

2

During these swift and confusing spring days of 1945 when the European war was being brought to a close, MacArthur still faced heavy fighting both in Luzon and in the central and southern islands. In Lt. General Eichelberger, commander of the Eighth Army, he had found his Stonewall Jackson. What "Old Jack" meant to Lee in swift and sure obedience and energy, the tall, fearless Buckeye meant to the Southwest Pacific Commander-in-Chief.

In place of the rolling hills and sweet villages of northern Virginia and the beautiful Shenandoah Valley, Eichelberger was
382

now to operate on a sea, air and land battlefield more than 500 miles square. In the short five-month period from March 15 to August 15, 1945, he was to be credited with 52 separate landings, covering the vast areas of all the central and southern islands south of Luzon.

The Visayas came first, with landings on Panay on March 15; then on Cebu on the 28th, and on sugar-rich Negros the following day. In western Negros alone there were 14,000 enemy troops. Already Eichelberger had other units operating far to the south, and toward the end of March he landed near Zamboanga in Mindanao and seized the air strip. There was no slacking of his whirlwind attacks.

Eichelberger now brought his skill to the difficult task of liberating Mindanao, the second largest island in the Philippine group. It was a razzle-dazzle type of football-war his team played. He drove from three sides across the great mountainous island toward the Japanese base at Davao. On May 4 he personally led the advance column of troops of his 24th Division and suddenly broke into the outskirts of the battered town.

Three days later came the news of the German surrender. The end of the European war was to bring certain changes in the Pacific setup. There would now be almost unlimited ground and air reinforcements to draw from, and plans were swiftly made for the transfer of numerous units half-way around the world. General "Hap" Arnold, Air Corps representative on the Joint Chiefs of Staff, flew to Manila with General George E. Stratemeyer, air commander in China, to confer with MacArthur and George Kenney. Kenney had already consolidated his own immortal Fifth with the experienced Thirteenth to form the Far East Air Force. To many it appeared that the imaginative Kenney should have the over-all air command of the entire Pacific. But Arnold had his own ideas.

The top U. S. air commander announced his plan to bring in Doolittle and probably Twining from the European theatre and give them the long-range Superfortresses to be assigned to the new Eighth and Twentieth forces. These two would constitute the Strategic Air Force, and General Spaatz would probably be placed in command. But as executive agent of the Joint Chiefs of Staff Arnold personally would be in command of all air.

No single ship of the magnificent B-29s had been assigned to MacArthur's theatre, and none would be. Many of the men of the original Fifth Air Force, who from early Guinea days had fought on a shoestring, did not fully appreciate the necessity of importing European air commanders, who from the start had had ten times their number of planes and supplies, and who, as one of Kenney's commanders complained, "had been eating high on the hog." Kenney and his officers, Whitehead, Wurtsmith and Hutchison, Crab and Cooper, may have resented the newcomers slightly, now that the Pacific war was obviously drawing to a close and the terrible days of half-starvation in men and equipment were over. But they all wanted to finish the war and get home.

In June MacArthur journeyed south by cruiser to witness the landings of the Australian troops at Brunei Bay in Borneo. Kenney's air had cleared the beaches there and broken the set defenses of the Japanese on that side of the great island. MacArthur had insisted on going ashore within an hour after the first waves had landed at 9:15.

The weather was unbearably hot and muggy, but MacArthur appeared fresh and cool as he strode in the lead of the little party toward the advance elements. Men years his junior were dripping with sweat and falling behind. Rifle fire broke out ahead, and MacArthur seemed to increase his pace as he hurried to the point. The Aussies were moving up a few Matilda tanks of the vintage of the dark days of Buna and Gona. One tall lad from Down Under, looking up as the brass strolled by, recognized the General and remarked: "Well, ain't that a bit of bloody all right!"

The tanks struck a trap and were held up. Suddenly two Nips in ditches on opposite sides of the road, and less than a hundred feet away, opened up. The Aussies killed them. MacArthur walked up to where one lay, and leaning over opened his leather cartridge box. That second an army photographer dropped to one knee to take a picture. A bullet ripped into his shoulder. MacArthur saw that the man was not badly wounded and then led the way ahead. He walked as if he were actually exalted by the danger he faced. (He was wearing his "lucky hat," as usual.)

Brigadier General Fellers of his staff turned to George Kenney and whispered that someone should get the Old Man to turn back. "If MacArthur goes, there is no one else who can hold this Southwest Pacific together," Fellers said to the air commander. "He won't listen to me any more. He just tells me I can go back if I want to, but that he's going on. Wish you'd try him, General."

Kenney had his own way of doing things. He walked up alongside of MacArthur and remarked that if he wanted to collect a bullet as a souvenir, he was sure going after it the right way. Pretty soon they'd be running into a Jap outpost, but that was the infantry's affair and not the commander-in-chief's business. How about heading back toward the shore and the cruiser *Boise?* MacArthur grinned down at his air commander and chuckled: "All right, George, we'll go back. You mustn't miss that chocolate ice cream soda they've got for you."

All this had happened on the Sunday morning of June 10, 1945. On Tuesday the party was at the beautiful harbor of Jolo on the Sulu Sea. Eichelberger, fresh from his great triumph in Mindanao, flew in for a conference. With Kenney and Jens Doe, the 24th Division commander, they called at the regimental headquarters to meet the Sultan of Jolo, who had come in to pay his respects. He was a weazened little old man, who in 1905 at the end of the Moro War had surrendered to John J. Pershing, then a cavalry captain. He had been loyal to the Americans in all the years since that time, and his people had enjoyed killing Japanese soldiers who had wandered out from the old Walled City.

That night after dinner on board the *Boise* the General unburdened himself for a full hour on his conclusions about the war and the mistakes being made in the Central Pacific, about the Russians and about the world in general. He explained, for instance, how he had decided on the Brunei Bay operation only after he had studied the enemy dispositions for several months. When the Japanese pulled out their fleet from Brunei, he figured they would also pare down their garrison. He watched intelligence reports, studied photographs of landing areas and finally concluded that his keystone dictum of knowing exactly "when and where to fight" had been satisfied. It was the companion piece to "hittin' 'em where they ain't."

Turning to the larger strategy of the future, he explained that if it was necessary eventually to land on the enemy's home islands, a prerequisite should be to have the Russian Army strike in northern Manchuria before America tried to invade Kyushu, the lowermost island of the Japanese chain. The Russians should engage the million Japanese soldiers in Manchuria and dull the edge of the Nip Air Force. It would take up much of the shock of the American landings and save thousands of American lives.

The Japanese soldier was tough physically and spiritually, he went on. He could live on very little, and he would willingly die. From a purely military point of view it was too bad to see such courageous soldiers suffer from such stupid leadership. Yamashita was the best general the Emperor had, but he had fought a very poor campaign on Luzon, MacArthur concluded.

Two days later MacArthur went ashore at Zamboanga. There had been sharp fighting here a few weeks before, and some thousand starving enemy soldiers, including Lt. General Hojo, had escaped to the hills. Again that night MacArthur, puffing away on his corn-cob, talked of the great battle of Iwo Jima and the desperate struggle for Okinawa, both under supreme naval command and over which he had not the slightest control or authority.

At Iwo Jima the fighting had begun in February 1945, and in the terrible days that followed the American casualties had been more than 20,000, with some 4,500 killed. This did not include the losses of naval personnel, which were well over 1,000. The counted Japanese dead had been 21,000. King and Nimitz and the Joint Chiefs of Staff had decided that the little island, 4 miles by 2, was necessary as a half-way base for the crippled B-29 bombers returning to their airfields in Saipan and the Marianas after bombing the Tokyo area. And the Joint Chiefs of Staff considered that it was needed as a base for fighters accompanying the heavy American bombers on their long-range raids.

Not even the expensive and deadly Iwo battle had checked

the Navy and the JCS in their determination to capture the large island of Okinawa, which lay almost directly below the lower tip of the southern home island of Kyushu. The over-all command was in the hands of Admiral Raymond A. Spruance, with Vice Admiral Richmond K. Turner in charge of the amphibious forces: the ground operations were assigned to Lt. General Simon B. Buckner, whose Tenth Army included both Marine and Army divisions. (Four days after this discussion aboard the *Boise,* the brave Buckner was killed by a shell as he surveyed his front area. He was replaced by Lt. General Roy Geiger, of the Marine Corps. After the island had fallen Lt. General Joseph W. Stilwell replaced Geiger.)

The Okinawa landings began on April 1 and the fierce and heroic fighting did not end until June 21. During the week before final victory, MacArthur and his officers on the *Boise* had only a rough estimate of the losses and the frightening cost the Marines and the Army, and the Navy as well, paid for their triumph. Total American ground casualties on the island eventually were put at 65,631 men, including 7,300 dead. The Japanese Air, largely suicide planes, had sunk 36 ships and damaged 332 others. Naval casualties afloat were estimated as high as 27,000 men, with 4,907 killed on the U. S. ships. Japanese dead totalled 107,500, with 7,400 prisoners.

The night closed in with the *Boise,* moving northward through the quiet Sulu Sea. It was a serious and disturbed group who quietly analyzed the costly Okinawa venture. Why had American casualties been so high? Could they have been prevented? Had there been serious errors in tactics? There was some question, in the first place, whether Okinawa was an absolutely essential objective. Smaller islands nearby might have been taken swiftly without serious losses and fighter bases established if it still had been felt that Okinawa was absolutely essential.

The kamakaze suicide planes had injected an element into the long battle that involved the ancient law of self-preservation. Naturally, the first duty of the naval aircraft carriers and escorts was to protect themselves and their sister ships. Consequently, during enemy air attacks few of the carrier planes could give the ground forces the needed help and protection. They had first to protect their own ships. In doing this, possibly as many as 90% of the American carrier-borne missions flown were to protect the fleet.

Once the upper two-thirds of the 68-mile-long island had been secured, the lower tip could have been sealed off, and the troops there allowed to starve. Most of the American ground casualties had occurred in the exhausting series of deadly frontal attacks against this southern nest. The Japanese there might have been made prisoners of their own barricades, and the captured airfields and bases in the central part of the island could rapidly have been put into operation.

Within two weeks after the initial landings an area 50 miles long and the width of the island and well beyond enemy artillery range was firmly held by the Americans. It was space enough to build a great and useful air base and staging area for the coming assault on the Japanese home islands, without regard for the doomed enemy troops trapped below. This was precisely what was done near the end of the costly campaign.

Even when the frontal attacks against the lower pocket were proving so costly, no bold attempts were ordered at surprise amphibious landings or great air drops behind the enemy lines that might have permitted double envelopment. Excellent and brave as the ground commanders certainly were, the situation called for an over-all leader who had the imagination and expert know-how—as well as the authority—to depart from staid, old methods of direct assault.

Such was the conclusion arrived at that late June night on the warm Sulu Sea.

3

On July 1 Eichelberger and his Eighth Army took over the fighting on Luzon and throughout the entire Philippines. Krueger and his mighty Sixth Army were released to rest and reequip for the desperate undertaking that lay ahead.

This Sixth Army had fought long and gallantly. All Luzon was now cleared, save the almost impenetrable Caraballo mountains in the north, and portions of the great Sierra Madre chain that ran along the eastern side of the island. Tens of thousands of utterly fanatical Japanese still held like grim death to their caves and mortar pits and dugouts along the steep slopes and narrow, roadless valleys that led into the high places. To capture a single key mountain track, less than three miles long in the Caraballos, had taken weeks of cruel fighting before the series of 214 caves had been blasted and burned out, and the last of the 9,000 half-crazed defenders killed. The final link in the steel chain that was now pulled taut around Luzon had been forged with the American landings at Legaspi in the south and at Aparri in the extreme north.

By middle August less than 50,000 Japanese troops remained alive of the total 400,000 who had guarded the scattered islands when MacArthur on October 20, 1944, made his first landing at Leyte. On Luzon alone there were now 192,000 counted Japanese dead, and 9,700 captured. The total cost had been 7,933 American dead and 32,632 wounded and missing.

The ratio furnished an accurate table of the small American losses against enemy killed in MacArthur's Southwest Pacific campaigns. The comparative figures possibly had never been equalled in war between more or less equal forces. Krueger's Sixth Army alone had counted more than 250,000 Japanese dead since it fought its first meager and handicapped battles in Guinea. It had by-passed and left to die on the vine at least another quarter-million. Yet its own losses for almost three years of war, including Leyte and Luzon, had been 13,199 killed, 51,162 wounded and 528 missing—a total casualty list of 64, 889. For every Sixth Army casualty suffered, the American soldiers in MacArthur's command had demanded almost four dead Japanese, and an equal number by-passed and left behind to starve. Yet MacArthur's naval forces and amphibious units were but a fraction of those available to the Central Pacific.

The MacArthur strategy and tactics had paid off handsomely in American boys who came home.

MacArthur will go down as the first great commander who fully understood and practiced the new 4th dimension in war—psychological warfare. It can well be called the battle for the mind of the enemy. Its principal weapons were air-drop leaflets, radio beamings and front-line broadcasts on loud-speakers. It had been developed in the New Guinea campaigns but it reached its full effectiveness in the Leyte and Luzon battles.

4

The sudden death of Roosevelt on April 12 left many highly important matters regarding the Pacific war hanging in the air. No final decision had been reached regarding Japanese peace moves and possible surrender terms. Nor had a conclusion been evolved whether Japan could be defeated by sea blockade and air bombings alone, or if the actual ground invasion of the home islands must go ahead.

This last desperate move might eventually cost as many as a quarter-million American casualties, and was connected irrevocably with the proposition of Russia entering the Pacific war as a result of the promises made at Yalta. In Washington there was much confusion as a result of the sudden succession as President of Harry S. Truman, who had had no part in the tragic conference nor any real knowledge of the unrevealed commitments.

Washington had withheld from MacArthur knowledge of the secret efforts Japan's Emperor had begun as far back as February 14 to get Russia to act as a mediator between America and Japan. Through intelligence and the early breaking of the Japanese code the overtures became known to both the State Department and General Marshall. It was not until the Potsdam Conference at the end of July that Stalin acknowledged the attempt and admitted his refusal to raise his hand to stop the war.

On April 7, 1945, the radical Koiso Ministry of the Japanese War Party resigned in Tokyo. It was shortly replaced by a cabinet headed by the 77-year-old conservative Kantaro Suzuki, chamberlain to the Emperor, who was recognized as a moderate. It was perfectly clear to MacArthur that the drastic move was a signal to the world that the Emperor was in the saddle and that Japan might be prepared to move toward peace talks.

All through the early days of 1945 there were bitter and constant attacks on the Japanese Emperor and the monarchy in the radical and pro-administration press of America. Men who had advocated the utter crushing of Germany under the disastrous guise of unconditional surrender, were now clamoring for some such ruin for Japan and for her whole system of government. Both points of demand had been strenuously advocated by the extreme radical press, the Communist *Daily Worker* in New York setting the pace. Communist sympathizers over the country joined in the cry for revenge against the Emperor and his authority. Yet it was the one issue that would insure the stubborn and uncompromising resistance of the Japanese people.

MacArthur's concern was limited to the stern realities of the situation as they involved the American military forces in the Pacific. As long as four million Japanese soldiers in Asia and the Pacific islands and another two million in Japan were still armed and unbeaten, it was uncertain whether the Emperor himself could handle them, even if he agreed to a surrender.

On May 26, twelve days after the German surrender, formal orders were issued by the Joint Chiefs of Staff in Washington setting the target date of November 1, 1945, for the invasion of Kyushu, and March 1, 1946, for the invasion of the Tokyo Plain. Before the first landings in either island, Japanese cities, harbors, factories, concentrations and communications were to be pulverized by constant air bombardment.

According to MacArthur's information there had been little obvious weakening in the fanatical Japanese resistance, and even if the Emperor and his more moderate cabinet members wanted peace, there was no assurance that the War Party would consent and make invasion unnecessary. From army intelligence sources the General knew something of the enemy plans of resistance on the home islands. Great connecting caves and tunnels, well behind the landing beaches, had already been prepared with their caches of food and ammunition, and here fanatical soldiers could fight on until the last man was killed. Approximately two and a half million regular soldiers still were garrisoned on the home islands, and there were hundreds and possibly thousands of suicide planes hidden in wooded areas and cemeteries with camouflaged security.

But MacArthur had no means of knowing the mass of intrigue, subterfuge and pro-Soviet politics that was being played in Washington during these late spring months of 1945 when President Truman was new to his job. Nor had he been fully informed as to the secret sections of the Yalta Agreement. His chief concern was victory and the least possible loss of American lives.

At best he had only vague knowledge of how the State Department was split wide open over the questions: first, whether the Japanese Army at home and on the Asiatic mainland would surrender at the command of the Emperor: second, whether there should be a peace proposal by the United States Government that would guarantee the continuation of the Emperor's life and authority: third, whether the entrance of Russia into the Japanese war would bring on all kinds of dangerous complications into the Far East and the Western Pacific.

In the State Department under the direction of Assistant Secretary Dean Acheson, there had been slowly developing a leftist crowd calling themselves liberals, who were supported by a number of men of internationalist sympathies, both within and without the Department. They were vigorously opposed by several old China hands, headed by Joseph Grew, one-time ambassador to Japan and now Undersecretary of State, and his former Tokyo Counsellor Eugene H. Dooman. Eventually this small, moderate bloc numbered among its supporters Secretary of War Stimson and Secretary of Navy James V. Forrestal. General George Marshall and most of the army people around him seemed dominated by the group that demanded that the Emperor must go, that Russia must be brought into the war, and that no terms other than unconditional surrender should be offered Japan.

Toward the end of May, when Secretary of State Stettinius was still in San Francisco, Undersecretary of State Grew ordered Dooman, who was chairman of a three-man State-War-Navy coordinating committee for the Pacific, to complete the preparation of a paper to be presented to the President that would be the basis for Japanese surrender. At a subsequent meeting of the Policy Committee of the State Department, the paper was studied. There were no objections until it came to the part suggesting a constitutional monarchy for Japan once a peaceful regime was assured. Both Dean Acheson and Archibald MacLeish violently objected to this. Acting Secretary Grew announced that he would present the paper to the President as it stood despite the objections.

A day or two later Grew and Judge Samuel I. Rosenman went to see the President, who carefully read the document. According to the later testimony of Dooman before the Senate Internal Security Sub-committee, the President said "he would approve and accept the document, provided it was agreeable to the armed services." Eventually a number were convinced that a prompt submission of the peace proposal to Tokyo might have brought on a Japanese surrender before Russia came into the war, with all the deadly consequences of that act.

The following day a meeting was called at the Secretary of War's office, attended by Grew, Dooman, Judge Rosenman, Stimson, Forrestal, McCloy, Elmer Davis, George Marshall and several officers of the armed services. Copies of the proposed peace document had been handed out, and Stimson explained that he approved the paper as it stood. Secretary of Navy Forrestal and John J. McCloy both gave their assent. Elmer Davis, Director of the Office of War Information, however, appears to have objected and is quoted as stating that he did not approve of anything that might be construed in any way as forming a basis for negotiated surrender. Unconditional surrender and the idea of morgenthauing Japan seemed to suit most of the group.

It was now that General Marshall intimated that the document be pigeonholed because its publication at this time would be premature. It was apparently this decision by Marshall that destroyed any chances of a definite peace proposal being made in late May 1945. Russia was still not ready to enter the Pacific war. The delay would certainly be most satisfactory and helpful to her.

Two weeks later Owen Lattimore called on President Truman and remonstrated against the government taking any position which would enable the monarchy to remain in Japan. But Secretary of War Stimson took the surrender proposal to the Big Three Conference, which opened in Potsdam near Berlin in July, and after securing Churchill's approval presented the document to President Truman and Byrnes, the new Secretary of State. It was accepted by both men, and its contents wirelessed to Chiang Kai-shek. On July 29, exactly two months to a day after it had been branded and shelved as premature by General Marshall, it was thus promulgated as the Potsdam Proclamation to Japan, and it was largely on this basis that Japan surrendered 16 days later. Its presentation to the Japanese government in May might have cut short the war and automatically solved the problem of Russia invading Manchuria and Korea at the ultimate cost of the loss of China, the Korean war and its deadly aftermath.

One more item of the devious and complicated episode still remains to be told. On May 28, the day before the historic meeting at the Secretary of War's office in the Pentagon when the peace proposal was turned down by the Marshall crowd, a radio was received from Harry Hopkins, reporting the result of his third interview with Stalin in Moscow. Its opening sentence read:

> By August 8 the Soviet Army will be properly deployed on the Manchurian border. . . . Stalin left no doubt in our mind that he intends to attack during August.

5

When the terms of the Potsdam Declaration to Japan were received in Manila in late July, there was considerable skepticism regarding its effect. MacArthur was far from certain that it would bring an early peace. He understood how tough and fanatical the Japanese militarists were and how deeply entrenched.

He realized fully the terrible damage the constant bombing was doing to the home islands and that the ultimate doom of Japan had long ago been sealed. While he could fervently hope for peace, he must continue in his preparation for the desperate Kyushu landings, scheduled three months ahead.

On the last day of July Admiral Sherman, Nimitz's chief of staff, flew in with the suggestion that it would be well to prepare plans for a Japanese surrender. His idea was that the Navy should receive simultaneous surrender of the enemy forces in

394

all the principal Japanese and Asiatic harbors. After that was accomplished and peace was assured, MacArthur could gradually land his troops and take over.

MacArthur made no attempt to conceal his complete disapproval of the Navy plan. He was certain that local Japanese port and naval commanders in many instances would neither believe nor understand the surrender terms and some might even refuse to recognize their validity. The result would be confusion, with the possibility of fighting breaking out in practically every harbor entered by the American Navy. Nor would the Navy be able adequately to garrison the ports immediately after their surrender was effected.

MacArthur contended that a bloodless surrender of the enemy forces was possible only if it were made in Tokyo at the direct order of the Emperor. Once Hirohito's personal surrender orders were made known to his field commanders, they would almost certainly obey them. MacArthur was firm in his belief that American demands to the enemy ground, sea and air commanders, if unsupported by the Emperor's mandate, would lead to heavy local fighting wherever Japanese forces were intact.

Time was the critical factor, and MacArthur insisted that when the actual capitulation neared, he and a reasonable number of troops should be landed in Tokyo without a moment's delay. Here in the Emperor's palace he planned to receive the formal surrender and arrange for similar actions in the various Pacific islands and on the Asiatic mainland. Otherwise it was almost certain that Japanese reaction would result in a terrible and completely unnecessary loss of American life.

When Admiral Sherman would not agree, MacArthur explained that he would then have George Kenney fly him to Tokyo at the proper time. He would order the Japanese to clear and guard an airdome near Tokyo; then he would have an American army division brought in by air lift, and he personally would receive the surrender and assume command of all Allied forces as they landed.

With the interview over, Admiral Sherman, flabbergasted at the startling and realistic proposal, went to Lt. General Sutherland, MacArthur's chief of staff, for a re-checking. Sutherland gave his opposite number little satisfaction. "Well, he's personally landed at Manus, Hollandia, Morotai, Leyte, Lingayen, Brunei Bay and Balikpapan," Sutherland explained, "and if he said he'd land at Tokyo, he will do it—and I shall not try to talk him out of it."

MacArthur's G-3, Major General Chamberlain, then met with Admiral Sherman and details of the MacArthur plan were shortly worked out. But the war was still on, and peace was still uncertain.

The early August days were crowded with rumors and counter rumors, with bright hopes and pessimistic reactions. Meanwhile taking out the Japanese cities and their war potentials went on. The waters of the Inland Sea were daily mined from the air, and all Japanese shipping was blasted around-the-clock. On flying days as many as 1,500 of Kenney's bombers alone carried out their missions of death and destruction against Japanese bases and installations all the way from Kyushu to Borneo. At the same time the deadly B-29s were piling up their scores.

On August 5, Manila time, a special messenger arrived in Manila with the top secret information that an atomic bomb would be dropped on an industrial area south of Tokyo the following day. There had been a trial explosion in mid-July at Los Alamos, New Mexico, but no one could be sure what would be the result of this full-scale effort. The A-bomb dropped on August 6 did not actually rock the Eastern world, as some believed it might, but the early reports estimated that a hundred thousand human beings were destroyed or maimed in Hiroshima.

There was still no final news on that historic day of August 6 or on the next day about any direct peace answer from Tokyo. On the 8th MacArthur received the word that the Soviets had actually entered the war and that great Russian forces were lunging into Manchuria, some directly toward Korea, against light Japanese opposition. It was now clear to him that under no circumstances would he have to send Americans to their death on the beaches of Kyushu and Honshu while a million Japanese troops still remained as possible reinforcements in Manchuria.

MacArthur had been kept at least partially informed of the general Manchurian invasion plans of the Russian armies. For several weeks previous to the Soviets entering the war, negotiations had been going on between Washington and Moscow for a military liaison team to be sent from Manila to contact the Russians and join their advances south into Manchuria and coordinate the Russian-American air strikes. MacArthur had chosen his military secretary, Brigadier General Fellers, to head the liaison mission as a major general. The Russians had delayed their acceptance of the plan, although they had their own mission in the Philippines, and when the fighting shortly ended, they refused the proposed American mission the right to enter their war zones.

The day following Russia's declaration of war and march into Manchuria, correspondents urged MacArthur to make a statement, and on August 9 he released the following:

> I am delighted at the Russian declaration of war against Japan. This will make possible a great pincer movement which cannot fail to end in the destruction of the enemy. In Europe, Russia was on the eastern front, the Allies on the west. Now the Allies are on the east and Russia on the west, but the result will be the same.

Apparently MacArthur continued to be concerned over the possibility that the Japanese armed forces would refuse to surrender peacefully, and that they might have to be dug out and killed. For four years he had watched the almost inconceivable mass suicide tactics of Japanese soldiers when they could have saved their lives by a mere gesture of surrender. Time and again he had seen the kamakaze fliers dive to their death, and he had long pondered over such senseless disregard of human life, even if it be their own, that dominated millions of Japanese.

There still remained the terrible possibility that these strangely devoted and dedicated enemy forces would refuse the Emperor's orders to lay down their arms, and an actual invasion of these battered islands would be necessary. The Emperor was the key. But even so, MacArthur understood the great risk involved, and that Russian intervention in Manchuria would save thousands of American lives *if* the actual invasion of the Japanese homeland was necessary. He had been rigidly excluded from the great international policy-making meetings and had little knowledge of the secret agreements arrived at and the cost Roosevelt and Marshall had paid in broken pledges to China for the promise of Stalin's intervention. He could only view the situation from the isolated borders of his own theatre—and not with the full knowledge of the intrigues and betrayals at Yalta and later at Potsdam, in which General Marshall had actually participated. It was purely the human equation that influenced MacArthur.

The day following his statement the second atomic bomb was dropped on Nagasaki. Fortunately it did not hit the center of the city, but the damage was ghastly. The two A-bombs made every previous act of war or atrocity or revenge seem puny and inconsequential.

A day later, Domei, the official Japanese news agency, broadcast the statement that the Potsdam Declaration would be accepted if the Emperor's dynasty was permitted to remain intact. On the 11th a note was sent to Tokyo through the Swiss Minister in Washington explaining a little ambiguously that the Emperor and the government would be subject to the orders of the Supreme Commander of the Allied Powers. When there was no reply, the following day orders were sent out for the several American air forces to continue the bombings.

On the morning of the 13th the Emperor for a second time called his Supreme Council together and ordered them to prepare a radio script. This, the Emperor personally recorded on a platter as a rescript of surrender to be broadcast that same night. It had been a dramatic meeting, and the imperial order had barely been carried out when a mob of a thousand inflamed soldiers broke into the palace. Only by hiding in his bomb-proof shelter did the Emperor save himself from probable assassination. He had held firm to his belief that the people would support him because they now knew the war was lost and that the military had lied to them. He, too, had read the American propaganda pamphlets that had been air-dropped by the millions over Japan and had aided so materially in the psychological preparedness of the masses for their surrender and occupation.

The surrender terms were received in Washington on the 14th. Early that evening President Truman broadcast the acceptance of what he called "the unconditional surrender of Japan."

In his short broadcast the President added that General Douglas MacArthur had been appointed Supreme Allied Commander to receive the surrender.

For three years the able and determined Admiral King had constantly fought to insure the Pacific getting even the small part of the total war effort that Roosevelt and Churchill begrudgingly allotted it. The Navy's Central Pacific areas kept most of the entire Pacific allotments, but without King's sustained efforts up to late 1944 the Japanese war would have been even more neglected than it was.

The terrible losses in the Navy-controlled Okinawa battle had shocked President Truman, and this had helped influence him in favor of MacArthur. Nimitz was the Navy's choice for the post of supreme allied commander.

The new President had not as yet succumbed to the bitter hatred and envy that the leftist groups around the White House, along with certain individuals in the Pentagon and State Department, had for MacArthur. He could still make his own decisions.

So it was that the bitter controversy over command and allotments that had plagued the Pacific for so long, came to an end with victory. The Navy no longer would stand out against MacArthur.

But other strong forces of even a more deadly nature would shortly combine to oppose his ideas and his methods. Washington would continue a very real and devastating second front for him.

6

The day following Japan's acceptance of the surrender terms MacArthur ordered that enemy emissaries fly at once to Manila to receive final instructions. He stated that they were to make the first leg of the journey in one of their own planes, with green crosses painted on the fuselage and wings. They were to use the call letters B-A-T-A-A-N, and they would land at Io Shima, an island off the northwest tip of Okinawa, and from there an American plane would carry them to Manila.

The Japanese radioed that it was uncertain whether the representatives were to sign the surrender or merely negotiate the terms. MacArthur sternly answered that his instructions were clear and to carry them out. A subsequent message that they would use the call letters J-N-P met with a terse order that the call letters B-A-T-A-A-N had been given them.

The envoys arrived in Manila at 6 P.M. August 19. Major General Willoughby, Chief of Intelligence, and Colonel Sidney F. Mashbir, fluent Japanese-language scholar and head of the Japanese interpreter section of the staff, met the small delegation. There was no show of the amenities, and hand shakes were refused by General Willoughby and Colonel Mashbir. The enemy group was led directly to a hotel. That night Chief of Staff Sutherland received them with cold formality. They were told exactly what to do and what was expected of their defeated country. There was not the slightest effort at humiliation or brutal intimidation such as Wainwright had received. It was all strictly stern, impersonal business.

MacArthur's instructions to them were clear and precise. The Japanese were directed to prepare the airdrome at Atsugi, 10 or 15 miles from Yokohama, for the landing of an airborne division. They were to arrange hotel accommodations and billets and transportation. Their troops were to be withdrawn first from the Atsugi area and then from Yokohama and finally from the Tokyo area. All forces were to be disarmed and demobilized as swiftly as possible. The air landings would begin August 28, weather permitting, and the formal surrender would come two days later.

The following day the emissaries flew back to Japan. MacArthur had decided not to see them, but he had arrived at the definite impression that they would honorably and completely carry out the spirit as well as the letter of their instructions. They had also left the feeling that the military and civilian population would be guided by the Emperor's wishes that they peacefully lay down their arms and accept the occupation of their country.

For the next ten days he mulled over the risk he and his soldiers would be taking in landing almost in the center of a vast armed camp. He would be dealing with the psychology of an Oriental people, and he would be successful only if overnight they could be led to abandon their fanaticism and hate and to accept orders from their Emperor that were the exact antithesis of all that they had been taught by the military. Here was the unprecedented gamble he was taking.

It was obvious that his hope of success lay in his own assurance that the Japanese military leaders and population would obey the orders of the Emperor, and that the pledges made by the emissaries would be carried out.

MacArthur unhesitatingly decided to take the long chance. He called in Eichelberger, whose Eighth Army was to furnish the occupation troops, and had him limit his initial landing operation to the 11th Airborne Division and cancel the former coordinated plan to push the 24th Division ashore in Tokyo Bay at the same time. Sea-borne troops could come later.

Eichelberger suggested that MacArthur at least permit him to fly in with a part of his division two days before the Supreme Commander's arrival so that he could make sure everything was safe. MacArthur shook his head. Eichelberger could have a two-hour start.

At 9:00 on the morning of August 29 the Supreme Commander in Manila boarded the *Bataan* for Okinawa. Brigadier General Fellers, military secretary, and Colonel Mashbir, interpreter, and his medical aide, Lt. Colonel Roger Egbert, and two Filipino orderlies accompanied him. The Japanese had radioed that they were having trouble preparing Atsugi airdrome and that a short delay was requested. Unsatisfactory weather conditions helped out in granting the request. MacArthur did not know at the time that the delay asked for was largely due to the fact that Japanese Army troops had been forced into a sharp little fight before the 300 kamakaze pilots

401

billeted at Atsugi could be disarmed and the propellers of their planes removed and destroyed.

At 2:00 in the afternoon of the 29th the *Bataan* dropped down on Okinawa. Later MacArthur called on Major General Swing, whose 11th Airborne Division had been flown up from the Philippines in 250 C-54's that had been loaned Kenney by General Arnold. They could fly from Okinawa to Tokyo and return without refueling. Kenney had never before had such long-range transports, and never for a day had he the use of the mighty Superforts.

General Swing remarked to MacArthur that his air-borne troops were landing in fighting clothes ready for anything. MacArthur answered casually that it wasn't the clothes the men wore that counted but the way they wore them. He added that he was especially anxious that the landings and occupation be made without any serious incidents.

That night MacArthur sat on the little porch in front of his Quonset hut and outlined to a member of his staff his ideas about the Japanese occupation and the great task that lay ahead. They had been formulated into exact phrases and conclusions in his mind during the ten days since the Japanese emissaries arrived at Manila. But they were based on his own deep background and knowledge of the Far East that covered a full four decades.

It was a seven-point policy he proposed, and all was to be implemented through the Emperor and the machinery of the Imperial government.

1. Disarm all Japanese forces.
2. Demobilize and send the men to their homes.
3. Divert such heavy industry as remains from war activity.
4. Open all schools with no check on instruction save to end all pre-military teaching and add courses in civics.
5. Give the vote to women.
6. Hold free elections.
7. Permit labor to organize and bargain for its rights.

Although far-seeing and humane, it seemed a rather large order. At best it would take many years to fulfill the complex mission. He was well into his 67th year, and he had had no single day of relief for more than four years. And it had already been eight and a half years since he had stepped foot on his homeland.

Lt. General Sutherland joined MacArthur's plane at 9:00 on the morning after his arrival at Okinawa, and rode in the cockpit on the five-hour flight to the Atsugi airfield. Brigadier General Whitney also accompanied the party. Eichelberger and some 500 soldiers, with the band of the 11th Airborne Division, were on hand to welcome the *Bataan* when it landed at 2:00 P.M., August 30. For some minutes the men on the plane had been keeping their eyes on a sight that certainly none of them would ever see again. Far below on the broad waters of Tokyo Bay lay the hundreds of warships comprising the great Pacific armada that had had so much to do with victory.

MacArthur was puffing on his corncob pipe when he led the way down the landing ladder of his plane. Eichelberger saluted him as he stepped to the ground.

"Bob, this is the payoff," he said with a grin.

They talked over the arrangements that had been made. Two bombers roared in, three minutes apart. One belonged to General George Kenney and the other to General Carl Spaatz. When the air generals walked from their planes, all had the butts of their automatic pistols showing in their shoulder holsters. The firearm had long been part of their battle dress. MacArthur quietly suggested to Kenney that maybe they'd better leave their guns in the planes. Within marching distance were some 15 enemy divisions, and if the Japanese didn't mean what they had pledged, a dozen or so pistols wouldn't make any difference. Later it was discovered that this gesture created a most favorable impression among the Japanese.

The automobiles that were furnished were old and worn out, and the procession to the New Grand Hotel at bombed-out Yokohama was made at a slow pace. Every hundred feet or so an armed Japanese soldier stood with his back to the little cavalcade. They were guarding the American Supreme Commander in the exact fashion that they guarded their Emperor. This was significant.

MacArthur was shown to his hotel suite and offered a private dining room. He shook his head and answered that he would eat in the regular dining room with his officers. So far, everything was clicking according to schedule.

The following day the details regarding the surrender procedure on board the U. S. S. *Missouri* were threshed out. MacArthur had insisted that both Generals Wainwright and Percival, the American and British Commanders at Manila and Singapore, who had been so humiliated and mistreated, should be flown in from the prison camps in Manchuria and be present at this high moment of triumph. He also insisted that each commander of the several Allied forces that had helped in the victory share in the great day.

And now one of the great Sundays in all American history was at hand. A bright sun shone on the steel quarter-deck of the battleship *Missouri*. The moment of actual surrender had arrived.

The Japanese Minister of Foreign Affairs, Mamoru Shigemitsu, embarrassed that he could not fit his wooden leg under the small table, nervously fumbled with his pen, while he sought to find the line where he was to place his signature. MacArthur, tense, grim-faced, snapped out the words: "Sutherland! Show him where to sign!"

It was MacArthur's day. He dominated every moment of the great drama. As he played his part, he seemed to stand head and shoulders above them all.

The last signature had been affixed. Only one final gesture remained—MacArthur's report to his own people. For him, in a way, it was the most sacred and solemn part of the unforgettable ceremony. His voice was low and tense with emotion. Slowly he read:

My fellow countrymen:
Today the guns are silent. A great tragedy has ended. A great victory has been won. The skies no longer rain death—the seas bear only commerce—men everywhere walk upright in the sunlight. The entire world lies quietly at Peace. The Holy Mission has been completed. And in reporting this to you, the people, I speak for the thousands of silent lips, forever stilled among the jungles and the beaches and in the deep waters of the Pacific

which marked the way. I speak for the un-named brave millions homeward bound to take up the challenge of that future which they did so much to salvage from the brink of disaster.

As I look back on the long, tortuous trail from those grim days of Bataan and Corregidor, when an entire world lived in fear; when Democracy was on the defensive everywhere, when modern civilization trembled in the balance, I thank a merciful God that he has given us the faith, the courage and the power from which to mould victory. We have known the bitterness of defeat and the exultation of triumph, and from both we have learned there can be no turning back. We must go forward to preserve in peace what we won in war.

A new era is upon us. Even the lesson of Victory itself brings with it profound concern, both for our future security and the survival of civilization. The destructiveness of the War potential, through progressive advances in scientific discovery, has in fact now reached a point which revises the traditional concept of War.

Men since the beginning of time have sought peace. Various methods through the ages have been attempted to devise an international process to prevent or settle disputes between nations. From the very start workable methods were found in so far as individual citizens were concerned but the mechanics of an instrumentality of larger international scope have never been successful. Military alliances, balance of power, Leagues of Nations all in turn failed leaving the only path to be by way of the crucible of war. The utter destructiveness of war now blots out this alternative. We have had our last chance. If we do not devise some greater and more equitable system Armageddon will be at our door. The problem basically is theological and involves a spiritual recrudescence and improvement of human character that will synchronize with our almost matchless advance in science, art, literature and all material and cultural developments of the past two thousand years. It must be of the spirit if we are to save the flesh.

We stand in Tokyo today reminiscent of our countryman, Commodore Perry, ninety-two years ago. His purpose was to bring to Japan an era of enlightenment and progress by lifting the veil of isolation to the friendship, trade and commerce of the world. But alas the knowledge thereby gained of Western science was forged into an instrument of oppression and human enslavement. Freedom of expression, freedom of action, even freedom of thought were denied through suppression of liberal education,

405

through appeal to superstition and through the application of force. We are committed by the Potsdam Declaration of Principles to see that the Japanese people are liberated from this condition of slavery. It is my purpose to implement this commitment just as rapidly as the armed forces are demobilized and other essential steps taken to neutralize the war potential. The energy of the Japanese race, if properly directed, will enable expansion vertically rather than horizontally. If the talents of the race are turned into constructive channels, the country can lift itself from its present deplorable state into a position of dignity.

To the Pacific basin has come the vista of a new emancipated world. Today, freedom is on the offensive, democracy is on the march. Today, in Asia as well as in Europe, unshackled peoples are tasting the full sweetness of liberty, the relief from fear.

In the Philippines, America has evolved a model for this new free world of Asia. In the Philippines, America has demonstrated that peoples of the East and peoples of the West may walk side by side in mutual respect and with mutual benefit. The history of our sovereignty there has now the full confidence of the East.

And so, my fellow countrymen, today I report to you that your sons and daughters have served you well and faithfully, with the calm, deliberate, determined fighting spirit of the American soldier and sailor based upon a tradition of historical truth, as against the fanaticism of an enemy supported only by mythological fiction. Their spiritual strength and power has brought us through to victory. They are homeward bound—take care of them.

It was as if he, too, were signing off for good. He had reached the end of the long trail. From now on it seemed certain that everything that came to his life would necessarily be in the nature of anti-climax.

But Time was to prove how wrong was this surmise.

20

MACARTHUR SAVES JAPAN FROM THE REDS

Six days after the formal surrender on the great battleship *Missouri*, MacArthur drove the 30 miles from Yokohama to Tokyo. Much of the ride was through devastated areas. On all sides was ruin and desolation.

A Guard of Honor from the old 7th Cavalry Regiment, of the 1st Cavalry Division, was drawn up in front of the U. S. Embassy Chancery, which was the scene of the simple and memorable ceremony of raising the American flag. In some ways it was almost as touching to MacArthur as the actual surrender on board the battleship. His voice betrayed the intensity of the moment, as he gave the order:

> General Eichelberger: Have our country's flag unfurled and in Tokyo's sun let it wave in its full glory as a symbol of hope for the oppressed and as a harbinger of victory for the right.

Two years later in a short message to the Daughters of the American Revolution MacArthur described an incident that occurred that day while he was inspecting the bombed chancery, which was some little distance from the Embassy itself. It can best be told in his own words:

> I recall that in Tokyo, at the end of the bloody Pacific trail, after unfurling our flag over the American Embassy on September 8, 1945, while inspecting the fire-gutted Chancery building I saw hanging upon the wall as I approached an uninjured portrait of George Washington. It moved me more than I can say. It seemed peculiarly appropriate that he should be there calmly awaiting the arrival of American arms. For it is from the example of his wise and resolute leadership in releasing the forces of human freedom from the shackles of tyranny and oppression, and

the indomitable qualities of his compatriots, our forebears, that has come much of the inspiration which since has fired American hearts with the will to victory, as we stubbornly have fought to defend that freedom, won for us by the grace of God and the invincibility of our Continental Arms.

It required little time to refurbish the Embassy residence sufficiently for MacArthur to occupy it; the American bombers had smashed everything around it, but it had come through without a scratch. He remained at the Grand Hotel in Yokohama less than a week, and then a comfortable house owned by the Sun Oil Company in a part of the city called The Bluff was turned over to him. Here a small mess was set up that included his military secretary, his language expert and his personal doctor, who was also acting as his aide. Within a matter of two or three weeks he moved, lock, stock and barrel, to the beautiful Embassy, and a few days later Mrs. MacArthur and Arthur flew from Manila to join him there.

The first steps in the difficult occupation procedure had gone ahead without a hitch. The Japanese government faithfully carried out every detail of the surrender agreements, and the swift demobilization and disarming of the millions of enemy soldiers proceeded even more swiftly than was expected. It was already evident that the great gamble involved in trusting and then making use of the Emperor's authority and his government was working out perfectly.

But back in America, and particularly in Washington and New York, there was an increase in the violent criticism in press and radio against retaining the Emperor. It was a part of the positive demand that Hirohito and his dynasty and the entire fascist government must be destroyed root and branch. The bell-wether of the attack was the Communist *Daily Worker,* and its lead was followed by a group of papers that included two or three of the largest and most respected newspapers in New York City. Hand in glove with the press assaults went the same type of intense criticism by a number of broadcasters with nation-wide hookups.

The "line" had been laid down before the surrender, but within a few days after its formal announcement by President

408

Truman, a concerted attack was opened by the *Daily Worker* against both MacArthur and the Emperor. Over the country generally the same voices and the same publications that had demanded turning Germany into a pastoral state were now urging a similar policy toward Japan. In many instances the propaganda for a harsh peace included bitter smears of General MacArthur personally.

On Friday, September 14, the *Daily Worker* ran a full-page story under the heading:

MACARTHUR LINKED TO FASCISTS SEIZING POWER IN PHILIPPINES

It was signed by one José Balahap, and was announced as the first of three articles. It claimed that MacArthur owned stock in several business ventures in Manila, and that he was associated with a number of capitalists there. The intimation was that the Supreme Commander in Japan would now protect the fascists and the capitalists in Japan.

On the same morning that the *Daily Worker* printed its personal blast against MacArthur the General issued a statement in answer to the flood of adverse comment that had been directed against himself and the occupation. It read:

> I have noticed some impatience in the press based upon the assumption of a so-called soft policy in Japan. This can only arise from an erroneous concept of what is occurring. . . .
>
> The first phase of the occupation must of necessity be based upon military considerations which involve the deployment forward of our own troops and the disarming and demobilization of the enemy. . . .
>
> When the first phase is completed, the other phases as provided in the surrender terms will infallibly follow. No one need have any doubt about the prompt, complete and entire fulfillment of the terms of surrender. The process, however, takes time. . . . The surrender terms are not soft and they will not be applied in kid-gloved fashion.
>
> Economically and industrially, as well as militarily, Japan is completely exhausted and depleted. She is in a condition of utter collapse. Her governmental structure is controlled completely by the occupation forces and is operating only to the extent

409

necessary to insure such an orderly and controlled procedure as will prevent social chaos, disease and starvation. . . .

It is extraordinarily difficult for me at times to exercise that degree of patience which is unquestionably demanded if the long-time policies which have been decreed are to be successfully accomplished without repercussions which would be detrimental to the well-being of the world, but I am restraining myself to the best of my ability and am generally satisfied with the progress being made.

Instead of succeeding in its obvious intent at conciliation, the statement seemed to have the exactly opposite effect. Radio commentators and many important newspapers continued to pound away at MacArthur and his occupation methods with constant demands that the Emperor be pushed aside and punished.

Three days after his initial statement MacArthur sought to enlighten his critics and the public by a report so reassuring and optimistic that there could no longer be any legitimate criticism of his work. America was in the midst of a vast emotional urge that her soldiers everywhere be brought home. The near-miracle of bloodless occupation that had occurred in Japan played directly into this sentimental demand, and the bright hope that MacArthur now held out gave a tremendous importance to his announcement. Its implied promises had been well augmented a few days before when General Eichelberger had been quoted as saying, "If the Japs continue acting as they are now, within a year this thing should be washed up."

The MacArthur statement read:

The smooth progress of the occupation of Japan has enabled a drastic cut in the number of troops originally estimated for that purpose. . . .

By utilizing the Japanese governmental structure to the extent necessary to prevent complete social disintegration, insure internal distribution, maintain labor and prevent calamitous disease or wholesale starvation, the purposes of the surrender terms can be accomplished with only a small fraction of the men, time and money originally projected. . . . Probably no greater gamble has been taken in history than the initial landings where our ground forces were outnumbered a thousand to one, but the stakes were worth it.

Then came the proposal that was to bring on a violent reaction from those who wanted a harsh and bitter revenge on Japan:

As a consequence of the saving in men the occupation forces originally believed essential are being drastically cut, and troops will be returned to the United States as rapidly as ships can be made available. Within six months the occupational force, unless unforeseen factors arise, will probably number not more than two hundred thousand men, a size probably within the framework of our projected regular establishment, and which will permit the complete demobilization of our citizen Pacific forces which have fought so long and so nobly through to victory. Once Japan is disarmed, this force will be sufficiently strong to insure our will. . . .

It was ready-made for the headline writers and for sensational radio announcers. But somehow the happy news it carried to mothers and wives and to millions of American families fell like a deadly bomb on the Department of State in Washington.

Two days after the statement was issued in Tokyo Acting Secretary of State Dean Acheson held a press conference in his office. The secret pro-Russian and anti-Japanese groups within the Department obviously had found their hoped-for leader in the Acting Secretary. In answer to a question by a reporter, Acheson formally replied:

I have no comment to make on the military aspects of what General MacArthur stated. That is a purely military matter with which the State Department is not properly concerned.

I think I can say that I am surprised that anybody can foresee at this time the number of forces which will be necessary in Japan. That may come from my inadequate knowledge of the military field, however, and it is not very important.

The important thing is that the policy in regard to Japan is the same policy which has always been held by this Government and is still held so far as I know—and I think I know.

In carrying out that policy the occupation forces are the instruments of policy and not the determinants of policy, and the policy is and has been that the surrender of Japan will be carried out, that Japan will be put in position where it cannot renew

411

aggressive warfare, that the present economic and social system of Japan which makes for a will-to-war will be changed so that will-to-war will not continue, and whatever it takes to carry this out will be used to carry it out.

The day before, President Truman at his regular press conference had quietly explained that he had not been informed of the possibilities of the drastic cut in the Japanese occupation forces until he had seen it in the General's statement. MacArthur had first estimated that he would need an army of occupation of 500,000. He had later reduced that estimate to 400,000, and now there was a possibility that it might be as low as 200,000. The President's calm appraisal was quite different from the somewhat ill-tempered viewpoint of Acheson, Acting Secretary of State.

Acheson's appointment as Undersecretary of State was yet be confirmed, and when it came up before the Senate five days later it brought on a four-hour debate, with Senator Wherry, Republican of Nebraska, and his Democratic colleague, Senator Chandler of Kentucky, vigorously challenging the remarks and the attitude of Acheson toward MacArthur. Acheson's appointment was in the end confirmed by a Senate vote of 69 to 1, although previously a motion to send the nomination back to the Senate Foreign Relations Committee for clarification had been voted down by 66 to 12.

The rather violent reaction against MacArthur by Acheson at least brought two things into the clear: the definite proof where MacArthur's most determined and bitter opposition at home lay, and the release by the President of the full text of the initial policy relating to Japan as prepared by the Far East Sub-committees of the Coordinating Committee of the State, War and Navy Departments and approved by the President.

The paper had been drawn shortly before the occupation began and had been radioed out to Manila for MacArthur's suggestions and approval. Four days after the Japanese surrender on the *Missouri*, a special messenger arrived by plane from Washington with the full text for MacArthur. It had been kept a top secret, however, and its publication now apparently relieved MacArthur of much of the personal attacks being made against him on account of his conciliatory attitude toward the Emperor and the Japanese government.

The sections of the long directive that applied particularly to the Supreme Commander's relation with the Emperor and the government read:

The authority of the Emperor and the Japanese government will be subject to the Supreme Commander, who will possess all powers necessary to effectuate the surrender terms and to carry out the policies established for the conduct of the occupation and the control of Japan.

In view of the present character of Japanese society and the desire of the United States to attain its objectives with a minimum commitment of its forces and resources, the Supreme Commander will exercise his authority through Japanese governmental machinery and agencies, including the Emperor, to the extent that this satisfactorily furthers United States objectives.

The Japanese government will be permitted, under his instructions, to exercise the normal powers of government in matters of domestic administration. This policy, however, will be subject to the right and duty of the Supreme Commander to require changes in governmental machinery or personnel, or to act directly if the Emperor or other Japanese authority does not satisfactorily meet the requirements of the Supreme Commander in effectuating the surrender terms.

One other paragraph gave MacArthur the exact powers that would prove of inestimable value a little later in the occupation:

Although every effort will be made, by consultation and by constitution of appropriate advisory bodies, to establish policies for the conduct of the occupation and the control of Japan which will satisfy the principal Allied powers, in the event of any differences of opinion among them, the policies of the United States will govern.

2

The sudden outbreak against General MacArthur by the Acting Secretary of State tended to bring into the open the tight little group within the Department that had quietly been wielding a considerable influence in Far Eastern affairs. Acheson, whose successful law firm had often represented foreign governments in financial dealings with the United States government, had long been one of the principal members of this group. Associated with him in various degrees at this time were John Carter Vincent, John Paton Davis, head of the China Division, John Stewart Service, Lauchlin Currie, Owen Lattimore, Alger Hiss (chief of the department of political affairs) and a number of others. Later it was to come out that at least one member of this group was a member of a Communist cell exerting tremendous influence in many matters that concerned the whole of the explosive Western Pacific and East Asia.

The subversives concerned were largely occupied with the general premise that Chiang Kai-shek and his Nationalist Government must be defeated and replaced by the Chinese Communist "agrarian reformers." At the same time they secretly insisted that the whole involved fascist government of Japan must go, and the doors be opened for a large-scale infusion of Red agents. The ultimate fate of Korea was tied into the idea that some day this long abused country of 30,000,000 inhabitants would become a Communist People's Republic.

There had been, however, a definite opposing right-wing group in the State Department led by Undersecretary Joseph C. Grew that included Dr. Stanley Hornbeck, Joseph Ballantine, Eugene Dooman, Adolf Berle, James C. Dunn and a number of other able and highly patriotic men. During the war years President Roosevelt had largely functioned as his own Secretary of State, but with his death and the succession of the inexperienced Truman the State Department had been able to regain some of its former power and influence.

When Stettinius succeeded the ailing Cordell Hull in late 1944, he devoted most of his energy to establishing the United Nations, and the direction of the important Far Eastern affairs was left to the older permanent department officials. Consequently, during the spring and summer of 1945, Grew and his associates were able to a considerable extent to check the Acheson crowd of liberal left-wingers, to supervise the general terms of surrender laid out at Potsdam and to control the drafting of the wise and liberal terms in the initial policy statement following Japan's collapse.

Byrnes had been appointed Secretary of State only a few days before the Potsdam Conference opened in Berlin early in July. Upon his return to Washington, Undersecretary Grew, worn and discouraged over the sudden strength being developed by the Achesonites, presented his resignation. Eugene Dooman, long associated with Grew in Tokyo, and now in charge of the important Far Eastern section, likewise resigned.

Thus by August of 1945 there had disappeared most of the opposition to the infiltration of the Communist line into the sections of the State Department that made policies concerning Japan, China, the Philippines and Korea. In the place of the loyal and devoted Americans who had been in control, there now appeared a group of men who were anti-Japanese, anti-Chiang Kai-shek, anti-free Korea, but decidedly pro-Communist Chinese.

A short time before this date, Dean Acheson had resigned as first assistant secretary, but when Grew and Dooman resigned Secretary Byrnes at once telephoned Acheson and asked him to return to the State Department to take Grew's place in the far more powerful position of undersecretary. Acheson lost no time in re-orienting the Department regarding the four vital areas: China, Korea, the Philippines and Japan. He assigned John Carter Vincent as head of the Far Eastern Section, replacing the experienced and conservative Eugene Dooman. Vincent, as an advisor to the American Embassy in China, had long shown and exercised his determined pro-Communist leanings regarding China. He called in John Stewart Service (who shortly before this had been arrested in connection with stolen documents in the famous *Amerasia* magazine case) to head the important State Department information service. George Atcheson, who had been sent back from China by Ambassador Hurley for his then pro-Chinese Communist attitudes, was now dispatched to Tokyo as one of MacArthur's advisors. Owen Lattimore, standing quietly in the background, was a most vital adjunct of this new and dominant radical group in the State Department.

There was neither time nor opportunity for the new crowd

to change materially the context of the over-all Policy Directive given to MacArthur on September 6. Nor did the group really show its hand until Dean Acheson shortly blustered into public view with his outbreak against MacArthur's pronouncement that the Japanese occupation had progressed so smoothly that the number of American occupation troops might be reduced to 200,000 within six months.

President Truman had backed MacArthur, and the General's Senate friends had shown their teeth against the new undersecretary, so that any immediate attempt on Acheson's part to harass MacArthur too openly was postponed.

MacArthur was by no means unaware of the dangers and stresses that faced the Far Eastern world. He had many lines of information that led from Washington to his own office. A continuous flow of visitors from America kept him alerted to many of the secret moves within the Washington government and administration. A number of his friends who came to see him in Tokyo were deeply concerned over the state of affairs and by the betrayal into Communist hands of the fruits of Allied victory in both Europe and Asia.

His chief concern was his own problem of building the new life in Japan and guarding it against attacks from without and within. But China, too, was close to his heart, and he watched with misgiving and despair as the China tragedy unfolded.

The first objective of the Acheson-Lattimore crowd in regard to China had been to get rid of tough and wise Ambassador Patrick J. Hurley and replace him with a man they could handle. Their second and third tasks would be to win over President Truman to their plan, and then quietly discredit Lt. General Albert Wedemeyer and conceal the recommendations he had made regarding the integrity of China and Korea.

Acheson planted political advisors George Atcheson, John Service and other fellow-travelers at MacArthur's headquarters. Their strategy would now be to peck away at MacArthur, while their columnist, newspaper and radio friends in America continued to denounce him and the Emperor. One of the first steps would be quietly to force MacArthur to accept an Allied Council that would include a strong Soviet representative, who could thus get his foot in the door.

Early in October 1945, at the meeting of the Council of Foreign Ministers in London, Secretary of State Byrnes had his own troubles with Molotov, Soviet Minister, who demanded that an Allied Control be set up in Tokyo that would give Russia an actual voice in decisions. British Foreign Minister Bevan did not entirely disapprove of the Russian suggestion. But Byrnes was able to check the move to turn the purely advisory Allied Council into a projected Control Council. However, the final decision in the matter was put off until the coming December meeting of the Foreign Ministers in Moscow.

When a twin plan of control, as a result of this later Moscow meeting, was finally released, the Associated Press carried the statement that General MacArthur had seen and did not object to the new Japan Control Plan before it was approved at Moscow. The report further stated that he had been kept informed throughout the conference of matters dealing with Japan and Far Eastern affairs. MacArthur, harassed and resentful, issued a formal denial on the last day of December 1945:

The statement attributed to a Far Eastern Commission Officer that I "did not object to the new Japan Control Plan before it was approved at Moscow" is incorrect. On 31 October my final disagreement was contained in my radio to the Chief of Staff for the Secretary of State, advising that the terms "in my opinion are not acceptable." Since that time, my views have not been sought. Any impression which the statement might imply that I was consulted during the Moscow conference is also incorrect. I have no iota of responsibility for the decisions which were made there.

I might add that whatever the merits or demerits of the plan, it is my firm intent, within the authority entrusted to me, to try to make it work. The issues involved are too vital to the future of the world to have them bog down. With good will on the part of those concerned, it is my fervent hope that there will be no insuperable obstacles. As I said before, it is "my full purpose to see it through."

Later an additional paragraph was issued by MacArthur that read as follows:

General MacArthur never received any information or communication whatsoever from the Moscow conference during the meeting, and did not even know Japan was being discussed until he saw it announced in the daily press.

In Washington the newly created Far Eastern Commission composed of Allied members was apparently to be the final governing body, but Byrnes had slipped in a clause or two at Moscow that to a great extent left the actual power in American hands. Before any of the Allied Commission's instructions reached MacArthur, they must first be passed by the Commission, then drafted by the State Department, then approved by the Joint Chiefs of Staff, then finally sent on to the Supreme Commander.

As a matter of fact the Commission included at various times such distinguished American members as Major General Frank McCoy and Nelson T. Johnson, former ambassador to China. Early in January 1946 the Commission visited Tokyo, and its contact with MacArthur was pleasant; and in general its suggestions were most acceptable to him. Much time was to elapse before it was discovered that the pinks had planted a man squarely in the center of the commission as an advisor to wise old General McCoy.

The four-power Allied Council for Japan, set up in Tokyo, however, was a horse of another color. The United States, China, the British Commonwealth and the Soviet Union were represented, but the Russians had high hopes that through their machinations within this Council they would be able to take a strong hand in the actual occupation and begin their tactics of Red infiltration. But when MacArthur addressed the Allied Council at its opening session on April 5, 1946, he skillfully reduced it to its actual status of a purely advisory capacity. Never once did he make a direct move of any kind against the Russian delegation. The 185 members of the Soviet mission in Tokyo were permitted to go and come as they pleased, and no attempt to supervise them was ever undertaken. But they shortly found they were utterly powerless to interfere.

MacArthur's initial talk at the Council was a masterpiece of gentle but complete deflation:

I welcome you with utmost cordiality in the earnest anticipation that, in keeping with the friendship which has long existed among the several peoples represented here, your deliberations throughout shall be governed by goodwill, mutual understanding and broad tolerance. As the functions of the Council will be advisory and consultative, it will not divide the heavy administrative responsibility of the Supreme Commander as the sole executive authority for the Allied Powers in Japan, but it will make available to him the several viewpoints of its members on questions of policy and action. I hope it will prove to be a valuable factor in the future solution of many problems.

. . . Any advice the Council as a whole or that of any of its individual members may believe would be helpful to the Supreme Commander will at all times be most welcome, and given the most thorough consideration. As my manifold other duties will not normally permit me to sit with the Council, I have designated a deputy to act as Chairman thereof. To promote full public confidence in its aims and purposes, it is advisable that all formal sessions be open to such of the public and press as existing facilities will accommodate. There is nothing in its deliberations to conceal, even from the eyes and ears of our fallen adversary. Through such a practice of pure democracy in the discharge of its responsibilities, the world will know that the Council's deliberations lead to no secret devices, undertakings or commitments. . . .

The local Russian representatives found themselves completely frustrated in their ambition first to gain some real authority and then to stir up as much trouble as possible. MacArthur's conduct had been meticulous. But any time that it became necessary to check interference, he had a clear directive to fall back on as the source of his assumptions.

Here in Tokyo it was quite a different situation that faced the usually victorious and arrogant Russians, accustomed to dictating and dominating the inter-Allied conferences and then pushing through their treaty-breaking moves in Europe.

3

During the very earliest days of the occupation a matter of utmost importance began quietly to come to a head. One of the first Japanese callers at SCAP (Supreme Commander Allied

Powers) Headquarters in the Dai-Ichi Building in Tokyo was Prince Konoye, who had replaced a militarist as Prime Minister and on the previous April 7 had himself been succeeded by the elderly Kantaro Suzuki. MacArthur received Konoye with courtesy and listened attentively while his worried guest blamed the militarists for the war, with the additional excuse that the new government had long feared the rise of Communism and social unrest among the Japanese masses.

MacArthur replied that reform for the people was necessary, and that there must be a strong minister of education who would insist that the truth of the war be taught in the schools. He pointed out that the world did not trust Japan, and that only through education would she regain true respect.

In effect MacArthur made it clear that the Japanese government need no longer worry about the militarists, for he could handle them. The government's problem now was to get the truth to the civil population.

Exactly three weeks later Prince Konoye sought a second interview with MacArthur. Again he blamed the militarists and the old threat of Communism for the country's downfall, but he carefully exonerated both the Emperor and the great capitalist groups of all responsibility. MacArthur promptly laid out a four-point program that must be started at once: Liberalize the constitution; extend suffrage to women; hold elections; clear militarists out of all control.

When the Minister protested that the Cabinet completely lacked the authority to accomplish these things, MacArthur quietly pointed out that the entire Japanese government existed by the Supreme Commander's sufferance, and that he personally proposed to authorize all these changes. The Emperor and the government must assist in every way possible.

Both visits apparently were preliminary moves for a visit by the Emperor. A member of the Imperial Household quietly broached the subject. MacArthur sent back word that the Emperor's call would be most welcome, and that the General would receive him informally at the Embassy and not at his office. It would have humiliated the Emperor to require him to come to his conqueror's office in a public building.

The Supreme Commander had his military secretary waiting

to meet the Emperor when he stepped out of his old-fashioned black limousine at the entrance to the Embassy. The Emperor was so emotionally disturbed that he was actually shaking. Brigadier General Fellers saluted, and the Emperor almost timidly reached for his hand. The officer greeted him most cordially, and they walked side by side to the study. The friendly reception had a marked effect. The Emperor realized immediately that he faced no trying ordeal.

MacArthur had sent word that the Emperor was to bring his own interpreter, and when the two entered the study the door closed behind them. Only the three were there, and the whole atmosphere was one of complete friendliness and good will. They talked over certain phases and incidents in the long war and other matters of immediate concern. The total result was of immense significance.

Back in America the announcement of the meeting brought violent reactions. The leftist hang-the-Emperor advocates insisted that instead of receiving him so courteously, MacArthur should have had him tried and condemned.

It is possible that no single move by MacArthur during his five years in Japan had a more profound effect on the Japanese people than this. As the story of Hirohito's visit spread throughout the Japanese islands, it seemed to put a final stamp of complete acceptance of the realities of the occupation and of the series of great reforms that were being initiated. MacArthur had proved that he had no intention of publicly humiliating their Emperor. The people everywhere began to understand that the American Commander who had had such a part in their defeat was now a true friend who was trying his best to help them into a new way of life.

MacArthur never left any doubt for a single moment, however, where the real authority lay. Again and again he quietly broke up Japanese schemes and smart little dodges to circumvent his wishes. At one point Foreign Minister Shigeru Yoshida called on him to announce that the Cabinet now headed by Baron Shidehara had decided to resign, because of a directive ordering a purge of totalitarian-minded Japanese officials. After the protest registered by their resignations had been publicized, the Baron would duly succeed himself.

421

MacArthur did not raise his voice when he answered: "Mr. Minister, you tell Baron Shidehara that there is no one for whom I have greater respect or in whose ability to carry out my directives I have greater confidence. However, if he and his Cabinet resign tomorrow, it will be clear to the people of Japan that they are unable to carry out my objectives. Baron Shidehara may thereafter be acceptable to the Emperor as the next Prime Minister, but he will not be acceptable to me."

Brigadier General Courtney Whitney, who had charge of civil affairs on the Staff of SCAP, was present during the interview, and when he had walked down the hall with the Minister, he asked him if it was quite clear what the General meant. The Foreign Minister answered, "Too clear!"

4

The end of the Japanese war had brought many changes within the high command in Washington. The Joint Chiefs of Staff still functioned, but Admiral King was replaced by Admiral Nimitz, after King refused to agree to the amalgamation of the Navy in a single Department of National Defense.

General Marshall asked for retirement, and in October 1945 he was replaced as Army Chief of Staff by General Eisenhower. In the State Department the collaborators of Undersecretary Acheson with their definite internationalist and pro-Red Chinese views had absorbed many of the key positions, particularly those dealing with the Far East, Russia and the United Nations. A vast flight of left-wingers from the Office of War Information (OWI), the Federal Economic Agency (FEA), Office of Strategic Services (OSS) and Office of Inter-American Affairs landed in the State Department. In the single year of 1945 some 5,000 outsiders infiltrated into this once conservative Department and began to take over. The vital move gave State a new and dangerous pink complexion.

[A one-time Deputy Assistant Secretary of State, J. Anthony Panuch, several years later testified to a Senate Internal Security Sub-committee that the final design of this transfused ideology was "a socialized America in a world commonwealth of Communist and Socialist states, dedicated to peace through collective security, political, economic and social reform, and the redistribution of national wealth on a global basis." Hundreds of these new radical State Department recruits, he pointed out, were shunted over the world, particularly into China and Korea and into MacArthur's occupational machinery in Japan. The extent of the damage they were able to do is beyond computing. Most of their subversive work is deeply hidden in secret State Department files or long ago has been taken out and destroyed. Even if a determined and sincere effort were to be undertaken, it is doubted if the full story could ever be pieced together. The stark results, however, stand out in all their overpowering terror: a Red China, an uncertain Formosa, a broken and almost helpless Korea, and an entire Far East handicapped, weakened and at the mercy of a ruthless international Communism.]

Ambassador Patrick J. Hurley flew back to Washington from China. Partly because of his poor health and partly because of his angry report criticizing the personal loyalty of certain of his aides belonging to the State Department group of pro-Communist Chinese, his immediate resignation, submitted November 26, 1945, was accepted. General Marshall had been relieved as Army Chief of Staff only six days when President Truman sent for him and insisted that he must replace Hurley in China. While his instructions were being formulated, Marshall was busy before a Senatorial committee that was investigating the Pearl Harbor disaster—and in particular trying to jog his usually keen memory into recalling where he was the night before and the morning of December 7, 1941.

Who drew up Marshall's actual instructions in China still remains a mystery, but it appears that they were partly written by John Carter Vincent, leftist head of the Far Eastern section of the State Department. The document was carefully gone over both by the President and General Marshall, as well as by Dean Acheson, Undersecretary of State. It was based on the general proposition that the civil war must end, and there must be unity and peace in China; Chiang Kai-shek must open the inner circles of his Nationalist government to the representatives of Mao Tse-tung's Communist group, and Red Chinese troops must ultimately be incorporated into the armies of a United China. This proved to be the exact sort of deadly tactics that gave the Chinese Communists the power ultimately to weaken and render impotent the Nationalist government.

At this time the Chinese Communists held only a small part of China. On August 14, 1945, the day Japan surrendered, a Sino-Soviet pact was signed in Moscow in which Stalin promised to recognize and sustain Nationalist China as the single government for the vast country. But as the Russian armies in Siberia drove down into Manchuria and Northern Korea, it was immediately evident that they were concerned primarily in helping to arm and direct the Chinese Communists, in their losing fight against Chiang Kai-shek's Nationalist government. Chiang's army had been wearing itself out for more than seven consecutive years in fighting the Japanese and at the same time opposing the Chinese Communists.

The pro-Mao leftist crowd within the U. S. State Department, backed by the endless barrage of American writers and radio commentators who followed the line laid down by Lattimore's Institute of Pacific Relations, had long before this decided who should win. The phrase "China unity" apparently meant that Chiang Kai-shek's exhausted government was eventually to be forced by both the United States and Russia (with the United Nations' approval) to accept the collaboration of the Communist Chinese revolutionary government or to go down before it.

The unrealistic document that General Marshall took with him to China pointed the way to this ultimate Communist domination. He was met at the Shanghai airport by Lt. General Albert C. Wedemeyer, military advisor to Chiang Kai-shek and head of American armed forces in China. Wedemeyer was experienced, astute and long-headed. He understood the nuances embodied in Marshall's instructions and the impossibility of Chinese unity, Red style, save by completely giving way to the Chinese Communists. He was aware that the Chinese Reds were far from the simple and independent agrarian reformers that the Lattimore-inspired writers and radio commentators and their misguided liberal friends had told America they were.

But Marshall insisted that the Chinese Communists comprised only a minority political party that must be brought into Chiang's government to attain unity. In his eyes the two opposing Chinese groups were not too dissimilar from the two great political parties in America.

Wedemeyer respectfully asked his old chief how he would feel about the Republican party at home, for instance, if it were armed to the teeth and was determined to gain control by force and as the result of an open civil war. But apparently Marshall had been too well indoctrinated by Acheson's men to heed the advice of one of the few senior American soldiers who understood how dangerous it was to try to effect compromises or make political deals with the Kremlin and its tools.

Marshall's first move was on January 13, 1946, when he arranged a tentative truce with both armies frozen in their positions of that moment. There was, however, a provision that Nationalist troops could restore Chinese authority in certain portions of Manchuria long held by Japan. The Chinese Communists soon broke the truce, and civil war was resumed. Shortly after this Marshall flew home for consultation with the President and with Acheson's left-wing advisors.

On his return in March of 1946 he was met at the Tokyo airfield by MacArthur. Not once did Marshall mention his difficult China assignment or discuss with MacArthur how the turn of affairs there might affect the whole Far Eastern situation and the problems involved in the occupation of Japan. The isolation of MacArthur from the currents of policy in Washington was deliberate and complete.

From the time of his arrival in China, Marshall exercised continued pressure on the Nationalist government to bring in the Communist groups. Finally, in July 1946, when he met with no success, he declared an embargo on the sale of all arms and munitions to both sides in China. Chiang Kai-shek's struggle with the Reds called for large quantities of small arms and ammunition as well as motor transport and aircraft. Now he was completely cut off from fresh supplies.

But the embargo had little effect on the Chinese Communists. The Soviets saw to it that they were well supplied with arms and ammunition. The Russian agreement with America had arranged that the surrender and disarming of the Japa-

425

nese forces in China and Manchuria was to be made to Chinese Nationalist representatives. But vast quantities of arms and munitions were turned over by the Japanese to the busy Russian troops, and the almost inexhaustible military dumps were deliberately left unguarded by the Soviet troops so that the Chinese Communist forces could supply themselves as they wished.

Less than a month after Marshall's embargo was ordered, President Truman, won over to the United-China-at-any-price idea and to the left-wing conception of the Chinese Communists as being simple agrarians, now issued an additional executive order that China was not to be allowed to secure any surplus American army weapons "which could be used to fight a civil war."

This embargo was greatly responsible for the slow but certain whittling away of the resistance of the Nationalist government. The growing pressure of the Chinese Communist forces was revitalized by the arms and munitions the Russians furnished and by secret Red military aid and advice.

Lt. General Wedemeyer did everything in his power to offset the working of the unfair embargo that denied aid to the Nationalist government while Russia armed the Communist elements. Even after the embargo was formally lifted in May 1947, the State Department managed to keep all real military help from reaching the Nationalists by simply holding up shipping permits. Marshall, then Secretary of State, eventually ordered Wedemeyer to make a full investigation of both the Chinese and the Korean situations. The report Wedemeyer delivered was an extraordinarily wise and far-seeing analysis, but neither its findings nor its solemn warnings were followed. Instead, its suggestions concerning the formation of a strong defense organization in South Korea were pigeonholed by order of Secretary of State Marshall, who ordered General Wedemeyer to step out of the picture.

In April 1948 the Republican-controlled Congress voted the sum of $125,000,000 for definite military aid for Nationalist China. But once again the move was effectively scuttled by the action of the State Department, and its collaborators in the Department of Commerce, in holding up the delivery of the desperately needed arms and ammunition. Months went by until all chance of blocking the Moscow-supported Red Chinese advances had gone, and Chiang Kai-shek was actually forced to flee to Formosa. Here from December 1949 on he was virtually abandoned to his fate by China's oldest and most trusted friend, the United States, while Britain and other important United Nations members did their best to force America to follow their lead and recognize the Chinese Communist régime and do business with it.

5

Even during his first year in Japan MacArthur had no illusions regarding the nature of the forces that opposed him both in Washington and in Moscow. During the early days of the occupation the State Department had sent out to him as a special advisor, with the rank of minister, George Atcheson, an attractive career officer. Atcheson had been one of Ambassador Patrick J. Hurley's people in China, but he had been won over to the pro-Communist Chinese side by certain Americans who opposed Grew. When Atcheson arrived in Tokyo, MacArthur sent for him and showed him a letter he had received frankly warning the Supreme Commander that Atcheson was a pink.

Atcheson's face reddened, but he made no attempt at disavowal when he handed the letter back to MacArthur.

"I just wanted you to see this so we can start off on a fair and square basis," MacArthur explained without the slightest bitterness. "The cards are now face up on the table."

Never again did MacArthur make any reference to the letter, nor did he exclude Atcheson from policy meetings or in any way show any resentment against him. Gradually Atcheson began to understand the problems MacArthur faced in Japan and to appreciate how mistaken he had been regarding the true ambitions of the Chinese Communists. Soon he was as loyal and ardent a member of the MacArthur team as there was in Tokyo.

On his way home to Washington for a conference Atcheson lost his life in the mid-Pacific when his plane was forced down through lack of gas. Investigation showed suspicious evidence of sabotage at the Guam base, where the reserve gas tanks, checked as full at Tokyo, had been emptied. MacArthur was shocked and deeply grieved at the loss of Atcheson.

He was well aware that there were a number of Japanese Communists working under the secret direction of the Soviet mission in Tokyo. The legalizing of labor unions had been one of the original tenets of MacArthur's occupation directives, and it was evident that Red influences were penetrating these circles, and that serious trouble might break out. On May 20, 1946, he moved quickly to forestall what might have become a most difficult situation. He realized that there would be sharp reaction in America against his bold step, and he met it head-on in his statement:

> I find it necessary to caution the Japanese people that the growing tendency towards mass violence and physical processes of intimidation, under organized leadership, present a grave menace to the future development of Japan. While every possible rational freedom of democratic method has been permitted and will be permitted in the evolution now proceeding in the transformation from a feudalistic and military state to one of democratic process, the physical violence which undisciplined elements are now beginning to practice will not be permitted to continue. They constitute a menace not only to orderly government but to the basic purposes and security of the occupation itself. . . .

Again MacArthur was attacked by large groups in America, who were either unconscious of the intent of Red agents operating over the world or were converts to their ideas. He personally was unimpressed by their promises or their threats, and on the first anniversary of the Japanese surrender he issued a lengthy statement that restated his own beliefs:

> A year has now passed since the surrender terms were signed on the battleship *Missouri*. Much has been accomplished since then—much still remains to be done. But over all things and all men in this sphere of the universe hangs the dread uncertainty arising from impinging ideologies which now stir mankind. For our homeland there is no question, and for the homelands of others, free as are we to shape their own political order, there is no question. But which concept will prevail over those lands now being redesigned in the aftermath of war? This is the great

issue which confronts our task in the problem of Japan—a problem which profoundly affects the destiny of all men and the future course of all civilization. . . .

Should such a clash of ideologies impinge more directly upon the reorientation of Japanese life and thought, it would be no slight disadvantage to those who seek, as intended at Potsdam, the great middle course of moderate democracy, that a people so long regimented under the philosophy of an extreme conservative right might prove easy prey to those seeking to impose a doctrine leading again to regimentation, under the philosophy of an extreme radical left. . . .

The goal is great—for the strategic position of these Japanese Islands renders them either a powerful bulwark for peace or a dangerous spring-board for war.

Carefully phrased as was this gentle rebuke against Communism, it drew the fire of the radical cabal in the State Department. In Japan there continued to be constant Red pressure on the Japanese labor leaders to embarrass the new government in every possible way. And there was no letup on the interference from Moscow and the efforts to discredit MacArthur.

About the middle of September 1948, the Soviet ambassador in Washington publicly assailed the occupation and charged that MacArthur's policies were in direct violation of Allied policy and the Potsdam Declaration. MacArthur did not bother to answer directly this charge, but he used the opportunity to explain his reaction to the Communist intrusions in Asia and over the world. The final paragraph of his statement showed how fully aware he was of the rising danger. It read:

Perhaps the most unsuccessful effort made anywhere by world wide propaganda to instill communistic principles has been in Japan. Here concepts leading to disorder, discontent and ultimate chaos have made little headway. Despite frantic communistic efforts to achieve the contrary, Japan continues calm, stable and well ordered. The Communists and those who adhere to their cause thus have a growing sense of frustration at their failure in Japan. If they had their way they would repeat there the deplorable state of affairs which they have brought about in certain unhappy European centers.

429

Four months later the Soviet ambassador, using as his sounding board the Far Eastern Commission, renewed his attacks on MacArthur. The General fully understood how all-important it was to hold this strong Pacific outpost of Japan against the constant Communist pressure and intrigue. He decided that the time had arrived when he must fight back openly and with everything he had. His statement was blunt and concise:

I have noted the statement of the Soviet Ambassador before the Far Eastern Commission in derogation of American policy and action with reference to Japan. It has little validity measured either by truth or realism and can be regarded as mainly a continuation of the extraordinary irresponsibility of Soviet propaganda. Its basic cause is the complete frustration of the Soviet effort to absorb Japan within the orbit of the Communistic ideology. This effort has been incessant and relentless from the inception of the Occupation.

It has sought by every means within its power to spread discord and dissension throughout this country, reduced by the disasters of war to an economy of poverty, originally threatening the actual livelihood of the entire nation. It has hoped to so mutilate the masses that there could be imposed through the resulting despair and misery a Godless concept of atheistic totalitarian enslavement.

It has failed, due largely to the innate common sense and conservatism of the Japanese people, the concepts of democratic freedom implanted during the Occupation, and the progressive improvement in living conditions. The resulting rage and frustration has produced, as in the present instance, an unbridled vulgarity of expression which is the sure hallmark of propaganda and of failure.

In a way it was almost a lone fight that he was making. He could not have been unconscious of the many roadblocks that were constantly being erected against him. But he had his own way of getting around them.

He knew, too, that there were powerful interests within the United Nations that were far from happy over the sturdy new Japan he was helping build. He was approaching the completion of the great task of a Japanese treaty that must be able to withstand the demands and intrigues of nations and ideologies concerned with their own selfish interests in the Far East and with their problems of appeasing or actually fostering a marching Communism.

A Red China was swiftly rising. Between the Sea of Japan and the Yellow Sea lay the peninsula of Korea, divided, helpless and uncertain. It might well be next on the Red schedule of doom.

Within the shadowy inner circle of Lake Success, where the United Nations often met in confusion and uncertainty, there were currents and tides that seemed to be moving not only against the best interest of America, but against a free and democratic world. Proof was yet to come of the treacheries and perfidies of innocent-looking groups and individuals within the U. S. government who had long been betraying America and poisoning the minds of the public and officials alike. Later would break the great exposés of the Hiss trial and conviction; the startling facts of Communist penetration eventually brought out by the McCarthy and McCarran committees and later by the Jenner and Velde investigations.

Shortly after his arrival in Tokyo, MacArthur's alert intelligence officer, Major General Charles A. Willoughby, unearthed the sordid ramifications of the Sorge Red spy ring, which extended from Moscow and Tokyo to Shanghai and Chungking. The findings had proved beyond any doubt the extent and enterprise of the Russian secret agents and their friends. Certainly MacArthur and his G.H.Q. were alive to what was going on in China and Korea.

Here in Tokyo he had by one means or another been able to check through Washington friends and visitors the many attempts by forces within the administration to undermine his stewardship. Time and again he had countered the efforts of the Russians to force an entering wedge into Japan. He knew that only by keeping a tight rein on the expanding Japanese labor unions and the small radical native groups could he keep Communist agents from fostering Red movements that might lead toward bitter internal trouble and eventual civil war. It

431

was the usual Communist tactics: infiltrate, then divide and rule. From the beginning of the occupation he had never failed to nullify all such attempts.

He was fully conscious, too, of the scores of State Department liberals who had been dumped in his lap as advisors and specialists. They had been specially chosen for the job, and for the most part they were far more concerned with at least a partial socialization of Japan and the accompanying humiliation of the Emperor than in building a sturdy, free state that might be on the side of America in her ultimate fight for survival. He was aware, as well, that radical converts and troublemakers of the same type were being sent out from Washington to muddy the waters of South Korea and to forestall her attempt to establish a free, united republic of Korea.

China was swiftly approaching the crisis in her long civil war. It was all too evident to MacArthur that the Communist sympathizers and the innocent dupes in the State Department were materially aiding in the collapse and defeat of Chiang Kai-shek's forces.

He could do little more than wait for the final tragedy of Nationalist China's fall, just as he had been forced to wait while doom closed about him in Manila in the late autumn of 1941.

21

. . . WHILE WASHINGTON
LETS CHINA GO COMMUNIST

Despite the constant official tension and the eternal excursions and alarms, the days and weeks slipped by pleasantly for the little MacArthur family in Tokyo.

Life under the expansive roof of the American Embassy was gracious and satisfactory. To a large degree the old daily routine that MacArthur had begun back in the summer of 1919 when he had been appointed superintendent of West Point was again in order. He had continued it on through his days as Army Chief of Staff in Washington, and then after his marriage to Jean Faircloth in his years in Manila. Even as commanding general of the Southwest Pacific theatre in Brisbane and finally at the end of the bitter war campaigns, he had largely followed his own quiet way of life here in Tokyo.

In attempting to describe his unique schedule it probably would be fair to say that quite without realizing it he was complete master of his own house and as well of all his waking hours. The devoted Jean found her own full measure of happiness in taking care of her husband and their growing boy Arthur. It never for a moment occurred to any of them, including himself, that the Supreme Commander was not the final figure of authority in regard to every detail of the life about him. He did not demand it to be so; it simply was an accepted fact.

In that observation there may be the key to his sometimes misunderstood personality. Without consciously meaning to do it, he quietly dominated everything that came within his orbit. Yet in a strange way he was a complete creature of habit. His own personal wants were very few. He cared little for food and nothing for drinks. He enjoyed an occasional cigarette and his pipes and a cigar at night. At no time in his life did he have more than a handful of really intimate friends, and never did he lean heavily on them. He was sentimentally attached to a few men who had fought the wars with him and with whom he enjoyed reminiscing, but they were not necessary to his happiness or existence. His one true adult companion was his beloved Jean.

He attended no parties, dinners or receptions, save at the one or two rare moments when he looked in at some official gathering of special significance. He worked seven days a week at his office. During the early periods of the war and occupation he was always on tap for any emergency business that came up day or night. Jean, likewise, had little or no social

433

life, and her only public appearances were on occasions where she semi-officially represented the General. Oddly enough, this austere and secluded existence appealed strongly to the Japanese. In their eyes it gave to General MacArthur the distinct touch of a superior and removed being, separated by several degrees of caste from ordinary mortals.

When the day's work was done and dinner was over, he usually found an hour's relaxation in an evening movie shown in the large reception room at the Embassy, attended by the members of the household and any soldiers of the Embassy guard who were off duty and cared to look in. Only on rare occasions was there an outsider or house guest.

The General ordinarily arose a little before 8. He leisurely shaved with one of a set of old-fashioned straight razors that his father had given him as a West Point graduation present, and then he methodically went through a few simple calisthenics. He was still addicted to the worn and shabby black-gold-and-gray cadet bathrobe that had been his companion through the years. After he breakfasted with Jean, he read whatever papers were at hand, and around 10 o'clock started for his office. He usually remained there until somewhere between 1:30 and 2:00. Then he returned to the Embassy for lunch. If there were no guests, he ate alone with Jean. But two or three times a week there was a fairly large semi-official luncheon party for very important people of one kind or another from Stateside. All his official entertaining was at these luncheon parties.

After the business of eating was ended, the General would push back his chair and embark for an hour or longer on an uninterrupted discourse on some phase of the occupation or the Far Eastern problem or the latest Russian move. These informal sessions seemed to give him a chance to let off steam and to further the development of his own ideas and conclusions. Almost invariably his guests left with the definite impression that they had been listening to one of the profound and brilliant intellects of the time. It was not unusual for men who had arrived in Japan bent on finding proofs for their preconceived theories and criticisms regarding the Japanese occu-

434

pation or the Supreme Commander to be completely won over by this after-luncheon magic.

After the party had been dismissed, the General invariably went to his bedroom and enjoyed an hour's sleep. Then he returned to his office, usually to remain at work until 7 or 8 or even later. It was a killing schedule for the members of his immediate staff, but they did little grumbling. Their affection for their chief was expressed in loyalty and devotion almost beyond measure.

The General's evening meal was usually simple and almost frugal. Jean would have supper with him regardless of the hour, and after the meal they would usually take their regular seats in the front row of the chairs arranged before the moving picture screen. The General's personal choice still remained the westerns, but he found relaxation in almost any action film.

After the movie he and Jean would usually spend an hour or two alone, and then he would pace back and forth across the wide reception room and into the great hall. He had a clear path of more than 100 feet and as he walked his beat he usually gave wings to his thoughts, laying out the immediate problems that faced him. "Thinking out loud" comes the nearest to interpreting this nightly pacing.

Jean would almost literally see to it that he was tucked in bed, open the windows and then check in on Arthur. The General was doing exactly as he wanted to do, and the same thing could be said about his wonderful wife. She had found her complete role in looking after the man and the boy to whose comfort and happiness she had dedicated her life.

From the days in Manila in the late 1930s, when the war clouds began to settle down over the China Sea, the General had given up his ancient habit of long hours of reading before he went to sleep. The library of his penthouse atop the Manila Hotel had been lined with books from his father's own large and carefully chosen collection. But he no longer felt the driving need for concentrated reading. Besides most of his favorite military and historical books had been lost in the war.

When the decision had been made on the afternoon of Christmas Eve in 1941 that the military command and the Philippine government would transfer immediately to Corregidor, the lovely penthouse with all its books and silver, its pictures and priceless mementos was left in the care of the Filipino houseboy, Castro.

At the time the city was recaptured in March and April 1945, the Manila Hotel was found burned and completely gutted. MacArthur had hardly settled in one of the civilian homes still standing, when Castro came to headquarters and in broken English explained that he had something that belonged to the General.

One of the various enemy dignitaries who had used and abused the penthouse had been an official from the Japanese Foreign Office, who eventually had changed residences to one of the fashionable homes on the Luneta. The old MacArthur houseboy had gone along with him, his eye on a heavy box of silver that the Japanese diplomat had taken. The loyal servant had quietly put the long, heavy box in a darkened space under the stairs, well behind cases of documents and food. When the diplomat had hurriedly pulled out shortly before the Americans landed on Luzon, the special box had been overlooked. It was this priceless cache that was now turned over to the General in Manila.

Both he and Jean accepted the fact that the books in the library that had meant such a warm, intimate touch with the father would never be recovered. However, two or three small batches of books that had been sequestered by hotel servants began to appear.

And later in Tokyo the same houseboy who had promptly joined up with the family in Manila accompanied Jean to Japan. Once settled in the Embassy, he took over his old job. One day late in the fall of 1945, he came to Jean with a newspaper that had a picture of a Japanese general who had just been taken into custody in Tokyo as a war criminal. The loyal Castro was burning with anger and excitement as he jabbed at the picture and insisted that he was one of the looters.

" 'At him! 'at him!" he insisted. "He General in Manila hotel. He took! He took!"

Jean and Colonel Sidney Huff called a car and with the servant drove to the house where the Japanese general had been arrested. Inside they found a hundred or more precious military books looted from MacArthur's library in Manila.

MacArthur's personal relation with the key members of his G.H.Q. staff had long been a matter of considerable speculation and of some adverse criticism. He had at one and the same time been accused of being too loyal and easy going with his official family and of being too little concerned with their rewards and advancement.

Apparently he had always taken a good deal for granted. During his years as Army Chief of Staff in Washington, in the years in Manila and during the war and occupation periods, he had been fully absorbed with matters of the highest importance to the armed services and often to the very life of his country. He personally thought out most of the great moves and decisions involved in his responsibilities. The members of his staff were primarily occupied in implementing them. He was completely and exhaustingly absorbed by the larger aspects of military strategy and statesmanship.

To many who knew him well he seemed to have little time left for the people who served him. The problems he faced used up the last ounce of his time and energy. For the ten years beginning in 1940 and even during most of the previous decade he struggled against terrific odds. As a consequence he left the routine of running his headquarters and its many details in the hands of his chief of staff. This included the very sensitive matter of promotions and decorations for his senior commanders and for the important members of his headquarters staff. To many critics it seemed that MacArthur failed to appreciate how much these personal matters meant to the officers serving under him and how badly they were often handled by his responsible subordinates.

Nor did he seem to be greatly concerned over rifts and angry feuds within his own personal staff. There were so many enervating problems on a seemingly higher level that called for his personal decisions that the human equation often was ignored or pushed aside. He had removed himself largely from all unnecessary contacts, and the barriers raised to relieve him from what appeared to be the small items involving such things as men's pride and rewards often reflected against him.

There can be little doubt that there were injustices and oversights, and certainly in a number of individual cases there was real bitterness left. For instance, many of the friends of Lt. General Eichelberger felt that a grave injustice had been done him when he did not receive his fourth star. Eichelberger had gone out to MacArthur in the summer of 1942 as a lieutenant general and had fought through all the campaigns from Buna to Mindanao. During the first three trying years of the Japanese occupation he had commanded the Eighth Army. At the end of more than six years of loyal and magnificent service in the Pacific he had retired and returned to the States with the same three stars on his shoulder. In the summer of 1954, in retirement, he was awarded his fourth star by the Army.

In the entire Southwest Pacific Command only Lt. Generals Kenney and Krueger and Vice Admiral Kinkaid received their fourth stars. Additional high promotions may have been prevented by roadblocks erected in the Pentagon against MacArthur and his theatre.

In 1946 Sutherland, his chief of staff who had been with him even before Bataan and Corregidor, returned to America and was replaced by Major General Dick Marshall who had long been deputy chief. Eventually Marshall retired to become superintendent of the Virginia Military Institute, and he was succeeded by Major General Stephen J. Chamberlain, who had served MacArthur as G-3 through the war from his arrival in Australia. Subsequently Chamberlain was replaced by Major General Paul John Mueller.

As the old Bataan gang—a tight little corporation of great pride and zeal—along with other members of his intimate staff who had been with him for a number of years retired or were relieved, MacArthur found himself leaning more and more on Courtney Whitney, who had joined his staff in Brisbane in 1943 as a colonel and finally was promoted to major general. Six months after Whitney's arrival in the Pacific he was made chief of the civil affairs at G.H.Q. He had resigned from the Regular Army in 1927 and for a number of years had practiced law in Manila.

On the long road back to the Philippines from Australia

Whitney had been assigned to the section of the staff that handled in its office at G.H.Q. the operations of the Filipino guerillas. Once back in the Philippines, he was given the civil section dealing with the many problems of local reconstruction and later with delicate and important civil affairs in the Japanese occupation. He had to a most unusual degree a talent for translating to paper MacArthur's wishes and thoughts, and he became extremely valuable in the important task of writing out statements and announcements that gave the exact shade of meaning the General desired.

2

Here in Tokyo during his years as Supreme Commander MacArthur came into complete and final maturity. Almost 20 years before these Tokyo days he had reached the top rung of the peace-time military ladder as Army Chief of Staff. Certainly no additional military honors remained for him to gain. He then graduated from soldiering into the higher echelon of statesmanship.

As a matter of fact, his service ever since 1935, when he embarked on his handicapped and misunderstood career as military advisor to President Quezón, had cast him into the definite and sustained role of soldier-statesman. Part of his formal task with Quezón was actually called "diplomatic representation," and his influence on the thinking of both the Philippine commonwealth leaders and the Filipino people was of immense importance.

This statesman side of his duties in Australia, and then again in the liberation of the Philippine Islands, was almost as valuable to his country as his purely military victories. With the momentous decision to send him to Japan as the proconsul of the wrecked and helpless nation, he stepped into a position that carried with it the personal responsibility for the life or death of American interests in these key islands of the Pacific. The subsequent moves he made and somehow was able to get Washington to accept had been decided on the highest moral and patriotic plane.

Issues automatically became moral issues, his decisions resting on the simple test of what is right and what is wrong. Plain truth and honor had almost been lost sight of by many during the years when America was being led into the war largely by the pressure of deceptions and downright lies.

But the ancient verities still remained the basis of the great decisions that MacArthur made. Their simple honesty was the outward expression of his own moral character.

Strong as had been his personal ambitions to be at the head in every endeavor, there had also been planted deep within him a high character standard from which there could be no deviation. The definitely superior mind he inherited had been supported and improved by his own energy and singleness of purpose. These qualifications tended to mark him with certain of the attributes of genius. As the years went by and his responsibilities increased, he never betrayed the West Point motto that had sustained him from his cadet days—"Duty, Honor, Country."

It was unfortunate that in the eyes of many people certain little human weaknesses apparently blurred the hard and rigid outlines of this unusual soldier. His need for study and meditation and for a quiet existence where he could work out his own solutions and decisions often made him liable to imputations of snobbishness and aristocratic superiority. He was accused of being aloof and lacking the common touch.

Apparently he could never quite reconcile his inherent shyness to the roar of the crowd. In his mature years he wanted personal success only when it coincided with the success of his country; and his country always came first. He was sensitive to criticism, but there was a tough fiber in his character that made him invincible and incorruptible. As was evidenced in his handling of beaten Japan, he harbored no revenge but rather a broad humanitarianism and an understanding of the human needs of these broken and helpless people.

3

It was with deepest concern that MacArthur watched the gradual deterioration of the Nationalist government in China, brought about by America's lack of any intelligent long-range policy and by the deliberate plotting of Communist agents and their followers in high position in Washington and elsewhere. He had never met Chiang Kai-shek, but he looked upon him as a true comrade-in-arms and a thoroughly devoted Chinese patriot. He knew the details of the Generalissimo's unbroken fight against Russian-inspired Communist intrusion since the early 1920s, and he knew that Moscow considered Chiang Kai-shek as its No. 1 enemy.

From 1937 to V-J day the Generalissimo had been fighting for his life against Japan, and never for a day had he succumbed to any outside pressures that would compromise the integrity of his country. During these years he had to fight also the Communist Chinese armies, which had never aided him by making a single decisive move against the Japanese invaders. Always he must fight these two enemies, who, oddly enough, had a bitter and eternal hatred for each other. Always it was the long arm of the Kremlin that helped set the evil forces moving against Chiang Kai-shek.

Since the turn of the century America had been the one permanent and unselfish friend that China could depend upon. John Hay's Open Door Policy had stood the test of time. Hay, as Secretary of State under President McKinley, had been in the forefront of the little group of men who at the turn of the century had remained steadfast in their belief not only that did much of America's destiny lie in the western Pacific but that her well-being rested to a large degree on her close friendship with China. A distinguished list of statesmen followed this political philosophy—Theodore Roosevelt and Elihu Root, Senators Lodge and Beveridge, Herbert Hoover and Charles Evans Hughes and, in the earlier days of his administrations, Franklin D. Roosevelt.

The pattern of Stalin's global strategy for ultimate Communist world domination had assumed dangerous proportions by the early spring of 1948. The Soviets' immediate designs in Europe had been accomplished with terrifying completeness. The bankruptcy of the Roosevelt-Churchill policies, followed by the failure of Truman and his American advisors to oppose Stalin at Potsdam in July 1945 had resulted in the complete betrayal of Poland, the division of Germany and the isolation of Berlin. No effective opposition was made to the brutal conversion into Soviet satellites of the Eastern European border states from the Baltic to the Mediterranean and Black Seas. There had been nothing subtle or mysterious about these deadly Red operations; the confused and often leftist-advised American statesmen simply had not the experienced intelligence, the long-range view or the courage to demand a show-down with Stalin, while America's military strength was at its maximum and her power beyond question. The dead hand of Roosevelt pulled the strings at Potsdam in July 1945, while Red influences were broadening in Washington.

4

Early in March of 1948 MacArthur sent to a House committee an answer to a request for his own opinion of the Far East situation. It was almost in the nature of a declaration of faith. Part of his lengthy statement read:

Because of deep-rooted racial and cultural and business ties, we are prone to overconcentrate on happenings and events to our East and to underemphasize the importance of those to our West. America's past lies deeply rooted in the areas across the Atlantic, but the hope of American generations of the future to keep pace with the progress of those of the past lies no less in the happenings and events across the Pacific. While fully availing ourselves of the potential to the East, to our western horizon we must look both for hope of a better life through yet untapped opportunities for trade and commerce in the advance of Asiatic races, and threat against the life with which we are even now endowed. For beyond that horizon upon the outcome of the ideological struggles to which opposing forces are now engaged and the restoration of political, economic and social stability, rests war or peace, assurance or threat, hope or fear.

5

It was in the latter part of 1947 that a new element entered the Tokyo scene in a definite attempt to boom MacArthur again for President. The campaign that shortly got under way could hardly be expected to enhance MacArthur's popularity with the men who were in control of the Pentagon and the administration, and particularly with President Truman, who was interested in succeeding himself. The changes in the high command that shortly took place involved the succession to General Eisenhower as Army Chief of Staff by General Bradley on February 15, 1948, and the replacement a year later of General Marshall as secretary of state by Dean Acheson.

Probably MacArthur had no exaggerated idea of his own chances in the coming Presidential campaign, but he did not feel he should evade any demand made on him. On March 9, 1948, he issued a statement in which he made clear his own position. It read:

I have been informed that petitions have been filed in Madison, signed by many of my fellow citizens of Wisconsin, presenting my name to the electorate for consideration at the primary on April 6. I am deeply grateful for this spontaneous display of friendly confidence. No man could fail to be profoundly stirred by such a public movement in this hour of momentous import, national and international, temporal and spiritual. While it seems unnecessary for me to repeat that I do not actively seek or covet any office and have no plans for leaving my post in Japan, I can say, and with due humility, that I would be recreant to all my concepts of good citizenship were I to shrink because of the hazards and responsibilities involved from accepting any public duty to which I might be called by the American people.

The fact that the Wisconsin primary did not turn out too favorably for the MacArthur enthusiasts obviously made little difference to the General. The following day there was some concern among his political friends whether he would now withdraw his name from future consideration. He met the issue head-on with the following cable:

9 April 1948

To: Mrs. Mary E. Kenney,
 1746 Harwood Avenue,
 Lincoln 2, Nebraska.
 Thank you for your message. You may be sure that my statement of March 9 that I was available for any public duty to which I might be called by the American people was not delimited to any particular political test but was a restatement of

443

a concept of the responsibility of citizenship on which I then stood, I now stand, and I shall continue to stand as long as I live.

MACARTHUR.

The national MacArthur campaign for the Republican nomination was making small progress in its conflict with the machine-controlled candidacy of Governor Dewey when Mac-Arthur was invited to appear in Washington before the Senate Appropriations Committee. In a few weeks the nominating conventions would open, and a number of friends in America were urging upon him the idea that a great home-coming welcome, skillfully arranged at the right moment, might swing the Republican nomination in his favor.

MacArthur would have none of it. How sensitive he was to making any possible political use of his formal invitation to appear before the Senate Committee was indicated in his answer to Senator Bridges in which he turned down the invitation. His statement dated May 29, 1948, concluded with the following paragraphs:

. . . As to this theatre, I have already, directly and through representatives, expressed my views on such details and there is little that I could add to what has already been said thereon and is now before the Congress.

Apart from this, it would be peculiarly repugnant to me to have it felt that I sought to capitalize to political advantage, as many have frankly urged, the public goodwill which might manifest itself upon my first return to American soil following the Pacific war. For such goodwill would find its inspiration in the victory which crowned our Pacific war effort to which countless gallant Americans, living and dead, contributed by unfailing and invincible devotion. Usurpation of such goodwill by me to serve a political end would be a shameful breach of their faith and a betrayal of the mutual trust on which was erected the cornerstone to the Pacific victory. . . .

The subsequent July convention in Philadelphia brought a distressing awakening to many of his followers. The memory of the post-midnight treatment the Dewey machine meted out to the frail and pathetic figure of General Wainwright as he seconded the nomination of General MacArthur was not to be quickly forgotten.

444

There can be little doubt that there was a steady hardening of the opposition against MacArthur in the inner circles of the administration, including the White House, the Department of State and the Pentagon as the crisis in the China situation advanced, and the Korean problem became more threatening.

Underneath the seeming calm in the exchange of cables and directives beween MacArthur and the men who were running affairs in Washington, there was brewing an intense and bitter personal conflict that sooner or later would almost certainly burst out into the open.

6

By the close of 1949 the plot succeeded: China was lost to America and the free world. The once mighty bulwark against the advancing Russian Empire was now a Moscow satellite. Some 400,000,000 Chinese had been swept from the orbit of the democratic world into the Communist international net. By the *fait accompli* the situation of both Formosa and Korea became desperate.

At the Cairo Conference in late 1943 Roosevelt, Churchill and Chiang Kai-shek had mutually pledged that with victory against Japan "in due course Korea shall become free and independent." Formosa was allocated to the Republic of China. When the Japanese made their offer of surrender on August 10, it was hurriedly arranged in the Pentagon that Russia would receive the surrender of the Japanese troops north of the 38th parallel in Korea, and the Americans would do the same below the line. This 38th parallel was thus accepted as the line of demarcation between the American and Russian zones of surrender if and when victory came.

On August 12, six days after Russia declared war, her Siberian troops broke across the Korean frontier. The Japanese surrender came three days later, but Russia continued her march across Korea and drove deeply into Manchuria as well.

Three weeks after the Russians crossed the northern Korea border, Lt. General John R. Hodge hurriedly disembarked in southern Korea with the first elements of his U. S. Corps. Immediately there was confusion, uncertainty and grave trouble. The Russian troops to the north were arrogant and uncooperative, and shortly afterward all communication between the two zones was severed.

It was obvious from the start that the Soviet occupation forces in Korea knew exactly what they wanted to do and had drawn complete plans how to do it. All during the Japanese war Korean escapees had been gathering in Siberia, and from these Koreans, who had in the meantime been Communist-indoctrinated, the Russians had organized a fair-sized army. This group became the nucleus of the native North Korean Red Army, and it was now rapidly expanded in the rugged, mountainous country above the 38th parallel.

Anti-Red opposition was promptly crushed, and local Communist governments were set up under the full control of the Soviet representatives. The infiltration of Communist agents into South Korea followed at once, with assassination and terror as their principal weapons.

Arrayed against this Russian plan to turn all Korea into a Communist satellite, General Hodge and his troops in South Korea operated under an unrealistic and flabby series of directives sent out from Washington. In 1947 Lt. General Wedemeyer had been ordered to look into the situation, but his final report with its key recommendation for a South Korean force capable of guaranteeing freedom was pigeonholed. Soon a swarm of experts from the State Department arrived in South Korea. Many of them should actually have been under the pay and patronage of Moscow.

As far back as December 1945, at the Big Three Conference in Moscow, a Korean trusteeship for five years was agreed upon by Russia, Britain and the United States. But five months later negotiations for a unified country completely broke down, and the middle border was closed by the Communists. A year and a half later the United Nations set up a Korean Commission empowered to hold nationwide elections over the whole country, but Communists in North Korea not only boycotted the elections but sealed the border even tighter. On August 25, 1948, the Communists held elections within North Korea for what they had proclaimed back in May as the People's Republic of North Korea. The well-supervised free elections in South Korea took place ten days after the rival Russian-dominated state was announced. On September 9 Dr. Syngman Rhee was inaugurated in Seoul as President of the Republic of Korea.

Almost immediately after the inauguration, at which MacArthur made the principal address, the United Nations instructed all foreign troops to leave Korea. It was a directive made to order for the Soviets. They had not only raised, trained and equipped a force of 125,000 native North Korean Communists, but they had brought in thousands of Red Koreans who had been serving in the Chinese Communist armies. More and more North Korean troops were enlisted, until eventually the army numbered 187,000 well-equipped and trained Red Koreans. They were furnished ample Russian-built artillery, 173 tanks and 200 planes. On January 1, 1949, the Russian troops pulled out, for they were no longer needed to guarantee the success of the Red plans.

Six months after these Russian forces had been removed from the north the last of the American troops left for home. An American military mission of a scant 450 army personnel responsible directly to the Department of State was left behind to carry on the tail end of the very possibly insincere American effort to prepare the Republic to meet the advancing threat of Communist North Korea. A training school for officers had been established, small arms plants had been opened, and American military equipment, at one time valued at $100,000,000, was used in arming a force of some 96,000 South Korean soldiers, roughly one-half the number of the North Korean force. Unfortunately there was an almost complete lack of tanks and anti-tank weapons, heavy artillery, fighter planes, proper signal equipment and the innumerable items that go into the making of even a small modern army.

In October 1949 the U. S. Congress passed a Military Assistance Act appropriating $10,000,000 for South Korea. But once again the State Department delayed interminably over the export permits so that only a dribble of the badly needed supplies ever actually arrived.

The do-nothing policy apparently had the support of Owen

Lattimore, who had very clear-cut ideas of just what he wanted to happen in Korea. On July 17, 1949, he wrote in the radical New York *Daily Compass*: "The thing to do is let South Korea fall, but not to let it look as if we pushed it."

The following month Lattimore was requested by the State Department to submit a memorandum regarding Korea. He suggested that "South Korea is more of a liability than an asset," and that the "United States should disembarrass itself as quickly as possible from its entanglements in South Korea."

With the formation of the Republic of Korea and the withdrawal of American Army forces, MacArthur's official concern with Korea was ended. He had never actually been in control of the occupation. From August 15, 1948, the doomed little country was under the complete charge of the State Department. MacArthur's headquarters were not even favored with such intelligence reports as were secretly issued.

His own experienced intelligence section under Major General Willoughby was well aware of the distinct possibility of an attack by the North Korean Communists during the spring or summer of 1950. Civil war might be postponed until fall when the rice crop had been harvested, but it was fairly clear that it was only a matter of time before hostilities would begin.

Already the complete liquidation of Chiang Kai-shek's resistance to Communist encirclement on the continent had occurred. On December 9, 1949, the last legions of the Generalissimo were forced to retreat to the island of Formosa, 100 miles or so off the mainland of China.

Around Christmas time of this tragic year of 1949, MacArthur's attention was drawn to a statement regarding Formosa sent up by the State Department under date of December 23 to its representatives abroad. On January 3, 1950, a friendly United Press reporter in Tokyo managed to secure a copy of the statement and immediately cabled a sensational dispatch to America. The news story read in part:

> The United States State Department has notified its attachés that the loss of Formosa, island redoubt of the Chinese Nationalists, to the Communists was to be anticipated.
> The Department said the public must be sold on the idea that

448

the island is of no strategic value in order to prevent the loss of prestige at home and abroad. . . .

The document said all available material should be used "to counter false impressions" that the retention of Formosa would save the Chinese Government, and that its loss would damage seriously the interest of either the United States or of other countries opposing communism.

"Without evidencing undue preoccupation with the subject," it continued, "emphasize as appropriate any of the following main points.

"Formosa is exclusively the responsibility of the Chinese Government. Formosa has no special military significance."

The unfavorable publicity given the apparently secret plan tapered off until June 2, 1950, when Senator Robert A. Taft in a formal speech insisted that Formosa should be protected from Communist invasion by the U. S. Seventh Fleet. Three days later President Truman bluntly declared that no more military aid or assistance would be given to the Chinese Nationalists there.

On January 12 in a major address before the National Press Club in Washington Secretary of State Acheson virtually wiped Formosa off the American map. He called it outside "our defense perimeter." South Korea had likewise been excluded from the American defense outposts. His words could be interpreted as meaning that America was no longer interested in Formosa or Korea.

MacArthur's own Eighth Army in Japan had been reduced until it consisted of four understrength divisions made up largely of recruits whose battle training had been grievously limited by the nature of their occupational duties. The Seventh Fleet still remained in Western Pacific waters, and a moderate-sized Far East Air Force, under Lt. General George Stratemeyer, was based on Okinawa and Japanese home airfields.

MacArthur's attempts to expose the overwhelming Communist threats in his part of the world appeared almost pathetic against the general apathy and the inspired pro-Communist propaganda that continued in America. It is clear that MacArthur sensed through some strange foreboding that a storm of

449

events was about to sweep down on these western Pacific shores.

Willoughby's special intelligence reports on Korea during the spring days of 1950 told of the unrest along the 38th parallel and of obvious preparations for a large-scale invasion by the North Korean Reds. There had been much border trouble, but most of it centered on the rice raids that the Korean Communists made now and again into the country below the 38th parallel. For several months there had been rumors of a coming North Korean Communist invasion, but as the pleasant June days drifted by, there seemed a bare hope that the war might be postponed.

John Foster Dulles was spending some time in Tokyo, working with MacArthur and Whitney on the final terms of the coming Japanese Treaty. Near the end of June Dulles flew to Korea for a quick look around before he returned to America.

On June 22 Dulles motored from Seoul toward the closed border along the 38th parallel. His swift survey caused him no great alarm. To his militarily inexperienced mind the South Koreans seemed fairly well prepared to meet any attack from the north. Neither Dulles nor the South Korean leaders apparently realized how inferior in training, equipment and numbers the democratic forces were to their Communist neighbors north of the 38th parallel. It was, however, fully known to MacArthur and his headquarters.

At 4:00 on Sunday morning three days later thousands of Red Korean troops poured over the border, overwhelming the South Korean advance outposts and moving southward with a speed and power that swept aside all opposition.

MacArthur was just rising on this tragic morning of June 25 when the first news of the attack was brought to him. The only immediate military obligation involving his own forces had to do with the evacuation of 2,000 American and United Nations personnel in the area of the Korean Republic.

He must have recalled that it was on a Sunday morning, nine and a half years before this, that the Japanese invading planes first loosed their bombs on Luzon.

450

22

A WAR
HE WAS NOT PERMITTED TO WIN

At dawn on Sunday, June 25, 1950 (Far Eastern time), eight divisions of North Korean Communist armies broke across the 38th parallel. The columns on the west lunged swiftly toward the capital city of Seoul, 30 miles away.

At the same time other Red forces drove down the railroad and highways on the east coast and through the roads and trails in the mountainous center of the peninsula. The South Koreans suffered from an almost total lack of anti-tank guns and heavy artillery. The marching columns of the North Koreans, plentifully supplied with tanks and artillery, soon turned the entrenched lines of the confused South Koreans into little more than papier-mâché defenses.

Frantic calls for help from President Rhee's tottering Republic were sent to Washington, Lake Success and Tokyo.

President Truman hurried back to Washington from Independence, Missouri, while plans were being made to call a hurried meeting of the United Nations Council. Reverting now to Washington time, at 3 Sunday afternoon the Council adopted a resolution declaring that North Korea had committed a breach of peace and that hostilities must end at once and the North Koreans withdraw their forces. Fortunately the Soviet Union had been boycotting the Council because of the continued presence of the representative of Nationalist China.

Sunday night, Washington time, the President and his advisors from the Pentagon and the State Department decided to use American ships and planes to evacuate American civilians in South Korea, and to give President Rhee arms. MacArthur was immediately informed of the decision. At the same Blair

House meeting it was argued that Formosa should be guarded and isolated from the war. The final decision was delayed for 24 hours.

The following night MacArthur was cabled that he was in command of any military action taken. So far his opinions had not been asked, nor had he volunteered any suggestions. At a meeting that same evening the decision was reached to use American air and naval forces, but there was to be no action above the 38th parallel. After the close of this meeting Louis Johnson and the Joint Chiefs of Staff hurried to the Pentagon and a call was placed to MacArthur over the scrambled-voice telephone. MacArthur was personally given the new orders. The following noon the President announced the decision to the world.

Wednesday there was only bad news from Korea. MacArthur scrupulously relayed such reports as he received. Two South Korean divisions had distintegrated, and the following day MacArthur was permitted to make a front-line inspection. The weather report of conditions over Japan and Korea was about as bad as it could be, but early in the morning Major Tony Storey, pilot of MacArthur's *Bataan,* phoned the Tokyo Embassy that the low ceiling was breaking over Korea and there was a chance they might make it. MacArthur said to get ready for take-off.

It was a risky landing Storey made on a dangerous airfield near Suwon, to the south of Seoul. During the next 9½ months he was to fly MacArthur 17 times to Korea, and always there were hazards to face. The General had complete faith in Storey's judgment and hunches, and as long as the pilot was willing to take a long chance he never hesitated.

After an eight-hour inspection of the battlefront MacArthur was certain that the South Koreans were utterly doomed unless ground help quickly arrived. It was the only thing that could save them, and even that was problematical. A near panic had been brought on during the early withdrawal of South Korean forces across the broad Han river just below Seoul when key bridges were blown up leaving thousands of troops still on the north bank. If anything was to be done to save the desperate situation, it must be done at once.

452

MacArthur flew back to Tokyo, and around 3 in the morning of June 30, Washington time, held a long telecon conversation with Chief of Staff Collins and high Pentagon officers. He outlined the situation as he had just seen it, and answered questions. He was prepared to deliver only a professional military analysis regarding the desperate outlook. He was giving no advice and suggesting no high policy decisions—save that only American troops could salvage the desperate situation. Secretary of the Army Pace was immediately informed.

At 4:57 that morning Secretary Pace awakened President Truman and laid out the alarming facts. The President almost immediately made his decision; alone and on his own responsibility, he directed MacArthur to send in American ground troops from Japan and do everything he could to check the North Korean aggression. One U. S. regiment was to be sent at once from Japan, and a few hours later Truman gave the decision to dispatch 2 divisions. The war was on.

The odds that MacArthur now faced brought to his mind the somewhat similarly discouraging conditions he had been forced to meet in the Philippines in early December 1941. Once again, he would simply do the best he could with what little he had. When the orders came on June 27 to contribute sea and air support, he hurried to Korea a G.H.Q. Advanced Command Group under Major General John H. Church. It was vigilant and active well before the arrival of the orders of June 30 to throw in ground forces, and it was of immeasurable value in securing information, in picking a vital spot for the first American troops and in expediting delivery of key supplies.

It is an ancient maxim of war never to feed in troops piecemeal. Nine times out of ten it is fatal, but MacArthur, probably because he had no alternative, immediately took that chance. He ordered Major General William F. Dean, of the 24th Division, to fly in a small fighting group, named Task Force Smith for its commander, Lt. Colonel Charles B. Smith, of the 21st Infantry. It would be difficult to conceive of a smaller outfit being dispatched alone into actual fighting against heavy enemy attacks: two companies of infantry, a battery of 105-mm. howitzers, two 4.2-inch mortar platoons, a platoon of 75-mm. recoilles rifles and six 2.36-inch rocket-launcher teams.

On July 4, 1950, this little group of fighting men established contact with the enemy near Osan, 25 miles below Seoul, and the following day it received the full impact of a Communist division, supported by Russian T34 tanks. For seven bloody hours these Americans stood against this frontal attack, while enemy units enveloped their flanks. They held out until they were forced to blow up their heavy weapons and fight their way on foot to the south.

The rest of the U. S. 21st Regiment with the 34th Infantry was rushed by boat across the Tsushima Strait to the port of Pusan and then raced north by rail and unloaded almost on the fighting lines. The Americans were now directly across the main rail and road system that led from the capital south to the key defense communication center of Taejon. The double-tracked rail lines then cut 65 miles southeast to Taegu, and then on straight south to the port of Pusan.

For 15 days the two American regiments, with the addition of the 19th Infantry of the 24th Division, fought with wild courage to hold the rail and road lines to Taejon. Colonel Bob Martin of the 34th Regiment sacrificed his life in the early fighting when he calmly fired the last round of his bazooka at a Red tank less than 15 yards away. A few days later Major General Dean, personally leading a forlorn attempt to check a Communist charge, simply disappeared in the wild mêlée accompanying the withdrawal. "Trade space for time" was the order; gain at all costs the precious time to land two more of the U. S. divisions remaining in Japan—time to bring in heavy weapons and tanks and supplies.

In broad terms South Korea is a rough, mountainous peninsula with three main corridors running north and south below the 38th parallel. Close to the east and west shorelines are both highways and railroads, with a third irregular passageway going down in the center between the two flanking routes. With the American troops now arriving in force and placed in battle positions, MacArthur's first military objective was to fight a series of delaying actions that would check the Red drives down the great corridors of approach. The main enemy drive

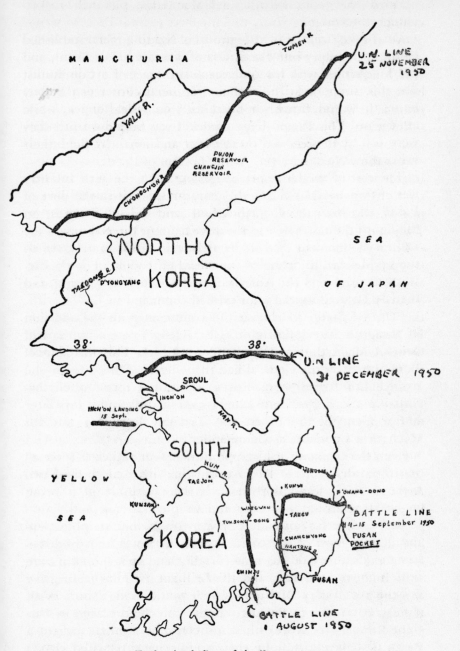

The key battle lines of the Korean war.

was now from the northwest, and MacArthur planned to stop it along the Naktong river, which curves eastward for 40 miles above the key center of Taegu. The Naktong then turns to the south to empty into the Straits of Tsushima.

If MacArthur with his Americans and South Koreans could hold this rectangle at the extreme southeast corner of the Republic, it would furnish a beachhead 90 miles long and 60 miles wide. This Pusan defense pocket was bound on the east and south by the sea, and on the west and north by the broad and shallow Naktong river. At the bottom of the defensive perimeter was the modern port of Pusan, and to the east lay the port of Pohang. The heaviest enemy pressure, it should be repeated, was from the victorious Red army driving down from Taejon on the northwest to the west bank of the Naktong.

From the moment that orders arrived to throw in his ground troops, MacArthur assumed unofficial direction of both the South Koreans and the American troops. On July 7 the U. N. Security Council agreed on a unified command in Korea, with the United States to choose the commander and act as the U. N. agent. The following day President Truman appointed General MacArthur as Commander-in-Chief. This was almost six months after the General had turned 70.

Since the Republic of Korea was not a member of the United Nations, President Rhee issued on July 19 his own formal approval of the U. N. and Truman decision regarding MacArthur's position as Commander-in-Chief.

From the moment of his appointment—or rather as soon as the initial drive of the Red Koreans had been checked—MacArthur's mind was absorbed with the possibility of a great by-pass that would not only relieve the battered and hard-pressed South Korean and American troops but possibly trap and destroy most of the North Korean Army that had driven far to the south. He was now certain that the U. S. 24th and 25th Infantry Divisions, and the brilliant 1st Marine Brigade and the 1st Cavalry Division—which would soon disembark at the east coast port of Pohang—along with the remnants of the eight Republic of Korea divisions, could hold on to the great Pusan beachhead, while he engineered some spectacular envelopment from the north, far north of the fighting.

Shortly the buddy system was introduced into the American units whereby each American company integrated 100 South Koreans into its structure. Many of the Koreans were green, young recruits but they were brave and willing, and they blended into the American outfits in a way that increased the American unit's efficiency and power by a full third. The 7th Infantry Division, kept back in Japan for some such great stroke as MacArthur was brewing, took into its organization 8,000 South Korean recruits, bringing its depleted strength well above the tables for war.

The most obvious spot on either coast for a great surprise amphibious landing was at the Yellow Sea port of Inchon, 30 miles to the west of the capital city of Seoul. It offered the possibility of cutting squarely across the enemy's main supply lines leading to the south, thus isolating almost his entire army. It was an ideal point but it had two serious drawbacks which would make a successful landing operation all but impossible: its 29-foot tides and the difficult approaches to its shorelines.

But the more MacArthur studied the maps and the information regarding the Inchon harbor and the off-shore island of Wolmi with its two-mile-long causeway leading to the mainland, the more the project fascinated him. His planning staff back in G.H.Q. in Tokyo, however, thought that the chances of failure were too great for it to be seriously considered.

The very fact that his own officers as well as the Joint Chiefs of Staff in Washington doubted its feasibility made him certain that the North Koreans likewise would never suspect that a vast amphibious landing would ever be attempted at Inchon. He ordered his planners to use the greatest secrecy in laying out the operation.

On July 20 he issued his first formal estimate of the Korean situation. American troops had been fighting 15 days when the statement was released:

> With the deployment in Korea of major elements of the Eighth Army now accomplished, the first phase of the campaign has ended and with it the chance for victory by the North Korean forces. The enemy's plan and great opportunity depended upon the speed with which he could overrun South Korea, once he had breached the Han River line and with overwhelming num-

bers and superior weapons temporarily shattered South Korean resistance. This chance he has now lost through the extraordinary speed with which the Eighth Army has been deployed from Japan to stem his rush. When he crashed the Han line the way seemed entirely open and victory was within his grasp. The desperate decision to throw in piecemeal American elements as they arrived by every available means of transport from Japan was the only hope to save the situation. The skill and valor thereafter displayed in successive holding actions by the ground forces in accordance with this concept, brilliantly supported in complete coordination by air and naval elements, forced the enemy into continued deployments, costly frontal attacks and confused logistics which so slowed his advance and blunted his drive that we have bought the precious time necessary to build a secure base. . . .

. . . Our hold upon the southern part of Korea represents a secure base. Our casualties despite overwhelming odds have been relatively light. Our strength will continually increase while that of the enemy will relatively decrease. His supply line is insecure. He has had his great chance but failed to exploit it. We are now in Korea in force, and with God's help we are there to stay until the constitutional authority of the Republic is fully restored.

2

One week later after a thorough reconnaissance of the front MacArthur returned to Tokyo. The sound of battle was still ringing in his ears when he started on the 1,500-mile flight to Formosa to see first-hand the Nationalist China forces there and to talk with Chiang Kai-shek. It was some consolation for him to know that President Truman had done an almost complete turn-about from his statement in Chicago, January 3, 1950, formally washing Formosa off the slate. The President then declared that the United States would furnish no more military aid to Chiang Kai-shek. Yet on June 27 when he had ordered MacArthur to give sea and air aid to the hard-put South Koreans, Truman announced that the United States would protect Formosa from invasion.

At the same time, however, the President denied Chiang Kai-shek the right to assume operations against the Communist

Chinese mainland. Thus the very same U. S. Seventh Fleet blocked the sea-roads both to and from Formosa.

This meant that the Communist China leaders need have little worry about a possible Nationalist landing on the mainland opposite Formosa, and that they could move Red troops northward to the Manchurian country above the Yalu river with perfect safety. It gave their Korean war plans a tremendous impetus, because Red China could now enter the Korean war at any time she chose without fear of being attacked on her flank and rear by the Nationalist troops on Formosa. What seemed to the muddled public to be a far-sighted move by the President to save Chiang Kai-shek from invasion was actually nullifying all use for the present of the large Nationalist Army on Formosa as a fighting force against Red China. In one significant gesture it banged the door shut in Chiang's face, and it opened the door into Korea for the Chinese Communists. Possibly as many as a million Red Chinese could now be released from the mainland opposite Formosa and made available for future assignment in Manchuria.

Less than a week after the North Koreans had crossed the 38th parallel the Nationalist Chinese ambassador in Washington offered the State Department an advance force of 33,000 troops that could be embarked for Korea within five days after the offer was accepted. The suggestion was politely refused. To some it seemed that the negative decision by the State Department was definitely abetted by the dual facts that Britain had long recognized the Red China government, and that the Indian ambassador at Peiping was on intimate terms with the Communist regime.

MacArthur spent the day and a half of his Formosa visit inspecting the Nationalist troops and equipment and in friendly private talks with Chiang Kai-shek and his wife. Immediately upon his return to Tokyo he issued a carefully worded statement that avoided any possible criticism of the administration in Washington:

> My visit to Formosa has been primarily for the purpose of making a short reconnaissance of the potential of its defense against possible attack. The policy has been enunciated that this

island, including the Pescadores, is not under present circumstances subject to military invasion. It is my responsibility and firm purpose to enforce this decision.

My conferences here on all levels have been most cordial and responsive in every respect. Among the problems which were discussed was the prompt and generous offer of the Chinese Government to send troops to join the United Nations forces in Korea. The belief of all concerned however was that such action at this time might so seriously jeopardize the defense of Formosa that it would be inadvisable.

Arrangements have been completed for effective coordination between the American forces under my command and those of the Chinese Government, the better to meet any attack which a hostile force might be foolish enough to attempt. Such an attack would, in my opinion, stand little chance of success.

It has been a great pleasure for me to meet my old comrade-in-arms of the last war, Generalissimo Chiang Kai-shek. His indomitable determination to resist Communist domination arouses my sincere admiration. His determination parallels the common interest and purpose of Americans, that all peoples in the Pacific area shall be free—not slave.

Nothing MacArthur could have done would have precipitated a greater storm of angry criticism among his old detractors in the State Department than his visit to Formosa and his subsequent report. Not only was he violently attacked by critical foreign groups within the United Nations, but he was assailed by certain of his own countrymen who were still following Britain and India in the appeasement of the Soviet Union and Red China.

Within ten days after his first statement regarding Formosa, the General felt the need for a fuller report. Busy as he was with the desperate Korean war, he took the time to release the following on August 10:

There have been so many misstatements made with reference to my recent trip to Formosa that in the public interest at this critical moment I feel constrained to correct them.

1. This trip was formally arranged and coordinated beforehand with all branches of the American and Chinese Governments.

2. It was limited entirely to military matters, as I stated in

my public release after the visit, and dealt solely with the problem of preventing military violence to Formosa as directed by the President—the implementation of which directive is my responsibility. It had no connection with political affairs, and, therefore, no suggestion or thought was ever made from any source whatsoever that a political representative accompany me.

3. The subject of the future of the Chinese Government, of developments on the Chinese Mainland, or anything else outside the scope of my own military responsibility, was not discussed or even mentioned.

4. Full reports on the results of the visit were promptly made to Washington.

Fully aware of the dangers he faced in sneak attacks against him, MacArthur went far out of his way to be conciliatory to the men in Washington who held the whip hand. There was nothing else for him to do at this stage. His statement continued:

This visit has been maliciously misrepresented to the public by those who invariably in the past have propagandized a policy of defeatism and appeasement in the Pacific. I hope the American people will not be misled by sly insinuations, brash speculations and bold misstatements invariably attributed to anonymous sources, so insidiously fed them both nationally and internationally by persons ten thousand miles away from the actual events, which tend, if they are not indeed designed, to promote disunity and destroy faith and confidence in American purposes and institutions and American representatives, at this time of great world peril.

Contrary to these propaganda efforts calculated to create the impression of friction and disunity between this Headquarters and various executive agencies in Washington, there could be no greater unity of purpose and complete coordination and cooperation than now exist. I have never known so high a degree of mutual support, without the slightest friction or misunderstanding.

But this last obviously was for public consumption. He knew he was once again fighting a two-front war. During most of the early days of the Japanese struggle his Southwest Pacific theatre had been throttled down and handicapped by Roosevelt and the Joint Chiefs of Staff working closely with Prime Minister Churchill in their strategy of "Hitler First." Throughout almost five years of occupation duties in Japan he had faced the steady and relentless pressure of the Russian Soviet, aided by skillful propaganda and the secret conniving of strong anti-Nationalist China groups within the U. S. State Department. Now, for a second time, he had a difficult foreign war on his hands, while bitter opposition was mounting against him behind his back in Washington. Always he was menaced by the definite but unpredictable possibility of a sudden intervention into the Korean war by Communist Chinese armies, backed and equipped by Communist Russia. And he could not be too sure of the reaction of certain powerful and allegedly friendly nations in the Security Council of the U. N. should Red China actively interfere.

The half-million Chinese Nationalist troops in Formosa must have been a matter of extreme military importance in his eyes. Yet already he found that Britain's Socialist Prime Minister Attlee and India's left-wing Socialist Nehru carried far more weight in many official American quarters than he, himself, the Commander-in-Chief on the actual front.

In middle August, while he was actively engaged in the prospect of the great Inchon landing, a request came from Clyde A. Lewis, Commander-in-Chief of the Veterans of Foreign Wars, asking MacArthur to send a message to the 51st Annual National Convention in Chicago on August 27. MacArthur agreed to prepare a speech to be read there.

A week before the convention opened he sent his long message to Commander Lewis and turned over copies to the news agencies and one or two news magazines with a release date to correspond to the reading of the paper on the floor of the Convention. A copy was sent through ordinary channels to the Pentagon. Late on the night of August 25, two days before the formal release, a Washington reporter called the attention of Averell Harriman to the MacArthur statement, which he had seen in his office. A copy was hurried to the President. At 9 the following morning the angry Truman called in his chief military and civilian advisors.

When the President found that the speech had not been cleared at the Pentagon, but that the release had been merely sent in from Tokyo at the same time a copy had been sent to the V.F.W. convention in Washington, he was incensed. The President's snap judgment was to fire MacArthur at once. Secretary of Defense Louis Johnson was able, however, to dissuade Truman from relieving MacArthur, especially in view of the critical situation in Korea. The President ordered Johnson to cable MacArthur immediately to withdraw the speech. The General promptly stopped its delivery on the convention floor, but it was too late to check its general circulation, since a news weekly actually had gone to press with the full text.

The reaction from London, Delhi, Lake Success and Washington was immediate and angry. It was apparent that from now on MacArthur would be held in open suspicion and distrust by the Red appeasers who were becoming fearful that MacArthur might actually be winning the war. His statement, intended for the V.F.W., though officially cancelled, was given world-wide circulation. It read in part:

> In view of misconceptions currently being voiced concerning the relationship of Formosa to our strategic potential in the Pacific, I believe it in the public interest to avail myself of this opportunity to state my views thereon to you, all of whom having fought overseas understand broad strategic concepts. To begin with, any appraisal of that strategic potential requires an appreciation of the changes wrought in the course of the past war. Prior thereto the Western strategic frontier of the United States lay on the littoral line of the Americas, with an exposed island salient extending out through Hawaii, Midway and Guam to the Philippines. That salient was not an outpost of strength but an avenue of weakness, along which the enemy could and did attack us. The Pacific was a potential area of advance for any predatory force intent upon striking at the bordering land areas.
>
> All of this was changed by our Pacific victory. Our strategic frontier then shifted to embrace the entire Pacific Ocean, which had become a vast moat to protect us as long as we hold it. Indeed, it acts as a protective shield for all of the Americas and all free lands of the Pacific Ocean area. We control it to the shores of Asia by a chain of islands extending in an arc from the Aleutians to the Marianas, held by us and our free allies. From this island chain we can dominate with air power every Asiatic port from Vladivostok to Singapore, and prevent any hostile move-

ment into the Pacific. Any predatory attack from Asia must be an amphibious effort. No amphibious force can be successful without control of the sea lanes and the air over these lanes in its avenue of advance.

So important in MacArthur's eyes was the purely strategic conception of Formosa's position that he now reiterated his military threats:

> With naval and air supremacy and modest ground elements to defend bases, any major attack from continental Asia toward us or our friends of the Pacific would be doomed to failure. Under such conditions the Pacific no longer represents menacing avenues of approach for a prospective invader—it assumes instead the friendly aspect of a peaceful lake. Our line of defense is a natural one and can be maintained with a minimum of military effort and expense. It envisions no attack against anyone, nor does it provide the bastions essential for offensive operations, but properly maintained would be an invincible defense against aggression. If we hold this line we may have peace—lose it and war is inevitable. . . .

> As a result of its geographic location and base potential, utilization of Formosa by a military power hostile to the United States may either counterbalance or overshadow the strategic importance of the central and southern flank of the United States front line position. Formosa in the hands of such a hostile power could be compared to an unsinkable aircraft carrier and submarine tender ideally located to accomplish offensive strategy and at the same time checkmate defensive or counteroffensive operations by friendly forces based on Okinawa and the Philippines. This unsinkable carrier-tender has the capacity to operate from ten to twenty air groups of types ranging from jet fighters to B-29 type bombers, as well as to provide forward operating facilities for short-range coastal submarines. In acquiring this forward submarine base, the efficacy of the short-range submarine would be so enormously increased by the additional radius of activity as to threaten completely sea traffic from the south and interdict all sea lanes in the Western Pacific. Submarine blockade by the enemy, with all its destructive ramifications, would thereby become a virtual certainty.

> Should Formosa fall and bases thereafter come into the hands of a potential enemy of the United States, the latter will have acquired an additional "fleet" which will have been obtained

and can be maintained at an incomparably lower cost than could its equivalent in aircraft carriers and submarine tenders. . . .

It was this evil shadow of the ever-expanding Communist global domination by Russia that had now fallen directly across the strategic island. MacArthur, the hater of war, could only point out the real and immediate dangers of confusing appeasement with peace. This was not the time for expediency and retreat. He went on:

Nothing could be more fallacious than the threadbare argument by those who advocate appeasement and defeatism in the Pacific, that if we defend Formosa we alienate continental Asia. Those who speak thus do not understand the Orient. They do not grasp that it is in the pattern of Oriental psychology to respect and follow aggressive, resolute and dynamic leadership— to quickly turn from a leadership characterized by timidity or vacillation—and they underestimate the Oriental mentality.

Nothing in the last five years has so inspired the Far East as the American determination to preserve the bulwarks of our Pacific Ocean strategic position from future encroachment, for few of its peoples fail accurately to appraise the safeguard such determination brings to their free institutions. To pursue any other course would be to turn over the fruits of our Pacific victory to a potential enemy. It would shift any future battle area 5,000 miles eastward, to the coasts of the American continents, our own home coasts; it would completely expose our friends in the Philippines, our friends in Australia and New Zealand, our friends in Indonesia, our friends in Japan and other areas, to the lustful thrusts of those who stand for slavery as against liberty, for atheism as against God.

The decision of President Truman on June 27 lighted into flame a lamp of hope throughout Asia that was burning dimly towards extinction. It marked for the Far East the focal and turning point in this area's struggle for freedom. It swept aside in one great monumental stroke all of the hypocrisy and the sophistry which has confused and deluded so many people distant from the actual scene.

President Truman's personal ambassador, Averell Harriman, was rushed by plane to Tokyo to set MacArthur straight on some of his apparent deviations from the Washington and

465

U.N. party line. Harriman was back in Washington within five days after he had taken off for his distant mission.

Pressure on the Pusan beachhead was at its highest when MacArthur addressed a note to the Joint Chiefs of Staff asking for permission to bomb the highly important North Korean city of Racin, which lies thirty-five miles southwest of the Siberian-Korean border. It was the key supply center for this entire northern area, and the destruction of its transportation facilities by air would have been a perfectly safe and reasonable proposition. Both Lt. General George E. Stratemeyer, commander of the Far East Air Force, and his bomber chief, Major General Emmett (Rosey) O'Donnell, had vigorously appealed to MacArthur for the right to take out this troublesome North Korean supply center during the critical summer period before the Inchon landing. The Red Koreans were then attacking the Pusan defense pocket from three sides, and supplies coming down the east coast by sea and land from Racin were of great importance to the enemy. But MacArthur's request was promptly turned down by Washington and the U.N.

MacArthur's mind was already turning to the complicated problems connected with the Inchon landing. Before he issued the final directives, he was visited by the Army Chief of Staff J. Lawton Collins on two occasions, but Collins remained skeptical about its success. Only Defense Secretary Louis A. Johnson, now to be relieved, had openly and courageously approved the bold venture since the start.

The North Korean pressure on the Pusan beachhead had been increasing rather than abating. MacArthur was putting all his eggs in one basket, but he was superbly confident on September 13 when he boarded a warship for Inchon on the west Korean coast, so as to be on hand if some unforeseen tragedy befell the great landing operation.

Since the beginning of the war MacArthur had been using psychological warfare to a far greater extent than even in the Philippines. At his first staff conference after American troops had been committed he called for the full use of this new dimension in war. Colonel Woodall Greene, chief of the special branch, immediately prepared the leaflets and 10 million were dropped behind the enemy lines within the first few days. Each month tens of thousands of front-line broadcasts, promising good treatment for all who surrendered, were directed toward the Red positions. There can be no question that all this helped materially in breaking down the morale of the enemy when the pressure came, and some 200,000 Reds were either captured or surrendered. MacArthur, the old master of three-dimensional war, was now the champion of the new weapon in complete envelopment—land, sea, air and mind.

Back across the world in Washington a matter of considerable importance to MacArthur and to the conduct of the war occurred on the 12th of September, 1950, when General George C. Marshall, who had resigned as Secretary of State in late 1948, was appointed to succeed Louis Johnson as Secretary of National Defense on September 17. It took a special act of Congress to by-pass the law that made any active military officer ineligible to fill the high post.

Secretary of State Dean Acheson now had formidable allies close at hand or within his own department: Lt. General Bedell Smith as head of the highly important Central Intelligence Agency: Emerson and Joseph E. Davies and other partisans in key posts in the State Department; Marshall's own choice, General Collins, in the Pentagon; and Marshall himself, who had played second fiddle to Roosevelt at Yalta but first fiddle to Truman in the tragic play that led to the loss of China. More than once President Truman had referred to Marshall as "the greatest living American."

Marshall, many felt, would now have a good chance to prove his greatness by his official contribution to the success or failure of this desperate undeclared war going on in the mud and stench and death of the river valleys and deadly hills of this far-away and lonely land of Korea. In many ways he dominated both American military and foreign policies.

The appointment, however, could hardly have appeared a happy one to MacArthur, the hard-pressed commander-in-chief of the American and South Korean forces and their sparse but fighting allies.

3

In none of the many amphibious landings MacArthur had made in the long march up the New Guinea coast and intervening islands to Leyte and Lingayen Gulf, had he faced such a hazard as the 29-foot tides that rose and fell in Inchon harbor in middle September. Only for a scant three-hour stretch each twelve hours, could landing craft get close to the shores. Split-second timing with complete coordination of all arms was an old story to him, but never before had he faced this peculiar problem of abnormal tides.

His plan called for the 1st U. S. Marine Division to make the initial landing. The 1st Marine Brigade, which had fought so magnificently in Korea, was pulled back to Japan, where it was reinforced by six Marine battalions from the United States and the Mediterranean, and by its own Marine-trained combat air support. The 7th Infantry Division that had been kept in Japan and built up by the induction of 8,000 South Koreans comprised the other half of the new X Corps he now placed under the command of Major General Edward M. Almond, who had recently been relieved of his duties as chief of staff to G.H.Q. in Tokyo.

Two days before the landings two American and two British cruisers entered the harbor, and four American destroyers fearlessly pointed close in, inviting fire from hidden enemy shore batteries. Although without an air force, the North Koreans rose to the bait, and at once the warships opened up on the exposed batteries. Four great aircraft carriers standing over the horizon furnished air power, and every spot that looked like an enemy position was heavily blasted. The strategic surprise was so complete that the enemy was in no position to oppose the landings.

At 6:30 in the morning of September 15, and one hour before high tide, a battalion of the 5th Marine Regiment was put ashore on the key island of Wolmi. Men and guns poured onto the restricted beaches, and the two-mile stone causeway to Inchon was secured. Twelve hours after the first landing the 29-foot tide rose again, and this time the Marine assault lines pushed directly ashore and over the city's 9-foot sea wall. When the tide receded the long, gangling LSTs squatted helplessly in the mud far back from the high points of the beaches, while tanks and vehicles still waddled ashore.

The Marine columns with their tanks in the lead fanned out toward the city of Seoul, 30 miles inland, and toward the Kimpo airfield and the great supply arteries running north and south. On the 18th the 7th Division came ashore and moved swiftly toward the outskirts of the capital and the vital communication avenues below it. Eleven days after the initial landings, Seoul fell, after heavy fighting by men of the two U. S. divisions aided by four sturdy battalions of South Korean marines.

[Throughout the entire Korean war the U.S. Navy, with limited Allied naval assistance, played a highly important and brave part in the long and involved struggle. No mission was too hazardous for these tireless sailors—and their air arm—to undertake. Eventually the navy men on the spot boasted that MacArthur had been a superb General of ground and air forces before this particular war, but that now he was a first-rate Admiral.]

4

On the day Seoul was freed a free-wheeling battalion of the 7th Cavalry broke out of the Pusan beachhead, far to the south, and in a single wild night raced on rubber and steel tracks 100 miles northwest to a junction with the outposts of the 7th Division standing across the principal north-south highway below Seoul. Since the initial landing at Pusan there had been much desperate fighting far below by the United Nations troops within the bridgehead, attempting to break through the steel wall that the enemy had built around the embattled U. N. defenders. Here, more than 100 miles to the south of the 38th parallel, the North Korean attacking force now suddenly found the tables reversed. The 13 infantry divisions and the single tank division the Red Koreans had sent into the fighting were no longer the trappers but the trapped.

With the main northern supply and escape lines cut below Seoul, a full two-thirds of the total enemy troops were immediately thrown on the defensive on the west side of the Pusan beachhead. The sharp 100-mile thrust of the mechanized 7th Cavalry Regiment up the northwestern road, linking U. N. communications with the troops from the Inchon landings, had sprung the upper jaws of the pincer that now closed down on the North Koreans. Thousands of Reds were killed and wounded in their desperate attempt to escape the trap, while other thousands threw away their weapons and disguised in peasant garb tried to make their way northward through the central mountain passes toward the 38th parallel. In the two weeks between September 15 and 30 the United Nations forces took 23,600 prisoners. Main roads and rail escape lines to the north of the old Pusan beachhead were quickly blocked in the center and along the eastern shorelines.

The dual movement of the great Inchon by-pass and the subsequent breakout from the Pusan beachhead had been perfectly executed. MacArthur and his forces were showered with congratulatory messages from President Truman, Secretary of Army Pace, the Joint Chiefs of Staff and a personal message from George Marshall, now Secretary of National Defense. MacArthur's reply to Marshall's cable could be branded as a classic example of overstatement. After all the neglect he had suffered at the hands of Marshall it seems logical to suppose that MacArthur's eyes were sparkling with the irony of the situation as he wrote out the words:

> Thanks, George, for your fine message. It brings back vividly the memories of past wars and the complete coordination and perfect unity of cooperation which has always existed in our mutual relationships and martial endeavors. Again my deepest appreciation for your message and for your unfailing support.

There is, however, no reason to doubt the complete sincerity of the message received from the British Chiefs of Staff or of MacArthur's answering note. The British professional soldiers, regardless of their meddling politicians, were unsparing in their praise of the great deeds of their comrade-in-arms:

> We send you our warmest congratulations on your brilliant victory. We have admired not only the skill with which you have conducted an extremely difficult rear guard action against

great odds over many anxious weeks, but equally the bravery and tenacity with which the forces under your command have responded to your inspiring and indefatigable leadership. We believe that the brilliant conception and masterly execution of the "Inchon" counter stroke, which you planned and launched whilst holding the enemy at bay in the south, will rank amongst the finest strategic achievements in military history.

British Chiefs of Staff

MacArthur's perfect touch was shown in the few words of his reply:

My thanks and deepest appreciation for your inspiring message. British Forces played a large part in the victory.

Within two weeks after the opening of the Inchon by-pass, the South Korean troops rapidly pushed up the east coast railroad and highway, and on October 1 reached the disputed 38th parallel. For days the U. N. halls at Lake Success crackled with bitter debate over the right of MacArthur to enter the Red areas of North Korea. Even before his capital had been restored to him, President Rhee had announced on September 19 that his South Koreans would continue their attacks, with or without U. N. assistance. Finally on October 1 MacArthur with the full approval of Washington called upon the enemy to surrender in the following proclamation:

To: The Commander-in-Chief
North Korean Forces

The early and total defeat and complete destruction of your armed forces and war-making potential is now inevitable. In order that the decisions of the United Nations may be carried out with a minimum of further loss of life and destruction of property, I, as the United Nations Commander-in-Chief, call upon you and the forces under your command, in whatever part of Korea situated, forthwith to lay down your arms and cease hostilities under such military supervision as I may direct—and I call upon you at once to liberate all United Nations prisoners of war and civilian internees under your control and to make adequate provision for their protection, care, maintenance, and immediate transportation to such places as I indicate.

North Korean Forces, including prisoners of war in the hands of the United Nations Command, will continue to be given the

471

care dictated by civilized custom and practice and permitted to return to their homes as soon as practicable.

I shall anticipate your early decision upon this opportunity to avoid the further useless shedding of blood and destruction of property.

That same day he ordered the ROK troops on the east coast to cross the border line and head north. He had ample justification, he was certain, in the original Security Council resolution of June 27, "to repel the armed attack and to restore international peace and security in the area." Only by crushing the North Koreans in their own territory could this peace and security be gained. The Security Council's resolution of July 7 gave further authority in its repetition of the declaration of June 27.

But for a period of nine days the United Nations forces, which at the moment included the five U. S. divisions and the British Commonwealth, Canadian and Turkish brigades and token units of several other countries, were held back of the line. The South Korean Republic was not a member of the U. N., although its troops were under MacArthur's orders.

On October 3 at Lake Success and while a Korean debate was under way, the Indian delegate, Sir Benegal Rau, transmitted a message sent to him by Prime Minister Nehru, which in turn had come to the Indian Premier from his ambassador in Peiping. The warning that had been given the Indian ambassador by the Communist China Foreign Minister, Chou En-lai, was that the Chinese Communists would send troops to the Korean frontier if U. N. or U. S. troops entered North Korea. This would not happen, the threat continued, if South Korean troops alone invaded the territory north of the 38th parallel. The warning was considerably watered down by the Indian diplomat, who explained to the Political Committee of the General Assembly that "our fears may turn out to be wrong, but each government has to judge the situation upon its best information and act accordingly." The particularly dire suggestion of intervention was ignored, and on October 7 a new resolution passed the Assembly that indicated but did not formally give full authority to MacArthur to order U. N. troops forward. Again MacArthur was forced to accept the responsibility without a definite and written directive. This was to become the pattern of most of his dealings with the Joint Chiefs of Staff and with the U. N.

The following day MacArthur addressed a formal note to the Premier of the government of North Korea. His first call for surrender had been sent to the Commander-in-Chief of the North Korean Forces. This second attempt at peace went to the head of state, but, as in the first effort, the result was nil.

There was nothing to do but continue the fighting.

5

With Seoul captured and the great Kimpo airdrome in U. N. hands, MacArthur on October 7 sent by sea to the east coast the 1st Marine and 7th Infantry divisions of Almond's X Corps that had completed the great Inchon by-pass. Two days later the 1st Cavalry Division and I Corps, with other U. N. units operating on the west coast under the Eighth Army commander, drove across the 38th parallel and advanced toward the North Korean capital of Pyongyang. On the other side of the peninsula, and along the Sea of Japan, the ROK (Republic of Korea) I Corps secured the important port of Wonsan, and other ROK units won the central town of Inchon. All the fighting, save the tough job of mopping up the North Koreans who had adopted the guise of peasant guerillas, was now taking place north of the 38th parallel.

MacArthur's tactics of striking on both coast lines and up through the center of the rough, mountainous country had given the enemy no moment to reorganize his shattered divisions and dig in for strong defense. Toward the end of September the U. S. 187th Airborne Regimental Combat Team was flown to Kimpo airdrome, and 2,800 paratroopers of the same outfit on October 20, with 300 tons of combat equipment, were dropped behind the enemy lines at Sunchon, and on the airstrips in the west coast port of Sukchon, well above the 38th parallel. MacArthur accompanied this fleet of air transports in his sturdy old *Bataan*.

Two days after this initial drop here in North Korea, an additional 1,200 troops parachuted down. There was no lull in the varied attacks and envelopments. By the end of October a total of 135,000 enemy troops had been captured and were in POW pens.

The war had every appearance of going along extremely well, but the pressure on the President to stand for no dictatorial attitudes from MacArthur, and the demand that the President make it perfectly clear to the soldier just who was boss was too strong for Truman to resist. A meeting of the two had been suggested but instead of bluntly ordering MacArthur to report to him, Truman courteously offered to meet him halfway and let the General choose Wake Island rather than Hawaii. On October 15 the cable arrived for MacArthur to meet the President at Wake Island. The mid-term elections of 1950 would be held in less than 3 weeks, but the General unquestionably sensed a political implication in the meeting.

American morning papers on October 11 gave the President's announcement of the coming meeting. The General took with him only Major General Courtney Whitney and his aide, Colonel Larry Bunker. He was not at all certain what might develop, for reports had reached him of the violent criticism levelled at him for his action in sending U. N. troops north of the 38th parallel without specific orders.

MacArthur, arriving first, met the plane bearing the President and his formidable group of advisors, which included Averell Harriman, Special Assistant to the President; Secretary of the Army Frank Pace; Chairman of the Joint Chiefs of Staff Omar Bradley; Commander-in-Chief of the Pacific Fleet Admiral Radford; Assistant Secretary of State Dean Rusk; and Ambassador at Large Philip C. Jessup.

For an hour the President and General MacArthur talked privately, and then they were joined by the impressive entourage for a general discussion. MacArthur had no way of knowing that a female stenographer brought from Jessup's office in Washington had been secretly placed behind a door conveniently left ajar so that she might hear and transcribe every word of the meeting. [The facts regarding this unusual procedure, along with the transcript of the conversation and additional notes, were secretly turned over to a friendly newspaper man in Washington some six months later, but probably MacArthur

474

would not have made any changes in his frank contributions to the give-and-take exchange had he known of the presence of the surreptitious stenographer.]

A copy of the document was sent to MacArthur's headquarters within a few days of the meeting, but there is a possibility that press of war matters left him no time to go over it carefully.

At the moment of the conference it seemed that the total destruction of the North Korean forces and the overrunning of all the Korean territory north of the 38th parallel would necessitate only a few weeks more fighting. The fresh U. S. 2nd and 3rd Infantry divisions had arrived or would shortly arrive in Korea, and it was apparent that nothing but full-scale action by the Chinese Communists could check the rapid and complete liquidation of the North Korean Forces. To all intent and purpose the war was almost over.

Toward the end of the extremely top secret session on Wake Island the President turned to the General and put the blunt and straightforward question: "What are the chances of Chinese or Soviet interference?" MacArthur answered:

Very little. Had they interfered in the first or second month it would have been decisive. We are no longer fearful of their intervention. We no longer stand hat in hand. The Chinese have 300,000 men in Manchuria. Of these probably not more than 100,000 to 125,000 are distributed along the Yalu River. Only 50,000 to 60,000 can be gotten across the Yalu River. They have no air force. Now that we have bases for our Air Force in Korea, if the Chinese tried to get down to Pyongyang there would be the greatest slaughter.

With the Russians it is a little different. They have an air force in Siberia and a fairly good one, with excellent pilots equipped with some jets and B-25 and B-29 planes. They can put 1,000 planes in the air with some 2,000 more from the 5th and 7th Soviet fleets. They are probably no match for our Air Force. The Russians have no ground troops available for North Korea. They would have difficulty putting troops into the field. It would take six weeks to get a division across, and six weeks brings the winter. The only other combination would be Russian air support of Chinese ground troops.

Russian air is deployed in a semicircle through Mukden and Harbin, but the coordination between the Russian air and the

Chinese ground would be so flimsy that I believe Russian air would bomb the Chinese as often as they would bomb us. Ground support is a very difficult thing to do. Our Marines do it perfectly. They have been trained for it. Our own air and ground forces (coordination) are not (as good) as the Marines, but they are effective. Between untrained air and ground forces an air umbrella is impossible without a lot of joint training. I believe it just wouldn't work with Chinese Communist ground and Russian air. We are the best.

Averell Harriman broke in at this point with a question regarding war criminals, and there was no further reference to the chances of Communist China or Russian intervention. MacArthur had given his frank opinion regarding the complex and unfathomable situation as it stood on October 15, 1950. He had stated that there were 300,000 Chinese Communist troops in Manchuria and from 100,000 to 125,000 directly along the Yalu. It was his impression that not more than from 50,000 to 60,000 could be gotten across the broad river at present, and that it would not be frozen over for some weeks. No Russian jet fighters had been seen in Korean territory, but there were plenty of Russian planes in both Siberian and Manchurian fields that could be utilized.

It seems logical that MacArthur's negative answer to the President's direct question regarding the possibility of Red Chinese intervention was based on the assumption that the Red leaders would reason this way: if a large invasion force struck the U.N. armies, MacArthur would then be permitted to use his air arm, with its deadly potential of atomic bombs. Within a matter of hours this unwrapping of his air would mean the destruction of the bridges over the Yalu, of enemy airfields, troop concentrations, supply lines and every important base and target in Manchuria. The invading Red army, regardless of its size, would be cut off from its supplies and soon defeated. It was incredible to MacArthur that the shrewd Chinese leaders would dare risk an all-out attack with such air odds against them. MacArthur could not conceive the possibility that the Communists might already be tipped off that, regardless of what happened to U.N. forces, certain Allied powers were influential enough to keep America from giving him the full use of his

476

air arm, even to save his own armies. He simply could not believe such craven perfidity possible. And here lay the key to his answer that there was "very little chance of Chinese intervention."

When the conferences ended, the President and the General rode alone together over the coral roads of the Island in a battered old American car. The conversation was free and easy and friendly.

Here in the warm and colorful atmosphere of Wake Island MacArthur encouraged Truman to speak his mind on matters that touched Truman's own political future. The General suggested that the President might have to run again to see that his own policies were carried out.

The President's answer was a trifle vague: "I want only three words as my epitaph—'He Brought Peace.'"

MacArthur again referrred to the election that was still almost two years away.

"I can assure you of one thing, Mr. President," the General went on. "If you ever have to run against a military man, his name won't be MacArthur."

Truman jumped at the bait and launched into a tirade against General Eisenhower, whose name was being frequently mentioned as a candidate, and who was shortly to be sent to Europe as supreme commander of the recently organized and highly touted NATO forces. Truman's description of the younger 5-star general was proof that he had once driven mules in Missouri.

Despite the outwardly friendly nature of the visit there seem to have been very few, if any, tangible results. Two men who were most directly concerned with the desperate and changing Far Eastern situation, and with the rise or fall of General Mac-Arthur—Secretary of State Dean Acheson and Secretary of Defense George Marshall—had remained behind in Washington. The whole affair had been most perfunctory.

23

"THE CRIME OF THE CENTURY"

On October 15, 1950, the day that MacArthur boarded the *Bataan* at Wake Island to fly back to Tokyo, Russian-made anti-aircraft batteries, planted on the Manchurian side of the Yalu and manned by Red Chinese, shot down their first American plane patrolling below the south bank of the river. The following day it was discovered that elements of the 307th Regiment of the 124th Division of the Chinese Communist 24th Army had crossed the Yalu and were proceeding toward the Choshin and Fusan dams in the northcentral area. Eventually they came in contact with U. N. forces some 60 miles north of Hamhung on the east coast.

On the 20th of October the Chinese Communist 56th Task Force, consisting of approximately 5,000 troops, crossed the Yalu at Antung, near the mouth of the river. MacArthur, in a special report to the U. N. Security Council, gave additional information regarding the sudden turn of events: "A captured Communist soldier of this Task Force states that his group was organized out of the regular Chinese Communist 40th Army, stationed across the river in Manchurian Antung."

On October 30 there was an interrogation of 19 Chinese Communist prisoners belonging to the two regiments now north of the western port of Chŏngjin, and by November 4 a total of 35 Communist Chinese prisoners of war had been examined. Some wore North Korean uniforms.

There no longer remained the slightest doubt that regular Chinese Communist units had now crossed the Yalu in force and had met U. N. troops. There was still a possibility, however, that they were at least partially volunteers. MacArthur, with the approval of the Joint Chiefs of Staff, and with a scant month left before deadly winter closed in, pushed his advances northward toward the Yalu as rapidly as possible.

He might still destroy the remaining North Korean forces before they were too heavily reinforced by Red China and before winter came.

On October 26 the 7th Regiment of the ROK 6th Division reached the international border town of Chosan on the Yalu river, but soon was forced to retire. By early November the U. S. 24th Division advanced up the West Coast toward the temporary North Korean capital of Sinuiju at the mouth of the Yalu. It encountered strong resistance and pulled back.

Here on the western side of the peninsula Lt. General Walton Walker, the 8th Army commander, had three corps comprising four American divisions, four ROK divisions and the British Commonwealth and Turkish brigades, as well as small units from five other United Nations countries that had sent token fighting forces. On to the east a long arm of North Korean country stretched straight on up the Sea of Japan and came to an end some 70 miles below the Russian port of Vladivostok. Here on the Sea of Japan sector the X Corps, still under independent command of Major General Almond, mustered the U. S. 1st Marines, the 7th Infantry Division and two ROK divisions, with the fresh U. S. 3rd Division about to disembark at Wonsan, some 50 miles below the port of Hungnam. In the rugged central mountains, northwest of this coastal city of Hungnam, was the highly important Choshin reservoir, which was hooked into the vast Japanese-built electric power system that gave North Korea its industrial importance. Its power lines reached to the small-arms factories of the Chinese Communists at Mukden and to the mines and industrial plants of eastern Manchuria.

MacArthur's two field commanders, Walker and Almond, drove cautiously northward up both coasts despite the double threat of the Chinese Communists and the approaching winter. Victory was in sight—if their luck held out.

But always MacArthur had to depend largely on his own enthusiasm and demand for victory and his own will to win, with little real help from Washington. From the moment of the great success of the Inchon landing on, he had the whip hand and would have remained complete master of the battlefield if Washington had supported him with honest vigor. But this was not the case. General Collins had initially opposed him in the Inchon venture and only the backing of Louis A. Johnson, the then Secretary of Defense, had given him the chance to put it over. Johnson was now replaced by General Marshall, although it took a special act of Congress to permit a general on the active rolls to serve. Collins was still Army Chief of Staff, and Bradley head of the Joint Chiefs of Staff. Obviously MacArthur could hope for no real enthusiasm from the Pentagon clique.

Instead of the Washington crowd being full-heartedly behind a great surge for victory, the State Department seemed to give way to hidden pressures and secret threats by the timid or interfering members of the U. N. who, combined, had less than 10% of the total of American troops in Korea but demanded a major share in all decisions. How much of this tragic failure to stand squarely behind the American commander and Syngman Rhee may have influenced the Red Chinese in their decision to enter the war may never be known, but the inertia of the U. N. and its absurd power over the American State Department were largely responsible for the situation that soon resulted.

MacArthur knew he was taking a long chance to push boldly northward in the face of winter, but the enemy was groggy and ripe for the kill. It seemed certain that there must be secret and vicious interests working against him, but the possibility of victory was too strong to permit him to abandon this great chance to end the war. His worries were ceaseless and he was almost as one acting in the dark and far from home.

Around November 6 he cabled the Joint Chiefs of Staff that he could not be held responsible for what might happen unless he was given permission to bomb the Yalu bridges if affairs took a sudden turn for the worse. This was not forthcoming, but MacArthur still could not believe that if his armies actually faced a new war and the possibilities of destruction, he would continue to be denied the use of any and every weapon he possessed. Throughout the history of war this had been a recognized and unbroken tenet.

It was still impossible for him to understand fully the weight of the outside power exercised by the U. N. on the

480

American State Department—and, in turn, the overwhelming influence of the State Department on the White House and Pentagon. Under no circumstances could he believe he would be virtually abandoned.

2

Suddenly around November 10 much of the pressure against the advancing U. N. and ROK forces seemed to slacken. On the East the alert ROK Capital Division pushed rapidly up the coast along the Sea of Japan to Chongjin, only 60 miles from the Russian border. Meanwhile elements of the U. S. 1st Marine and the 7th Infantry Divisions, with the fresh 3rd Infantry Division supporting them, drove toward the great Choshin reservoir, 60 miles inland from the coast.

Cold blasts and light snowstorms began sweeping down from the north, and a weird sort of uncertainty gripped the front. On November 1 Russian-built jet Migs first appeared in combat. Well before this time enemy anti-aircraft batteries, secure in their protected nests north of the Yalu, were regularly shooting down American planes, which were scrupulously observing their restrictions to keep south of the border. To all this was added the definite intelligence that tens of thousands of Chinese Communist troops were now well below the Yalu.

Into the already crazy-quilt pattern there was violently injected a curious event that proved how deep-rooted were the global desires to conciliate and appease Russia, influenced in part by the demand among certain friendly nations for trade relations with Red China at any price. Sir Gladwyn Jebb, the British representative in the U. N., rose in the Security Council and proposed that Peiping be invited to send envoys to Lake Success to take part in the discussion of the Korean situation. (Sir Gladwyn was said to have shared in working out the details of the Yalta Agreement.)

On November 8 a formal invitation to put their case before the United Nations was sent to the Chinese Communists in Peiping, and their emissaries arrived in New York on November 24. It was to be a day of double significance in the swiftly unfolding tragedy on the Korean front.

Eight days before this, President Truman released a carefully worded statement regarding a Security Council resolution pledging that the Chinese frontier would be kept inviolate and that all U. N. forces would be withdrawn when a unified, independent and democratic government was established throughout Korea. What he said on November 16 showed his complete approval of the MacArthur strategy, and of the general point of view of the fighting leaders at the front:

> United Nations forces are now being attacked from the safety of a privileged sanctuary. Planes operating from bases in China cross over into Korea to attack United Nations ground and air forces and then flee back across the border. Chinese Communist and North Korean Communist forces are being reinforced, supplied and equipped from bases behind the safety of the Sino-Korean border.
>
> The pretext which the Chinese Communists advance for taking offensive action against United Nations forces in Korea from behind the protection afforded by the Sino-Korean border is their professed belief that these forces intend to carry hostilities across the frontier into Chinese territory.
>
> The resolutions and every other action taken by the United Nations demonstrate beyond any doubt that no such intention has ever been entertained. On the contrary, it has been repeatedly stated that it is the intention of the United Nations to localize the conflict and to withdraw its forces from Korea as soon as the situation permits.
>
> Speaking for the United States Government and people, I can give assurance that we support and are acting within the limits of the United Nations policy in Korea, and that we have never at any time entertained any intention to carry hostilities into China. . . .

It was the first time that the phrase "privileged sanctuary" had been used in a public document. It struck a bell in the minds of the worried field commanders, 10,000 miles away, who realized the desperate task they were undertaking but who had supreme confidence in their troops and in MacArthur's leadership—and in the old-fashioned vigor of American sovereignty and integrity.

Besides, these harassed soldiers were always sustained by

482

their belief that should the Red Chinese attack in great force, MacArthur would not be denied the right to use his bombers against the supply lines, bases and concentrations north of the Yalu.

It was the crux of the momentous decision he was shortly to take. His Intelligence, gathered from the several conventional agencies and the usual native spies, disclosed that an alarming infiltration of Red troops in small groups was beginning. The rugged nature of the terrain and the sub-zero weather made it most difficult for his G-2 spies to operate on both sides of the Yalu. And his own government had forbidden all aerial reconnaissance north of the river.

At best the entire operation was a desperate one. He had the remnants of the North Korean Army rocking on its heels. With luck he could push ahead for the knockout. All his commanders and intelligence groups realized the possibility of a sudden attack by infiltrated Red Chinese. However, to hold fast and await developments would probably have been disastrous. If the Red Chinese forces proved to be light in numbers, it would have been a fatal blunder not to have finished off the war. If the Chinese proved to be overwhelmingly strong, then not to move forward at this moment, with winter swiftly coming on, would have permitted the enemy to strike in force, infiltrate southward between MacArthur's armies, and cut off his supplies.

To withdraw his troops at this crucial moment would also have put him in an extremely dangerous position. If there were strong, organized groups of the Red Chinese, they could then attack his exposed flanks and rear. To lunge ahead in one great, final effort might still be effective, despite the very real possibility of disaster. If the Chinese should prove dangerously strong, it might, nevertheless, be safer to attack immediately than to try to hold his ground or attempt withdrawal.

On November 24 MacArthur flew to an advance air strip for a final conference and personal reconnaissance. In semi-private conversation with a division commander he dropped the remark that if the great attack succeeded, "the boys might be home by Christmas." "Home," to MacArthur, with Christmas 31 days away, meant the rest areas around Pusan or across the narrow straits to Japan. Newsmen picked up the sentence and sent it spinning around the world.

MacArthur had no illusions about the gamble he was taking in this final great effort. He and Walker and Almond knew well the formidable nature of the high mountainous area in the center of the peninsula. They were all concerned over the wide rugged gap that stretched between the Eighth Army and the independent X Corps, in the neighborhood of the difficult country around the great Choshin dam, 60 miles from the east-coast port of Hungnam. They understood clearly that they lacked the troops to guard the frozen passes in this central range running from north to south. If all-out Chinese intervention came, they had insufficient ground forces to stop its initial drive and shock. It would become a new war.

The 1st Marine Division and units of the 7th Division held both sides of the Choshin reservoir. On to the northeast along the coast where the upper border of Korea stretched to a width of almost 400 miles, the 17th Regiment of the U. S. 7th Division had driven straight to the hilltops and north slopes that looked down on the narrow Yalu river, far from its mouth. On the northern side of the river lay the "privileged sanctuary" of Manchuria. Here, far from its mouth, the Yalu was hardly more than a little stream, reminding the lonely, homesick American soldiers of little rivers they knew in their own far-away homeland.

It was a thin and tenuous U. N. line that ran on to the west at various distances below the river. In spots the uneven front was little more than a hard night's march from the Yalu for the swift-moving intruders, lightly equipped and fired by fanatical courage and bitter hatred.

On this November 24, 1950, after MacArthur drove by jeep from one division headquarters to another, he returned to his plane and as soon as it was airborne ordered his pilot, Tony Storey, to head for the west coast. When they picked up the river's mouth at Sinuiju, he told him to turn sharply to the right and fly eastward up the Yalu. The plane with its fighter escort kept two or three miles south of the broad river, and with perfect visibility at 16,000 feet MacArthur studied both sides of the river valley, rimmed in for the most part by snow-covered hills and mountains. It was a motionless front, with no evidence from the skies of enemy movement or build-up of any kind.

Back in Tokyo MacArthur's communiqué gave a definite impression of his high hopes. How much of his confidence was for troop consumption and how much to deceive the enemy, and how far he himself might have been in error is pure speculation. His statement, which later was so bitterly criticized, read:

> The United Nations massive compression envelopment in North Korea against the new Red armies operating there is now approaching its decisive effort. The isolating component of the pincer, our Air Forces of all types, have for the last three weeks, in a sustained attack of model coordination and effectiveness, successfully interdicted enemy lines of support from the north so that further reinforcement therefrom has been sharply curtailed and essential supplies markedly limited.
>
> The eastern sector of the pincer, with noteworthy and effective naval support, has steadily advanced in a brilliant tactical movement and has now reached a commanding enveloping position cutting in two the northern reaches of the enemy's geographical potential. [A reference to the fact that the 17th Regiment of the U. S. 7th Division had approached the Yalu at Hysanjin.]
>
> This morning the western sector of the pincer moved forward in general assault in an effort to complete the compression and close the vise.
>
> If successful this should for all practical purposes end the war, restore peace and unity to Korea, enable the prompt withdrawal of United Nations military forces, and permit the complete assumption by the Korean people and nation of full sovereignty and international equality. It is that for which we fight.

Within 48 hours after MacArthur's reconnaissance all uncertainty had ended. The great gamble had lost.

3

Little opposition was met the first day on either the west or east fronts by the advancing U. N. and ROK troops. But by the end of the second day a strong counteroffensive by Chinese Communist troops drove down the narrow, twisting valleys of the central north-south range, penetrating to a depth of as much as 20 miles. The Red columns then turned sharply to the west to overwhelm two ROK divisions on the right of the Eighth Army. The U. S. 2nd Division, backing up the two ROK divisions, suddenly faced on its right flank the full fury of this great enveloping movement. The shoe was now on the other foot.

What had seemed ample plans for an orderly retirement of the U. N. forces had been prepared, in case overwhelming Chinese numbers were encountered. But there had been little advance information concerning this powerful attack of no less than seven Chinese divisions, which swiftly drove a wedge down through these rugged and apparently impassable mountains between the U. N. east and west forces.

These attacking Red units had been carefully hidden above the U. N. lines, and then thousands of lightly equipped Chinese foot soldiers, each carrying his own slender rations of ground grain and 200 rounds of rifle ammunition, poured down through the mountain passes despite the sub-zero weather. Others, packing light machine guns and mortars, moved straight to the flanks and rear of the surprised U. N. and ROK troops, cutting their supply lines, blocking the roads of retreat and going to their own death with the same fanaticism displayed by the Japanese in the great war.

Meanwhile the Eighth Army divisions to the left or west of the U. S. 2nd Division, fighting with superb courage on the flank of Walker's Eighth Army, were being assailed by direct frontal attacks, launched by the Chinese without regard to casualties. The U. N. forces gave ground, but they were able to evacuate all their heavy guns and equipment. Within six days the Eighth Army was driven below the Chongchon river, and when the Chinese assaults gradually weakened, the American, South Korean and U. N. forces crossed the Taedong river to the south to positions that permitted them to regroup and reorganize their units. Only the U. S. 2nd Division, fighting desperately to hold the Eighth Army's flank, had lost heavily in this vicious action on the west side of the peninsula.

Over toward the central area, parts of the U. S. 1st Marine

Division and units of the 7th Division of Almond's X Corps found themselves surrounded in a mountainous pocket below the great Choshin reservoir. Chinese forces in large numbers had quickly turned eastward from their middle wedge, to cut in below the reservoir, and were now driving hard for the east coast, in a vast enveloping movement that would deny the U. N. and the South Korean forces of the X Corps all escape except by sea. But more of this battle later.

Two days after the U. N. offensive had commenced, MacArthur's intelligence estimate of the Chinese strength rose to 80,000, and within a week the figure was set at 200,000. Later a revised figure gave the number of Chinese Communists at a quarter-million, while the estimate of additional freshly organized and re-equipped North Korean troops rose as high as 150,000.

MacArthur apparently had not anticipated the unique ability of the Chinese leaders to slip tens of thousands of troops across the Yalu without detection. These lightly armed Red Chinese soldiers, clad only in padded coolie garments, operated in small, self-contained units, and by night marches they moved safely into Korean mountain hide-outs. From these their Chinese leaders secretly poured them down the central mountain valleys for their surprise flank attacks.

No single agency of information of the several that belonged to the U. S. Central Intelligence, the State Department and the G-2 sections of the U. N. and ROK armies had fully warned of the presence of such gigantic hordes that seemed to spring up from nowhere. It had been a brilliant and superbly executed enemy surprise move, the strength of which was fully uncovered only when MacArthur ordered his attack of November 24.

He was long to face bitter criticism for this failure to esti mate properly the size of the Red invading forces. But probably had he known the full facts, there would have been no alternative better than the course he followed. Certainly he would have exercised the greatest caution in what promised to be the final battle for victory, had he sensed the almost unbelievable fact that he would be denied the full use of the only weapon—his offensive air arm—that could swing the tide in his

487

favor. It was easy for his critics to see the picture after the disaster was over. The fact that no less than two million North Korean refugees fled southward, crowding the roads and hampering troop movements, brought fresh complications to MacArthur's commanders.

Four days after he had begun what was now described as a great "reconnaissance-in-force," MacArthur issued a communiqué that made no attempt to conceal the facts.

Enemy reactions developed in the course of our assault operations of the past four days disclose that a major segment of the Chinese continental armed forces in army, corps and divisional organization of an aggregate strength of over 200,000 men, is now arrayed against the United Nations forces in North Korea.

There exists the obvious intent and preparation for support of these forces by heavy reinforcements now concentrated within the privileged sanctuary north of the international boundary and constantly moving forward.

Consequently, we face an entirely new war. This has shattered the high hopes we entertained that the intervention of the Chinese was only of a token nature on a volunteer and individual basis as publicly announced, and that therefore the war in Korea could be brought to a rapid close by our movement to the international boundary and the prompt withdrawal thereafter of United Nations forces, leaving Korean problems for settlement by the Koreans themselves.

It now appears to have been the enemy's intent, in breaking off contact with our forces some two weeks ago, to secure the time necessary surreptitiously to build up for a later surprise assault upon our lines in overwhelming force, taking advantage of the freezing of all rivers and roadbeds which would have materially reduced the effectiveness of our air interdiction and permitted a greatly accelerated forward movement of enemy reinforcements and supplies. This plan has been disrupted by our own offensive action, which forced upon the enemy a premature engagement.

Possibly due to orders or suggestions from Washington the General added a concluding paragraph to his comment:

This situation, repugnant as it may be, poses issues beyond the authority of the United Nations military council—issues which must find their solution within the councils of the United Nations and chancelleries of the world.

Already a surge of violent personal attacks and bitter criticism against MacArthur began to appear. Certain correspondents at the front, who had for some time been more or less unfriendly to him, made no attempt to soften their attacks on him. He was accused of making "a momentous blunder." One Washington columnist declared that "MacArthur thus walked into a huge, well-laid trap." And the correspondent of a weekly news magazine insisted that "perhaps it might become the worst military disaster in American history."

On December 1, the day that a special message was sent to Congress by the President, MacArthur gave out a statement in answer to a series of questions cabled him by Hugh Baillie, President of the United Press. Part of the statement read:

Never before has the patience of man been more sorely tried nor high standards of human behavior been more patiently and firmly upheld than during the course of the Korean campaigns. From the initiation of the North Korean aggression against the Republic of Korea until the total defeat of the North Korean armies, support from the Communist Chinese from behind the privileged sanctuary of neutral boundaries was open and notorious and all-inclusive. . . .

The existing situation under which the United Nations Command is confronted with a new and fresh and well trained and equipped enemy of vastly superior and ever increasing numbers initiating an entirely new war to cover the North Korean defeat, results largely from the acceptance of military odds without precedent in history—the odds of permitting offensive action without defensive retaliation. These odds have been and are being cheerfully accepted in the effort to uphold the high principles and standards which have characterized guiding policy and given nobility to the cause for which we fight, and to further the universal desire that the war be localized. Indeed, throughout the war against the North Koreans we meticulously respected and held inviolate the international boundary, and I at no time even recommended that authority be granted to retaliate beyond it. Against such odds, officers and men of all services and participating nations have fought, and if need be, will continue to fight, with unexcelled gallantry.

MacArthur's patience had almost reached its breaking point. Open and frequent angry criticism now appearing in the foreign press seemed to be the last straw. Washington and the U. N. at Lake Success might be impressed by the logic of these adverse opinions, but certainly he was not. He spared no effort to show exactly how he felt, as he continued in the special statement:

> With this background of devotion to high principles and invincible determination to achieve the stated objectives of the United Nations, it is disturbing indeed to note the irresponsible comments appearing in responsible sections of the European press. There appears to be a general failure, intentional or from misinformation, to comprehend the mission prescribed for this Command by resolutions of the United Nations of which their governments were joint architects and directors, or fairly to recognize that in success or adversity this Command has proceeded unerringly in compliance with controlling policies and directives.
>
> I can only attribute this to a somewhat selfish though most short-sighted viewpoint. To the European the welfare and security of Europe is naturally paramount. He has no fear of attack from the West, solely from the East. It is not unusual therefore that he sees in every dedication of friendly resource toward the stabilization of Asia but a subtraction from that available for the betterment and security of Europe. This is of course fallacious reasoning. Any breach freedom in the East carries with it a sinister threat to freedom in the West. The issue is a global one and failure to comprehend this fact carries the germs of freedom's ultimate destruction. If the fight is not waged with courage and invincible determination to meet the challenge here, it will indeed be fought, and possibly lost, on the battlefields of Europe. . . .

There were immediate and violent retorts to the General's remarks on the "somewhat selfish though most short-sighted viewpoint" of certain European nations. He was accused of entering the field of international politics and of overstepping the boundaries of a field commander. During the next two days he answered no less than five cabled requests from newspapers and news magazines for public statements.

For possibly the first time in his life his professional military reputation was being attacked. He tried his best to hold his

490

temper and to explain as simply as he could how he had arrived at his decision to move against the Red Chinese, even though far from certain of their real strength. In answer to one of several questions from a list submitted by a group of Tokyo correspondents, he wrote out a concise explanation. It read:

> This probing movement [of November 24] was essential to develop the Chinese purpose and strength. The only other recourse would have been to resign ourselves to the possibility of a devastating strike in such power as to completely destroy the Eighth Army. It was the only chance we had to ascertain the truth or falsity of the Chinese contention that his intervention was merely on a volunteer and individual basis. The proximity of the main borderline to the battlefront, only a night's march separating them, and the impossibility of reconnoitering beyond the border lines by our planes made it imperative to develop the true state of affairs.
>
> I agree completely with General Walker's estimate that this probing effort was made none too soon. Had our forces remained indefinitely impassive, it would not only have foregone all chances of concluding the North Korean campaign which would have signalled the withdrawal of main forces from Korea and the avoidance of a long winter stalemate, but prolonged inertia would have greatly increased our jeopardy by permitting an indefinite build-up of the enemy force, which might well have resulted in the complete destruction of the Eighth Army. The present adverse situation is not in the slightest degree due to our assault tactics but is the sole result of the enemy's predominant strength in numbers. In my opinion, it was a fortunate move.

Suddenly the White House stepped into the picture. The all-powerful State Department and its comrades in the U. N. had their own twisted versions and desires to be turned out by the official propaganda machine. On December 6, ten days after the disastrous turn of events, the Joint Chiefs of Staff dispatched a cable to MacArthur embodying a general Presidential order allegedly sent to all responsible officials. One paragraph read that "no speech, press release, or other statement concerning military policy should be released until it has received clearance from the Department of Defense."

A special clause directed to the Secretary of State and Secretary of Defense was obviously intended for MacArthur. It said:

> Officials overseas, including military commanders and diplomatic representatives, should be ordered to exercise extreme caution in public statements, to clear all but routine statements with their departments, and to refrain from direct communication on military or foreign policy with newspapers, magazines or other publicity media in the United States.
>
> The above is transmitted to you for guidance and appropriate action.

There was nothing for MacArthur to do but to accept what he knew was a full-fledged gag.

Meanwhile the Chinese Communist emissaries from Peiping had arrived in New York City and were arrogantly announcing that before they would enter into a discussion over Korea, the United States must be put on trial before the United Nations for its actions in entering the civil war.

4

By late December it was clear that Walker had saved his Eighth Army, although his 6th and 8th ROK Divisions were overrun, and his fine U. S. 2nd Division was badly cut up. The "human-wave" tactics of the Communists had been difficult and costly to stop, but Walker and his commanders had discovered within a week after the first attack started that the Reds seemed to lack the ability fully to exploit their gains. Once the momentum of their attack was lost, they had to stop and re-group and bring in fresh troops and supplies. Walker made full use of these lulls, and by December 15 his forces were in defensive positions below the Imjin river and along the 38th parallel.

From November 27, when the Chinese counteroffensive started, on to December 12, Walker's four U. S. divisions had suffered casualties that totalled 6,326, with an additional 1,011 for other U. N. units involved. This did not include the ROK divisions. Only the U. S. 2nd Infantry had been disastrously hit; its losses numbered 4,131 in killed, wounded and missing, roughly 25% of its total strength during the fifteen days it had fought to protect the vulnerable right flank of the Eighth Army. It was hardly comparable to the 60% casualties by the U. S. division principally involved during the first fourteen days of fighting in the Bulge in December of 1944. That catastrophe, due almost entirely to faulty and inexcusable intelligence, had been accepted as merely one of the misfortunes of war. But not so for MacArthur in Korea.

On the eastern side of the peninsula the great counter-offensive had caught Almond's X Corps stretched from a position 60 miles from the Siberian border to a point westward on the Yalu, and then on southwest to the Choshin reservoir, in the mountainous areas in the center. From here the lightly held U. N. front ran in a wide arc that swung to the south-eastward as far down the Sea of Japan as the port of Wonsan. At the moment the Reds struck, the ROK Capital Division held the post near the Siberian border at Hyesanjin: the 17th Regiment of the U. S. 7th Division looked down on the Yalu; and the rugged country around the Choshin reservoir on the southwest was defended by the 1st and 7th Regiments of the U. S. 1st Marines, and a battalion each from the 31st and 32nd regiments of the 7th Division, with a reinforced company of British Marine commandos. Such were the dispositions on the east when the Red Chinese started their vicious counteroffensive.

Orders were received for the Marines of the X Corps to attempt the relief of the hard-pressed right flank of Walker's Eighth Army on to the west of the central gap, but before they could undertake the mission, the Chinese attacked them in great numbers from the north and west. Withdrawing down the west side of the great reservoir, they were joined by the two battalions of the U. S. 7th Division and the British Commandos from the east side of the dam, only to discover that the enemy had cut their escape and supply route to the southeast toward the port city of Hungnam.

Fighting desperately, the embattled group attacked the enemy concentrations and roadblocks and foot by foot drove their way toward the coast. Enemy rifle and machine guns and mortars swept the slippery, frozen trails and hairpin curves.

At times the U. N. troops were completely enveloped, and there seemed little chance of escaping death or capture.

Their main hope lay in help from the air. Cut off from all supplies, they would have perished from the ceaseless attacks of the enemy and the cold and exposure, had it not been for the hundreds of air missions that brought them ammunition, food and medicine. Supplies of all sorts were parachuted to them, and wherever a makeshift air strip could be found, fearless C-47 pilots quickly landed their food and ammunition, and when they took off, they carried wounded and sick men. Time and again pilots from the Far East air force and the Marine and Navy air units risked their lives in these errands of mercy. A total of almost 5,000 U. N. wounded and sick men were evacuated by air. Many were the victims of frostbite, and were not listed as battle casualties.

At one spot on the endless 60-mile journey a 20-yard section of one-way road had to be carved out of a rock hillside and a new escape route established. A little later a key bridge was suddenly blown up by the Communists, and it seemed that only by abandoning all their vehicles and heavy equipment and even their wounded, could the Americans and their friends possibly escape from the trap. But the next day the Combat Cargo Command dispatched 8 C-119s, each carrying a two-ton bridge span, which was carefully dropped near the treacherous chasm. Army combat engineers attached to the ground force somehow managed to bolt together the spans and swing them across the gap, in the face of heavy mortar and machine-gun fire. Once again the road was open, and the trucks carrying the dead and wounded moved on toward the Sea of Japan.

MacArthur ordered that every possible effort be made to aid the survivors, and shortly a reinforced battalion of the 1st Marine Regiment, accompanied by a special force of Army combat engineers, rolled out of Hamhung, determined to fight its way to a junction with its comrades. It was a great day for the bruised and exhausted men of the retreating column when heavy firing was heard far down the escape route. Then the fighting came closer, and finally the rescuers broke through.

494

The heavy roadblocks in front had been broken, and now the weary men, braced by this fresh unit, battled their way down the high mountain passes and icy trails to the gentle slopes that led to the coast and freedom. For 13 days these men, who had at the beginning numbered almost 20,000, had fought for their lives.

The U. S. 3rd Division's 65th Regiment from Puerto Rico now formed the protecting rear guard as the survivors made their way to the port city of Hungnam.

MacArthur flew in on December 11 to meet them and to thank them for their brave fight. After all, it was the Chinese Communists and not these veterans who had really lost the campaign. The Reds had failed in both their east and west attempts at complete envelopment and destruction of the U. N. and South Korean forces. The enemy had taken terrible losses, in certain frontal attacks possibly running as high as 10 to 1 against them. The U. N. forces had been driven back, but they had not been annihilated, and with help and luck they could still win and Korea be free and united.

Here on the east Almond's three American divisions had up to December 12 suffered a total of 5,638 battle casualties—and probably an almost equal number of sick men, most of whom were hospitalized for frostbite. The 1st Marine Division led in battle casualties with 2,891; the 7th Infantry Division was next with 2,097; and the battle losses of the 3rd Infantry Division were 650.

The 17th Regiment of the U. S. 7th Division of Almond's X Corps, which reached the Yalu, and the ROK Capital Division, which had penetrated deep into the country toward Siberia, along with other scattered outfits, had safely pulled back shortly after the Red counterattack opened and had either embarked by sea or gone southward over the east coastal roads toward the great concentration port of Hungnam. A strong defense perimeter was now thrown around the city as preparations went ahead for a complete evacuation by water.

A total of 193 vessels was employed in the vast undertaking. It went smoothly ahead while the Chinese Communists fed in piecemeal thousands of fanatical troops, which were destroyed in their wild attempts to penetrate the defense perimeter.

From Hungnam and the two other ports of Wonsan and Sing-jin, a grand total of 105,000 U. N. and ROK troops were evacuated with 98,000 civilian refugees. In all 350,000 tons of cargo were salvaged, and 17,500 vehicles were safely loaded. Even a number of captured Russian-made self-propelled 76-mm. guns were taken out.

For two weeks the fighting around the great arc of the perimeter at Hungnam was desperate and almost continuous. Newly organized Red North Korean divisions were brought down through the mountain passes and thrown recklessly against the defending lines. Gradually the perimeter was shortened, until finally on the day before Christmas only the rear guard, comprising 9,000 men of the U. S. 3rd Infantry Division, manned the inner defense lines.

A scorched-earth policy had been followed by the U. N. forces, and on this final day, while carrier-based planes showered the enemy areas with rockets and bombs of every description, the remaining American troops took to the open-mouthed landing ships and shoved off. It was 2:46 on the afternoon of this day before Christmas 1950 when the last man was safely embarked.

5

The military crisis that MacArthur suddenly faced in the last week of November had been squarely and successfully met. Despite his heavy losses, both his Eighth Army on the west and his independent X Corps on the east had been withdrawn successfully. But all North Korea was in the hands of the Communists by Christmas.

MacArthur had been forced by Washington and the United Nations to fight this wholly new war with his offensive air arm tied behind his back. The speculative fear that Russia might start World War III if the Manchurian border was crossed in the air was still the No. 1 consideration in Washington, Lake Success, London, Delhi and a score of other capitals.

To this paralyzing effect of fear there was now added a general confusion and what appeared to many to be a devious shiftiness on the part of the leadership in Washington. Three days after the great Chinese Communist attack began on November 26, President Truman issued a statement that was followed on the next day by a special message to Congress. A threat that the atomic bomb might be used brought Prime Minister Attlee by fastest plane from London. He was assured by Truman and Acheson that no step would be taken that need alarm the Socialist Premier, regardless of what might happen to American and U. N. troops in Korea.

It would seem a complete psychosis of fear suddenly paralyzed all efforts by American leaders and their friends in the free world. They seemed unable longer to think clearly and logically about the possibility of the Soviet Union starting World War III in retaliation for an American and U. N. move against Red Chinese territory. The timid or designing men in control apparently subscribed to the theory that the moment an American plane crossed the Red Chinese border Russia would start a full global war.

Both Washington and the General Assembly of the U. N. apparently overlooked the fact that Red China had deliberately made open war against America and the United Nations and their ward Korea, and that it was their right and duty to fight the Red invaders with every available weapon—including the air arm. The pro-Russian appeasers apparently dominated all official thought and propaganda.

So strong was the pressure from England and India and European nations generally, that the patent argument that Russia herself did not want war and was not yet ready for war was overlooked or pushed aside. To MacArthur and his people under the gun it was abundantly clear that Russia needed several more years to build her long-range bomber planes and stock-pile her atomic bombs. Time was what Russia needed most, and MacArthur held to the solid belief that only an actual invasion of the homeland of the Soviet Union could have pulled her into war.

Yet so complete had been the poisoning of the American mind by Red-spy and fellow-traveller propaganda and by the terror-stricken and, in many cases, disloyal leaders that Amer-

497

ica was no longer master of her own fate. Her once brave and open mind was turned into a hotbed for carefully planted seeds of fear and confusion.

MacArthur was unable at this time fully to comprehend to what a great extent un-American forces and pressures had taken over the direction of American foreign policies. But he knew that never before in her history had his country been so deliberately handicapped in war that her field commanders, once they had their directives, were prohibited from using every force and every weapon they possessed to meet the enemy and defeat him quickly.

6

On December 14, 1950, the U. N. General Assembly "viewed with grave concern the situation in the Far East," and passed a resolution requesting the President of the Assembly, Nasrollah Entezam, of Iran, to appoint a group of three to determine a basis for a cease-fire. On December 23 Communist Peiping promptly turned down the suggestion. This was followed by a bitterly resisted resolution of the U. N. Security Council declaring the Chinese Communists to be the aggressors.

But what MacArthur needed was a clear-cut directive from the Joint Chiefs of Staff granting him the right to win the war, with the privilege of *hot pursuit* for his hamstrung planes, allowing them to enter the "privileged sanctuary" of Manchuria, when driving off Red planes attacking them from the far side of the Yalu.

The theory of hot pursuit is based on an ancient doctrine of criminal law that permits a peace officer who is closely pursuing a felon to cross beyond the area of his jurisdiction in order to capture the criminal. The granting of immunity from pursuit to Communist planes attacking U. N. air forces inside North Korea was in direct opposition to this old and accepted doctrine of criminal and international law.

During the days of late November and early December, 1950, when MacArthur's forces faced the possibility of destruction by invading Red Chinese forces from north of the

Yalu, he could secure no authority to pursue these attacking MIG's to their bases, nor was he permitted air reconnaissance over Manchuria. However, early in January of 1951 there seemed to be a unanimous agreement among MacArthur, the Joint Chiefs of Staff, the President and even the Secretary of State that his planes should be granted this right of hot pursuit after being attacked.

Sufficient authority for the action lay in the command function delegated by the U. N. to the United States government, but the Secretary of Defense George Marshall now hedged by asking Acheson to inform the thirteen U. N. nations having armed forces actually engaged in some form or other in the Korean conflict of the probable change in policy. Acheson took it upon himself not to inform the allies but to question them regarding their views on this matter—a matter that meant life or death to the men fighting against heavy odds in Korea. The first six nations approached, according to the subsequent testimony of the Secretary, stood out against the proposal of permitting MacArthur to exercise this needed military action of hot pursuit. So it was that the American Secretary of State's mind, if not already fixed, was made up for him by distinctly foreign pressures. Neither the needs of American soldiers and airmen nor traditional national honor had much or anything to do with his decision.

Shortly after MacArthur's request for hot pursuit was turned down by Washington, he asked a second time for the right to bomb troublesome Racin, the busy Red Chinese supply base in North Korea some 35 miles from the Siberian-Korean border. For a second time he was promptly turned down, although his bomber commanders had given him positive assurance that there was no chance of violating Siberian territory in the air attack.

Sometime before this MacArthur had helped in drawing up a study for victory that was made by the Joint Chiefs of Staff. The paper then was duly presented to Secretary of Defense Marshall. MacArthur's troops were now holding a line that roughly strung along the 37th parallel. This marked the low point of the great U. N. withdrawal. Pressure by the Communist Chinese was negligible, and the time was arriving when MacArthur and Ridgway felt they might regain the offensive and start the long march back up the peninsula. (Lt. General Matthew Ridgway, with the personal approval of MacArthur, was brought to Korea to command the Eighth Army, after the courageous Walker had been killed in a jeep accident just before Christmas. The X Corps would soon be evacuated from Hungnam to become a part of the Eighth Army.)

MacArthur and his commanders realized fully at this moment of decision how much it would mean if a driving will-to-win could replace the fear and the restraining attitude that prevailed in Washington and at the U. N. General Assembly. MacArthur, as always, thought only in terms of victory and in the spirit of the offensive. He had contributed four specific points to the over-all list of 16 suggestions about what should be done to win the war and remove the threat of a disastrous stalemate. Apparently his four clauses won the approval of the JCS, but on January 9 Secretary of Defense Marshall ordered that these specific MacArthur suggestions be thrown out. Who counselled Marshall in arriving at this momentous decision is still not known. The four proposals MacArthur made were:

1 intensification of the economic blockade against China
2 imposition of a naval blockade against the China coast
3 removal of restrictions on air reconnaissance of China's coastal areas and Manchuria
4 removal of restrictions on the forces of the Republic of China on Formosa, with logistical support to contribute to their effective operation against the Chinese mainland.

About this same time it appeared to MacArthur's G.H.Q. that there was a slacking off in the censorship gag that had been imposed by the President on December 6. As it was interpreted in Tokyo, the original directive applied only to formal public statements and not to communiqués, correspondence or personal conversations. At a press conference in Washington shortly after the turn of the year, the President had denied any curb on MacArthur's authority "to speak freely on the Korean war."

Exactly two months after the Chinese Communists entered the war in force, MacArthur ordered the launching of the first large U. N. counteroffensive. His battle lines were now roughly 200 miles south of the former extreme positions he had held on the North Korean front, from which his Eighth Army and the X Corps had begun their great attacks of November 24 and their subsequent retreat a few days later.

The X Corps, now re-grouped and re-organized, added materially to the power of Ridgway's Eighth Army. MacArthur had been severely criticized in certain military circles for retaining this X Corps under his own G.H.Q. after the Inchon landing and its subsequent dispatch to the east coast as an independent unit.

His critics claimed that the swift surprise penetration in late November by Red Chinese infantry divisions through the mountainous gap that separated the Eighth Army and the X Corps was primarily the cause for the vast disaster that followed. MacArthur's defenders answered that lack of troops alone had made it impossible to man adequately the gap between the two forces, and as a consequence it had seemed most practical to operate the two groups independently. When they were again in close contact after the end of the great Red attack, MacArthur ordered the X Corps to become a part of Ridgway's Eighth Army.

Toward the middle of January U. N. reconnaissance groups prodding the enemy front suddenly discovered little opposition, and on January 25, 1951, a concerted counteroffensive was begun. By February 10 the port of Inchon and the important Kimpo airfield were re-captured, but Seoul still remained in Communist hands. Resistance suddenly stiffened, and on the night of February 11 and 12 the enemy once again drove hard to the south down the lower middle corridor of the peninsula.

The following day MacArthur flew in from Tokyo for personal observation and for a front-line conference with Ridgway and his commanders. Probably due to the handicaps still put on his Air Force, his communiqué ended on a pessimistic note:

Talk of crossing the 38th parallel at the present stage of the campaign, except by scattered patrol action incidental to the tactical situation, is purely academic. From a military standpoint we must materially reduce the existing superiority of our Chinese Communist enemy engaging with impunity in undeclared war against us, with the unprecedented military advantage of sanctuary protection for his military potential against our counterattack upon Chinese soil, before we can seriously consider conducting major operations north of that geographical line. . . .

The new Red counterattack of middle February had won some success in the center of the peninsula, but within ten days the lost ground had been regained by the U. N. troops. MacArthur pondered the idea of a by-pass far up the west coast that might permit him to repeat his great strategic and tactical victory after the Inchon landing of September 1950. But he did not have the troops to dare undertake any such operation.

The establishment of NATO and its immediate implementation in December 1950 by the dispatching of General Eisenhower to Europe again placed European demands above American interests in the Far East. And without sufficient reinforcements and the right to wage a war for victory and to make full use of all available weapons and air here in Korea, MacArthur and his advisors knew perfectly well how little chance they had if they attempted any bold and decisive strategic move.

Once again a large-scale participation in Europe had assumed No. 1 priority over the Pacific. It was apparent that for a second time America was abandoning her own soldiers and their war for survival in the Far East, in favor of responding to the pressure for European help, when it was doubtful whether immediate military help was needed. Obviously there was still a lack of understanding in Washington of the fact that Asia was as important as Europe in the global strategy of checking the Communist expansion. Likewise there was a complete failure to estimate Europe's lack of a will to fight.

Some hidden directing power, some Red plan or Communist line exercising its controlling supervision in a secret web of intrigue seemed actually to be pulling the strings and calling the tunes for certain of the spiritless leaders in Washington and at the U. N. It seems certain that MacArthur glimpsed the plot that pointed to his own ultimate sacrifice and to a war stalemate as part of the appeasement policy to Russia and Red China. Suspicion must have entered his mind that he was not supposed to win the Korean war as long as there was the slightest chance of any retaliation by Russia. General Eisenhower and his NATO must now come first in everything.

[The influence of foreign political considerations and pressures in dictating the half-hearted directives that were sent to MacArthur were almost as clear to him at the time as they appeared later when he could see them in retrospect. His ultimate analysis of the motives behind his orders were eventually contained in a letter he sent to Senator Harry F. Byrd of Virginia on April 19, 1953, in response to a request by the Senator for information regarding the artillery shell shortages in Korea. Part of the statement covers so accurately the middle period of MacArthur's Korean days that it is well worth reading:

> The inertia of our diplomacy failed utterly to utilize the victory of Inchon and subsequent destruction of the North Korean armies as the basis for swift and dynamic political action to restore peace and unity to Korea.
>
> This was one of the great contributing causes to the subsequent new war into which we were later plunged by Red China. At this time a new war with this much more formidable foe was not foreseen. . . .
>
> My own military estimate was that with our largely unopposed air forces, with their atomic potential, capable of destroying at will bases of attack and lines of supply north as well as south of the Yalu River, no Chinese military commander would dare hazard the commitment of large forces upon the Korean peninsula. The risk of their utter destruction, through lack of supply would be too great.
>
> But by one process or another it was conjectured by, or conveyed to, the Red Chinese that even though they entered the fray in large force it would be under the sanctuary of being relieved from any destructive action of our military forces within their own areas. Such a limitation upon the utilization of available military force to repel an enemy attack has no precedent either in our own history or, so far as I know, in the history of the world.
>
> The results were disastrous beyond imagination and are still incalculable. When the Chinese Communists actually struck without warning, and my order to destroy the bridges at their

503

points of entry over the Yalu into Korea was immediately counter-manded from Washington, I realized for the first time the extraordinary decision which had been made to deny me the use of my full military power to safeguard the lives of my soldiers and ensure the safety of the army.

To me it clearly foreshadowed the tragic situation which has since developed and left me with a sense of shock I had never before experienced in a long life crammed with explosive reactions and momentous hazards. . . .]

7

On the eve of a new U. N. counteroffensive MacArthur again flew to the front and gave his full approval to the plans for a ground by-pass of Seoul, a surprise air-drop at Munsan, some 30 miles above the South Korean capital, and then a general drive northward on a broad front across the peninsula at the 38th parallel. He released his military comment in Tokyo on March 7, the day marked for the important U. N. counteroffensive. The statement seemed to bear the marks of a man desperately trying to keep himself under control and to fight on despite the inhibitions and restraints imposed on him by decisions that he held in great suspicion. His words reflected his futile attempts to fight a fire with half the water supply turned off. It read in part:

> Assuming no diminution of the enemy's flow of ground forces and matériel to the Korean battle area, a continuation of the existing limitation upon our freedom of counter-offensive action, and no major additions to our organizational strength, the battle lines cannot fail in time to reach a point of theoretical military stalemate.
>
> Thereafter our further advance would militarily benefit the enemy more than it would ourselves. The exact place of stabilization is of necessity a fluctuating variable, dependent upon the shifting relative strengths of the forces committed, and will constantly move up or down.
>
> Even now there are indications that the enemy is attempting to build up from China a new and massive offensive for the spring. . . .
>
> Vital decisions have yet to be made—decisions far beyond the

scope of the authority vested in me as the Military Commander, decisions which are neither solely political nor solely military, but which must provide, on the highest international levels, an answer to the obscurities which now becloud the unsolved problems raised by Red China's undeclared war in Korea.

The final paragraph epitomized to him the deep injustice of his position. He still could get no final decisions from Washington—"decisions far beyond the scope of authority vested in me as the Military Commander, decisions which are neither solely political nor solely military."

The confused and badgered Joint Chiefs of Staff under the authority of General Marshall, Secretary of Defense, apparently had succumbed completely to the dictates of the Department of State. As a result of this, MacArthur was constantly hampered by a complete lack of adequate directives or by half-hearted ones that held him responsible but refused to give him proper authority.

Here lay at least part of the growing differences between himself and the Big Three who were supposed to be running the war in Washington—President Truman, Secretary of State Acheson and Secretary of Defense Marshall.

In talks with friendly visitors General MacArthur made perfectly clear his own disturbed feelings. He had seen the great war victory in Europe dissipated and destroyed because of the unrealistic attitude of American political and military leaders who utterly failed to press the need for a long-range peace victory. And many of these same leaders were still in authority in Washington.

He had seen these same men or their approved successors stand by or actually take part in the series of events that let China go Red. They had been prepared to see Formosa fall and South Korea overrun. With rare patience he tried his best to get along with them. More than once members of the Joint Chiefs of Staff were sent from Washington to Tokyo to bend MacArthur to some phase of the administration's policy of conciliation and appeasement. Invariably MacArthur's eloquent and compelling logic and his appeal to pure American interests won over these emissaries to his point of view.

"Go back and sell this to Washington!" MacArthur would urge. "You believe it."

Invariably nothing happened. The arguments of what was good for America seemed of small consequence in Washington when placed against the constant pressures of those nations in the U. N. General Assembly that were bent on appeasement. Slowly MacArthur became convinced that the terrible sacrifices made in Korea for a righteous cause had assumed a distinctly second place, even in the minds of the highest American authorities. The Internationalists, the Europe-Firsters, the Red appeasers, the U. N. worshippers were in full control. Even the President, who had appeared to be definitely on Mac-Arthur's side during the late days of the great war and at the start of the Japanese occupation, now apparently had been fully won over by the Acheson-Marshall combination.

But deeper than this personal side, MacArthur unquestionably sensed the determination of certain of these top-level men of the administration to break down the American people's resistance to a One-World, internationalist attitude, and by propaganda and fear to appease the U. N. countries that were condoning the great Communist advance here in stricken Korea.

Vague rumors came to him in Tokyo that the trio in power were now prepared to buy a cease-fire that could only lead to a perpetual stalemate. It was to be bought at the price of the surrender of Formosa to Red China, and her recognition and ultimate seating in the United Nations in place of Chiang Kai-shek's Nationalist government. MacArthur's strong sense of realism and patriotism could not permit him to ignore what this would mean to his country and the free world.

His counteroffensive of March 7, 1951, was completely successful. Seoul was by-passed and swiftly abandoned by the enemy without a fight. On March 23, the U. S. 187th Regimental Combat Team was parachuted to the area near Munsan, well north of the battle lines, and an armored column drove straight through to contact it and complete the encirclement. But the Communists had retired before the threat, and there was no large bag of prisoners. Four days after the air-drop, two ROK corps crossed the 38th parallel near the east coast port of Yangyang, on the Sea of Japan.

MacArthur was now ready to send his U. N. troops north of the parallel as soon as he secured formal permission from the Joint Chiefs of Staff. His crippling air limitations still were a severe handicap, but once again he was master of the battlefield. With proper backing in material and morale he thought he could still drive out the Red Chinese invaders. Stubbornly he planned a great double envelopment north of Inchon. He could still win the war and return North Korea to the legal republic.

On March 20 he received a somewhat obscure message from the JCS. The word "State" in the message obviously referred to the State Department. It read:

To: Commander in Chief, Far East, Tokyo, Japan
From: Joint Chiefs of Staff.

State planning Presidential announcement shortly that, with clearing of bulk of South Korea of aggression, United Nations now prepared to discuss conditions of settlement in Korea. Strong UN feeling persists that further diplomatic effort toward settlement should be made before any advance with major forces north of 38th Parallel. Time will be required to determine diplomatic reactions and permit new negotiations that may develop. Recognizing that parallel has no military significance, State has asked JCS what authority you should have to permit sufficient freedom of action for next few weeks to provide security for UN forces and maintain contact with enemy. Your recommendations desired.

It was obvious to MacArthur that a big sellout was about to take place. Apparently the best he could hope for was a talk marathon, a futile effort to arrive at a settlement with a Moscow-dominated enemy that would accept no compromise short of a united Red Korea. Four days after he received the ambiguous message MacArthur wrote out a lengthy statement. It must have seemed to him that this was his last chance to help check a political move that might well be disastrous to both Korea and America. The Eighth Army, with its air arm still tied behind its back, was advancing and ready to cross the

507

38th parallel. He might still press for a conclusion of the war, despite the intrigues in Washington and in the General Assembly of the U. N.

There can be no question but that he was now personally proposing decisions "neither solely political nor solely military." And it is likewise evident that he was cutting squarely across what was probably a devious and far-fetched plan by the U. N. for an appeasement settlement, as suggested in the note from the Joint Chiefs of Staff. MacArthur knew the risks of personal censure and acid criticism he was running, but he was willing to pay the price. His public release of March 24, 1951, read:

> Operations continue according to schedule and plan. We have now substantially cleared South Korea of organized Communist forces. It is becoming increasingly evident that the heavy destruction along the enemy's lines of supply caused by our 'round-the-clock massive air and naval bombardment, has left his troops in the forward battle area deficient in requirements to sustain his operations.
>
> This weakness is being brilliantly exploited by our ground forces. The enemy's human-wave tactics definitely fail him as our own forces become seasoned to this form of warfare; his tactics of infiltration are but contributing to his piecemeal losses, and he is showing less stamina than our own troops under rigors of climate, terrain, and battle.
>
> Of even greater significance than our tactical success has been the clear revelation that this new enemy, Red China, of such exaggerated and vaunted military power, lacks the industrial capacity to provide adequately many critical items essential to the conduct of modern war.
>
> He lacks manufacturing bases and those raw materials needed to produce, maintain, and operate even moderate air and naval power, and he cannot provide the essential for successful ground operations, such as tanks, heavy artillery, and other refinements science has introduced into the conduct of military campaigns. . . .
>
> These military weaknesses have been clearly and definitely revealed since Red China entered upon its undeclared war in Korea. Even under inhibitions which now restrict activity of the United Nations forces and the corresponding military advantages

which accrue to Red China, it has been shown its complete inability to accomplish by force of arms the conquest of Korea.

The enemy therefore must by now be painfully aware that a decision of the United Nations to depart from its tolerant effort to contain the war to the area of Korea through expansion of our military operations to his coastal areas and interior bases would doom Red China to the risk of imminent military collapse. . . .

It was as if MacArthur was trying desperately to force the U. N. itself to think clearly about the playing of its final trump card of threatened bombing and destruction above the Yalu. On its face the long press release appeared to be directed as much to the U. N. as to the enemy. He continued:

These basic facts being established, there should be no insuperable difficulty arriving at decisions on the Korean problem, if the issues are resolved on their own merits without being burdened by extraneous matters not directly related to Korea, such as Formosa and China's seat in the United Nations.

The Korean nation and people which have been so cruelly ravaged must not be sacrificed. That is the paramount concern. Apart from the military area of the problem where the issues are resolved in the course of combat, the fundamental questions continue to be political in nature and must find their answer in the diplomatic sphere.

Within the area of my authority as military commander, however, it should be needless to say I stand ready at any time to confer in the field with the commander in chief of the enemy forces in an earnest effort to find any military means whereby the realization of the political objectives of the United Nations in Korea, to which no nation may justly take exceptions, might be accomplished without further bloodshed.

It was a bold and desperate move on MacArthur's part to force the Red commander to confer directly with him. Certainly it forestalled any half-way measures for appeasement that might have come out of the United Nations.

The fact that the Tokyo dateline was a day ahead of Washington time meant that this MacArthur statement, dated Tokyo March 24, was actually received in the capital on March 23. Newspapers the following morning carried the long dispatch; and the next day, March 24, Washington time, a directive was hurried off to MacArthur. It carried little more than a suggestion of the storm that was brewing in the minds of the President and his two most important advisors, Marshall and Acheson. The directive read:

> *To:* Commander in Chief, Far East, Tokyo, Japan
> *From:* Joint Chiefs of Staff, personal for MacArthur
> The President has directed that your attention be called to his order as transmitted 6 December 1950. In view of the information given you 20 March 1951 any further statements by you must be co-ordinated as prescribed in the order of 6 December.
> The President has also directed that in the event Communist military leaders request an armistice in the field, you immediately report that fact to the JCS for instructions.

It was apparent to the three men who were most concerned with bending MacArthur to their way of thinking that a crisis was near at hand. Neither of the two senior advisors to the President in this matter seemed interested in any effort to temper the President's growing personal bitterness against MacArthur.

In a way, history was repeating itself. MacArthur had long believed that Marshall, as the senior army advisor to President Roosevelt at Yalta, evaded his mandatory responsibilities when he had not tried to stop the President from signing the secret clauses of the Yalta Agreement. In MacArthur's eyes, the duty and responsibility that confronted Marshall now, six and a half years later, was very much the same; Marshall, he felt, should warn President Truman that a Korean stalemate would almost inevitably mean the eventual conquest of all Korea by the Chinese Communists backed by Russia even if it took several years of intrigue and cruel intimidation to bring it about.

During his years in Japan MacArthur had had considerable experience with Acheson and various fellow-traveller elements within the State Department, and he had no illusions where the Secretary stood regarding British and Indian interests in Korea, Formosa and Red China. The General knew how little

510

consideration he could expect from any of the three men who were dictating the foreign and military policies of America in collaboration with their Socialist friends in the United Nations and under the consistent pressures of Red spy cells and their growing influence. But he could hardly have anticipated the sudden startling turn of events.

On the afternoon of April 5 Joseph Martin, Minority Leader of the House, interrupted a speech he was making on Korea by reading a letter he had received from MacArthur a few days before. It had been written in answer to the following note from Martin:

> *Office of the Minority Leader,*
> *House of Representatives,*
> *Washington, D. C., March 8, 1951*
> *General of the Army Douglas MacArthur*
> *Commander in Chief, Far Eastern Command*
> *My dear General:* In the current discussions on foreign policy and overall strategy many of us have been distressed that, although the European aspects have been heavily emphasized, we have been without the views of yourself as Commander in Chief of the Far Eastern Command.
>
> I think it is imperative to the security of our Nation and for the safety of the world that policies of the United States embrace the broadest possible strategy and that in our earnest desire to protect Europe we not weaken our position in Asia.
>
> Enclosed is a copy of an address I delivered in Brooklyn, N. Y., February 12, stressing this vital point and suggesting that the forces of Generalissimo Chiang Kai-shek on Formosa might be employed in the opening of a second Asiatic front to relieve the pressure on our forces in Korea.
>
> I have since repeated the essence of this thesis in other speeches, and intend to do so again on March 21, when I will be on a radio hook-up.
>
> I would deem it a great help if I could have your views on this point, either on a confidential basis or otherwise. Your admirers are legion, and the respect you command is enormous. May success be yours in the gigantic undertaking which you direct.
>
> Sincerely yours,
> *Joseph W. Martin, Jr.*

MacArthur's answer was made in a completely routine manner. The General dictated it the day before receiving the message from the Joint Chiefs of Staff informing him that the President was shortly to release the statement that the U. N. was now prepared to discuss a settlement in Korea. To MacArthur his answer to the Martin letter was merely one of scores of replies he regularly sent to friends and admirers in the States. It read:

General Headquarters,
Supreme Commander for the Allied Powers,
Tokyo, Japan, March 20, 1951

Hon. Joseph W. Martin, Jr.
House of Representatives, Washington, D. C.

Dear Congressman Martin: I am most grateful for your note of the 8th forwarding me a copy of your address of February 12. The latter I have read with much interest, and find that with the passage of years you have certainly lost none of your old-time punch.

My views and recommendations with respect to the situation created by Red China's entry into the war against us in Korea have been submitted to Washington in most complete detail. Generally these views are well known and clearly understood, as they follow the conventional pattern of meeting force with maximum counter-force, as we have never failed to do in the past. Your view with respect to the utilization of the Chinese forces on Formosa is in conflict with neither logic nor this tradition.

It seems strangely difficult for some to realize that here in Asia is where the Communist conspirators have elected to make their play for global conquest, and that we have joined the issue thus raised on the battlefield; that here we fight Europe's war with arms while the diplomats there still fight it with words; that if we lose the war to communism in Asia the fall of Europe is inevitable, win it and Europe most probably would avoid war and yet preserve freedom. As you pointed out, we must win. There is no substitute for victory.

With renewed thanks and expressions of most cordial regard I am,

Faithfully yours,
Douglas MacArthur

MacArthur had placed no restrictions on the use of the letter, and probably even if Martin had cabled for permission to use it on the floor of the House, the General would not have raised the slightest objection. It concerned the subject nearest his heart. It had to do with his duty to his country now faced with grave peril.

8

Within a few minutes after the Minority Leader read MacArthur's communication on the floor of the House on that mid-afternoon of April 5, word of Martin's political use of the letter reached the White House. Truman was vociferously annoyed. It was too good an opportunity to get rid of MacArthur for his enemies to miss.

The following noon, immediately after the regular Cabinet meeting, the President called in Secretary of State Acheson, Secretary of Defense Marshall, Special Advisor Harriman and General Bradley, Chairman of the Joint Chiefs of Staff. For an hour there was a general discussion covering the possibility of permitting MacArthur to continue in authority until after a Japanese treaty had been negotiated. The four advisors were asked to study the situation and to gather again on Saturday morning at the White House offices.

At this Saturday meeting there was a discussion regarding splitting MacArthur's commands so that Ridgway could be made Commander-in-Chief of the United Nations Forces in Korea and MacArthur's authority would be limited to his single status of Supreme Commander in Japan. The President asked his advisors to ponder the problems over the week end, and Marshall was specifically instructed to obtain the views of the Chiefs of Staff. This was done on Sunday afternoon.

At the Monday morning meeting General Bradley informed the President that the Joint Chiefs of Staff unanimously agreed that MacArthur must go. On Tuesday, April 10, there was a further meeting with Truman at 3 o'clock, at which various drafts of the President's orders were discussed. Arrangements were made to have both MacArthur and Ridgway formally notified at the same time. Secretary of War Pace was the messenger chosen to inform MacArthur of his immediate relief, and General John E. Hull, of the General Staff, was to carry the word to Ridgway that he was to replace MacArthur. Both envoys were then in Korea on an inspection trip.

There was frantic scurrying about during this day of April 10, when a report reached the White House that apparently there had been a leak in the secret plan. Walter Trohan, aggressive head of the Washington Bureau of the Chicago *Tribune*, had telephoned the Pentagon requesting clarification of the report from Japan concerning a Tokyo tip that news of an important resignation was scheduled for the following afternoon, Tokyo time. It seems quite logical that the White House interpreted this to mean that MacArthur, although unaware of his fate but disgusted with the support he was receiving, might be planning to ask for sudden retirement before the secret orders for his relief would reach him.

After considerable discussion and several changes in the plans, because of the uncertainty of communications with Secretary of War Pace, it was finally decided to call in the regular White House correspondents at 1:30 in the morning of April 11, and give them the full directive, at the exact moment messages would be delivered to both MacArthur and Ridgway. Not since correspondents had been summoned to receive the carefully guarded news of the death of President Franklin D. Roosevelt on April 12, 1945, had there been such speculation and uncertainty as to the nature of the announcement that would be forthcoming.

To MacArthur in Tokyo there was no intimation of what was coming.

9

The General and Jean were finishing a lengthy lunch with a visiting Senator at the Embassy, when Colonel Sidney Huff phoned from his own apartment within the walled compound and left word for Jean to call him the moment she was free.

As soon as the MacArthurs reached their private quarters she called Huff. He explained he had been tipped off by an

American radio correspondent that there was something important regarding the President and the General that would be on the 3 o'clock broadcast. Then Huff blurted out the bad news.

He had just tuned in and at the very end of the newscast had come the flash announcement that the General had been relieved of all his commands. The news had broken only a few moments before Jean's return call had reached him.

It seemed incredible to the MacArthurs that they had received no advance hint of the unaccountable order.

A little later a small brown envelope was delivered by the Signal Corps message center. Colonel Huff immediately took the envelope to the door of the General's bedroom, where Jean was waiting. Huff felt that it was almost as if he were delivering a death sentence.

The General opened the envelope and took out the enclosed sheets. Swiftly his eyes raced through the messages that were clipped to the flimsy, recording the formal statement of their reception at the Signal Corps center. They read:

Message Relieving General MacArthur of Command,
April 10, 1951

I deeply regret that it becomes my duty as President and Commander in Chief of the United States military forces to replace you as Supreme Commander, Allied Powers; Commander in Chief, United Nations Command; Commander in Chief, Far East; and Commanding General, U. S. Army, Far East.

You will turn over your commands, effective at once, to Lt. Gen. Matthew B. Ridgway. You are authorized to have issued such orders as are necessary to complete desired travel to such place as you select.

My reasons for your replacement will be made public concurrently with the delivery to you of the foregoing order, and are contained in the next following message.

Statement of the President Relative to the Relief of
General MacArthur, April 10, 1951

With deep regret I have concluded that **General of the Army** Douglas MacArthur is unable to give his whole-hearted support to the policies of the United States Government and of the United Nations in matters pertaining to his official duties. In view of

515

the specific responsibilities imposed upon me by the Constitution of the United States and the added responsibility which has been entrusted to me by the United Nations, I have decided that I must make a change of command in the Far East. I have, therefore, relieved General MacArthur of his commands and have designated Lt. Gen. Matthew B. Ridgway as his successor.

Full and vigorous debate on matters of national policy is a vital element in the constitutional system of our free democracy. It is fundamental, however, that military commanders must be governed by the policies and directives issued to them in the manner provided by our laws and Constitution. In time of crisis, this consideration is particularly compelling.

General MacArthur's place in history as one of our greatest commanders is fully established. The nation owes him a debt of gratitude for the distinguished and exceptional service which he has rendered his country in posts of great responsibility. For that reason I repeat my regret at the necessity for the action I feel compelled to take in his case.

So it was that the General met his fate.

24

OLD SOLDIERS NEVER DIE . . .

To certain men in Washington, in Lake Success and in Moscow, London and Delhi the announcement must have come as most welcome and pleasant news. From 10 Downing Street to the Kremlin, and to the U. N. Assembly cocktail lounges, with their nests of intrigue, there was great rejoicing that the American soldier, who for so long had blocked one sinister scheme after another, was now out of the way.

It was a great day for the Reds and Internationalists and the faint-hearted American leaders. No longer would they be plagued by the soldier who opposed their brazen attempts to neutralize and emasculate American interests and betray American honor and courage. No longer would this old warrior, almost single-handed, attempt to block the surrender of the State Department, the Pentagon and the White House to a U. N. Security Council dominated by One-Worlders, Socialists and Communists and by nations more interested in trade with Russia and Red China than with the preservation of a free world.

No longer would this stalwart be able to hold out against the ever-growing government by fear, by the gigantic bluff of Russia and the Red Chinese threats and intimidations.

For a full two decades MacArthur had stood against the gradual surrender of the constitutional government to an imported creeping socialism and, for the last 10 years, to the spell cast by such foreign leaders as Churchill and Stalin, Attlee and Nehru. He had never given way to the secret pressures and the influences of the Red conspiracy and its corruption of the once free and unique American mind. He had watched with horror how the victory won at such cost in Europe and the Pacific had been lost by the ineptness and ignorance and lack of foresight of American leaders. He had been horrified at the treachery of American Pinks and Reds and their dupes, enmeshed in the web of betrayal within the high offices of the U. S. government; and how Nationalist China had actually been destroyed as a result of these influences.

With infinite courage and genius he had helped save South Korea from certain disaster, and he had led his victorious armies to the high cliffs of the Yalu. Only when a vicious new war broke and a hundred thousand hidden Red Chinese suddenly appeared from their caves and snow-camouflaged forests and attacked, had he felt the utter frustration of not being permitted to unwrap his air and turn defeat into a certain victory that might well have settled the whole Asiatic threat for a score of years to come.

And he was to live to see his able successors denied the same chance to win—and the icy hand of Russian fear and British trade demands closing tightly around the timid hearts of certain American leaders. Never for a day were either Generals

Ridgway, Van Fleet, or Clark permitted to win the Korean war by making full and fearless use of the weapons each had at hand. The psychosis of fear of Russia and the betrayal of American ideals before the pressure of her questionable Allies were to continue with the mockery of the surrender at Panmunjon and the disgraceful armed peace that followed, leading straight on into the vast problems of future local wars in the distant Pacific.

So it was that the rejoicing among little Americans and their foreign tutors was great that day in mid-April 1951. The brave sentinel had been stabbed in the back. Those who bent their knees to the Red Bear finally had seen their plots against this fearless soldier succeed.

Douglas MacArthur, the uncompromising American, had been destroyed.

Or so they thought.

2

Early in Tokyo on the morning following the orders for the General's relief, the flood of friendly messages from the United States began to pour in on MacArthur. He drew even tighter the veil of privacy that had surrounded him during his five and a half years in Tokyo. Trans-Pacific phone calls and cables were handled by aides, for, as in every other great crisis of his life, he wanted to make his decisions alone and without pressure from outside sources. This time, of course, he had the wise and loyal co-operation of Jean MacArthur.

A message relayed from Mr. Herbert Hoover that broke through the barricade advised MacArthur to "fly home as quickly as possible, before Truman and Marshall and their crowd of propagandists can smear you." The suggestion was added that MacArthur would be asked to speak before a joint meeting of Congress and would be received with a public ovation. But the important thing was to come home as quickly as possible before the public could be poisoned against him. He must not wait for a ship but return by plane.

MacArthur agreed that the suggestion was sound, and added

518

that he desired the ex-President to understand one thing; he wanted Mr. Hoover to be his sole advisor. This Mr. Hoover readily agreed to do.

Shortly an official invitation was cabled to the General asking him to address a meeting of the two Houses of Congress. MacArthur immediately expedited arrangements for his return. The date of April 19 was agreed on for his Congressional address. This would mean that his plane would have to leave Tokyo early on the fifth day after the original news of his dismissal had been phoned to him.

He made two short visits to his office to clear his desk and to arrange for shipping his personal belongings. Then he shut tight the doors to all friends and callers. In what spare moments he had he worked on his address to be delivered before Congress. Swiftly came the hour when the little party must start on the journey to the airport, where he was to make his departure at 7 in the morning.

All during the previous afternoon and night the narrow, winding roads that led to the airfield were filling up with thousands of Japanese people. They came from the tiny farms and shops and villages and from the great centers of Tokyo and Yokohama and neighboring cities. They made the journey on foot and bicycle and by bus and car and train, and they stood long hours in order to show their respect and affection for the great American who was now leaving them.

It was as if they were saying good-bye to a trusted friend who in some mystical way had given them a new sense of their own personal dignity and true freedom and hope. It was not a happy, cheering crowd but rather a stunned and bewildered outpouring of brave people, hardened to adversity and heartbreak. They lined almost every foot of the 15-mile route of the MacArthur party to the airport.

The brief farewell ceremony within the roped-off space that led to the landing ramp of the *Bataan* was of a quiet intensity of mood that reflected the true emotions of the high Japanese dignitaries, the members of the diplomatic corps and the old army friends who had gathered there.

The General, Jean and Arthur finally walked up the ramp

and while the army band played *Auld Lang Syne,* they turned and waved at the crowd. The door closed and a moment later the great ship rolled away.

At Honolulu, when MacArthur saw the vast crowd gathered at the airport, he remarked that he hoped they were not cheering because they felt sorry for him.

He was still completely unprepared for what was to come. The tragic conclusion of a half century of service had shocked him beyond words. In his own sensitive mind to be thus brutally and summarily relieved of all his commands could produce no reaction save a sense of injustice at the disgrace.

Before leaving Tokyo he had agreed to a public reception in San Francisco, and one at the Washington Monument, following his speech before Congress, and to a public appearance in New York a day or two later. He told Lt. Colonel Storey, his personal pilot, to draw up the time schedule so that they could slip into San Francisco after dark and get a good night's rest before the big reception the next day.

The wildly cheering, emotional crowd that welcomed MacArthur in San Francisco was his first intimation of the intensity of devotion and sympathy felt for him by all America. He still did not fully understand this patent evidence of the resentment of millions at his treatment by Washington. He still moved as one in a trance.

3

On April 19, eight days after his dismissal in Tokyo, the General made his historic address before a joint meeting of the Congress. In millions of homes, in offices and machine shops, in every nook and corner of the vast land, the people of America listened to his words with unconcealed emotion.

It is possible that at no previous moment in American history had there been such a universal outpouring of the human heart. Even his opening words seemed to ring with the peculiar quality of a great spirit enunciating what apparently would be his farewell:

> I stand on this rostrum with a sense of deep humility and great
> pride—humility in the wake of those great American architects

520

of our history who have stood here before me, pride in the reflection that this forum of legislative debate represents human liberty in the purest form yet devised.

Here are centered the hopes and aspirations and faith of the entire human race. I do not stand here as advocate for any partisan cause, for the issues are fundamental and reach quite beyond the realm of partisan consideration. They must be resolved on the highest plane of national interest if our course is to prove sound and our future protected. . . .

I address you with neither rancor nor bitterness in the fading twilight of life with but one purpose in mind: to serve my country.

A whole nation was gripped by the power and authority of his words and by the sheer beauty and magnificence of this master orator's voice. With majestic sincerity he approached the peroration:

In war there is no substitute for victory. There are some who, for varying reasons, would appease Red China. They are blind to history's clear lesson, for history teaches with unmistakable emphasis that appeasement but begets new and bloodier war. It points to no single instance where this end has justified the means, where appeasement has led to more than a sham peace. Like blackmail, it lays the basis for new and successively greater demands until, as in blackmail, violence becomes the only other alternative.

Why, my soldiers asked of me, surrender military advantages to an enemy in the field? I could not answer.

It was the question an entire nation was asking. The very fact that there was no answer shook the country to its inner soul. The strange pent-up anger involved and the endless pity and anguish of frustration brought tears to millions of citizens everywhere.

Then the mood swung from the grave injustice that had been done a brave and uncompromising fellow countryman, to a touching picture of an old soldier calmly facing the inevitable. His final words left their indelible imprint:

I am closing my 52 years of military service. When I joined the army even before the turn of the century, it was the fulfillment of all my boyish hopes and dreams. The world has turned over

521

many times since I took the oath on the Plain at West Point, and the hopes and dreams have long since vanished. But I still remember the refrain of one of the most popular barrack ballads of that day which proclaimed most proudly that—

"Old soldiers never die; they just fade away." And like the old soldier of that ballad, I now close my military service and just fade away—an old soldier who had tried to do his duty as God gave him the light to see that duty. Goodbye.

It was a proud moment for Douglas MacArthur.

His eyes had seen the glory of a grateful and bewildered nation laying its heartfelt thanks at his feet.

Time was to bring him the satisfaction of knowing that his country ultimately recognized that in his supreme struggle in the Pacific he had been right and those who opposed him—and finally punished him—had been wrong.

Millions of his countrymen still hoped he would be recalled to the service of his country. But no matter what the future might bring, to those millions he would forever remain the old soldier who would never die—or completely fade away.

INDEX

532